iPod® & iTunes®

FOR

DUMMIES®

10TH EDITION

by Tony Bove

WILEY

Wiley Publishing, Inc.

iPod® & iTunes® For Dummies®, 10th Edition

Published by
John Wiley & Sons, Inc.
111 River Street
Hoboken, NJ 07030-5774

www.wiley.com

Copyright © 2013 by John Wiley & Sons, Inc., Hoboken, New Jersey

Published by John Wiley & Sons, Inc., Hoboken, New Jersey

Published simultaneously in Canada

For general information on our other products and services, please contact our Customer Care Department within the U.S. at 877-762-2974, outside the U.S. at 317-572-3993, or fax 317-572-4002.

For technical support, please visit www.wiley.com/techsupport.

Wiley publishes in a variety of print and electronic formats and by print-on-demand. Some material included with standard print versions of this book may not be included in e-books or in print-on-demand. If this book refers to media such as a CD or DVD that is not included in the version you purchased, you may download this material at http://booksupport.wiley.com. For more information about Wiley products, visit www.wiley.com.

Library of Congress Control Number: 2012956419

ISBN 978-1-118-50864-0 (pbk); ISBN 978-1-118-55537-8 (ebk); ISBN 978-1-118-55550-7 (ebk); ISBN 978-1-118-50867-1 (ebk)

Manufactured in the United States of America

10 9 8 7 6 5 4 3 2 1

WILEY

MAY 2013

About the Author

Tony Bove has written about every iPad, iPod, and iPhone model and every update to iTunes from the very beginning, and not only provides free tips on his website (www.tonybove.com/tonytips) but also developed an app (Tony's Tips for iPhone Users). Tony is a technical publications manager for a software company and has written more than two dozen books on computing, desktop publishing, and multimedia, including *iPod touch For Dummies, iLife® '11 For Dummies, iPad Application Development For Dummies, iPhone Application Development All-in-One For Dummies* (all from Wiley), *Just Say No to Microsoft* (No Starch Press), *The GarageBand Book* (Wiley), *The Art of Desktop Publishing* (Bantam), and a series of books about Macromedia Director, Adobe Illustrator, and PageMaker. Tony also founded *Desktop Publishing/Publish* magazine and the *Inside Report on New Media* newsletter, and he wrote the weekly Macintosh column for *Computer Currents* for a decade, as well as articles and columns for a variety of publications including *NeXTWORLD,* the *Chicago Tribune* Sunday Technology Section, *Macintosh Today,* the Prodigy online network, and *NewMedia.* Tracing the personal computer revolution back to the 1960s counterculture, Tony produced a CD-ROM interactive "rockumentary" in 1996, *Haight-Ashbury in the Sixties* (which explains his taste in music in this book's examples). He also developed the Rockument music site, www.rockument.com, with commentary and podcasts focused on rock music history. As a founding member of the Flying Other Brothers, which toured professionally for a decade and released three commercial CDs (*52-Week High, San Francisco Sounds,* and *Estimated Charges*), Tony performed with Hall of Fame rock musicians.

Dedication

This book is dedicated to my sons, nieces, nephews, their cousins, and all their children . . . the iPod generation.

Author's Acknowledgments

I want to thank Kathy for putting up with my hectic writing schedule, and John and Jimi for being perfect examples of the iPod generation. I also want to thank Rich Tennant for his wonderful cartoons, and Dennis Cohen for technical expertise beyond the call of duty. And let me not forget my Wiley editor Jean Nelson for ongoing assistance that made my job so much easier. A book this timely places a considerable burden on a publisher's production team, and I thank the production crew at Wiley for diligence beyond the call of reason. I owe thanks and a happy hour or three to my agent, Carole Jelen at Waterside. And finally, I have executive editor Bob Woerner at Wiley to thank for coming up with the idea for this book and helping me to become a professional dummy — that is, a *Dummies* author.

Publisher's Acknowledgments

We're proud of this book; please send us your comments at http://dummies.custhelp.com. For other comments, please contact our Customer Care Department within the U.S. at 877-762-2974, outside the U.S. at 317-572-3993, or fax 317-572-4002.

Some of the people who helped bring this book to market include the following:

Acquisitions and Editorial

Project Editor: Jean Nelson

Executive Editor: Bob Woerner

Copy Editor: Jean Nelson

Technical Editor: Dennis Cohen

Editorial Manager: Jodi Jensen

Editorial Assistants: Leslie Saxman, Annie Sullivan

Sr. Editorial Assistant: Cherie Case

Cover Photo: © ariwasabi/iStockphoto.com

Cartoons: Rich Tennant (www.the5thwave.com)

Composition Services

Senior Project Coordinator: Kristie Rees

Layout and Graphics: Carrie A. Cesavice, Amy Hassos, Joyce Haughey

Proofreaders: ConText Editorial Services, Inc., Dwight Ramsey

Indexer: BIM Indexing & Proofreading Services

Publishing and Editorial for Technology Dummies

    Richard Swadley, Vice President and Executive Group Publisher

    Andy Cummings, Vice President and Publisher

    Mary Bednarek, Executive Acquisitions Director

    Mary C. Corder, Editorial Director

Publishing for Consumer Dummies

    Kathleen Nebenhaus, Vice President and Executive Publisher

Composition Services

    Debbie Stailey, Director of Composition Services

Contents at a Glance

Table of Contents

Part III: Playing It Back with Interest *205*

Introduction

*L*aunched on October 23, 2001, the iPod is ubiquitous throughout the world. How the first device came to be called "iPod" is still, to this day, a mystery, but the name not only stuck, it also spawned "iPhone" and "iPad." Some say a freelance copywriter came up with it after thinking of the phrase "Open the pod bay door, Hal!" from the movie *2001: A Space Odyssey*. According to a team member quoted by Steve Levy in *The Perfect Thing* (Simon & Schuster), back in 2001, the late Apple chairman Steve Jobs "just came in and went, 'iPod.' We all looked around the room, and that was it." It's certainly true that the late Steve Jobs rode hard on its design and user interface, making all final decisions. When one of the designers said that, obviously, the device should have a power button to turn the unit on and off, Jobs simply said no. And that was that. (We will all miss his insight.)

There were other MP3 audio players when the iPod was introduced, but none that offered as much capacity for holding music, and none that could change the entire experience of acquiring, playing, and storing your music the way the iPod did. And that's because the iPod is not alone: It is an integral part of an ecosystem that centers on the iTunes application on your computer, and includes iCloud and the iTunes Store and App Store on the Internet.

iTunes is the center of my media universe and the software that manages content for all my iPods, iPhones, and iPads. I bring all my content into iTunes — from CDs, the iTunes Store, and other sources — and then sync it wirelessly to my iPod touch, iPhones, and iPads for playback. Even though I buy content and apps directly with my iPod touch, everything I obtain is automatically synchronized with my iTunes library on my computer, and just about all my music is synchronized with my iTunes Match library in iCloud.

iTunes was originally developed by Jeff Robbin and Bill Kincaid as an MP3 player called SoundJam MP, and released by Casady & Greene in 1999. It was purchased by Apple in 2000 and redesigned and released as iTunes. Since then, Apple has released numerous updates of iTunes to support new devices, fix bugs, and add new features to improve your content library and your iPod experience. All the important features are covered in this book. iTunes is getting better all the time, and this book gets you started.

About This Book

The publishers are wise about book matters, and they helped me design *iPod & iTunes For Dummies,* 10th Edition, as a reference. With this book, you can easily find the information you need when you need it. I wrote it so that you can read from beginning to end to find out how to use iTunes and your iPod models from scratch. But this book is also organized so that you can dive in anywhere and begin reading the info you need to know for each task.

I didn't have enough pages to cover every detail of every function, and I intentionally left out some detail so that you won't be befuddled with techno-speak when it isn't necessary. I wrote brief but comprehensive descriptions and included lots of cool tips on how to get the most out of your iPod touch.

At the time I wrote this book, I covered the most recent iPod models and the latest version of iTunes. Although I did my best to keep up for this print edition, Apple occasionally slips in a new model or new version of iTunes between book editions. If you've bought a new iPod with features not covered in the book, or if your version of iTunes looks a little different, be sure to check out the free Tony's Tips section of my website (www.tonybove. com/tips) for more tips, bonus chapters, and updates on the latest releases from Apple.

Conventions Used in This Book

Like any book that covers computers, mobile devices, and information technology, this book uses certain conventions:

- **Choosing from a screen or menu:** With an iPod touch, when I write "Choose Settings⇨General from the Home screen," you tap Settings on the Home screen and then tap General on the Settings screen.

  With an iPod classic or iPod nano, when you see "Choose Settings⇨ Brightness from the iPod main menu," you scroll (rotate your finger clockwise around) the click wheel to highlight Settings on the main menu, press the Select button (the center button) to choose Settings, and then highlight and choose Brightness from the Settings menu.

  With iTunes, when I write "Choose iTunes⇨Preferences in iTunes," you click iTunes in the menu bar at the top of the display and then click Preferences in the iTunes menu that appears.

- **Sliding, scrolling, and flicking on an iPod touch:** When you see "Scroll the screen" I mean you need to drag your finger to slide the screen slowly. When I write "scroll the list on the iPod touch Settings screen," I mean you should drag your finger over the list so that it slides horizontally or vertically. When I write "Flick the screen," you should flick the screen with your finger to slide it quickly.

- **Clicking and dragging on the computer:** When you see "Drag the song over the name of the playlist," I mean you need to click the song name (in iTunes), hold the mouse button down, and then drag the song — while holding the mouse button down — over to the name of the playlist before lifting your finger off the mouse button.

- **Keyboard shortcuts on the computer:** When you see ⌘-I, press the ⌘ key on a Mac keyboard along with the appropriate shortcut key. (In this case, after selecting a content item or app, press ⌘-I, which opens the Information window in iTunes.) In Windows, the same keyboard shortcut is Ctrl-I (which means press the Ctrl key along with the I key). Don't worry — I always tell you what the equivalent Windows keys are.

- **Step lists:** When you come across steps that you need to do in iTunes or on the iPod touch, the action is in **bold,** and the explanatory part follows. If you know what to do, read the action and skip the explanation. But if you need a little help along the way, check out the explanation.

- **Pop-up menus:** I use the term *pop-up menu* for menus on the Mac that literally pop up from dialogs and windows; in Windows, the same type of menu actually drops down and is called a drop-down menu. I use the term *pop-up menu* for both.

A Quick Peek Ahead

This book is organized into six parts, and each part covers a different aspect of using your iPod touch and iTunes. Here's a quick preview of what you can find in each part.

Part I: Touching All the Basics

This part gets you started with your iPod: powering it up, recharging its battery, connecting it to your computer, and so on. You discover how to set up your iPod and install iTunes. You also find out how to use an iPod touch multi-touch interface and onscreen keyboard. I also impart all the techniques I use as an iPod road warrior: organizing apps into folders, setting your alarm and multiple clocks for time zones, keeping time with your stopwatch, changing your display settings, setting the passcode to lock up the device so others can't use it, and setting restrictions on content and the use of applications.

Part II: Managing Your Library

This part gets you started with iTunes on your computer, including playing and ripping audio CDs, adding videos, and downloading songs, albums, podcasts, audio books, movies, TV shows, and music videos from the iTunes Store, and applications from the App Store. You find out how to buy music, podcasts, videos, and applications directly on your iPod touch. I also show you how to synchronize your iPod touch with iCloud and synchronize all iPod models with the iTunes library on your computer, including your content, personal contacts, e-mail accounts, web bookmarks, and calendars. You also find out how to browse the content in your iTunes library, add and edit content information, and arrange content into iTunes playlists that you can transfer to your iPod. This part also contains crucial information about locating and backing up your iTunes library.

Part III: Playing It Back with Interest

In this part, I show you how to locate and play music on your iPod shuffle, and all types of content on your iPod touch, iPod classic, and iPod nano — music, audio books, podcasts, iTunes U courses, movies, TV shows, videos, and slide shows of your own photos. You also discover how to take photos and record videos with an iPod touch.

Part IV: Touching the Online World

This part describes how to use your iPod touch and the Safari application to surf the web. You also find out how to check and send e-mail, look at your stock portfolio, and check the weather in your city and other cities. I also show you how to display maps and driving directions.

Part V: Staying in Touch and Up-to-Date

In this part, I explain how to use your iPod touch to locate and communicate with friends on Facebook, Twitter, and Game Center; use the Messages app to send and receive text; and use the FaceTime app to make and receive video calls. I also show you how to enter and edit calendar entries, how to enter and sort contacts, and how to use the Siri personal assistant on your iPod touch. You also find out how to update or restore your iPod, and reset its settings.

Part VI: The Part of Tens

In this book's Part of Tens chapters, I provide ten tips that can help make your iPod experience a completely satisfying one, and I describe ten iPod touch apps that will rock your world.

Bonus Chapters and Tips

Lucky reader! You can take advantage of my previous forays into iPodland by checking out the online bonus chapters and free tips associated with this book in the Tony's Tips section of my website (www.tonybove.com/tips). Scattered through those tips and bonus chapters, you'll find even more great informational nuggets. Topics include the following:

- Choosing audio encoding formats and quality settings for importing music
- Adjusting the volume and equalizing the sound
- Preparing photo libraries, videos, address books, and calendars
- Managing multiple iTunes libraries and copying your library to other hard drives or computers
- Getting wired for playback and using accessories

Icons Used in This Book

The icons in this book are important visual cues for information you need.

Remember icons highlight important things you need to keep in mind.

Technical Stuff icons highlight technical details you can skip unless you want to bring out your inner technical geek.

Tip icons highlight tips and techniques that save you time and energy — and maybe even money.

Warning icons save your butt by preventing disasters. Don't bypass a Warning without reading it. This is your only warning!

On the Web icons let you know when a topic is covered further online on a website. For example, I call your attention to specific areas within Apple's site (www.apple.com), and I refer to the free tips and bonus chapters I provide on my site at www.tonybove.com/tips.

Part I
Touching All the Basics

The 5th Wave   By Rich Tennant

"Other than this little glitch with the landscape view, I really love my iPod touch."

1 touch all the basics in this first part to get you started with your iPod as quickly as possible.

I start you out with a power punch in Chapter 1: opening the box and powering up the iPod. You also find out how to get the most from your battery.

Chapter 2 describes how to set up your iPod and install the iOS operating system software on an iPod touch. It also describes how to install iTunes — on a Mac or Windows PC.

Next, in Chapter 3, I show you how to touch an iPod touch, tap an iPod nano, and thumb your iPod classic and iPod shuffle. You get a quick tour of the iPod touch Home screen, the icons, and the onscreen keyboard, including tricks like how to quickly type numbers, symbols, and accent marks.

Then, in Chapter 4, I set you up with the right time and date, clocks for different time zones, alarms, the timer, and the stopwatch. You discover how to set a passcode to lock your iPod so that no one else can use it. You learn how to set the display's brightness, turn the sound effects and ringtone on or off, and change the wallpapers that appear on the locked screen and behind the Home screen. You find out how to set notifications for your apps, and set restrictions so that your kids can't jump onto the web or download tunes or videos categorized as explicit in the iTunes Store. You also find out how to connect an iPod touch to the Internet using Wi-Fi.

Powering Your iPod

*T*he iPod has evolved into a range of mobile devices — from the current iPod shuffle, iPod nano, iPod classic, and iPod touch models described in this chapter, to the iPhone and iPad models described in books such as *iPhone For Dummies* and *iPad For Dummies*. Along the way, Apple has not only completely changed the way people play music, audio books, and videos, but also has changed the way people shoot photos and videos, play games, check e-mail, use computer applications, and use the Internet.

But don't just take my word for it. "It's hard to remember what I did before the iPod," said Grammy Award–winner Mary J. Blige in an Apple press release. "iPod is more than just a music player; it's an extension of your personality and a great way to take your favorite music with you everywhere you go." Pope Benedict XVI has an iPod engraved with his coat of arms. President Barack Obama gave the U.K.'s Queen Elizabeth II an iPod preloaded with rare songs by Richard Rodgers. And when Bono of U2 gave an iPod shuffle to George H. W. Bush, the former president joked, "I get the shuffle and then I shuffle the shuffle."

The convenience of carrying music on an iPod is phenomenal. For example, the least expensive iPod model — the $49 2GB iPod shuffle — can hold 500 songs, which is plenty for getting around town. The 64GB iPod touch ($399) can hold about 14,000 songs as well as run apps, connect to the Internet, make FaceTime video calls, and play video on a slick screen, whereas the $249 160GB iPod classic, which is designed more for playing music, can hold around 40,000 songs — that's more than 8 weeks of nonstop rock around the clock. (Prices may vary as Apple introduces new models.)

This chapter introduces the iPod models, and includes how to power them up and connect them to your computer, which are essential tasks.

Comparing iPod Models

The iPod was first invented for playing music, but now you can download movies and TV shows and select from a library of hundreds of thousands of applications (known as *apps*) for the iPod touch that offer everything from soup to nuts. The iPod touch can also shoot videos and still pictures. You can keep track of your calendar and contacts with an iPod classic as well as store loads of music, but with an iPod touch, you can also enter and edit calendar and contact entries, check and send e-mail, visit your favorite websites, get maps, obtain driving directions, read e-books and periodicals, take iTunes U courses, check the current weather, and even check your stock portfolio.

Introduced way back in the Stone Age of digital music (2001), each model of the iPod family has grown by several generations, now including:

- **The iPod touch (fifth generation):** This one looks and acts like an iPhone, but without cellular phone calls. It relies on Wi-Fi, which is short for *wi*reless *fi*delity, to connect to networks offering the Internet.

- **The iPod classic:** Following the original iPod design, the iPod classic offers the highest music capacity.

- **The iPod nano:** This is the ultra-portable iPod with the mighty 2.5-inch display that is small enough to hide in your palm and large enough to show videos. It comes in a variety of colors, and responds to multi-touch gestures like the iPod touch.

- **The tiny iPod shuffle:** This is an iPod designed just for audio, which you can clip to your sleeve.

To find out more about previous generations of iPods, including detailed information about cables and connections, see Bonus Chapter 1 in the free tips section of the author's website (www.tonybove.com/tips). For a nifty chart that shows the differences among iPod models, see the Identifying iPod Models page on the Apple iPod website (http://support.apple.com/kb/HT1353).

Getting in touch with iPod touch

I want to call it a *device,* but it's so much more — the iPod touch, shown in Figure 1-1, puts the entire world in your pocket. It's your passport to millions of songs as well as movies, TV shows, and other content on the iTunes Store. It lets you communicate with your friends and family with FaceTime video calls and instant messaging, and participate in social and gaming networks such as Facebook and the Game Center. It records stunning HD video as well as photos and lets you edit them before sharing them. And, of course, it offers a library of hundreds of thousands of applications (known as *apps*) that offer everything from soup to nuts, including thousands of games — but I get into that later in this chapter.

Figure 1-1: iPod touch in all its glory.

Enclosed in a single piece of anodized aluminum, less than a quarter of an inch thick, and weighing just a little over 3 ounces, the iPod touch is really a pocket computer — it uses a flash memory drive and the iOS operating system. It shares design characteristics and many of the features of its more famous cousin, the iPhone, with built-in speaker and volume controls, an accelerometer for motion detection (such as rotation and shaking), and Internet connectivity for surfing the Web and checking e-mail. Like the newest model iPhone, the newest model iPod touch sports a three-axis gyro for measuring or maintaining orientation (used extensively by games), and a

4-inch, widescreen, multi-touch Retina display that offers a stunning 1136-x-640 pixel resolution at 326 pixels per inch — so many pixels that the human eye can't distinguish individual ones.

The newest iPod touch also offers the 5-megapixel iSight camera on the back for recording HD (1080p) video at up to 30 frames per second (with audio). And you can use a front-facing 1.2-megapixel video camera for taking photos, recording HD (720p) videos, and making FaceTime video calls over the Internet.

The Siri intelligent personal assistant is also included with the newest iPod touch. With Siri and an Internet connection, you can talk in a normal voice to ask for directions, look up contacts, search the Internet, schedule appointments, and so on, as I describe in Chapter 18. For example, you can ask Siri for baseball scores. Any app that has a keyboard, such as Notes (as I show in Chapter 3), can use Siri to understand the text you speak, so that instead of typing, you can speak and your words will be entered as text.

Apple offers the following sizes of iPod touch models as of this writing, and they all use the same battery that offers up to 40 hours of music playback or 8 hours of video playback:

- **The 32GB model** holds about 7,000 songs, 40,000 photos, or about 40 hours of video. (With 7,000 songs, you could play a full week of non-stop music.)

- **The 64GB model** holds about 14,000 songs, 90,000 photos, or about 80 hours of video.

The newest model iPod touch can do nearly everything an iPhone can do, except make cellular-service phone calls or pinpoint its exact location with the Global Positioning System (GPS). Even so, the iPod touch can find its approximate location with Internet-based location services, and you can make the equivalent of a "phone call" using FaceTime, the Skype app, and an Internet connection, as I describe in Chapter 18. It also offers stereo Bluetooth for using wireless headphones and microphones.

Going mano a mano with iPod nano

Apple has brought its multi-touch technology to a screen the size of a credit card. The iPod nano is the thinnest iPod ever made and comes in a full spectrum of colors. It plays music, videos, podcasts, audio books, and music videos.

This mini marvel (see Figure 1-2) offers a 2.5-inch Multi-Touch display with 240 x 432 pixels of resolution at 202 pixels per inch, which can show videos and crisp images of your album cover art, and includes a motion sensor so that you can shake it to shuffle songs. Apple offers one 16GB model that holds about 4,000 songs. It also offers an FM tuner for listening to radio and a pedometer to keep track of your footsteps.

Figure 1-2: iPod nano plays FM radio as well as videos and music.

The battery in the iPod nano gives it the power to play up to 30 hours of music — all day and all of the night — or 3.5 hours of video.

Doing the iPod shuffle

If the regular iPod models aren't small enough to fit into your lifestyle or your budget, try the ultra-tiny 2GB iPod shuffle for $49 (see Figure 1-3). Its built-in clip lets you attach it to your clothing or almost anything. The iPod shuffle has no display but offers buttons on the front to control playback. This design keeps the size and weight to a minimum.

Figure 1-3: iPod shuffle is the iPod you can wear.

The iPod shuffle can also talk to you with the VoiceOver feature. Press the VoiceOver button on top of your iPod shuffle to hear the title and artist of the song. VoiceOver even tells you whether your battery needs charging.

The 2GB iPod shuffle holds about 500 songs, assuming an average of 4 minutes per song, using the AAC format at the High Quality setting for adding music (as described in Chapter 5). The battery offers up to 15 hours of power between charges.

Twirling the iPod classic

The iPod classic, shown in Figure 1-4, is an undeniable classic that Apple has kept in its product line for a good reason: Customers like it. It uses the same click wheel and buttons as previous models, combining the scroll wheel with pressure-sensitive buttons underneath the top, bottom, left, and right areas of the circular pad of the wheel. With the iPod classic, it's all about music storage on the road — Apple provides a single slim, 4.9-ounce 160GB model in black or silver that can hold 40,000 songs, 25,000 photos, or about 200 hours of video; and its battery offers up to 36 hours of music playback or 6 hours of video playback.

Figure 1-4: iPod classic can hold 40, 000 songs.

Thinking Outside the Box

Apple excels at packaging. Don't destroy the elegant box while opening it. Keep the box in case, heaven forbid, you need to return the iPod to Apple — the box ensures that you can safely return it for a new battery or replacement.

The iPod touch and iPod nano models come with stereo Apple EarPods, which are as good as some of the better earphones on the market — contoured to fit your ear and minimize sound loss. The iPod shuffle and iPod classic come with the Apple Earphones, which are suitable for most people. So you might be fine with what you get — except that if you want to use remote control buttons for playback or a voice microphone close to your mouth (which is useful for iPod touch voice calls and voice recording), you can get the Apple EarPods with Remote and Mic in the accessories section of the Apple Store. And, of course, there are many alternatives — a visit to a local Apple Store, or any electronics department or store (such as Fry's) can boggle your mind with displays of accessories, and you can order them online at the online Apple Store (easily accessed from www.apple.com) or other sites such as Amazon.com (www.amazon.com).

The iPod touch, iPod classic, and iPod nano are each supplied with a cable that connects your iPod (or a dock for the iPod) to your computer or to the AC power adapter using a Universal Serial Bus (USB) connection — a way of attaching things to computers and bussing data around while providing power. The iPod touch and iPod nano cables have a USB connector on one end and Apple's Lightning connector on the other end to connect either to a Lightning-compatible dock or directly to the iPod nano or iPod touch. The iPod shuffle includes a special cable to connect to a USB power adapter or to your computer. The iPod classic uses a cable with a USB connector on one end and Apple's older flat dock connector on the other end, which is compatible with the older docks.

You may want to have around a few things that are not in the box. For example, even though you don't really need an AC power adapter or dock (because you can connect the iPod directly to your computer to recharge your battery), a power adapter or dock is useful for keeping the battery charged without having to connect the iPod to your computer.

Although you can store your apps, content library, personal information, and settings for an iPod touch in Apple's iCloud, you may still want to use a computer and iTunes to manage these things and keep your iPod touch in sync with them. You need a computer and iTunes to manage and back up the content on an iPod nano, iPod shuffle, or iPod classic. Basically, that computer has to be a Mac running the most recent version of OS X (the operating system) or a PC running Windows XP, Vista, Windows 7, or Windows 8.

You've seen requirements before — lots of jargon about MB (megabytes), GB (gigabytes), GHz (gigahertz), and RAM (random access memory), sprinkled with names like Intel, AMD, and OS X. To see the most up-to-date requirements, visit the Apple download page (www.apple.com/itunes/download). This page is cool: It shows Macintosh requirements if you're visiting using a Mac (with a Windows Requirements link), or PC/Windows requirements if you're visiting using a PC (with a Macintosh Requirements link).

Applying Power to an iPod

All iPod models come with essentially the same requirement: power. You can supply power to your iPod (and charge your battery at the same time) by using the provided cable and your computer, or you can use an optional AC power adapter that works with voltages in North America and many parts of Europe and Asia.

Connecting to a computer or power adapter

An iPod can draw power from a computer or from a power adapter. There are also accessories such as *docks* that offer power and power strips with USB ports for recharging devices.

A dock can be convenient as a base station when you're not traveling with your iPod because you can remove any travel case and just slip it into the dock without connecting cables. Just connect it to an Apple or a third-party dock and then use the cable supplied with your iPod to connect the dock to your computer or power adapter. You can pick up a dock at an Apple Store, order one online, or take advantage of third-party dock offerings. Some docks, such as the Apple Universal Dock, keep your iPod classic or iPod nano in an upright position while connected. Some docks also provide connections for a home stereo or headphones, and some docks offer built-in speakers.

On the bottom of the iPod touch and iPod nano is the Lightning connector for connecting the USB cable or Lightning-compatible dock. You find the older, larger flat connector on the bottom of the iPod classic. The iPod shuffle uses the earphone connector with a special USB cable.

To connect your iPod touch, iPod nano, or iPod classic to your computer or power adapter, plug the Lightning connector or flat connector of the cable into the iPod (or into a dock holding your iPod), and then plug the USB connector on the other end of the cable into the USB 2.0 or USB 3.0 port on your computer or the USB connector on the power adapter.

The iPod shuffle is supplied with a special USB cable that plugs into the earphone connection of the iPod shuffle and draws power from the USB connection on the computer or from a USB power adapter. Plug one end of the included cable into the earphone connection of iPod shuffle and the other end into a USB 2.0 or USB 3.0 connection on your computer or power adapter.

When you first connect your iPod to a computer, iTunes starts up and begins the setup process (see Chapter 2). After syncing, the computer continues to provide power through the USB 2.0 or USB 3.0 port to the iPod.

Why USB 2.0 or USB 3.0 port? What happened to 1.0? Most PCs and all current Macs already have either USB 3.0 or USB 2.0, which is all you need to sync an iPod with your computer. Although you can use a low-speed USB 1.0 or 1.1 connection to sync an iPod, it's slower than molasses on a subzero morning for syncing.

To find out more about previous generations of iPods, including detailed information about USB and FireWire cables and connections, see Bonus Chapter 1 in the free tips section of the author's website (www.tonybove. com/tips).

Turning it on and off

Touch any button to turn on an iPod classic. To turn off an iPod classic, press and hold the Play/Pause button. To keep an iPod classic from turning on by accident, you can lock it with the Hold switch on the top. The Hold switch locks the iPod buttons so that you don't accidentally activate them — slide the Hold switch so that it exposes an orange layer underneath. To unlock the buttons, slide the Hold switch so that it hides the orange layer underneath.

If your iPod classic shows a display but doesn't respond to your button-pressing, don't panic. Just check the Hold switch and make sure that it's set to one side so that the orange layer underneath disappears (the normal position).

To turn on an iPod shuffle, slide the three-way switch to expose the green layer underneath. To turn it off, slide the three-way switch to hide the green layer. With the three-way switch or On/Off switch, iPod shuffle models don't need a Hold switch.

To turn on an iPod nano, press the Sleep/Wake button on top. Press it again to turn it off. To conserve battery life, the screen goes dark anyway if you don't touch it for a while — press the Sleep/Wake button to turn it back on.

Awaken your iPod touch by pressing the sleep/wake button, which is located on the top of the iPod touch. The iPod touch presents the Slide to Unlock slider at the bottom of the screen, and stays locked until you slide your finger across the slider to unlock it. If you press the sleep/wake button again, it puts the iPod touch back to sleep and locks its controls to save battery power.

You can turn the iPod touch completely off by holding down the sleep/wake button for about 2 seconds, until you see the Slide to Power Off slider; then slide your finger across the slider to turn it off. You can then turn it back on by pressing and holding the sleep/wake button.

After awakening but before unlocking your iPod touch, you can press the physical Home button twice quickly to display music controls. Slide the volume control to set the volume; tap the play/pause, back, or forward buttons to control playback (for details on music playback, see Chapter 12). You can also tap a camera icon to launch the Camera app. See Chapter 14 for details on taking photos and videos.

iPods can function in temperatures as cold as 50° F (Fahrenheit) and as warm as 95° F, but they work best at room temperature (closer to 68° F). If you leave your iPod out in the cold all night, it might have trouble waking, and it might even display a low-battery message. Plug the iPod into a power source, wait until it warms up, and try it again. If it still doesn't wake up or respond properly, try resetting the iPod as I describe in Chapter 19.

To save battery power, you should plug an iPod into AC power or your computer before turning it back on from a completely off state. And speaking of battery details, check out the next section.

Facing Charges of Battery

You can take a 6-hour flight from New York to California and watch videos on your iPod touch the entire time without recharging. The iPod models are supplied with built-in rechargeable lithium-ion batteries that offer the following playback time:

- ✒ The iPod shuffle offers 15 hours of music.
- ✒ The iPod nano offers 30 hours of music or 3.5 hours of video.
- ✒ The iPod classic offers 36 hours of music or 6 hours of video or photo display with music.
- ✒ The iPod touch offers 40 hours of music, or 8 hours of video, browsing the Internet using Wi-Fi, or displaying photo slide shows with music.

To find out more about the batteries in previous generations of iPods, see Bonus Chapter 1 in the free tips section of the author's website (www. tonybove.com/tips).

Recharging your battery

The iPod battery recharges automatically when you connect it to a power source. For example, it starts charging immediately when you insert it into a dock that's connected to a power source (or to a computer with a powered USB connection). It takes 4 hours to recharge the iPod touch or iPod classic battery fully from a drained state (less if partially charged), and only 3 hours for an iPod nano or iPod shuffle.

Need power when you're on the run? Look for a power outlet in the airport terminal or hotel lobby and plug in your iPod with your AC power adapter — the battery fast-charges to 80 percent capacity in 2 hours. After that, the battery receives a trickle charge for the rest of the time until it's fully charged.

Don't fry your iPod with some generic power adapter. Use *only* the power adapter from Apple or a certified iPod adapter, such as the power accessories from Belkin, Griffin, Monster, XtremeMac, and other reputable vendors.

You can use your iPod while the battery is charging, or you can disconnect it and use it before the battery is fully charged. A battery icon with a progress bar in the upper-right corner of the iPod touch, iPod nano, or iPod classic display indicates how much power is left. When you charge the battery, the battery icon displays a lightning bolt. The battery icon is completely filled in when the battery is fully charged, and it slowly empties into just an outline as the battery is used up. When you awaken an iPod touch that's plugged in to power, you see a large battery icon indicating how much juice you have. When you charge the battery, the large battery icon includes a lightning bolt.

You can check the battery of an iPod shuffle by turning it on or by connecting it to your computer. You can check the battery status without interrupting playback by quickly turning the iPod shuffle off and then on again. The tiny battery status light next to the headphone connector tells you how much charge you have:

- ✔ **Green:** The iPod shuffle is fully charged (if connected to a computer) or charged at least 50 percent.

- ✔ **Orange:** The iPod shuffle battery is still charging (if connected to a computer) or is as low as 25 percent. If the iPod shuffle is connected to your computer and blinking orange, this means that iTunes is synchronizing it — don't disconnect the iPod shuffle until it stops blinking.

- ✔ **Red:** Very little charge is left and you need to recharge it.

If no light is visible, the iPod shuffle is completely out of power, and you need to recharge it to use it.

To hear the VoiceOver feature speak your battery status ("full," "75 percent," "50 percent," "25 percent," or "low"), click and hold the center button of the earbud controls.

In iTunes, the battery icon next to your iPod shuffle's name in the Devices section of the source pane shows the battery status (you learn about the iTunes source pane in Chapter 5). The icon displays a lightning bolt when the battery is charging and a plug when the battery is fully charged.

Maintaining battery mojo

There are ways to keep your battery healthy. I recommend a lean diet of topping off your battery whenever it is convenient.

Using and recharging 100 percent of battery capacity is called a *charge cycle*. You can charge the battery many times, but there is a limit to how many full charge cycles you can do before needing to replace the battery.

Each time you complete a charge cycle (100 percent recharge), it diminishes battery capacity slightly. Apple estimates that the battery loses 20 percent of its capacity (meaning it holds 80 percent of the charge) after 400 full charge cycles. Recharging your battery when it's only half empty does not count as a full charge cycle, but as half a charge cycle. That means you can use half its power one day and then recharge it fully, and then use half the next day and recharge it fully again, and this would count as one charge cycle, not two.

It's a good idea to *calibrate* the battery once soon after you get your iPod; that is, run it all the way down (a full discharge) and then charge it all the way up (which takes at least 4 hours for an iPod touch or iPod classic, or 3 hours for an iPod nano or iPod shuffle). Although this doesn't actually change battery performance, it does improve the battery gauge so that the gauge displays a more accurate reading. This calibration occurs anyway if you fully recharge the battery, but if you've never done that, you can calibrate by disconnecting the iPod from any power for 24 hours to make sure the battery is empty and then fully recharging the battery.

Lithium-ion batteries typically last 3 years or more, but are vulnerable to high temperatures, which decrease their life spans considerably. Don't leave your iPod in a hot place, such as on a sunny car dashboard, for very long (don't leave it out in the rain, either — water can easily damage it).

For a complete description of how Apple's batteries work, see the Apple Lithium-Ion Batteries page at www.apple.com/batteries.

The iPod built-in rechargeable battery is, essentially, a life-or-death proposition. After it's dead, it can be replaced, but Apple charges a replacement fee plus shipping. If your warranty is still active, you should have Apple replace it under the warranty program (which may cost nothing except perhaps shipping — and with AppleCare service, even the shipping may be free). Don't try to replace it yourself because opening your iPod invalidates the warranty.

Keeping an iPod in a snug carrying case when charging is tempting, but it's also potentially disastrous. You could damage the unit by overheating it and frying its circuits, rendering it as useful as a paperweight. To get around this problem, you can purchase one of the heat-dissipating carrying cases available in the Apple Store.

If you don't use your iPod for a month, even while it's connected to power and retaining a charge, it can become catatonic. Perhaps it gets depressed from being left alone too long. At that point, it may not start — you have to completely drain and recharge the battery. To drain the battery, use it for many hours or leave it unconnected to power for 24 hours. Then, to fully recharge the battery, connect it to power for at least 4 hours without using it (or longer if you are using it).

Saving power

The iPod classic and older models include a hard drive — and whatever causes the hard drive to spin causes a drain on power. iPod nano, iPod shuffle, and iPod touch models use a flash drive, which uses less power but still uses power when playing content. The iPod touch also uses power doing things like accessing the Internet, using Bluetooth devices, keeping up with notifications, and running apps. Keeping these activities to a minimum can help you save power.

The following are tips on saving power while using your iPod:

- ✔ **Pause.** Pause playback when you're not listening. Pausing (stopping) playback is the easiest way to conserve power.

- ✔ **Lock it (with the iPod nano or iPod touch).** Press the sleep/wake button on top to immediately put it to sleep and lock its controls to save battery power. You can set your iPod touch to automatically go to sleep by choosing Settings➪General➪Auto-Lock from the Home screen, and then choosing 1 Minute, 2 Minutes, 3 Minutes, 4 Minutes, or 5 Minutes (or Never, to prevent automatic sleep).

- ✔ **Hold it (with the iPod classic).** Flip the Hold switch on the iPod classic to the locked position (with the orange layer showing underneath) to make sure that controls aren't accidentally activated. You don't want your iPod playing music in your pocket and draining the battery when you're not listening.

- ✔ **Back away from the light.** Turn down the brightness on an iPod touch by choosing Settings➪Brightness and dragging the brightness slider to the left. Turn it down on an iPod nano by tapping Settings➪General➪Brightness. Use the backlight sparingly on the iPod classic — select Backlight Timer from the iPod Settings menu to limit backlighting to a number of seconds or set it to Off. (Choose Settings from the main menu.) Don't use the backlight in daylight if you don't need it.

- ✔ **Don't ask and don't tell where you are (with an iPod touch).** Turn off Location Services if you aren't using apps that need it. Choose Settings➪Privacy➪Location Services from the Home screen, and tap On for the Location Services option at the top to turn it off (tap Off to turn it back on). See Chapter 4 for details.

✔ **Let the postman ring twice (with an iPod touch).** Check e-mail less frequently. You may want to turn off Push and change your Fetch settings, as I describe in Chapter 16. Turn off instant notifications from Facebook and other sources — see Chapter 4 for details.

✔ **Put a cap on Bluetooth (with an iPod touch or iPod nano).** Turn off Bluetooth (choose Settings⇨General⇨Bluetooth and tap the On button to turn it off) if you're not using a Bluetooth device.

✔ **Drop back in from the Internet (with an iPod touch).** Turn off Wi-Fi when not browsing the Internet or using Maps: Choose Settings⇨Wi-Fi and tap the On button to turn it off.

✔ **Fasten your seat belt (with an iPod touch).** Turn on Airplane Mode to automatically turn off Wi-Fi and Bluetooth at once, before the flight attendant reminds you to do it: Choose Settings and tap Off to turn Airplane Mode on.

✔ **Turn it off completely.** To turn off an iPod nano, press the Sleep/Wake button. To turn off an iPod classic, press and hold the Play/Pause button. To turn off an iPod shuffle, slide the switch to the off position, hiding the green layer underneath the switch. You can turn the iPod touch completely off by holding down the sleep/wake button for about 2 seconds, until you see the Slide to Power Off slider; then slide your finger across the slider to turn it off. You can then turn it back on by pressing and holding the sleep/wake button.

Starting an iPod touch or iPod classic that was completely turned off takes quite a bit of power — more than if it woke from sleep. If you do turn it off, plug it in to AC power or your computer before turning it back on.

✔ **You may continue.** Play songs continuously without using the iPod controls. Selecting songs and using the back and forward buttons require more energy. Also, turn off your iPod equalizer (EQ) if you turned it on — choose Settings⇨Music and tap EQ, and then tap Off.

Always use the latest iPod software and update your software when updates come out, as I describe in Chapter 19. Apple constantly tries to improve how your iPod works, and many of these advancements relate to power usage.

2

Setting Up iTunes and Your iPod

In This Chapter

▶ Installing iTunes on a Windows PC
▶ Installing iTunes on a Mac
▶ Setting up your iPod touch
▶ Setting up any iPod with iTunes

*i*Tunes manages your library of content and apps on your computer. It gives you the power to grab music from CDs and other sources and convert video to play on iPads and iPhones as well as iPods. iTunes also provides a quick and easy browsing experience for accessing the iTunes Store and App Store from your computer.

iTunes is essential for setting up an iPod classic, iPod nano, or iPod shuffle, and for updating its software and synchronizing content to it. You have more choices with an iPod touch — you can set up an iPod touch wirelessly using the iCloud service (as I describe in this chapter). You can also sync an iPod touch and update its software wirelessly with iCloud (as I describe in Chapter 8). But iTunes lets you do all that without an Internet connection, and provides finer control and more options for syncing content. You can also use iTunes to restore the device to its original factory settings if you need to (see Chapter 19 for details).

This chapter explains how to set up any iPod model using iTunes (including the iPod touch) and how to set up an iPod touch wirelessly with iCloud. During the setup process, you install the iPod software that controls the iPod nano, iPod classic, and iPod shuffle or the iOS operating system software that runs inside the iPod touch.

Installing iTunes

Setting up iTunes is a quick and easy process. The most up-to-date version of iTunes as of this writing is version 11. However, software updates occur rapidly, so you may end up installing a newer version by the time you read this. (If you already have iTunes installed, see Chapter 21 for instructions on updating it.) You can visit the Apple website to download the most up-to-date version of iTunes, which recognizes all iPod models.

Installing on a Windows PC

Before installing iTunes, make sure that you're logged on as a Windows administrator user. Quit all other applications before installing and be sure to disable any antivirus software.

To install iTunes for Windows, follow these steps:

1. **Download the iTunes installer from the Apple site.**

   Browse the iTunes page on the Apple website (`www.apple.com/itunes`) and click the Download iTunes button, as shown in Figure 2-1. You can then optionally enter your e-mail address, and click Download Now. Follow your browser's instructions to download the installer file (`iTunes64Setup.exe` for Windows 7) to your hard drive.

2. **Run the iTunes installer.**

   Double-click the installer file to install iTunes. At the Welcome screen, click the Next button. After clicking Next, the installer displays the iTunes installation options, as shown in Figure 2-2.

3. **Choose your iTunes installation options.**

   You can turn the following options on or off (as shown in Figure 2-2):

   - *Add iTunes Shortcut to My Desktop:* You can install a shortcut for your Windows desktop for iTunes.

   - *Use iTunes as the Default Player for Audio Files:* I suggest turning this option on, allowing iTunes to be the default audio content player for all audio files it recognizes. If you're happy with another audio player on your PC, you can deselect this option, leaving your default player setting unaffected.

4. **Choose the destination folder for iTunes.**

   By default, the installer assumes that you want to store the program in the Program Files folder of your C: drive. If you want to use a different folder, click the Change button to use Windows Explorer to locate the desired folder.

5. **Click the Install button to finish.**

   After you click Install, the installer finishes the installation and displays the Complete dialog.

6. **Click the Finish button.**

   Restarting your Windows PC after installing software is always a good idea.

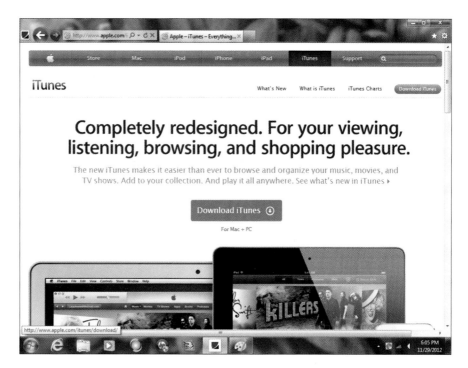

Figure 2-1: Download the newest version of iTunes from the Apple website.

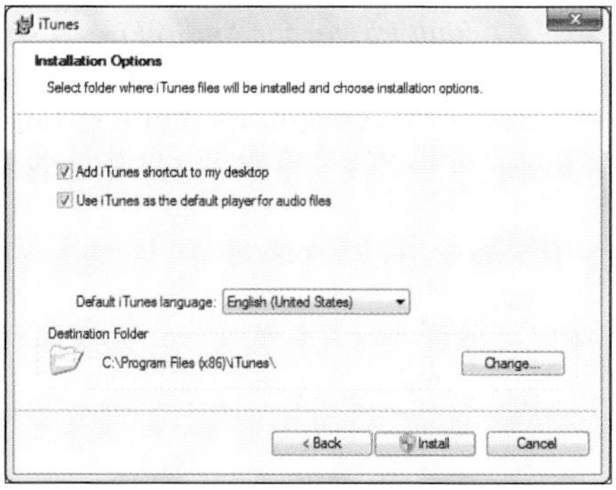

Figure 2-2: Choose iTunes installation options.

iTunes is now installed on your PC. To start using iTunes, double-click the iTunes desktop shortcut or use your Start menu to locate iTunes and launch it.

The first time you launch iTunes, an Apple license agreement appears. Feel free to scroll down to read the agreement, if only to appreciate legal minds at work. Whatever you do, you must click the Agree button to continue. After clicking Agree, the iTunes window appears with helpful links to tutorials on downloading music and importing music from CDs — unless you are replacing an older version of iTunes, in which case your iTunes window appears with your library of content.

Installing on a Mac

As a Mac user, you should already have iTunes installed because all Macs sold since 2003 come preinstalled with iTunes and OS X. The version of iTunes that's provided with the Mac might be the newest version; then again, it might not be. If iTunes displays a dialog with the message that a new version of iTunes is available and asks whether you would like to download it, choose Yes to download the new version. OS X not only downloads iTunes but also installs it automatically after you provide the administrator's password and agree to Apple's software license (of course).

You can set your Mac to automatically download the latest version of iTunes when it becomes available. Choose Preferences from the iTunes menu, click the General tab, and select the Check for New Software Updates Automatically check box at the bottom of the General preferences to turn it on.

The Mac App Store can update your version of iTunes. Launch App Store on your Mac and click the Updates button at the top of the screen to see the Updates screen. Your Mac checks for application updates, and if your version of iTunes is not the current version, an iTunes update appears on the Updates screen. Click the Update button for the iTunes update.

You can also set your Mac to check for all system software and Apple applications (including iTunes). Choose System Preferences from the Apple menu, and then choose Software Update from the System Preferences window. Select the Automatically Check for Updates check box to turn it on. You can also click the Check Now button to check for a new version immediately. If one exists, it appears in a window for you to select. Click the check mark to select it, and then click the Install button to download and install it.

If you want to manually install iTunes on your Mac or manually upgrade the version you have, you can browse the Apple website (www.apple.com/itunes) to get it, and follow the installation instructions. You can download iTunes free.

After installing iTunes, launch it by double-clicking the iTunes application or clicking the iTunes icon in the Dock. The first time you launch iTunes, an Apple license agreement appears. You must click the Agree button to continue. After clicking Agree, iTunes displays the iTunes window with links to tutorials on buying and importing music.

You can set up any model iPod using iTunes, as I describe in the upcoming "Setting Up an iPod Using iTunes" section. However, if you have an iPod touch, you can also set it up wirelessly using the Internet and Apple's iCloud service, as I describe in the next section.

Setting Up an Pod touch

After adding power, a new iPod touch comes alive and displays "iPod" and a slider with the word "Configure" or "Set Up" in different languages, as shown in Figure 2-3, left side). Follow these steps to set up your device to meet your needs:

1. **Slide your finger across the slider with the word "Configure" or "Set Up" in different languages.**

   After sliding across the slider, a brand new iPod touch shows the language screen. An iPod touch that has been set up before shows the Wi-Fi Networks screen, and you can jump to Step 4.

2. **Tap your language choice (if it's not already selected), and then tap the right-arrow icon in the top-right corner of the language screen.**

   After selecting a language, the Country or Region screen appears, showing a map of the world.

3. **Tap your country or region (if it's not already selected), and then tap Next.**

   To see more countries and regions, tap the Show More button. After tapping Next, the Wi-Fi Networks screen appears for choosing a Wi-Fi network, as shown in Figure 2-3, center.

   If you don't have a Wi-Fi network at your location, and no networks are within range (that you can log in to), you need to connect your iPod touch to your computer and use iTunes to continue with setup and syncing. Skip these steps and jump to the section, "Setting Up Any iPod Using iTunes," later in this chapter.

4. **Tap the network name if it is not already selected, and then tap Next in the upper-right corner of the screen.**

   The closest network with the strongest signal should already be selected (with a check mark next to it); if not, tap the network name (see Chapter 4 for details on connecting to Wi-Fi networks).

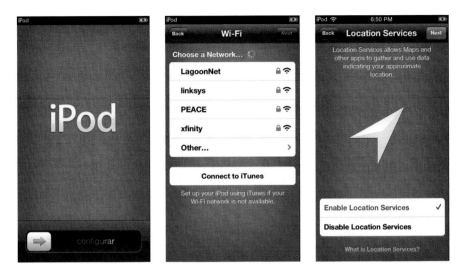

Figure 2-3: The iPod startup screen (left), choosing a Wi-Fi network (center), and enabling
Location Services (right).

5. **Tap a password for the Wi-Fi network if needed or log in to the network with your ID and password, and then tap Next in the upper-right corner of the screen.**

   Public networks typically require a username or ID and a password. Private networks are usually set up with a password — type the password for access.

   After choosing a Wi-Fi network, the Location Services screen appears, as shown in Figure 2-3, right side.

6. **Tap Enable Location Services, and then tap Next in the upper-right corner.**

   By choosing to enable Location Services, you are giving your iPod touch the chance to figure out the appropriate language and country for using your iPod touch. Apple offers country-specific iTunes Stores and many different languages. If you don't enable Location Services, you see screens that let you choose your language and your country. After tapping Next, the Set Up iPod touch screen appears, as shown in Figure 2-4, left side.

7. **Choose one of the following options (refer to Figure 2-4, left side):**

   • *Set Up as New iPod touch:* Select this option if you want to set up the iPod touch as new, and then tap Next.

Figure 2-4: Set up or Restore (left), sign in or create an Apple ID (center), and use iCloud (right).

- *Restore from iCloud Backup:* Select this option if you previously backed up your settings for an iPod touch, iPad, or iPhone to iCloud (as I describe in Chapter 19). You can then pick an iPod touch, iPad, or iPhone name from the pop-up menu to restore the previous device's name and settings. Your automatic sync settings are restored from the previous backup, and you can change your sync settings as I show you in Chapter 7.

- *Restore from iTunes Backup:* Select this option to restore a previous device's name and settings from an iTunes backup. You can then pick an iPod touch, iPad, or iPhone name from the pop-up menu. Skip to the next section, "Setting Up Any iPod Using iTunes," to use the iTunes backup.

After this step, the iPod touch displays the Apple ID screen shown in Figure 2-4, center.

8. **Sign in with your Apple ID or create a free Apple ID.**

Your Apple ID automatically sets up the iPod touch with your account in the iCloud service and the iTunes Store, which includes the App Store. Here's what you do:

- *If you have an iTunes Store, Apple Store, iCloud, or Apple developer ID,* tap the Sign In with an Apple ID option and enter the ID and password to swiftly move through the registration process. You then see a Terms and Conditions screen, and you have to tap Agree to continue. Apple automatically recognizes your iPod touch so that you don't need to enter the serial number.

- *If you don't have an Apple ID of any kind,* tap the Create a Free Apple ID option. You see a screen for entering your birthday (which is used as a question for retrieving your password if you forget it) and then a screen for entering an Apple ID and password combination. You then see a Terms and Conditions screen, and you have to tap Agree to continue. For details about setting up an iTunes Store account, see Chapter 6.

After signing in with your Apple ID, or creating a free Apple ID, the iPod touch displays the Set Up iCloud screen shown in Figure 2-4, right side.

   9. Tap Use iCloud and tap Next in the upper-right corner.

   Tap Use iCloud to set up the free portion of your iCloud service, which you can use to sync your iPod touch with content and personal settings (as I show in Chapter 8).

   If you did not use iCloud in this step, you're finished — and you need to continue setting up your iPod touch with iTunes on your computer, as I describe in the next section. If you are using iCloud, the iCloud Backup screen appears after you tap Next.

   10. Choose iCloud or your computer for backup, and then tap Next.

   Both iTunes on your computer and the iCloud service can back up your iPod touch settings when you sync the device, so that you can restore the settings you use to customize the device and its apps, including Wi-Fi network settings, the keyboard dictionary, and settings for contacts, calendars, and e-mail accounts. This backup comes in handy if you want to apply the settings to a new iPod touch or to one that you had to restore to its factory condition.

   If you generally sync your iPod touch with your computer using iTunes, tap the Back Up to My Computer option. If you sync your iPod touch from iCloud, as I describe in Chapter 8, you can tap Back Up to iCloud. Then tap Next to finish setting up your iPod touch. If you chose to use iCloud in Step 9, the Find My iPod touch screen appears.

   11. Turn on Find My iPod touch, and then tap Next.

   This option appears if you chose to use iCloud in Step 9. Tap the Use Find My iPod touch option to turn it on, or tap Don't Use Find My iPod touch to turn this option off. For details about this option, see Chapter 8. After this step, the Messaging screen appears.

   12. Deselect e-mail addresses that other people should not use to reach you with Messages or FaceTime, and then tap Next.

   Other people that use Messages or FaceTime on their iPhones, iPads, iPod touches, or Macs running Mountain Lion, can contact you at the e-mail addresses listed on the Messaging screen. By default, the e-mail address you use with your iTunes Store account is listed and active, along with any other e-mail accounts that were synced with this device previously (if you are upgrading to the new iOS rather than starting from scratch). Tap any e-mail address to deselect it so that other people can't use it to communicate to your iPod touch.

After this step, the iPod touch shows the Siri screen. (If you have a previous model without this screen, skip to Step 14.)

13. **Tap Use Siri, or Don't Use Siri.**

    Siri is Apple's voice-based personal assistant, which you can use to ask for directions, look up contacts, search the Internet, and schedule appointments, as I describe in Chapter 18. You can even use Siri to take dictation, as I show in Chapter 3.

    After this step, the Diagnostics screen appears.

14. **Automatically send (or don't send) diagnostics and usage information.**

    Tap Automatically Send to send the information, or tap Don't Send to not send it. This is your chance to help Apple improve the product — by automatically sending this info to keep Apple on its toes. Remember, however, that your location may also be sent with diagnostic information, depending on whether an app was using your location. To opt out of this, tap Don't Send. Either way, the Thank You screen appears.

15. **Start using your iPod touch.**

    Tap the Start Using iPod touch button on the Thank You screen.

That's it. Your iPod touch is ready to sync with iCloud if you chose to use iCloud in Step 9, and ready to back up its settings to iCloud if you chose that option in Step 10. This all happens wirelessly over the Internet, so you can do it in any location that offers a Wi-Fi Internet connection you can log in to. If you don't use iCloud, you can sync your iPod by connecting to iTunes, as I describe in the next section.

Setting Up Any iPod Using iTunes

You can set up any iPod model using iTunes, whether or not you are connected to a Wi-Fi network. With iTunes, you can set up your iPod touch from an iTunes backup and also customize the name of your iPod touch by following these quick setup steps with iTunes. (You can also rename your iPod when you use iTunes to sync it, as I describe in Chapter 7.)

When you connect a new iPod to your computer for the first time using a USB cable, iTunes displays the Welcome screen, as shown in Figure 2-5 for an iPod touch. Follow these steps to set up an iPod touch; skip to Step 2 to set up an iPod nano, iPod classic, or iPod shuffle:

1. **If you're setting up an iPod touch and you've synced it previously on the same computer, choose whether to use its settings by restoring from its backup or to set up the device as new.**

   iTunes first checks to see whether you have ever backed up an iPad, iPod touch, or iPhone before. If you haven't set one up before, skip to Step 2. Otherwise, iTunes gives you the following choices:

   - *Set Up as New:* Select this option if you want to set the iPod touch up as new.

   - *Restore from the Backup of:* Select this option, and pick an iPad, iPod touch, or iPhone from the pop-up menu to restore the previous device's name and settings. Your automatic sync settings are restored from the previous backup, but you can change them the way I show in Chapters 7 and 8.

2. **Click the Continue button on the Welcome screen.**

   iTunes displays the Sync with iTunes screen, showing you the iTunes tabs that you use to browse the iTunes library.

3. **Click the Get Started button.**

   After clicking Get Started, iTunes displays the Summary sync page, as shown in Figure 2-6 for an iPod nano.

4. **(Optional) Double-click the name and enter a new name for your iPod on the Summary sync page (refer to Figure 2-6).**

   Double-click inside the name so that it highlights and displays the text cursor, and type a new name.

5. **(Optional) Set your iPod sync settings as described in Chapter 7.**

   You can start syncing now, or sync later (after reading Chapter 7). If you sync now, wait for the message "Sync is completed" in the top status pane before continuing to the next step.

6. **Click Done and disconnect your iPod.**

   Disconnect the device from your computer by ejecting it. To eject your iPod, click the eject button next to its name in the iPod sync button (take a sneak peek ahead to Chapter 7 to see the eject button). You can then connect the iPod to its dock or power adapter to continue recharging its battery.

   After ejecting the iPod, wait for its display to show the main menu or the OK to disconnect message. You can then disconnect it from the computer. Never disconnect an iPod before ejecting it because such bad behavior might cause it to freeze and require a reset. (If that happens, see Chapter 19 for instructions.)

   You're done if you're setting up an iPod shuffle, and almost done if you are setting up an iPod touch, iPod nano, or iPod classic. Skip to Step 8 for an iPod nano or iPod classic.

Figure 2-5: Set your iPod touch up as new, or restore from an iPod touch, iPad, or iPhone backup.

Figure 2-6: Give your iPod a name and set sync options.

7. **iPod touch only: To finish setting up an iPod touch, follow the steps in the earlier section, "Setting Up an iPod touch."**

   This step requires access to a Wi-Fi network and the Internet so that you can access the iTunes Store and iCloud to set up your online account.

8. **iPod nano and iPod classic: Choose your language on the first screen.**

   Your iPod nano or iPod classic presents a list of languages. Choose your language (tap it on an iPod nano, or use the scroll wheel and click the select button to choose it on an iPod classic).

That's it, you're finished setting it up. Now go enjoy it!

3

Putting Your Finger on It

In This Chapter

▷ Touching and gesturing on an iPod touch or iPod nano

▷ Organizing apps on your iPod touch Home screens

▷ Typing on the iPod touch

▷ Thumbing through iPod classic menus

*T*he iPod is all about convenience. Apple designed the iPod classic and iPod shuffle models to be held in one hand so that you can perform simple operations by thumb. Even if you're all thumbs when pressing small buttons on tiny devices, you can still thumb your way to iPod heaven. The iPod shuffle's VoiceOver feature complements this arrangement by announcing each song, so you can quickly jump around.

With an iPod touch or iPod nano, your fingers do the walking. You can make gestures to do things, such as flicking a finger to scroll a list quickly, sliding your finger to scroll slowly or to drag a slider (such as the volume slider). You can double-tap a photo to zoom in to it and see more detail, and then drag the image to position the part you want to see in the center of the screen. On an iPod touch, pinch with two fingers to zoom out of a photo or pull apart with two fingers (also known as *unpinch*) to zoom in to the photo to see it more clearly.

This chapter gives you a quick tour of the iPod models, including the menus of an iPod classic, the iPod shuffle controls, and all the touch-and-gesture tricks to make your iPod nano or iPod touch dance and sing. I also give you a complete tour of the onscreen keyboard.

With the iPod touch or iPod nano, it's all touch and go. The device responds to tapping, flicking, and sliding your fingertip, among other gestures (such as shaking, tilting, two-finger tapping, and so on). One tap is all you need to run an app or select something, but sometimes you have to slide your finger to scroll the display and see more selections.

TIP

Sticky fingers are not recommended. To clean your iPod touch or iPod nano, make sure to unplug all cables and turn it off. (See Chapter 1.) Use a soft, slightly damp, lint-free cloth to wipe your screen clean — see Chapter 20 for cleaning tips.

Going on a Quick Tour of the iPod touch

After you press the sleep/wake button, the first screen you see on an iPod touch before unlocking it includes the time and date at the top, a nice color pattern as a background, the Slide to Unlock slider at the bottom, and a camera icon to the right of the slider. To unlock your iPod touch, slide your finger across the Slide to Unlock slider. Once unlocked, your Home screen appears in all its glory, as shown in Figure 3-1.

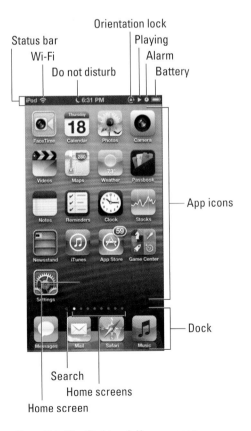

Figure 3-1: The iPod touch Home screen.

After awakening but before unlocking your iPod touch, you can quickly take a picture with the iPod touch camera by sliding the camera icon up to reveal the camera, which I show in Chapter 14. You can also press the physical Home button twice quickly to display music controls. Slide the volume control to set the volume, and tap the play/pause, previous/rewind or next/fast-forward buttons to control playback (for details on music playback, see Chapter 12).

Here are the touches and gestures you need to know to use an iPod touch (for touches and gestures with an iPod nano, see the later section, "Tapping Your iPad nano"):

- **Drag with your fingertip:** Scroll up or down lists slowly.

- **Flick up or down:** Swipe your fingertip quickly across the surface to scroll up or down lists rapidly.

- **Touch and hold:** Touch and hold an object in order to drag it, or while scrolling, touch and hold to stop the moving list.

- **Flick from left to right or right to left:** Quickly swipe your fingertip across the screen to change screens or application panes or to scroll a wide screen quickly.

- **Single tap:** Select an item.

- **Double tap:** Zoom in or out with Safari, Maps, and other applications.

- **Two-finger single tap:** Zoom out in Maps.

- **Pinch:** Zoom out.

- **Unpinch:** Zoom in.

Need to practice your tapping? Try Tap Tap Revenge, a rhythm game that plays music while requiring you to tap each of the colored balls when they reach the line at the bottom of the screen. If you tap the ball on the beat, you gain points; if not, it counts as a miss. You can also activate a revenge mode to score more points by shaking the iPod touch after setting a winning streak of 50 beats.

Sliding to the Home screen

There's no place like Home — it's the screen where you start. Everything is available from the Home screen at the touch of a finger (refer to Figure 3-1).

Application (also called *app*) icons appear on the Home screen, starting with the ones from Apple. (Touching Music, for example, brings up the Music screen with icons for Playlists, Artists, Songs, and so on.) The multi-touch interface changes for each app. Press the physical Home button below the screen (not shown in Figure 3-1) at any time to go back to the Home screen.

Shake, rattle, and roll

Your iPod touch can sense motion with its built-in accelerometer and orientation with its three-axis gyro. When you rotate it from a vertical view (portrait) to a horizontal view (landscape), the iPod touch detects the movement and orientation and changes the display accordingly. This happens so quickly that you can control a game with these movements.

For example, Pass the Pigs is a dice game in which you shake three times to roll your pigs to gain points. In the Labyrinth game, you tilt your iPod touch to roll a ball through a wooden maze without falling through the holes. And you can shake, rattle, and roll your way around the world in Yahtzee Adventures while you rack up high scores.

And if that's too tame for you, try Chopper, a helicopter game in which you need to complete your mission and return to base while avoiding enemy fire from tanks and bazooka-wielding madmen. You tilt the iPod touch to fly, and you touch the screen to drop bombs or fire the machine gun.

Xhake Shake lets you shake, flip, rub, and tap your iPod touch to challenge your hand-eye responses. And for scrolling practice, try Light Bike (loosely based on the Disney movie *Tron*) in which you scroll to maneuver a light bike from a third-person perspective against three computer-controlled light bikes. And infants can join the fun: Silver Rattle shows a screen that changes color and rattles with every shake. Big Joe Turner would be proud.

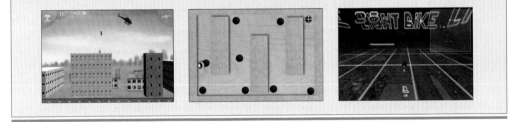

Apps you download from the App Store (as I describe in Chapter 6) show up as icons on the Home screen. You can also save Web Clips to your Home screen as icons that take you directly to those web pages (as I describe in Chapter 15). As you add apps and Web Clips, the iPod touch automatically creates more Home screens to accommodate them. (See the section "Cleaning Up Your iPod touch Home Screens," later in this chapter, to find out how to organize your icons into folders and rearrange icons on Home screens.)

The bottom row of the Home screen is called the *dock*. Icons in the dock remain on the screen when you switch from one Home screen to another. You can change the apps in the dock, as I show in the "Cleaning Up Your iPod touch Home Screens" section, later in this chapter.

The tiny dots above the dock indicate how many Home screens you have, and which Home screen you're viewing. To switch to the next or previous Home screen, flick with your finger to the left or to the right, or tap a dot on the right or left side of the row of dots. (The first dot is actually a tiny magnifying glass icon that represents the Search screen, which I describe in the "Searching for anything" section, later in this chapter.) Press the physical Home button under the screen to go directly from any other Home screen to the first Home screen.

Tapping the apps from Apple

The iPod touch Home screen (refer to Figure 3-1) offers the following apps supplied by Apple free:

- **FaceTime:** Use Wi-Fi to make FaceTime video calls to other people who have FaceTime (currently fourth-generation iPod touch and iPhone 4 models, iPad 2 models, and users running Snow Leopard, Lion, or Mountain Lion on their Macs). See Chapter 18 for details.

- **Calendar:** View your calendar — see Chapter 18 for details.

- **Photos:** Select photos by photo album or select individual photos on the iPod touch, as I show in Chapter 14.

- **Camera:** Snap a photo or shoot video using either the main back camera or front camera, as I show in Chapter 14.

- **Videos:** Play videos from your iTunes library — see Chapter 13.

- **Maps:** View maps and get driving directions, as I show in Chapter 17.

- **Weather:** View the weather in multiple cities — see Chapter 17.

- **Passbook:** Store all of your passes — boarding passes, tickets, store cards, and coupons. Find out how in Chapter 17.

- **Notes:** Add text notes — see the "Tickling the Keyboard" section, later in this chapter.

- **Reminders:** Add reminder notes and to-do tasks to a calendar and a list.

- **Clock:** View multiple clocks and use the alarm clock, timer, and stop-watch, as I show in Chapter 4.

- **Stocks:** Check the prices for financial stocks, bonds, and funds. Chapter 17 shows you how.

- **Newsstand:** Read magazines and newspapers downloaded from the iTunes Store — see Chapter 6 for a description of the iTunes Store.

- **iTunes:** Go to the iTunes online store to purchase content — see Chapter 6 for details.

- **App Store:** Go to Apple's online App Store to download other Apple and third-party apps, as I show in Chapter 6.

- **Game Center:** Discover and play games online with your friends, as I show in Chapter 18.

- **Settings:** Adjust settings for Wi-Fi, sounds, brightness, Safari, and other apps, as well as other settings for the iPod touch itself.

The following icons appear on the dock at the bottom of every Home screen:

- **Messages:** Send and receive text messages with other iPad, iPod touch, or iPhone users with the iMessage service — for details, see Chapter 18.

- **Mail:** Check and send e-mail. The postman always beeps once — see Chapter 16.

- **Safari:** Browse the Web, as I show in Chapter 15.

- **Music:** Select music playlists, artists, songs, albums, and more (including podcasts, genres, composers, audio books, and compilations). Find out all about the Music app in Chapter 12.

The Utilities icon also appears on the Home screen. This is a folder containing the following apps (if you restored from a backup, as I describe in Chapter 2, these apps may be loose on the Home screen rather than in Utilities):

- **Contacts:** View your contacts. To learn more about what you can do with your contacts, see Chapter 18.

- **Calculator:** You can use your iPod touch as a regular calculator for adding, subtracting, multiplying, dividing, and so on. Also, if you hold the iPod touch horizontally, it becomes a scientific calculator.

- **Voice Memos:** Record your voice.

For details on creating voice memos with iPod models and using the Voice Memos app on the iPod touch, see Bonus Chapter 4 in the free tips section of the author's website (www.tonybove.com/tips).

Additionally, you can download Apple's free iBooks app to read electronic books (e-books) from Apple's iBookstore and e-books from other vendors, as well as your own and downloaded PDF files.

Searching for anything

The tiny magnifying glass icon to the left of the dots above the dock (refer to Figure 3-1) is the search icon. Tap the search icon (or flick the first Home screen with your finger to the right) to show the Search screen. Search works just like the Spotlight Search feature of OS X. You can type a search term and immediately see suggestions.

Search looks through contacts, calendars, e-mail (the To:, From:, and Subject: fields, but not the message content), the content (songs, videos, podcasts, and audio books), and even the text in the Notes app. Tap a contact, calendar entry, e-mail, or note suggestion to open it, or tap the song, video, podcast, or audio book suggestion to play it.

You can set which types of information to search through and the order of information types to search first. Choose Settings⟹General⟹Spotlight Search. Tap any information type (Contacts, Applications, Music, Podcasts, Video, Audiobooks, Notes, Mail, and Calendar) to remove the check mark, which removes that type of information from the search; tap the information type again to bring back the check mark and include it in the search. To change the order of information types to search, touch and hold an information type, and then drag it to a new position in the list.

Checking the status bar

The iPod touch shows its current state in the status bar at the top of the screen (refer to Figure 3-1). The icons mean the following:

- **iPod:** Just in case you forgot you had an iPod in your hands (very existential).

- **Wi-Fi:** This icon says the iPod touch is connected to a Wi-Fi network. If the network offers Internet access (all commercial ones do), you're on the Internet. The more bars you see in the icon, the stronger the connection to the network. To find out more about using Wi-Fi, see Chapter 4.

- **Airplane mode:** This icon (not shown in Figure 3-1) replaces the Wi-Fi icon if you turned on Airplane Mode on the Settings screen. When you turn Airplane Mode on, the iPod touch automatically turns off Wi-Fi and Bluetooth. Note that you can turn Wi-Fi and Bluetooth back on while in Airplane Mode, so that you can use the airline's Wi-Fi (if offered).

- **Network activity:** This icon twirls to show that data is traveling from the network to your iPod touch (or vice versa). (Not visible in Figure 3-1.)

- **VPN:** If you have special network settings that access a virtual private network (VPN), this icon shows up next to the Wi-Fi icon to tell you that you are connected to it. Often used for corporate networks, a VPN provides secure information transport by authenticating users and encrypting data. (Not visible in Figure 3-1.)

- **Do not disturb:** If you tell your iPod touch not to disturb you with notifications, this partial moon icon appears. You can set the Notification Center to "do not disturb" by choosing Settings⟹Notifications, as I describe in Chapter 4

- **Play:** This icon tells you that a song, audio book, or podcast is playing (in case you didn't know — maybe you took your headphones off).

- **Orientation lock:** This icon appears if you locked the iPod touch in portrait display orientation. See the section, "Switching orientation," later in this chapter, for details.

- **Alarm:** This icon appears if you set an alarm. See Chapter 4 for details.

✔ **Location Services:** This icon appears to the left of the battery icon if an app is using Location Services to determine the location of the iPod touch. See Chapter 4 for details. (Not visible in Figure 3-1.)

✔ **Bluetooth:** This icon appears to the left of the battery icon only if Bluetooth is turned on (not shown in Figure 3-1). If Bluetooth is on and a device, such as a headset or keyboard, is connected, the icon is white; if it is on but nothing is connected, it turns gray.

✔ **Battery:** The battery icon shows the battery level or charging status. It's completely filled in when the battery is fully charged, and it slowly empties out into just an outline when the battery is used up. A lightning bolt appears inside the icon when the device is recharging, and a plug appears inside it when the iPod touch is connected to power.

Dragging down notifications

Red alert! A message just arrived; check your e-mail right now! Notifications are essential for people who need to know what's happening immediately. Your iPod touch can notify you about new e-mail messages, Facebook friend requests, Twitter messages, and lots of other things. iOS, the iPod touch operating system, offers the Notification Center to make it easy to keep track of them.

To see the Notification Center, swipe down from the status bar of any screen, including the Home screen or any app. The Notification Center includes stock and weather information as well as notifications from Mail and other apps. You can tap any message to see its contents or tap a notification from an app to launch that app.

To close the Notification Center, swipe up from the bottom of the screen. You return to the app you were using (or the Home screen, if you started from the Home screen).

You can customize the Notification Center to show only notifications from specific apps, and make other custom choices, by choosing Settings⤵ Notifications, as I describe in Chapter 4.

Multitasking your apps

You know what multitasking is — for example, talking on the cell phone, watching the kids, and grocery shopping at the same time. *Multitasking* on an iPod touch is roughly the same: doing multiple things at once. In this case, you are running *multiple apps* at once — or at least it seems that way.

With fourth-generation and newer iPod touch models, you can quickly switch to another app you were running previously without having to relaunch the app. When you first run an app, it runs in the *foreground* where the action with your fingers occurs, and the other apps you were just running hang out in the *background*. For example, after launching the Pandora app, it continues to work in the background to keep playing music from the Web while you run another app in the foreground. Other examples are voice-prompted navigation apps, Internet-calling apps, and apps that perform long downloads — they keep working while you're using another app in the foreground.

You can quickly move the currently running app to the background and switch to another background app by double-clicking the Home button. The four most recently used background apps appear in the bottom row of the screen, as shown in Figure 3-2 (left side). Tap any app on this row to immediately switch to that app and move it to the foreground. You can also flick left to see more apps that are running in the background and tap any one of them.

While running any app, or while viewing any Home screen, you can double-click the Home button to see the bottom row of apps in the background. You can also remove an app from the bottom row, terminating the app so it no longer runs in the background — touch and hold the app icon until all the icons in the bottom row start wiggling as if they were doing the jailhouse rock, with a circled minus (–) sign in the top-left corner of each app's icon. Tap the circled minus (–) sign to remove the app. You can free as many as you like. When finished, press the Home button once to stop the icons from wiggling. (The app appears again in the row of recently opened background apps the next time you run it and switch to another app.)

Figure 3-2: Switch to another app in the background (left) and flick the background for the Music player controls and portrait lock button (right).

Switching orientation

The iPod touch Home screens appear in portrait orientation, as do most apps. However, many apps, including Safari and Mail, change the orientation to landscape when you quickly rotate the iPod touch. For example, to view a web page in landscape orientation in Safari, rotate the iPod touch sideways. Safari automatically reorients and expands the page. To set it back to portrait, rotate the iPod touch again. You may prefer landscape for viewing web pages or entering text with the onscreen keyboard, which is wider in landscape orientation.

You can lock the iPod touch display in portrait orientation so that it doesn't jump to landscape even when you rotate the iPod touch. To lock the iPod touch in portrait orientation, double-click the Home button to see the bottom row of apps in the background, and then flick the bottom of the screen from left to right to show the Music player controls and portrait lock button, as shown in Figure 3-2 (right side). Tap the portrait orientation lock button to lock the iPod touch into portrait orientation. The portrait lock icon appears in the status bar (refer to Figure 3-1) when the orientation is locked into portrait.

Cleaning Up Your iPod touch Home Screens

You can easily go crazy in the App Store and end up with a mess of apps across several Home screens. Fortunately, you can organize your apps into folders, and rearrange your app icons over your Home screens, and even create additional Home screens to hold them.

To rearrange your app icons within a Home screen or over several Home screens, or to organize them into folders, touch and hold any icon until all the icons begin to wiggle. (That's right; it looks like they're doing the Watusi.) Then follow the instructions in the sections that follow. After rearranging icons or organizing folders of icons, press the Home button to stop all that wiggling, which saves your new arrangement for your Home screens.

You can also delete apps you download from the App Store by tapping the circled X that appears inside the icon as it wiggles. A warning appears, telling you that deleting the app also deletes all the app's data. You can tap Delete to delete the app, or Cancel. You can then press the physical Home button to stop the icons from wiggling, or continue to rearrange icons and organize them into folders.

Rearranging icons on your Home screens

When you have your icons dancing as I describe earlier, you can drag a wiggling icon to a new position on the Home screen, and the other icons move to accommodate, creating a new arrangement.

To move a wiggling icon to the next Home screen, drag it to the right edge of the screen; to move it to the previous Home screen, drag it to the left edge. If you have no Home screen on the right, the iPod touch creates a new one. You can flick to go back to the first Home screen and drag more wiggling icons to the new Home screen. You can create up to 11 Home screens.

While the wiggling icons are doing their show, you can also change the icons in the dock. Although you are limited to four icons in the dock, you can drag any icon out of the dock and then drag another one in to replace it.

To stop all that wiggling, press the Home button, which saves your new arrangement.

To reset your Home screens to their default arrangements, thereby cleaning up any mess you may have made on them, tap Settings⇨General⇨Reset⇨ Reset Home Screen Layout.

You can also quickly do some serious reorganization of your app icons on your Home screens by using iTunes to sync and arrange apps on your iPod touch, as I show in Chapter 7.

Organizing apps into folders

With the current version of iOS (and you should update your iPod touch software when prompted to do so — see Chapter 19 for details), you can organize your app icons into folders on your Home screens so that you can find them more easily. The iPod touch comes with three apps already organized into a folder — the Utilities folder, which holds the Contacts, Calculator, and Voice Memos apps. Folders also make it easier to find categories of apps — you can add all your social networking apps to a Social folder or add all your news-gathering apps to a News folder.

While your icons are wiggling (as I describe previously), drag the first app icon you want to include in the folder onto the second app icon you want to include. The system creates a new folder, including the two app icons, and shows the folder's name, which is based on the first icon you dragged (for example, if you drag a social app like Facebook over another social app, such as Twitter, the folder is automatically called Social, as shown in Figure 3-3, left side). You can then tap the folder's name field and use the keyboard to enter a different name.

To close a folder, tap outside the folder if you want to do more rearranging, or press the Home button to stop rearranging your app icons.

To add another app icon to a folder, touch and hold an app icon to start the icons wiggling again (if they're not already wiggling), and drag the app icon onto the folder. The app icons line up inside the folder as shown in Figure 3-3 (right side). To move an app icon out of a folder, start the icons wiggling again if they're not already, tap the folder to open it, and then drag the icon out of the folder. To delete a folder, move all the icons out of it. The folder is deleted automatically when empty.

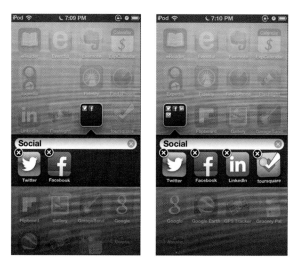

Figure 3-3: Drag one app icon over another to create a folder (left), and drag more app icons into the folder (right).

You can put up to 12 app icons into a folder. Like individual icons, folders can be rearranged by dragging them around the Home screens. You can also drag folders to the dock.

Tickling the iPod touch Keyboard

Got data? You can whip out your iPod touch and use its onscreen keyboard to type notes, contact information, calendar entries, map locations, stock symbols, and even the addresses for websites. You can also make selections for pop-up menus, and use Siri to take dictation.

Start practicing on the keyboard with just one finger. Tap a text entry field, such as the URL field for a web page in Safari (as I describe in Chapter 15) or the text of an e-mail message (as I describe in Chapter 16), and the onscreen keyboard appears.

Typing text, numbers, and symbols (using Notes)

You can practice your typing technique using the Notes app. Tap Notes on the Home screen, and the Notes screen appears. Tap the + button in the upper-right corner to type a new note, and the onscreen keyboard appears with letters of the alphabet, as shown in Figure 3-4 on the left.

The following list provides helpful tips to enter text, numbers, punctuation, and symbols on your iPod touch:

- **To enter letters,** tap the keys, and while you type, each letter appears above your thumb or finger. If you tap the wrong key, slide your finger to the correct key. The letter isn't entered until you lift your finger from the key.

- **To enter numbers, symbols, or punctuation,** tap the .?123 key at the bottom-left corner of the keyboard (refer to Figure 3-4, left side), which changes the keyboard layout to numbers (refer to Figure 3-4, center). After tapping the .?123 key, you can then tap the #+= key (refer to Figure 3-4, center) to change the keyboard layout to symbols, as shown in Figure 3-4, right side. To return to the alphabetical keys, tap the ABC key.

- **To quickly start a new sentence,** double-tap the spacebar. The iPod touch inserts a period followed by a space. The keyboard automatically capitalizes the next word after you type a period, a question mark, or an exclamation point. You can change this setting as I describe in the "Setting keyboard options" section, later in this chapter.

Figure 3-4: Type characters (left), numbers (center), and symbols (right).

✔ **To switch to the numeric keyboard layout and back to alphabetical layout automatically** (in order to type a number and continue typing letters): Touch and hold the .?123 key and then slide your finger over the keyboard to the number you want. Release your finger to select the number. The onscreen keyboard reverts immediately to alphabetical keys so that you can continue typing letters.

✔ **To type a letter with an accent mark,** touch and hold your finger on a letter (such as *e*) to show a row of keys offering variations on the letter. Slide your finger over the row to highlight the variation you want and then release your finger to select it. For instance, the word *café* should really have an accent mark over the *e,* and there may even come a day when you need to include a foreign word or two in a note — lycée or Autowäsche or también, for example. Although you can switch the language for the keyboard (as I describe in Chapter 20), you can also include variations of a letter by using the English keyboard.

To save your note, tap Done in the upper-right corner. A list of Notes appears with the last-modified date attached to each note. You can also delete a note by choosing the note and tapping the trash icon at the bottom of the note.

You can e-mail notes you type in Notes to yourself or others. Choose the note from the Notes screen and tap the envelope icon at the bottom of the note to display a ready-made e-mail message containing the text of your note — all you need to do is enter the e-mail address. See Chapter 16 for details on sending the message.

Editing text and handling word suggestions

Yes, you can edit your mistakes. To edit text in an entry field, touch and hold to see the magnifier, which magnifies portions of the text view, as shown in Figure 3-5 (left side).

Before releasing your finger, slide the magnifier to the position for inserting text. After releasing, the Select/Select All/Paste (or Select/Select All) bubble appears above the insertion point, as shown in Figure 3-5 (center), which is useful for selecting, copying, and pasting text (as I describe in the next section). You can then tap keys to insert text, or you can use the delete key — the key sporting the X in the lower-right side of the keyboard — to remove text.

The intelligent keyboard automatically suggests words (or corrections to words) while you type, as shown in Figure 3-5, right side (some languages only). You don't need to accept the suggested word — just continue typing. If you do want to accept it, tap the spacebar, a punctuation mark, or the Return key. iPod touch fills in the rest of the word.

Figure 3-5: Touch and hold for the magnifier (left), release when positioned correctly (center), and accept the word suggestion (right).

To reject the suggested word, finish typing the word or tap the tiny *x* next to the suggestion to dismiss it. Each time you reject a suggestion for the same word, your iPod touch keeps track and eventually adds the word you've been using to its dictionary. The iPod touch includes dictionaries for English, English (UK), French, French (Canada), German, Japanese, Spanish, Italian, Dutch, and other languages. The appropriate dictionary is activated automatically when you select an international keyboard. (See Chapter 20 for details about international keyboards.)

You can turn off suggestions by choosing Settings⇨General⇨Keyboard from the Home screen and tapping On for Auto-Correction. (On changes to Off when you tap it.)

Copying (or cutting) and pasting

You can copy or cut a chunk of text and paste it into another app — for example, you can copy a paragraph from a note in Notes and paste it into an e-mail message in Mail, or vice versa. You can even copy paragraphs from a web page and paste them in Notes or an e-mail message, as I show in Chapter 15.

To copy a single word, double-tap the word. The word appears selected with handles on either end of the selection and a Copy bubble above it. Tap Copy to copy the word. To do more than just copy a single word, touch an insertion point first, so that the keyboard appears, and then double-tap the word.

The Cut/Copy/Paste bubble appears above it with a right-arrow icon showing more options, as shown in Figure 3-6, left side (Paste appears in the bubble if text has already been cut or copied).

Tap the right-arrow icon to show Suggest and Define in the bubble, as shown in Figure 3-6, center. You can then tap Suggest to suggest a spelling for the selected word. You can also see a definition of a word by tapping Define. The dictionary definition appears, as shown in Figure 3-6 (right). Tap Done to return to your note.

Now that the keyboard is visible for editing, you can also select the nearest word or the entire text by touching and holding an insertion point to bring up the magnifier, and then releasing to show the Select/Select All/Paste (or Select/Select All) bubble. (Refer to Figure 3-4, left side and center.) You can then tap Select to select the nearest word or tap Select All to select all the text. The Cut/Copy/Paste (or Cut/Copy) bubble appears above the text, which is selected with handles on either end. Tap Cut to cut the selection, or Copy to copy it.

You can also make a more precise selection by dragging one of the handles. A rectangular magnifier appears for dragging the handle precisely, as shown in Figure 3-7 (left side). After you remove your finger to stop dragging, the Cut/Copy/Paste bubble appears for copying (or cutting) the selection, as shown in Figure 3-7 (center). Tap Copy to copy the selection or Cut to cut it.

To paste the copied or cut text somewhere new, open a note (or create a new note) in Notes, or start a new e-mail message, or open any app that lets you enter text. Touch and hold to magnify the text view so that you can mark an insertion point precisely. After you remove your finger, the Cut/Copy/Paste bubble appears, or if the message or note already contains text (such as the "Sent from my iPod" message that appears automatically as part of your signature in an e-mail message), the Select/Select All/Paste bubble appears, as shown in Figure 3-7 (right side). Either way, you can then tap Paste to paste the text at the insertion point, and it shows up in your message.

Take a letter, Siri

Siri is Apple's intelligent personal assistant that you can speak to in order to get things done. The more you use Siri, the better it will understand your natural speech. You can use Siri to understand the words you speak, so that instead of typing, you can speak and your words will be entered as text. You can use Siri to do lots of things with apps such as Maps, Contacts, Calendar, Reminders, and Clock — see Chapter 18 for details. With any app that has a keyboard, such as Notes, Siri can take dictation.

Figure 3-6: Select a word to cut or copy (left); suggest a spelling or define a word (center); see the definition (right).

Figure 3-7: Make a precise selection (left); copy a text selection (center), and tap an insertion point to paste the selection (right).

You can use Siri directly by holding down the physical Home button until the Siri microphone icon appears, as shown in Figure 3-8 (left side). The microphone shows a purplish-pink glow at the bottom, which indicates that it's listening. To show how Siri can take a note for you, I told Siri, "Create a note that says 'I spent $10 on breakfast.'" Siri created the note, as shown in Figure 3-8 (center). The note appears as a new note in the Notes app, as shown in Figure 3-8 (right side).

To dictate to Siri, use an app that offers use of the onscreen keyboard (such as Notes) and tap the microphone button on the onscreen keyboard. You can start talking as soon as you see the Siri microphone, as shown in Figure 3-9 (left side). To stop dictation, tap Done. I said, "Hello exclamation point can you hear me question mark," and the text, with punctuation, appears in the note as shown in Figure 3-9 (right side). You can even dictate in another language by adding another language keyboard, as I describe in Chapter 20. For more about Siri, see Chapter 18.

Setting keyboard options

To set keyboard options, choose Settings⟳General⟳Keyboard from the Home screen. The Keyboard settings screen appears, with options for Auto-Capitalization, Auto-Correction, Check Spelling, Enable Caps Lock, and Shortcut (which, by default, is set for inserting a period and a space by double-tapping the spacebar).

Auto-Capitalization automatically capitalizes the next word after you type a period, question mark, or exclamation point (punctuation that ends a sentence). It also automatically capitalizes after you tap the Return key. The assumption is that you're starting a new sentence or new line of text that should begin with a capital letter. Tap the On switch to turn this feature off if you want; tap Off to turn it back on.

Tap the On switch to turn off Auto-Correction if you don't want the keyboard to suggest typing corrections. Tap Off to turn it back on.

Enable Caps Lock is normally turned on, so that you can then double-tap the Shift key to turn on caps lock (uppercase letters). The Shift key turns blue, and all letters you type are uppercase. Tap the Shift key again to turn caps lock off. To turn off Enable Caps Lock, tap the On switch to turn it off.

The Shortcut option is set for inserting a period by double-tapping the spacebar, which inserts both a period and a following space. The assumption is that you want to finish a sentence and start the next one. Tap the On switch to turn this feature off if you want; tap Off to turn it back on.

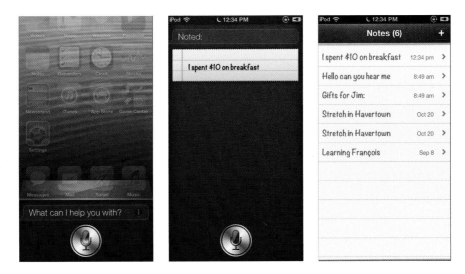

Figure 3-8: Tell Siri to take a note (left); stop talking and Siri does the job (center) and saves the note (right).

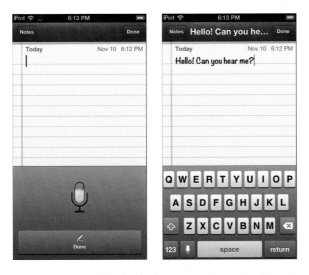

Figure 3-9: Start talking (left); after you tap Done, the dictated text appears (right).

Tapping Your iPad nano

You control the iPod nano in a similar fashion as the iPod touch: by tapping and swiping. After turning on the iPod nano, the first Home screen appears, as shown in Figure 3-10, with two dots along the bottom indicating two Home screens. As you swipe left or right, you move to the next Home screen — and the dot representing the current screen is highlighted.

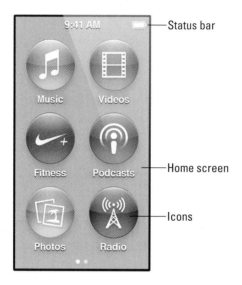

Status bar

Home screen

Icons

Figure 3-10: The iPod nano's first Home screen.

The icons on the Home screen represent choices for playing your synced music, videos, audio books, iTunes U courses, or podcasts; or for using other features like the Clock (with its Stopwatch and Timer functions) or Photos to display your synced photos.

The iPod nano offers the following icons on its first Home screen:

✔ **Music:** Show a menu with the following options: Now Playing (the currently playing song), Genius Mixes (if you synced any Genius Mixes), Playlists, Artists, Albums, Songs, Genres, Composers, Compilations, Audiobooks, Podcasts, and iTunes U. Tap an option to select the next menu, such as Playlists; you can then tap a playlist to play it. You can sync music and other content from your iTunes library, as I describe in Chapter 7. To learn more about playing music on your iPod nano, see Chapter 12.

To discover advanced iPod nano techniques, such as creating playlists directly on your iPod nano, see "Tips on Using iPod and iPhones" in the free tips section of the author's website (www.tonybove.com/tips).

✔ **Videos:** Show a menu with the Movies, TV Shows, Music Videos, and Video Playlists options. Tap an option to select the next menu, such as TV Shows; you can then tap a TV show episode to play it. Only the items you synced to the iPod nano show up — if you didn't sync any TV shows, the TV Shows option doesn't appear.

✔ **Fitness:** Tap to use the built-in pedometer and see your workout history (see Chapter 4 for details). If you have a Nike + iPod receiver connected to your iPod nano, you can access the Nike + iPod features, as I describe in Chapter 20.

✔ **Podcasts:** Tap to see an alphabetical list of podcasts; tap a podcast to see its episodes. A podcast is similar to a syndicated radio or TV show, except that you can download a podcast episode to iTunes and then play it at your convenience. You can sync podcasts from your iTunes library to your iPod nano. Chapter 13 has the details.

✔ **Photos:** Tap to see a list of photo albums, and tap an album to view its photos. See Chapter 14 for details on syncing photo albums to your iPod nano.

✔ **Radio:** After connecting earphones to your iPod nano, tap Radio to use the FM radio tuner and hear radio broadcasts. See Chapter 13 for details on playing the radio.

The iPod nano offers the following icons on its second Home screen:

✔ **Clock:** Tap to display the clock and use the built-in stopwatch and timer.

✔ **Settings:** Tap to change the settings for iPod nano features, many of which I cover in Chapter 4.

✔ **Audiobooks:** If you sync audio books from your iTunes library, you can tap this icon to show an alphabetical list of them. To find out how to sync audio books, see Chapter 7.

✔ **iTunes U:** If you sync iTunes U collections from your iTunes library, you can tap this icon to show an alphabetical list of them. iTunes U collections are electronic lessons (e-lessons) you can follow along and interact with, such as lectures, language lessons, and audio books. See Chapter 6 about the iTunes U section of the iTunes Store.

✔ **Voice Memos:** If you connect earbuds with a microphone, this icon appears on your second Home screen. Tap it to record voice memos. If you have voice memos already recorded on your iPod nano, you can tap this icon to select and delete them.

To find out how to record and manage voice memos, see Bonus Chapter 4 in the free tips section of the author's website (www.tonybove.com/tips).

After tapping an icon, you can tap choices in menus, and swipe sideways to move to the next or previous screen. Continually swiping right from any menu or choice (such as the Clock or the Now Playing screen) takes you to the first Home screen. You can also press the physical Home button on the front of the iPod nano to return to the Home screen.

Touch and hold an icon to rearrange icons on Home screens — when the icons begin to jiggle, drag them into a new order, and then press the Sleep/ Wake button to save the new arrangement.

The icons in the status bar at the top of the iPod nano screen tell you what's happening:

- ✔ The play icon (right-facing triangle) shows that a song, podcast, audio book, or iTunes U episode is playing.
- ✔ The pause icon (two vertical bars) shows that a song, podcast, audio book, or iTunes U episode is paused.
- ✔ The radio beacon icon shows that the radio is playing.
- ✔ The sneaker icon shows that the pedometer is turned on and counting steps.
- ✔ The Bluetooth icon appears only if Bluetooth is turned on.
- ✔ The battery icon shows the battery level or charging status.

Thumbing Your iPod Classic or iPod Shuffle

The circular click wheel on iPod classic makes scrolling through an entire music collection quick and easy. With your finger or thumb, scroll clockwise on the wheel to scroll down a list or counterclockwise to scroll up. As you scroll, options on the menu are highlighted. Press the Select button at the center of the wheel to select whatever is highlighted in the menu display.

The main menu for iPod classic offers the following selections:

- ✔ **Music:** Select playlists, artists, albums, songs, genres, composers, or audio books. You can also select Cover Flow to browse by cover art, or choose Search to search for a song or album title or artist (as I describe in Chapter 12).
- ✔ **Videos:** Select videos by video playlist or by type (movies, music videos, or TV shows), as I demonstrate in Chapter 13.
- ✔ **Photos:** Select photos by photo album or select all photos in the Photo Library (as I show in Chapter 14).
- ✔ **Podcasts:** Select podcasts by title and then select podcast episodes. Find out more in Chapter 13.

✔ **Extras:** View the clock, set time zones for clocks, set alarms and the sleep timer, use the stopwatch, and view contacts and your calendar, as I show in Chapter 4.

✔ **Settings:** Adjust menu settings, the backlight timer, the clicker, the date and time, and so on (see Chapter 4). You can also set the iPod's EQ (equalizer).

To find out how to set the iPod's EQ, see Bonus Chapter 3 in the free tips section of the author's website (`www.tonybove.com/tips`).

✔ **Shuffle Songs:** Play songs from your music library in random order.

✔ **Now Playing:** This selection appears only when a song is playing — it takes you to the Now Playing display.

The iPod classic click wheel has pressure-sensitive buttons underneath the top, bottom, left, and right areas of the circular pad that tilt as you press them. These buttons perform various tasks for song, podcast, audio book, and video playback. Here they are, in clockwise order from the top:

✔ **Select:** Press the Select button at the center of the wheel to select whatever is highlighted in the menu display.

✔ **Menu:** Press once to go back to the previous menu. Each time you press, you go back to a previous menu until you reach the main menu.

✔ **Next/Fast Forward:** Press once to skip to the next item. Press and hold Next/Fast Forward to fast-forward.

✔ **Play/Pause:** Press to play the selected item. Press Play/Pause when the item is playing to pause the playback.

✔ **Previous/Rewind:** Press once to start an item over. Press twice to skip to the previous item (such as a song in an album). Press and hold to rewind.

The buttons and click wheel on the iPod classic can do more complex functions when used in combination:

✔ **Turn on the iPod.** Press any button.

✔ **Turn off the iPod.** Press and hold the Play/Pause button.

✔ **Reset the iPod.** You can reset the iPod if it gets hung up for some reason. (For example, it might get confused if you press the buttons too quickly.) See Chapter 19 for instructions on how to reset your iPod.

✔ **Change the volume.** While playing a song (the display reads `Now Playing`), adjust the volume by scrolling the click wheel. Clockwise turns the volume up; counterclockwise turns the volume down. A volume slider appears on the iPod display, indicating the volume level as you scroll.

✔ **Skip to any point in a song, video, audio book, or podcast.** While playing an item (the display reads `Now Playing`), press and hold the Select button until the progress bar appears to indicate where you are, and then scroll the click wheel to move to any point in the song. Scroll clockwise to move forward and counterclockwise to move backward. Press the Select button again to see lyrics for the song (if available). Find out more about using these controls in Chapter 12.

The iPod shuffle offers the following buttons on its front side:

✔ **Plus (+) and minus (–) buttons (top and bottom):** Press plus (+) to increase the volume, or minus (–) to decrease the volume.

✔ **Next/Fast Forward (right side):** Press once to skip to the next item. Press and hold Next/Fast Forward to fast-forward.

✔ **Play/Pause (center):** Press to play the selected item. Press Play/Pause when the item is playing to pause the playback.

✔ **Previous/Rewind (left side):** Press once to start an item over. Press twice to skip to the previous item (such as a song in an album). Press and hold to rewind.

To discover advanced iPod techniques, such as creating playlists directly on your iPod, see "Tips on Using iPod and iPhones" in the free tips section of the author's website (`www.tonybove.com/tips`).

4

Clocking, Locking, Connecting, and Personalizing

In This Chapter

▶ Setting the time, date, clock, alarm, timer, and stopwatch

▶ Locking your iPod with a combination passcode

▶ Changing the brightness, wallpaper, sound effects, and other settings

▶ Connecting your iPod touch with the Internet

*Y*ou may think Apple designed the iPod just for listening to music or watching videos, but those thoughtful engineers crammed a lot more features into their invention. The iPod models offer settings you can adjust for daily operation in order to save battery power, change sound effects, lock it up for protection, connect to the Internet, determine your location, and so on. You can also use an iPod as a timekeeper to help you keep track of your personal life — setting an alarm, using the stopwatch, and displaying clocks of different time zones for traveling. And if you worry that your iPod might fall into the wrong hands, consider setting a combination lock.

This chapter covers settings for all iPod models, including those that are specific to the iPod touch, such as setting the brightness of the display, choosing the *wallpaper* (a stylin' background when it's locked, and another background for your Home screens), knowing your location, and placing restrictions on downloading and playing content. You also find out how to connect an iPod touch to a Wi-Fi network for Internet access.

This chapter also shows you how to set the backlight, the click sound, and even the display font for an iPod. I also show you how to check your calendar and your contacts on an iPod classic or iPod nano.

There's No Time Like the Right Time

Your iPod may already be set to the correct time, date, and time zone, depending on where you bought it (except, of course, the iPod shuffle, which doesn't offer these features). The iPod touch sets the time and date automatically after you connect it to your computer or the Internet. Other iPod models set the time and date when you set them up on your computer.

If you need to change the time zone, time, or date, you can do that yourself at any time (sorry for the pun). You can even set how the time appears in the status bar at the top of the screen.

On an iPod touch

To set the date and time for an iPod touch, follow these steps:

1. **From the Home screen, choose Settings⇨General⇨Date & Time.**

   The Date & Time menu appears with the Set Automatically option set to On, along with the 24-Hour Time and Time Zone options.

2. **(Optional) If you'd rather see military (24-hour) time, tap the Off button for the 24-Hour Time option to turn it on.**

   With the 24-hour display, 11:00 p.m. displays as 23:00:00, not 11:00:00. To turn off the 24-Hour Time option, tap the On button.

3. **Turn the Set Automatically option off in order to set the time and date manually.**

   The Set Automatically option is turned on by default. If this is okay with you, skip to Step 10 (you're done). If not, touch the On button to turn the Set Automatically option to Off, so that you can see the option for setting the time and date manually. After turning off the Set Automatically option, the Set Date & Time option appears under the Time Zone option.

4. **Tap the Time Zone option to set the time zone.**

   The onscreen keyboard appears; see Chapter 3 for instructions on how to use it. Type the name of the city you're in (or if you're in the middle of nowhere, the nearest big city in your time zone) and then tap the Return button on the keyboard. Your iPod touch looks up the time zone for you.

5. **Tap the Date & Time button in the upper-left corner of Time Zone screen to finish and return to the Date & Time menu.**

6. **Tap the Set Date & Time option.**

   Tapping the Set Date & Time option brings up the Date & Time screen with a slot-machine-style time wheel, as shown in Figure 4-1 (left side). The Time field is already selected.

7. **Slide your finger over the time wheel to set the hour, minutes, and AM or PM.**

   Slide until the selection you want appears in the gray window on the slot-machine wheel. The time in the Time field changes to reflect your new setting.

8. **Tap the Date field to see the date wheel.**

9. **Slide your finger over the date wheel to select the month, day, and year.**

Figure 4-1: Slide the wheel to set the time (left) and the month, day, and year (right).

10. **To finish, return to the Date & Time menu.**

    Tap the Date & Time button in the upper-left corner of the Date & Time screen (refer to Figure 4-1).

11. **Tap the General button in the upper-left corner of the Date & Time menu to return to the General menu for settings.**

On an iPod nano

To set the date and time on an iPod nano, follow these steps:

1. **Press the Home button to see the first Home screen, and then swipe to the left to see the second Home screen.**

2. **Tap Settings⇨General⇨Date & Time.**

   The Date & Time menu appears, with selections for setting the date, time, time zone, 24-hour clock, and the Time On Wake and Clock Face options.

   Skip to Step 5 if the correct time zone is set.

3. **Choose Time Zone.**

   After choosing Time Zone, a list of countries appears.

4. **Tap a country and then a city (or state).**

   Tap a country in the country list, and then tap a city (or state) for its time zone. After selecting the time zone, the Date & Time menu appears again.

5. **Choose Date from the Date & Time menu.**

   The date appears as a slot machine wheel with the month, the day, and the year cylinders you can scroll with your finger.

6. **Change the field setting by sliding your finger up or down to scroll each cylinder of the slot machine wheel.**

7. **Tap the Done button.**

   The Date & Time menu appears.

8. **Choose Time from the Date & Time menu.**

   The time appears as a slot machine wheel with the hour, the minute, and the AM/PM cylinders you can scroll with your finger.

10. **Change the field setting by scrolling the cylinders of the slot machine wheel.**

11. **Tap the Done button.**

   The Date & Time menu appears.

To show military time (so that 11:00 p.m. is displayed as 23:00), tap the Off button next to the 24-Hour Clock option in the Date & Time menu to turn it on; tap On to turn it off.

You can display the iPod nano's clock face every time you wake up the iPod nano — tap Off next to the Time On Wake option in the Date & Time menu to turn on the clock display. When you wake your iPod nano, the clock appears; swipe right to go back through the Now Playing screen to the Home screens. You can also switch the clock's face — tap Clock Face in the Date & Time menu, and then tap a different clock face.

On an iPod classic

To set the date and time on an iPod classic, follow these steps:

1. **Press the Menu button for the main menu.**

2. **Choose Settings⬆Date & Time.**

   The Date & Time menu appears, with selections for setting the date, time, time zone, and 24-hour clock. The Time in Title option appears to display the time in the menu title bar.

   Skip to Step 5 if the correct time zone is set.

3. **Choose Time Zone.**

   After choosing Time Zone, a map appears with a red dot set to your current time zone on the map.

4. **Scroll to choose a time zone.**

   Move the red dot to another zone by scrolling the click wheel — the red dot jumps from one region of the map to another, and the time zone appears below the map. Press the Select button to choose a zone. After selecting the time zone, the Date & Time menu appears again.

5. **Choose Date from the Date & Time menu.**

   The Date display appears with the month field highlighted.

6. **Change the field setting by scrolling the click wheel.**

   Scroll clockwise to go forward and counterclockwise to go backward.

7. **After scrolling to the appropriate setting, press the Select button.**

   The next date field is now highlighted.

8. **Repeat Steps 6 and 7 for the day and year.**

   After you finish scrolling and then selecting the Year field, the Date & Time menu appears automatically.

9. **Choose Time from the Date & Time menu.**

   The Time display appears with the Hour field highlighted.

10. **Change the field setting by scrolling the click wheel.**

    Scroll clockwise to go forward and counterclockwise to go backward.

11. **After scrolling to the appropriate setting, press the Select button.**

    The next date field is now highlighted.

12. **Repeat Steps 10 and 11 for minutes and AM/PM.**

    After finishing the AM/PM field, the Date & Time menu appears again.

To show military time (so that 11:00 p.m. is displayed as 23:00), choose the 24-Hour Clock option in the Date & Time menu and press the Select button to turn it on. The option changes from 12-hour to 24-hour. To switch back, press the Select button again.

To display the time on the menu title bar of an iPod classic, scroll to the Time in Title option in the Date & Time menu, and then press the Select button to turn this option on. To stop showing the time on the menu title bar, press the Select button again to toggle it to Off.

Rock Around the Clocks

You can always know what time it is — just look at the time on the locked screen or at the top of the Home screen of an iPod touch, or on the main menu title bar of an iPod classic or iPod nano. You can also tap the Clock icon on an iPod nano to see a clock face (you can change that clock face as I describe in this section).

On an iPod touch, you can also know what time it is in *other* time zones by displaying multiple clocks — using Apple's Clock app or a third-party app on an iPod touch, or Clocks in the Extras menu of an iPod classic. On an iPod nano, you can pick a clock face that shows the time in London and Tokyo below your time zone.

Alarms can be useful for waking up or just gearing up for an appointment, a stopwatch can help you exercise, and a timer can help you cook or monitor an activity. You can set an alarm and run a stopwatch on an iPod classic, and use the Stopwatch and Timer features of the Clock app on an iPod nano (you can use the timer as an alarm). On an iPod touch, you can use the Clock app to do all three — alarm, stopwatch, and timer.

Checking the time in Paris and Bangkok

With the Clock app on an iPod touch the Clock icon on an iPod nano, or the Clocks option in the Extras menu of an iPod classic, you can display clocks with different time zones, which is useful for traveling halfway around the world (or calling someone who lives halfway around the world).

To add clocks on an iPod touch, tap the Clock icon on the Home screen, and then tap the World Clock icon along the bottom of the display. It takes only two steps to add a clock:

1. **Touch the plus (+) button in the upper-right corner of the display.**

   The onscreen keyboard appears with a text entry field, as shown in Figure 4-2 (left side).

Figure 4-2: Add the city in a time zone (left) to the clocks (center) and add an alarm (right).

2. **Start typing a city name on the keyboard and tap one of the suggested cities, or type the entire name and tap Return (or tap Cancel next to the text entry field to cancel).**

   As you type, the iPod touch displays suggested cities. Tap a city (or continue tapping the name and then tap Return), and the iPod touch looks up the city's time zone and then displays the clock along with the initial clock of any other clocks you've added. (For details on how to use the onscreen keyboard, see Chapter 3.)

The clocks sport a daytime face (white background and black hands) from 6:00 a.m. to 5:59 p.m., as shown in Figure 4-2 (center), and a nighttime face (black background with white hands) from 6:00 p.m. to 5:59 a.m. If you add more clocks than can fit on the screen, you can flick to scroll the screen to see them.

To remove a clock, tap the Edit button in the upper-left corner of the display (refer to Figure 4-2, center) and then tap the circled minus (–) button next to the clock to delete it.

To create more clocks, edit the clocks, or delete additional clocks with an iPod classic, follow these steps:

1. **Choose Extras⇨Clocks from the main menu and highlight a clock.**

   One or more clocks appear (depending on how many you have created), showing the present time and location. If you have more than one clock and you want to edit one of them, scroll the click wheel to highlight the clock you want to edit.

2. **Press the Select button on the iPod to select the clock.**

   The Add and Edit options appear, along with a Delete option if you have more than one clock.

3. **Scroll the click wheel to select Add, Edit, or Cancel (or Delete if you have more than one clock already) and press the Select button.**

   If you select Add or Edit, a list of geographical regions appears in alphabetical order, from Africa to South America. If you select Delete, the clock is deleted, and you can skip the following steps.

4. **Scroll the Region list, choose a region, and press the Select button.**

   The City menu appears with a list of cities in the region in alphabetical order.

5. **Scroll the City list, choose a city, and then press the Select button.**

   You return to the list of clocks. You now have added a new clock (or edited a clock if you selected the Edit option).

On an iPod nano, you can pick a clock face that shows the time in London and Tokyo below your time zone. Tap Settings⇨General⇨Date & Time to show the Date & Time screen, and then tap Clock Face. A set of clock faces appears — flick up and down to see them all. Tap the clock face that shows London and Tokyo time underneath the regular time. After choosing this clock face, the World Clock option appears on the Date & Time screen. Tap World Clock, tap London or Tokyo to change the London or Tokyo clock, and the Time Zone screen appears. Tap the time zone on the Time Zone screen, and then tap a city to set the time zone for the clock.

Getting alarmed

Time is on your side with your iPod. On an iPod touch, you can set *multiple* alarms to go off on different days and set a variety of tones and sounds for your alarms that play through its speaker. On an iPod classic, you can even assign a playlist to an alarm to play through external speakers or headphones.

To set alarms on an iPod touch, follow these steps:

1. **Tap the Clock icon on the Home screen and tap the Alarm icon along the bottom of the display.**

2. **To add an alarm, tap the plus (+) button in the upper-right corner of the display.**

   The Add Alarm screen appears, as shown in Figure 4-2 (right side), with options and a slot-machine-style wheel for setting the alarm time.

3. **Slide your finger over the wheel to set the hour and minute and a.m. or p.m.**

   Slide until the selection you want appears in the gray window on the slot-machine wheel.

   Now you can set some optional features, or you can skip to Step 8 and be done with it.

4. **(Optional) Tap the Repeat option to set the alarm to repeat on other days.**

   You can set it to repeat every Monday, Tuesday, Wednesday, Thursday, Friday, Saturday, Sunday, or any combination of days. (You can select multiple days.)

5. **(Optional) Tap the Sound option to select a sound for the alarm.**

   A list of sounds appears; touch a sound to set it for the alarm.

6. **(Optional) Tap the On button to turn off the Snooze option or tap the button again to turn the option back on.**

   With the Snooze option, the iPod touch displays a Snooze button when the alarm goes off, and you tap Snooze to stop the alarm and have it repeat in 10 minutes (so that you can snooze for 10 minutes).

7. **(Optional) Tap the Label option to enter a text label for the alarm.**

   The label helps you identify the alarm in the Alarm list.

8. **Tap the Save button in the upper-right corner to save the alarm.**

When the alarm goes off, your iPod touch displays the message You have an alarm (and the date and time), along with the Snooze button if the Snooze option is turned on (refer to Step 6). Slide your finger to unlock the iPod touch to stop the alarm's sound, or tap the Snooze button to stop the alarm temporarily and let it repeat 10 minutes later. (When it goes off again, slide the unlock slider to turn it off — don't tap the Snooze button again; you're late for work!)

To delete an alarm on an iPod touch, tap the Clock icon on the Home screen and tap the Alarm icon along the bottom of the display. In the Alarm list, tap the alarm you want to trash, and then tap the Edit button in the upper-left corner of the display. The alarm appears with a circled minus (–) button next to it; tap this button, and then tap the red Delete button that appears to delete the alarm.

An iPod classic can do more than play a beep sound for the alarm — you can set a playlist, which you can hear by connecting the iPod to speakers or a stereo (or headphones, if you sleep with headphones on). To set an alarm on an iPod classic, follow these steps:

1. **Choose Extras➪Alarms from the main menu.**

   The Create Alarm and Sleep Timer options appear on the Alarms main menu.

2. **Choose Create Alarm and press the Select button.**

   The Alarms submenu appears.

3. **Highlight the Alarm option and press the Select button to turn it on.**

4. **Choose Date from the Alarms submenu.**

   The Date display appears with the month field highlighted.

5. **Change the field setting by scrolling the click wheel.**

   Scroll clockwise to go forward and counterclockwise to go backward.

6. **Press the Select button after scrolling to the appropriate setting.**

   The next field is now highlighted.

7. **Repeat Steps 5 and 6 for the day and year.**

   After you finish scrolling and then selecting the Year field, the Alarms submenu appears automatically.

8. **Choose Time from the Alarms submenu.**

   The Time display appears with the Hour field highlighted.

9. **Change the field setting by scrolling the click wheel.**

   Scroll clockwise to go forward and counterclockwise to go backward.

10. **Press the Select button after scrolling to the appropriate setting.**

    The next field is now highlighted.

11. **Repeat Steps 9 and 10 for minutes and AM/PM.**

    After finishing the AM/PM field, the Alarms submenu appears again.

12. **Choose Repeat from the Alarms submenu and choose a repeat multiple.**

    You can choose to set the alarm to go off once, every day, weekdays, weekends, every week, every month, or every year. After choosing a repeat multiple, the Alarms submenu appears again.

13. **Choose Alert from the Alarms submenu and choose a tone or a playlist.**

    The Tones and Playlists options appear in the Alerts submenu. Choose Tones to select a beep, or set Tones to None (no sound) if you want the iPod classic to display the alarm without making a sound. Choose Playlists to select a playlist (or None for no sound). After choosing a tone or a playlist, the Alerts submenu appears again; press Menu to go back to Alarms.

14. **Choose Label from the Alarms submenu to set a label to identify this alarm.**

    You can set labels for your alarms so that you can identify them easily in the Alarms main menu. Select a label from the prepared list, which includes labels such as Wake Up, Work, Class, Appointment, and so on. After choosing a label, the Alarms submenu appears again.

15. **Press Menu to return to the Alarms main menu, which now includes your new alarm with its label in a list of alarms under the Sleep Timer heading.**

You can create as many alarms, at different dates and times, as you need. To delete an alarm, select the alarm from the list on the Alarms main menu. The Alarms submenu appears with a list of options. Choose Delete.

When the alarm goes off, your iPod classic displays an alarm message along with the Dismiss and Snooze buttons. Choose Dismiss or Snooze by scrolling the click wheel and then select it by pressing the Select button. Dismiss stops the alarm's sound, whereas Snooze stops the sound temporarily and repeats it 10 minutes later.

Timing your steps

You can set an hour-and-minute timer for anything — baking cookies, baking CDs, or baking in the sun on the beach. The timer built into the Clock app on your iPod touch and the Clock feature of the iPod nano continues running even when playing music or running other apps. You might want to use a timer to see whether a set of activities — playing songs, playing videos, selecting from menus, and running apps — occurs within a specific time. (If you need to use seconds as well as minutes and hours, try using the stopwatch, which I describe in the next section.)

To use the timer on an iPod touch, follow these steps:

1. **Tap the Clock icon on the Home screen.**

    The Clock app's display appears, set to the screen you last used (World Clock, Alarm, Stopwatch, or Timer).

2. **Tap the Timer icon along the bottom of the Clock app's display.**

    The timer wheel for minutes and hours appears, along with the Start button.

3. **Flick the timer wheel to set the timer in hours and minutes.**

4. **Tap the When Timer Ends button, and then tap a sound to use when the timer is up.**

5. **Tap Set in the upper-right corner of the display to set the sound (or Cancel in the upper-left corner to cancel the sound).**

6. **Tap Start to start the timer.**

The timer runs backward. You can touch Cancel to cancel the timer or wait until it runs out. When it runs out, the iPod touch plays the sound (if a sound is set) and presents an OK button. Tap OK to stop the sound.

On an iPod nano, the Clock feature offers the Timer screen, which you can use to set an alarm or to set a sleep timer that turns off the iPod nano automatically. To use it, follow these steps:

1. **Tap the Clock icon (you can find it on the iPod nano's second Home screen — swipe left from the first Home screen to get to it).**

   The clock appears.

2. **Swipe left twice to see the Timer screen.**

   The Timer screen shows two cylinders you can flick to set the hours and minutes.

3. **Flick the hours and minutes cylinders to set the timer.**

   To use the Timer as an alarm, set it to the number of hours and minutes before the alarm should go off.

4. **(Optional) To set the ending alert sound, tap When Timer Ends, tap a sound, and then tap Set.**

   A list of sound effects appears (by default, the sound is set to Marimba). Tap an alert sound, and then tap Set.

5. **Tap Start to turn the timer on.**

   The timer runs backward. You can touch Stop on the Timer screen to cancel the timer or wait until it runs out. When it runs out, the iPod nano plays the sound over the headphones and presents an OK button.

6. **Tap OK to stop the sound and timer.**

Using the stopwatch

You can use a stopwatch with a lap timer for timing exercises, jogging, racing laps, seeing how long it takes the bus to travel across town, or finding out how long your friend takes to recognize the song you're playing. Whatever you want to measure with accurate time to the tenth of a second, the stopwatch is ready for you.

Even while you're running the stopwatch, you can still use the iPod to play music, videos, audio books, and podcasts. When you play a video, the stopwatch continues to count as usual; when you switch back to the stopwatch display, the video automatically pauses.

To use the stopwatch on an iPod touch, follow these steps:

1. **Tap the Clock icon on the Home screen, and tap the Stopwatch icon along the bottom of the display.**

   A stopwatch appears with Start and Reset buttons and 00:00.00 (minutes, seconds, and fractions of seconds) as the stopwatch counter.

2. **Tap the Start button to start counting.**

   The stopwatch starts counting immediately, the left button changes to Stop, and the right button changes to Lap.

3. **(Optional) Tap the Lap button to mark each lap.**

   Tap the Lap button to record each lap. Repeat this step for each lap — Clock creates a list of lap times.

4. **Tap the Stop button to stop counting.**

   The counter stops counting. The left button changes to Start, and the right button changes to Reset. You can resume the count from where you left off by tapping Start, or you can start the count again from zero by tapping Reset.

To use the stopwatch on an iPod nano, follow these steps:

1. **Tap the Clock icon.**

   The clock appears.

2. **Swipe left once to see the Stopwatch screen.**

   The Stopwatch screen shows zero time and Start and Reset buttons.

3. **Tap Start to start the stopwatch.**

The stopwatch starts counting immediately, the Start button changes to Stop, and the Reset button changes to Lap. To record lap times, tap Lap after each lap — each lap and its duration appears in a list on the screen. To pause the stopwatch, tap Stop. Tap Start to resume.

To reset the stopwatch, tap Reset when the stopwatch is paused, which deletes the lap information and makes the iPod nano ready to start a new session.

To use the stopwatch on an iPod classic, follow these steps:

1. **Choose Extras⇨Stopwatch from the main menu.**

   A stopwatch appears with the Play/Pause icon.

2. **Press the Select button to start counting.**

   The stopwatch starts counting immediately.

3. **(Optional) Press the Select button to mark each lap.**

   Press the Select button to record the current lap time while counting resumes accurately for the next lap. Repeat this step for each lap.

4. **Press the Play/Pause button to stop counting, and then press the Menu button.**

   The Stopwatch menu appears. The menu now includes the Current Log option to show the lap timings for the stopwatch session. Also included are previous stopwatch session logs. The iPod saves the stopwatch results in a session log for convenience, so you don't have to write them down.

5. **Select Resume to resume counting or New Timer to start a new stopwatch session.**

   You can resume the stopwatch session from where you left off, or you can start a new stopwatch session.

6. **(Optional) Read your stopwatch logs by choosing Current Log or the date of a previous log on the Stopwatch menu.**

7. **(Optional) Delete your stopwatch logs by choosing Clear Logs on the Stopwatch menu.**

Setting the sleep timer

As you can with a clock radio sleep timer, you can set your iPod to play music or videos for a while before going to sleep.

To set the timer on the iPod touch as a sleep timer, follow the instructions in the earlier "Timing your steps" section in this chapter. Then touch the When Timer Ends button and touch Sleep iPod at the top of the list to put the iPod touch to sleep when the timer ends. Touch Set in the upper-right corner of the display to set the Sleep iPod option (or Cancel in the upper-left corner to cancel). Finally, touch Start to start the timer. You can then play music or videos until the timer ends and the iPod touch automatically goes to sleep.

You can use the Timer on an iPod nano to set a sleep timer. Flick to set the hours and minutes, as I describe in the "Timing your steps" section earlier in this chapter, and then tap When Timer Ends to see the ending options. Tap Sleep iPod, and then tap Set. Tap Start when you're ready to start the timer.

To set the sleep timer on an iPod classic, choose Extras from the main menu; then choose Alarms⇨Sleep Timer. A list of intervals appears, from 0 (Off) to 120 minutes (2 hours). You can select a time amount or the Off setting (at the top of the list) to turn off the sleep timer. After the iPod shuts itself off or you turn it off, the preference for the Sleep Timer is reset to the default status, Off.

Working Out with Your iPod nano

The Fitness icon on the iPod nano provides a Walk option for a pedometer that keeps track of your steps, and a Run option for setting goals and soundtracks for your workouts and runs. Both work in the background, so that you can continue to play music or watch videos while walking, running, or working out.

Setting your personal info

To use Fitness properly, have a great time with it, and also get accurate workout information, set your personal info — your height and weight, your daily step goal, and your "power song" for those moments during a workout or run when you need an audio boost.

Follow these steps to set your height and weight:

1. **Tap the Fitness icon on the first Home screen, and then tap the *i* (info) icon in the lower-right corner.**

   The Settings screen for Fitness appears.

2. **Tap Personal Info on the Settings screen.**

   The Personal Info screen appears with Height and Weight options.

3. **Tap Height and set your correct height, and then tap Done.**

   The Height screen appears with two cylinders (feet and inches). You can flick the cylinders to set the height, and then tap Done. The Personal Info screen appears again.

4. **Tap Weight, set your correct weight, and then tap Done.**

   The Choose Weight screen appears with the weight in three cylinders (units, decimals, and pounds). You can flick the cylinders to set the weight, and then tap Done. The Personal Info screen appears again.

5. **Swipe right to see the Settings screen again.**

If you'd rather measure your height and weight using the Metric system (centimeters and kilograms rather than English feet, inches, and pounds), tap Units of Measure on the Settings screen. On the Units of Measure screen, tap Metric (or tap English to return to English measurement). To change distances from miles to kilometers or back to miles, tap Distances on the Settings screen, and then tap Miles or Kilometers.

To set your daily step goal for walking, tap Walk on the Settings screen, and tap the Off button to turn on Daily Step Goal. A screen appears with cylinders for the number of steps, which you can scroll to set. Tap Done to set the goal. Note that the steps you take during a Run workout are not counted toward reaching your daily step goal for walking.

To set your power song, tap Run on the Settings screen, and then tap PowerSong. You can then tap a song from the song list, or tap Playlists to choose a playlist (the first song of the playlist is considered the power song).

To view your Fitness history, tap Fitness on the Home screen, and then tap the clock-encircled-by-arrow icon in the lower-left corner of the Fitness screen. The History screen appears, and you can tap Personal Bests or Workout Totals. Sessions listed by date show details of start and stop times, distance, steps, and calories burned for each session. To clear your fitness history, swipe the History screen down to reveal the Clear button and tap Clear.

Walking to new wellness

To use the pedometer, tap Walk on the Fitness screen. The sneaker icon appears in the status bar to indicate that the pedometer is on. It runs in the background until you stop it, so you can listen to music and walk about while it counts your steps. After midnight, any steps you take are automatically tracked for the new day, so you can leave the pedometer on all the time and get an accurate daily count.

The Walk option's pedometer counts each step you take by detecting the motion. It can measure your progress and perhaps provide the motivation to exercise more (or motivate you to take a break). For more accurate results, keep the iPod nano in your pocket or near your waistband. Even so, pedometers also record movements other than walking, such as tying your shoes or shakin' your booty, so don't expect complete accuracy.

You can pair a Bluetooth heart rate monitor to your iPod nano to monitor your heart rate. To turn on Bluetooth, choose Settings➪Bluetooth and tap the Off switch to turn it on. Then tap the Fitness icon on the Home screen, tap the *i* (info) icon in the lower-right corner of the Fitness screen, and tap Nike + iPod Sport Kit. Tap Heart Rate Monitor and tap the Off switch to turn it on.

To find out more about using Bluetooth devices, see "Tips on Using iPods and iPhones" in the free tips section of the author's website (www.tonybove.com/tips).

Running for your life (and health)

To measure your performance against goals and set soundtracks for your workouts and runs, tap Run on the Fitness screen. The Run screen appears. Tap one of the following workout types:

✔ **Basic:** A basic workout with music, radio, podcast, or audio book as the soundtrack. Set the soundtrack on the Workout Music screen that appears.

✔ **Time:** Set a workout with a time goal, and then set the soundtrack on the Workout Music screen.

✔ **Distance:** Set a distance goal, and then set the soundtrack on the Workout Music screen.

✔ **Calorie:** Set the number of calories you want to burn, and then set the soundtrack on the Workout Music screen.

To select custom time, distance, or calorie goals, tap Custom after choosing the Time, Distance, or Calorie workout type. You can then scroll the time, distance, or calorie cylinders to set a value for the goal.

When the Workout Music screen appears, tap Playlists and select a playlist, Radio and select a radio station, Podcasts and select a podcast episode, or Audiobooks and select an audio book. You can also tap Shuffle Songs to shuffle the songs on your iPod nano or tap None for no audio.

After choosing the soundtrack, the workout screen appears — tap Start Workout to start your workout and your soundtrack.

To pause or stop your workout, press the play/pause button between the volume buttons on the side of the iPod nano; to resume, press it again. You can also tap the pause icon on the workout screen (you may have to press the sleep/wake button first) — a menu appears, and you can tap Resume to resume your workout, Change Music to change the soundtrack, or End Workout to stop.

To change the song while working out with a playlist, press the play/pause button between the volume buttons *twice*. The soundtrack skips to the next song in the playlist. To set a different playlist or set the workout soundtrack to radio, podcasts, or audio books, tap the pause icon on the workout screen, and then tap Change Music. To choose your power song at any time during the workout or run, tap PowerSong on the workout screen.

After choosing End Workout, the Workout Summary screen appears with the duration, start time, end time, pace, distance, and number of calories burned. You also hear a spoken version of the workout summary. If you're using Apple EarPods that include a remote switch, press and hold the center button to hear statistics while working out.

To choose a previous workout, tap My Workouts on the Run screen, and then tap a workout that appears in the list on the My Workouts screen.

Calibrate your iPod nano at least once and preferably more often — each time you calibrate, its accuracy improves. Tap Run on the Fitness screen, choose a workout type (such as Basic), and walk or run for at least one quarter of a mile (0.4 kilometers). Then end your workout by tapping the pause button and tapping End Workout. Tap the Calibrate button, which appears at the bottom of the Workout Summary screen if the workout was good enough to be used for calibrating walking, or running. You can calibrate or recalibrate any time the Calibrate button appears at the bottom of the Workout Summary screen.

To reset the calibration, tap the *i* (info) icon in the lower-right corner of the Fitness screen, and then tap Walk Calibration to reset the calibration for walking, or Run Calibration to reset the calibration for running.

You can upload your iPod nano workout data to the Nike+ website to compare and share with other folks. See Chapter 20.

Setting the Passcode for Your Lock

You can set a passcode for the iPod touch or iPod classic to lock it and thereby prevent others from navigating through your content (not available for the iPod nano or iPod shuffle). Setting a passcode also turns on data protection for an iPod touch, which uses your passcode as the key for encrypting mail messages and their attachments. (Data protection may also be used by some apps.)

The lockup works only when your iPod is not attached to a computer.

An iPod touch locks itself when it goes to sleep, and as you already know, you have to slide your finger over the `Slide to unlock` message to unlock it. But you can also set a passcode to keep the iPod touch protected from access — so that you need to supply the passcode to unlock it.

If you're playing music when your iPod classic is locked, the music continues playing — and you can even use the Play/Pause button to pause and resume playback — but if you set a passcode, no one can navigate the iPod classic or even change the volume without providing the passcode.

To conserve power, you can force your iPod touch to go to sleep by pressing the Sleep/Wake button — but you still need the passcode (if you set one) to use it after waking it up. Similarly, you can force an iPod classic to go to sleep by pressing the Play/Pause button, but you still need the passcode to unlock it. When the iPod awakens, it remembers everything — including its passcode.

Don't bother to call Apple to see whether the company can unlock your iPod for you. If you can't enter the correct passcode or attach it to the computer you set it up on, your only recourse is to restore the iPod — see Chapter 19.

To set a passcode for your iPod touch, follow these steps:

1. **Choose Settings↪General↪Passcode Lock from the Home screen.**

   The Passcode Lock screen appears with the Simple Passcode and Turn Passcode On options.

2. **To use a four-number passcode, leave the Simple Passcode option turned on; if you want to use a more complex alphanumeric password as a passcode, tap the On switch for Simple Passcode to turn it off.**

3. **Tap Turn Passcode On at the top and enter the passcode.**

   If you left the Simple Passcode option turned on in Step 2, you see a telephone-style keypad — enter a four-number passcode by touching numbers in the keypad. If you turned off the Simple Passcode option in Step 2, you see a full keyboard — enter an alphanumeric password as a passcode using the keyboard. If you change your mind, tap the Cancel button to cancel the operation.

4. **Enter the same passcode again to confirm the passcode.**

   After reentering the passcode, the Passcode Lock screen appears with passcode options.

5. **Choose Passcode options.**

   - You can choose Turn Passcode Off to turn it off or choose Change Passcode to change it. You need to enter the passcode to do either.

   - You can set the Require Passcode option to Immediately, After 1 Minute, After 5 Minutes, After 15 Minutes, After 1 Hour, or After 4 Hours.

   - You can turn the Siri, Passbook, and Reply with Message options on or off. These options are normally on so that you can talk to Siri, show items in your Passbook, and reply to a message without having to enter a passcode. As a security measure, you may want to turn it off, so that the iPod touch must be unlocked with the passcode first before using Siri, using Passbook, or replying to a message.

   - You can turn the Erase Data option on or off. This option erases all the information and content on the iPod touch after ten successive failed passcode attempts.

6. **When you're done, tap General to return to the General menu.**

The passcode screen appears immediately after you slide the `Slide to unlock` message. After correctly entering the passcode, the iPod touch unlocks.

To unlock a passcode-locked iPod touch, you must enter the same passcode or restore the iPod touch to its original factory settings, as I describe in Chapter 19. Restoring erases everything — this is, of course, a measure of last resort. You may want to perform the restore operation on the computer you synced the iPod touch with, so that you can resync it to your iTunes library.

To set a passcode (combination lock) for your iPod classic, follow these steps:

1. **Choose Extras⇨Screen Lock⇨Lock.**

   The Screen Lock icon appears with your combination lock set to zeros.

2. **Select the first number of the passcode by scrolling the click wheel.**

   While you scroll with your iPod, the first digit of the passcode changes. You can also press the Previous/Rewind or Next/Fast Forward button to scroll through numbers.

3. **Press the Select button to pick a number.**

   This sets your choice for the first number and moves on to the next number of the passcode. Repeat this step for each number of the passcode. When you pick the last number, the message `Confirm Combination` appears.

4. **Confirm the passcode.**

   Repeat Steps 2 and 3 for each number of the passcode to confirm it. After confirming, your iPod is locked.

On a locked iPod classic, the lock icon appears if you press any key. To unlock the iPod after locking it, press any button and repeat Steps 2 and 3 to enter each number of the passcode. After correctly entering the passcode, the iPod classic unlocks and returns to the last viewed screen.

To reset the passcode, unlock the iPod, choose Extras⇨Screen Lock⇨Reset Combination, and then repeat Steps 2 through 4. To turn off the lock, reset the combination to all zeroes.

If you don't know the passcode, attach the iPod classic to the computer you used to set it up and synchronize it with iTunes. When you disconnect it after synchronizing with iTunes, the iPod classic is no longer locked with a passcode.

Getting Personal

Your future might be so bright that you gotta wear shades, but your iPod display might not be bright enough. You can change the timer for the backlight on an iPod classic and set the brightness of the display on all models, as well as set the contrast of the black-and-white displays of older models.

You have plenty of other settings to consider when giving your iPod touch a personal touch. Besides wallpapering the display, you can set keyboard clicks and alert sounds to indicate that e-mail has arrived, that something in your calendar needs attention, and so on. You can also wallpaper your iPod nano.

If you share your iPod touch with children or adults who act like children, you may want to place restrictions that prevent explicit music from the iTunes Store from being displayed in playlists, or stop any access to the iTunes Store or App Store.

Adjusting the backlight of your iPod classic

The iPod classic and older iPods use a display backlight that turns on when you press a button or use the click wheel and then turns off after a short amount of time. You can set the backlight on the iPod classic to remain on for a certain interval of time. From the main menu, choose Settings⟳Backlight. A menu appears, giving you the options of 2 seconds, 5 seconds, 10 seconds, 15 seconds, 20 seconds, 30 seconds, and Always On. Select one by scrolling to highlight the selection and pressing the Select button.

REMEMBER

Using the backlight drains an iPod battery; the longer you set the interval, the more frequently you need to recharge the battery.

To set the backlight to *always* be on, choose Always On. If you want the backlight to *always* be off, choose Always Off. If you set it to always be off, the backlight doesn't turn on automatically when you press any button or use the click wheel — and the display is much darker, of course.

Brightening and wallpapering

To adjust the brightness of the display for an iPod classic, choose Settings⟳Brightness. The Brightness screen appears with a slider that shows the brightness setting, which ranges from low (a quarter-moon icon) to high (a bright sun icon). Scroll clockwise to increase the brightness (toward the bright sun) and counterclockwise to decrease the brightness (toward the moon).

To adjust the brightness on an iPod nano, tap Settings⟳General⟳Brightness from the second Home screen. The Brightness screen appears with a slider that shows the brightness setting, which ranges from low (a dim sun icon) to high (a bright sun icon). Slide the brightness slider's knob with your finger to the right to increase the brightness (toward the bright sun) and to the left to decrease the brightness (toward the dim sun). Of course, the brighter the screen, the more power is drawn from the battery.

On an iPod nano's Brightness screen, tap Restore to Default to set the brightness back to its default setting (a bit dimmer than half). You can also wallpaper your iPod nano screen with one of the built-in wallpapers: tap Settings⇨General⇨Wallpaper, and then tap a wallpaper design.

To adjust the brightness of an iPod touch, tap Settings⇨Brightness & Wallpaper. The Brightness & Wallpaper screen appears as shown in Figure 4-3, left side, with a slider that shows the brightness setting, which ranges from low (a dim sun icon) to high (a bright sun icon). Slide with your finger to the right to increase the brightness (toward the bright sun) and to the left to decrease the brightness (toward the dim sun).

While you're at it, why not wallpaper your display? You can make your iPod touch display different stylish wallpaper backgrounds for your lock screen and Home screen — one wallpaper image appears on the lock screen, and another appears behind the icons on your Home screens (or you can use the same image for both). You can also put up photos or other images from your Photo Library as your wallpaper choices. On an iPod nano, you can set a colorful pattern as your wallpaper on the Home screens.

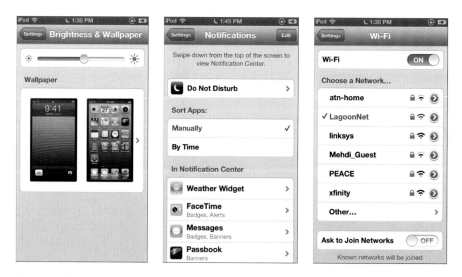

Figure 4-3: Set the brightness and wallpaper (left), set notifications (center), and connect to Wi-Fi (right).

You set the wallpaper on an iPod touch the same way as setting brightness: Choose Settings⇨Brightness & Wallpaper from the Home screen. To see the menu of wallpaper options, tap the combined lock screen and Home screen thumbnail that appears below the Wallpaper heading (refer to Figure 4-3, left side). On the wallpaper options menu, you can choose from among stylish built-in wallpaper images by tapping the Wallpaper button at the top. To choose from the photo library you synchronized with your iPod touch, tap a photo album. You can instead choose photos captured on the iPod touch by tapping Camera Roll, or photos in your photo stream by tapping My Photo Stream. (For more about photos and your photo stream, see Chapter 14.)

On an iPod touch, tap the thumbnail of a wallpaper image to select the image for your wallpaper, or tap the Back button in the upper-left corner to return to the Wallpaper menu. After tapping a wallpaper image thumbnail, the Wallpaper Preview screen appears; tap Set to set the image as your wallpaper or tap Cancel to cancel.

If you tap a thumbnail of a photo, your iPod touch displays the Move and Scale screen, which lets you optionally pan the photo by dragging your finger, and optionally zoom in or out of the photo by pinching and unpinching with your fingers. Tap the Set button to set the image as your wallpaper or tap Cancel to cancel.

After setting your image, a menu pops up with the Set Lock Screen, Set Home Screen, Set Both, and Cancel buttons. Tap Set Lock Screen to use the image for the locked screen, tap Set Home Screen to use the image for your Home screens, or tap Both.

Sound effects and ringtones

The click wheel of an iPod classic makes a clicking sound you can hear through its tiny speaker. You can turn it off by choosing Settings from the main menu and selecting Clicker once so that Off appears next to it on the right. Selecting Clicker again turns it back on.

Don't want to hear the iPod touch keyboard click while you type or hear the snap noise as you swipe your finger over the unlock message? You can set which events can trigger sound effects as well as the volume of the sound effect. Choose Settings⇨Sounds from the iPod touch Home screen. You can then turn on or off the sounds for new messages (the ringtone), new mail, sent mail, calendar alerts, Twitter tweets, Facebook posts, locking and unlocking, and using the onscreen keyboard. Tap the On switch to turn off the sound for each option (or vice versa).

You can also set the Do Not Disturb option for an iPod touch to not be disturbed by sounds — see "Setting and changing notifications" in this chapter for details.

When someone calls your iPod touch with FaceTime (see Chapter 18 for details), it plays a ringtone just like a cell phone. And when you get a text message (using the iMessage service) from the Messages app (which I describe in Chapter 18), your iPod touch plays a *text tone* — a ringtone set for text messages.

You can decide what the ringtone sounds should be for FaceTime calls and messages by choosing the ones supplied by Apple or by downloading ringtones from the iTunes Store. You can even make them yourself using a sound-editing program such as GarageBand on a Mac. After downloading ringtones from the iTunes Store or importing ringtones to the Library section of the iTunes source pane, you can sync the ringtones with your iPod touch as I show in Chapter 7.

You can also assign individual ringtones and text tones to people in your Contacts list, so that you can tell by the ringtone which person is calling, or by the text tone which person the message is from — see Chapter 18 for details.

To set ringtones, choose Settings⇨Sounds from the iPod touch Home screen, and tap Ringtone to set the tone for a FaceTime call, or tap Text Tone to set the tone for a text message. You can then select a built-in tone, or if you sync ringtones from iTunes, you can select a synced tone. You can also tap the Buy More Tones button to buy ringtones from the iTunes Store.

Tap the Sounds button in the upper-left corner to return to the Sounds screen, and then drag the volume slider to adjust the volume of the ringtone and alert sounds. If you turn on the Change with Buttons option under the volume slider on an iPod touch, you can also use the volume buttons on the side to set and change the volume.

Location, location, location

Perhaps nothing is more personal than your physical location. With Location Services on your iPod touch, apps like Maps (and lots of third-party apps like Google Earth, SkyOrb, Eventful, Foursquare, and various travel apps) can grab this physical location information and use it to help you find things closer to you. For example, the Maps app can find your location on the map, which is very useful for getting directions (see Chapter 17). The Camera app adds location information to each photo or video you shoot, which is very useful when browsing pictures using the Places icon in the Photos app. (See Chapter 14 to discover more about the Camera and Photos apps.)

An iPod touch can find itself in the physical world by leveraging the most extensive Wi-Fi reference database in the world. You need to be connected to Wi-Fi to use Location Services on an iPod touch (see the section, "Going Online with your iPod touch," later in this chapter).

You can turn Location Services on or off by choosing Settings⇨Privacy⇨ Location Services from the Home screen, and then tapping the Off button for Location Services at the top of the screen to turn it on or tapping the On button to turn it off.

The Location Services setting at the top of the screen turns on the services for all apps. You can also decide which apps can use Location Services. Each app you used that requested your location within the last 24 hours appears in the Location Services screen, showing whether Location Services has been turned on or off for that app. Tap the On button for each app to turn it off for that app.

A purple icon appears next to any app that has recently used your location, or a gray icon appears if the app used your location within the last 24 hours. An outlined icon appears if the app uses geofencing — a virtual perimeter around a location that provides the app (such as Reminders) with a way to notify you when you arrive at or leave the location.

Turn Location Services off if you are not using apps that make use of it, to conserve battery power or maintain privacy about your location. After turning it off, your iPod touch prompts you to turn it back on if you run an app that makes use of Location Services (such as Maps).

Setting restrictions

Are you lending your iPod touch to a youngster (or an adult acting like one)? You may want to set restrictions that

- Prevent access to explicit music, podcasts, and videos according to ratings
- Prevent the use of apps such as FaceTime and Safari
- Prevent installation of new apps
- Restrict use of the Camera app (see Chapter 14 about taking pictures or capturing video)
- Disallow in-app purchases
- Stop access to the iTunes Store, iBookstore, or App Store

Choose Settings⇨General⇨ Restrictions from the Home screen to see the Restrictions screen. Tap Enable Restrictions and set up a restrictions passcode (which is separate from your Passcode Lock passcode). Enter a four-number passcode by touching numbers on the telephone-style keypad. (If you change your mind, tap the Cancel button to cancel the operation.) Then enter the same passcode number again to confirm the passcode; the restrictions are enabled and ready for you to change.

Set the restrictions you want by tapping each control's On switch to turn it off. By default, all controls are on, which means that usage is allowed (not restricted). Turn off a control to restrict its use.

If you restrict access to Safari, the Camera, the iTunes Store, and/or the App Store (for installing apps), those icons are removed from the Home screen so that they can't be accessed. If you turn off Location Services, location data is no longer provided to applications. Restricted content does not appear when accessing the iTunes Store. To access the icons and the restricted content, you need to turn off the restrictions first (or turn off all restrictions).

You can turn In-App Purchases on or off, choose a ratings system based on your country, and set restrictions based on the chosen ratings system for music, podcasts, movies, TV shows, and apps. For example, tap Music & Podcasts and turn Explicit on (to allow explicit material) or off (to keep it clean). To allow movies rated PG-13 and lower (PG, G) but not R or NC-17, tap Movies and then tap PG-13 to set the limit. For TV shows, you can set the limit based on their ratings (TV-G, TV-MA, and so on).

For Apps, you can set the age limit, such as 4+ (essentially anyone), 9+ (must be at least nine), 12+ (must be 12 or older), and 17+ (must be 17 or older).

To turn off all restrictions, choose Settings⟹General⟹Restrictions and enter the passcode. Tap Disable Restrictions and reenter the passcode. Your iPod touch is now free.

Setting and changing notifications

Notifications can automatically appear on an iPod touch from apps with new information, such as Facebook friend requests, even when the app isn't running. (You can see notifications instantly in the Notification Center by swiping down from the top of any screen, as described in Chapter 3.) Notifications differ depending on the app — some notify you with alerts (text or sound), and some display a numbered badge on the app icon (for example, to show that you have messages on Facebook or Twitter). You can control what type of notification you receive from each app, and you can turn notifications off or on for each app.

To turn notifications on or off, choose Settings⟹Notifications to see the Notifications screen, as shown in Figure 4-3 (center). You can then set a Do Not Disturb schedule to not be disturbed by notifications — tap the Do Not Disturb button to see the Do Not Disturb screen. If you tap the Off switch for Scheduled to turn it on, you can then tap the From/To button to see the Quiet Time screen, where you can set the "from" and "to" times using the same type of slot wheel you use to set the real time. This setting defines the "quiet time" — to actually turn on the Do Not Disturb option and use this quiet time, choose Settings from the Home screen and tap the Off switch for Do Not Disturb to switch it on.

On the Notifications screen you can also tap Allow Calls From to specify which FaceTime calls you will accept: from everyone, from no one, from your list of favorites, or from certain groups of contacts (see Chapter 18 for details on favorites and contacts). If you turn on Repeated Calls, you are allowing FaceTime caller to call twice within three minutes.

To set notifications for specific apps, scroll the Notifications screen to see the apps in the Notification Center. Tap an app, and then tap On next to the Notifications Center option to turn it off, or tap Off to turn it back on.

You can also specify the type of notification for each app: Select the app in the Notifications screen, and then tap the options for the alert styles. Turn on the Badge App Icon option at the bottom of the app's notification options screen to show a badge on the app's icon. Turn on View in Lock Screen to see the app's notifications on the lock screen when the iPod touch is locked.

You can also sort the app notifications in the Notification Center — tap Manually at the top of the Notifications screen to sort notifications manually, or By Time to sort them by time.

Going Online with Your iPod touch

Going online means connecting to the Internet using a Wi-Fi network. To surf the Web, check e-mail, use the iTunes Store or App Store (or any other app that uses the Internet), or use Location Services on your iPod touch, you must first connect to the Internet.

An iPod touch can join Wi-Fi networks at home, at work, or at Wi-Fi hotspots around the world. Although some public Wi-Fi networks are free, others require logging in first, and still others require logging in and supplying a credit card number. Still others are detected but locked — if you select a locked network, a dialog appears asking for a password.

If you don't have Wi-Fi at home, but you do have a broadband Internet connection (such as cable or DSL), I recommend buying an AirPort Express or AirPort Extreme; or if your computers include a Mac, check out Time Capsule, which combines the AirPort Extreme with a backup drive — all are available in the Apple Store. You can then connect your Internet connection to the AirPort to extend Internet access over Wi-Fi throughout your home.

Turning Wi-Fi on or off

To turn Wi-Fi on, choose Settings⟳Wi-Fi from the Home screen to display the Wi-Fi Networks screen. Tap the Off button for the Wi-Fi setting to turn it on (tap it again to turn it off).

When Wi-Fi is turned on, your iPod touch detects and automatically acquires a Wi-Fi signal you've used before, or it can detect one or more signals in the area and present them in a list for you to choose. The list of available Wi-Fi networks appears below the Wi-Fi setting, as shown in Figure 4-3, right side.

If your iPod touch isn't already connected to Wi-Fi, it's set by default to look for networks and ask whether you want to join them whenever you use something that requires the network (such as Safari, Mail, and so on). You can stop your iPod touch from looking and asking: Scroll down to the end of the list of Wi-Fi networks on the Wi-Fi Networks screen and then tap the On button for the Ask to Join Networks option to turn it off. You can still join networks manually, but you won't be interrupted with requests to join them.

You should turn off Wi-Fi if you're not using it to save battery power and to keep your iPod touch from automatically receiving e-mail. (You can also change your Push settings to stop automatic e-mail — see Chapter 16.) Choose Settings➪Wi-Fi, and then tap the On button for the Wi-Fi setting to turn it off.

Choosing a Wi-Fi network

You can scroll the list of networks on the Wi-Fi Networks screen to choose one by tapping its name. Networks are named by their administrators. (If you set up your own home Wi-Fi, you get to name yours whatever you want.)

When connected to a Wi-Fi network, your iPod touch displays the Wi-Fi icon in the status bar at the top of the display. This also indicates the connection strength — the more arcs you see in the icon, the stronger the connection.

If a Lock icon appears next to the Wi-Fi network name, it means that the network is locked and you need a password. When you select a locked network, the iPod touch displays an Enter Password screen and the onscreen keyboard. Tap out the password using the keyboard. (For details on how to use the onscreen keyboard, see Chapter 3.) Tap Join to join the network or tap Cancel in the upper-right corner to cancel joining.

To join a Wi-Fi network that requires either a credit card or an account for you to log in to, select the network and use Safari to open the network's web page. (For more on using Safari, see Chapter 15.) The first web page you see is typically the login page for the service (for example, a commercial Wi-Fi service or a hotel service). Follow the instructions in Chapter 15 for interacting with web pages and entering information.

Your iPod touch remembers most Wi-Fi connections and their passwords and automatically uses one when it detects a network within range. If you've used multiple Wi-Fi networks in the same location, it picks the last one you used.

You can also stop your iPod touch from automatically joining a Wi-Fi network — such as a paid or closed Wi-Fi service that somehow got hold of your device and won't let you move on to other web pages without typing a password. See Chapter 20 for this tip.

Part II
Managing Your Library

The 5th Wave · By Rich Tennant

"Okay, the view's just up ahead. Everyone switch to 'America the Beautiful' on your playlist."

As soon as you start building your iTunes library, you'll want to know how to organize all your content, add or change the content information, add ratings, build playlists, burn CDs, and make a backup of your library.

First, in Chapter 9, you put iTunes to work — adding and editing the content information (such as the artist or title), changing the artwork, adding ratings, changing the List tab view options, and searching and sorting your library.

In Chapter 10, you discover how to play music, audio books, videos, and podcasts in your iTunes library. You also find out how to create your own playlists and take advantage of the iTunes Genius feature.

Then, in Chapter 11, I show you how to match or upload all of your songs in iCloud with iTunes Match. The chapter is also a guide to burning audio CDs and MP3 CDs as well as copying media files and making backup copies of your iTunes library.

By the time you finish all this, you've earned a degree in iTunes Library Management and you're ready to play!

5

Getting Started with iTunes

In This Chapter

▸ Opening the iTunes window

▸ Adding audio and video files

▸ Browsing your iTunes library content

▸ Playing music tracks on a CD

▸ Ripping music from CDs

▸ Setting your music importing preferences

*1*f iPods were spaceships, iTunes would be the space station they dock with to get supplies. iTunes is the central repository of all content. You can bring your music from audio CDs into iTunes to preserve the music forever in digital format and play the music on your iPod without having to fumble for discs. You can import sound and video files downloaded from the Internet into iTunes to keep all your content organized, and then you can take your content with you in your iPod by syncing the device to your iTunes library (as I show in Chapter 7). iTunes also provides a quick and easy browsing experience for accessing the iTunes Store and App Store from your computer.

In this chapter, I show you not only how to import music from audio CDs but also how to import music and videos from the Internet or other sources into your iTunes library. You get started in the simplest way possible: opening the iTunes window and using iTunes to play music tracks on a CD, before importing the CD's music. You can use iTunes just like a jukebox, only better — you don't have to pay for each song you play, and you can play some of or all the songs on an album in any order.

Toulouse Street
Doobie Brothers

What Were Once Vices...
Doobie Brothers

The Door

Morrison Hotel
Doors

The Soft Parade
Doors

Strange

Doors

Welcome to the iTunes Machine

You can run iTunes any time (with or without an iPod) to build and manage your library. You don't have to connect your iPod unless you want to transfer content to it (as I describe in Chapter 7) or update or restore the device's system (as I describe in Chapter 19).

When you first launch iTunes, you see the Welcome screen shown in Figure 5-1. You can click the Watch Tutorials link to see movies of iTunes in action. But before continuing, Apple needs to know whether or not you are willing to share details about your iTunes library. Apple uses this information to provide artist images, album cover art, and Genius music suggestions from the iTunes Store. (I show how Genius suggestions work in Chapter 10.) Click Agree to allow Apple to use this information or click No Thanks to skip it.

If you choose No Thanks, you can always change your mind and enable Apple to use this information later by choosing Preferences from the iTunes menu on a Mac or from the Edit menu on a Windows PC, clicking the Store tab, and clicking the check box for the Share Details About Your Library With Apple option.

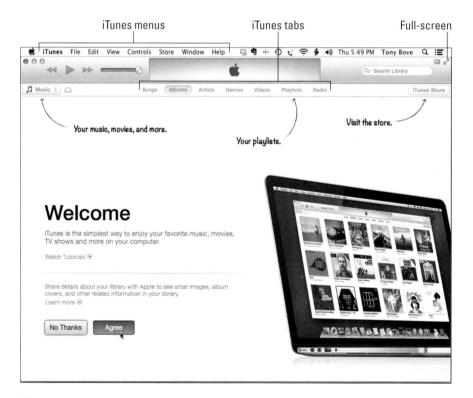

Figure 5-1: The iTunes Welcome screen.

After clicking Agree (or No Thanks), the iTunes Music screen appears, as shown in Figure 5-2, with the Go to the iTunes Store and Scan for Music buttons if you haven't used iTunes before and have no content in your library. If you're updating your version of iTunes and you already have content in your library (such as music purchased from the iTunes Store stored in the iCloud service), iTunes displays the Albums screen with album cover art. (You can skip ahead to find out how to browse your library content in the "Browsing Your Library Content" section, later in this chapter.)

To add content to your library from the iTunes Store, you can click the Go to the iTunes Store button to go directly to the store and start downloading content; to find out how to do this, see Chapter 6. To add music to your library, read the next section, "Adding Audio Files"; and to add video to your library, read the "Adding Videos" section, later in this chapter.

Figure 5-2: Start adding music from the iTunes Store or your hard drive.

The OS X and Windows versions of iTunes are nearly identical, as you can see by comparing Figure 5-1 and Figure 5-2. The dialogs and icons look a bit different between the two operating systems. Also, OS X shows the iTunes menus at the top of the screen above the iTunes window, while Windows includes the iTunes menus within the iTunes window — some are in the shortcut menu in upper-left corner (refer to Figure 5-2), and if you choose Show Menu Bar from the shortcut menu, the full iTunes menu bar appears at the top of the iTunes window.

To fill the screen with the iTunes window on a Mac, click the full-screen button in the top-right corner — the pair of diagonal arrows pointing out toward the corners of the screen (refer to Figure 5-1) — or choose View⇨ Enter Full Screen. To leave full-screen mode, hover your Mac's pointer over the very top of the screen to show the iTunes menus and choose View⇨Exit Full Screen. You can also press the Control-⌘-F key combination to enter or exit full-screen mode.

To fill the screen with the iTunes window on a Windows PC, use the ever-familiar Windows full-screen button. Click it again to reduce the iTunes window size.

Other differences may affect which version you should use for your library, assuming you have both a Mac and a Windows PC:

- ✓ The Windows version lets you import unprotected Windows Media (WMA) songs.

- ✓ The Mac version, like other iLife applications, can integrate its library directly within iPhoto to use with slide shows, iMovie to include in movies, and GarageBand to mix recorded music with your instruments.

Adding Audio Files

If you have music, audio books, or other audio files — MP3, AAC, AIFF, or WAV files — that you downloaded or copied to your hard drive, you can click the Scan for Music button (refer to Figure 5-2) if you haven't used iTunes before and have no content in your library.

If you already have content in your library, you can add more audio files to your library by simply dragging them over the iTunes window. If you drag a folder of audio files, all the audio files are added to your iTunes library. You can even drag a folder of mixed media files, such as audio files, video files, and PDFs of electronic books, to your iTunes library. You can also choose File⇨Add to Library on a Mac, or File⇨Add File to Library and File⇨Add Folder to Library on a Windows PC, as an alternative to dragging. For details on where iTunes stores the file, see Chapter 11.

MP3 CDs are easy to add because they're essentially data CDs. Simply insert them into your computer's CD-ROM drive, open the CD in the Finder or Windows Explorer, and drag and drop the MP3 audio files into the iTunes window.

Adding Videos

Besides purchasing and downloading videos from the iTunes Store, as I describe in detail in Chapter 6, you can also download video files (such as files that end in `.mov`, `.m4v`, or `.mp4`) from the Internet or copy them from other computers and bring them into iTunes. From iTunes, you can sync them to your iPod after converting them into a format that looks best for an iPod.

You can drag a video file into iTunes just like an audio file. Drag each video file from the Mac Finder or Windows Desktop to the iTunes window. The video files that you import into iTunes show up in the Movies section of your iTunes library (see the later section, "Browsing other content," for browsing instructions). You can use iTunes to change the media type (for example, to change a video file from Movie to Music Video) — see Chapter 9 for details. Video files are organized in folders and stored in the iTunes Media library on your hard drive just like audio files — see Chapter 11 for details.

There are lots of different video formats, and not all of them are supported by iTunes. If you drag a video file that is not supported, you get a warning that the video won't play in iTunes. You may also have a problem playing a video on an iPod if it is not properly converted for iPod playback, but iTunes lets you convert those videos to formats that can play back on an iPod, iPad, iPhone, or Apple TV.

To convert a video for use with an iPod, select the video and choose File⇨ Create New Version⇨Create iPod or iPhone Version. The selected videos are automatically copied when you convert them, leaving the originals intact.

To find out more about bringing videos, including MPEG files, from other sources into iTunes and converting videos for use with an iPad, iPod, iPhone, and Apple TV, see Bonus Chapter 2 in the free tips section of the author's website (`www.tonybove.com/tips`).

Browsing Your Library Content

You import a few music CDs, buy some songs, TV shows, and movies from the iTunes Store, and you're hooked. You keep adding more and more content to your library and forget how to find items you added last month. It's time to discover how to navigate your iTunes library.

After you add music to your library or if you already have music in your library, iTunes displays the music album covers under the Albums tab, as shown in Figure 5-3.

Does viewing an album cover whet your appetite for the music inside? Of course it does. Album covers provide a context that simply can't be put into words or conveyed by sound. One fantastic innovation of iTunes is how it integrates cover art from music albums, books, podcasts, and videos with your library so that you can flip through your content to find items based on the artwork.

You can also view your music library by artist by clicking the Artists tab. The artists are listed in the left column, with the All Artists option at the top, and the albums and album contents are listed in the wider right column. Select All Artists to see all albums or select an individual artist to see only the albums by that artist.

To view your music library by genre, click the Genres tab. The genres are listed in the left column, and the albums and album contents for each genre are listed in the wider right column.

iTunes tabs   Search

Figure 5-3: Albums in your iTunes library.

Your music library may also contain playlists — you can view them by clicking the Playlists tab (I show you how to create and use playlists in Chapter 10). You can also tune into Internet radio stations by clicking the Radio tab.

You can search your entire library by entering search terms into the search field in the upper-right corner of the iTunes window. I cover searching for content in Chapter 9.

To see music videos in your music library, click the Videos tab. You can hover your pointer over a music video thumbnail to show the play button and then click the play button to start playing the music video. For details about playing videos, see Chapter 10.

Browsing albums

If you switched to another view, click the Albums tab to show the Albums view of your music library (refer to Figure 5-3). You can scroll the Albums view to see all the albums in your library. By default, the albums are sorted by artist name, although you can change this sorting, as I describe in Chapter 9.

To quickly jump to an album, enter the first character of the artist's name, and the Albums view jumps to the first album by the first artist whose name begins with that character. Enter more characters of the artist's name to jump directly to the artist.

To see the contents of an album, click the album cover. The list of songs appears as shown in Figure 5-4. Click a song title to select the song or double-click the title to start playing the song. (To find out more about playback controls, see Chapter 10.)

You can find more songs or albums by the artist in the iTunes Store by clicking the In the Store link in the upper-right corner of the album's contents (refer to Figure 5-4). Click the Songs button to return to the album contents.

To fill your library automatically with cover art, get yourself an iTunes Store account (if you don't already have one), as I describe in Chapter 6. If you agreed to share your library information with Apple, as I describe in the earlier section, "Welcome to the iTunes Machine," iTunes grabs the cover art for not only content downloaded from the iTunes Store — including movies, TV shows, audio books, and podcasts — but also for CDs you import, if the albums are also available in the iTunes Store. Even if you downloaded or imported only one song of an album, you get the album's cover art for that song.

To enable Apple to use your library information, choose Preferences from the iTunes menu on a Mac or from the Edit menu on a Windows PC, click the Store tab, and select the Share Details about Your Library with Apple check box.

Selected song is playing   In the Store

Figure 5-4: View the contents of an album.

You can also get your cover art from other places that sell CDs, audio books, and DVDs (including Amazon.com, www.amazon.com) or even scan it from the actual CDs, DVDs, or books. You can then add cover art from a scanned or downloaded image file to any content item in your iTunes library, as I describe in Chapter 9. The optimal size for cover art is 300 x 300 pixels.

Browsing songs

To browse songs in the more traditional layout of genres, artists, and albums, click the Songs tab. The Songs view shows the column browser at the top (with columns for Genre, Artist, and Album), and the songs in a list on the bottom, as shown in Figure 5-5. The list shows the title of each song in the Name column, the artist or band name in the Artist column, and the title of the album in the Album column.

The column browser organizes music content into Genres, Artists, Albums, Composers, and Groupings columns — you can choose which columns to display by choosing View⟹Column Browser⟹Genres, View⟹Column Browser⟹Artists, and so on — to select each category to show (or deselect each category to remove). For example, in Figure 5-5, I included only the

Genres, Artists, and Albums columns in the column browser. To browse all the songs in your library, select All at the top of each of the columns — Genres, Artists, and Albums. To be more specific, select a genre in the Genres column to see artists in that genre in the Artists column or select All at the top of the Genres column to see all artists for all genres. When you select an artist in the Artists column, the album titles appear in the Albums column (on the right). When you select an album, iTunes displays only the songs for that album in the list pane below the column browser.

To hide the column browser, choose View⇨Column Browser⇨Hide Column Browser (or press ⌘-B on a Mac or Ctrl-Shift-B on a Windows PC). To bring back the column browser, choose View⇨Column Browser⇨Show Column Browser (or press ⌘-B on a Mac or Ctrl-Shift-B on a Windows PC).

To see the songs for more than one album from an artist at a time, press ⌘ (Mac) or Ctrl (Windows) while clicking each album name.

After selecting an album in the Albums column, the songs in the list are sorted in the proper album track order, just as the artist, producer, or record label intended. (You can even edit the song information easily in this view. I describe how to get and edit track information in wondrous detail in Chapter 9.)

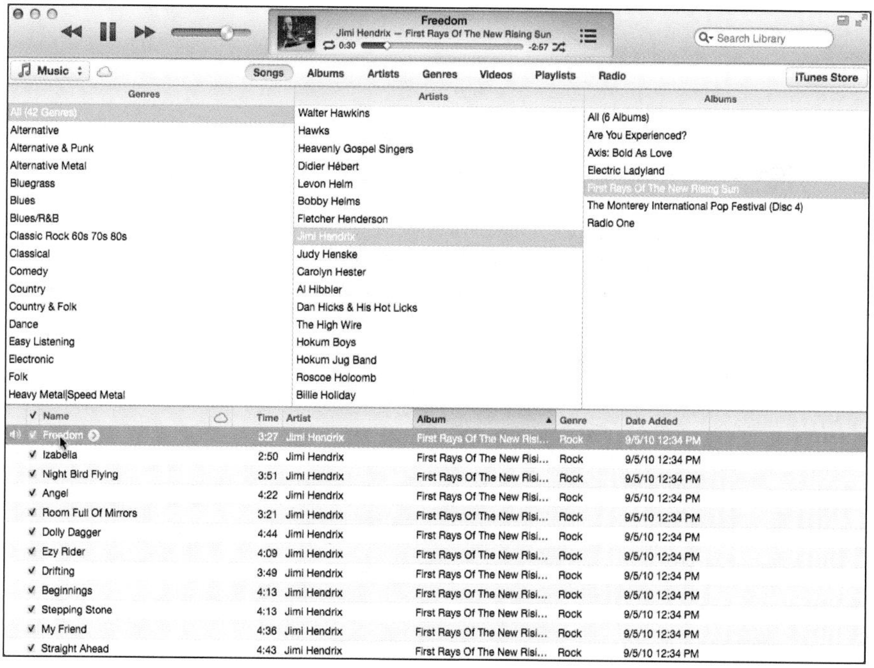

Figure 5-5: Select an artist in the column browser to see the list of albums for that artist.

Browsing other content

To browse other content, choose a source from the source list menu shown in Figure 5-6, which offers these choices in its Library section:

- **Music:** Shows the songs and music videos purchased, downloaded, imported, or copied into the library. This choice also shows Internet radio stations.

- **Movies:** Shows movies downloaded from the iTunes Store and video files you've added to your library.

- **TV Shows:** Shows TV shows downloaded from the iTunes Store. This choice also shows video files you've imported and then changed to TV Show in the Media Kind pop-up menu of the Options pane of the Info dialog — see Chapter 9 for details on adding or changing the media type.

- **Podcasts:** Shows the podcasts you've subscribed to. (See Chapter 10 for details on subscribing to and browsing podcasts.)

- **iTunes U:** Shows courseware, lectures, and other items downloaded from or subscribed to in the iTunes U section of the iTunes Store.

- **Books:** Shows the audio books downloaded from the iTunes Store or from www.audible.com, and electronic books downloaded from the iBookstore and other sources (such as PDF files from Project Gutenberg).

- **Apps:** Shows the iPod touch apps downloaded from the App Store or iTunes Store, and iPod games downloaded from the iTunes Store.

- **Tones:** Shows the ringtones and text tones downloaded from the iTunes Store or from other sources, as well as those created in GarageBand on a Mac and added to your iTunes library.

If you'd rather see the source list as a fixed pane for switching back and forth between sources quickly, choose View⇨Show Sidebar. The Library section shows the same source list; the sidebar also includes the Store, Genius, and Playlists sections of your library. To hide the sidebar, choose View⇨ Hide Sidebar.

To browse the audio books and e-books in your library, select Books in the Library section of the source list pop-up menu, and then click the Audiobooks tab to see your audio books or the Books tab to see your e-books. You can also click the PDFs tab to see books in the standard Portable Document Format (PDF).

You can browse by author by clicking the Authors tab; click the List tab to see a list of book titles. Under the List tab, you can use the column browser by choosing View⇨Column Browser⇨Show Column Browser (or press ⌘-B on a Mac or Ctrl-Shift-B on a Windows PC). To hide the column browser, choose View⇨Column Browser⇨Hide Column Browser (or press ⌘-B on a Mac or Ctrl-Shift-B on a Windows PC).

Source list

iTunes tabs

Figure 5-6: Select a content source from the source list.

To browse podcasts, select Podcasts in the Library section of the source list. You can select podcasts in the left column, as shown in Figure 5-7, and then select an episode of the podcast in the wider right column. You can click the Unplayed tab to show only unplayed podcast episodes, or the List tab to show a list of podcasts and episodes. For details on playing episodes, see Chapter 10.

To browse movies, select Movies in the Library section of the source list. You can then click Genres to browse by genre or Unwatched to show only the movies you haven't watched yet. You can click the List tab to see a list of movies by title. Under the List tab, you can use the column browser by choosing View⇨Column Browser⇨Show Column Browser (or press ⌘-B on a Mac or Ctrl-Shift-B on a Windows PC).

Most video files you add to your library from sources other than the iTunes Store are classified as movies, and some, such as EyeTV recordings, are classified as TV shows. You can change the media type, as I describe in Chapter 9, so that, for example, a video shows up as a TV show or music video rather than a movie. You can also find in the Movies listing those movies and short films you downloaded from the iTunes Store.

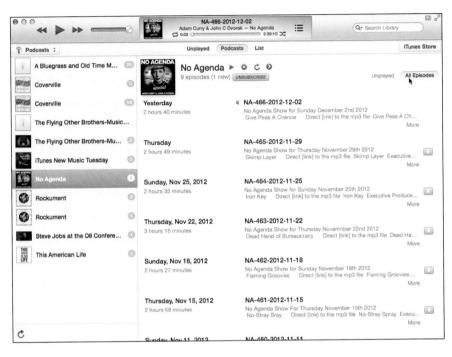

Figure 5-7: Select a podcast to see its episodes.

You can browse TV shows by selecting TV Shows in the Library section of the source list. You can then click Genres to browse by genre, or Unwatched to show only the shows you haven't watched yet. You can click the List tab to see a list of TV shows and episodes by title and use the column browser.

The mysterious blue dot next to a movie, a podcast episode, an audio book, an iTunes U course, or a TV show episode means that you haven't played it yet. As soon as you start listening to or watching it, the dot turns into a half-moon until you finish it (accompanied by the theme of Rod Serling's original *The Twilight Zone*).

Browsing apps and iPod games

The apps you download for your iPod touch, along with the games you download for your iPod classic (or older model iPod), show up in the Apps section of your iTunes library. Apps for the iPod touch are available in the App Store, and click-wheel games for the iPod classic and older iPod models are in the iTunes Store (see Chapter 6 for glorious details). And although you can't run the apps or play the games in iTunes, you can browse the list of apps and games you downloaded.

To browse your iPod touch apps, as well as iPod classic click-wheel games, select Apps in the source list. You can then click tabs to show only iPhone/iPod touch apps (which run on all three devices), iPad apps (which run only on the iPad models), and iPod Games (click-wheel games for iPod classic and older iPod models). Click All to see all apps and games, or List to see a list of all apps and games.

For details on how to play click-wheel games on your iPod classic, see Bonus Chapter 4 in the free tips section of the author's website (www.tonybove.com/tips).

Playing Audio CD Tracks

iTunes needs content. You can get started right away by importing music from CDs into your library, as I describe in the later section, "Importing Audio CDs." For more instant gratification, though, you can play music right off the CD first, before importing it. Maybe you don't want to put the music into your library just yet. Maybe you just want to hear it first, as part of your Listen First, Import Later plan.

To play a CD, insert any music CD — or even a CD-R that someone burned for you — into your computer. After you insert the CD, iTunes adds your CD to the source list menu and displays the contents of the CD, as shown in Figure 5-8. If you're connected to the Internet, iTunes displays the track information for each song automatically if the CD was commercially released. If the track information doesn't appear, you can grab it from the Internet or edit it yourself (see Chapter 9 for details). For burned mix CDs, you need to edit it yourself.

When you play a CD in iTunes, it's just like using a CD player. To play a CD, select a track and click the play button, which turns into a pause button as the song plays (refer to Figure 5-8) — or just double-click the track. You can control the volume by dragging the Volume slider.

When the song finishes, iTunes continues playing the songs in the list in sequence until you click the pause button or until the song list ends. You can skip to the next or previous song by using the arrow keys on your keyboard or by clicking the fast-forward/next or previous/rewind buttons (next to the play button). You can also double-click another song in the list to start playing it.

You can press the spacebar to perform the same function as clicking the play button; pressing it again is just like clicking the pause button.

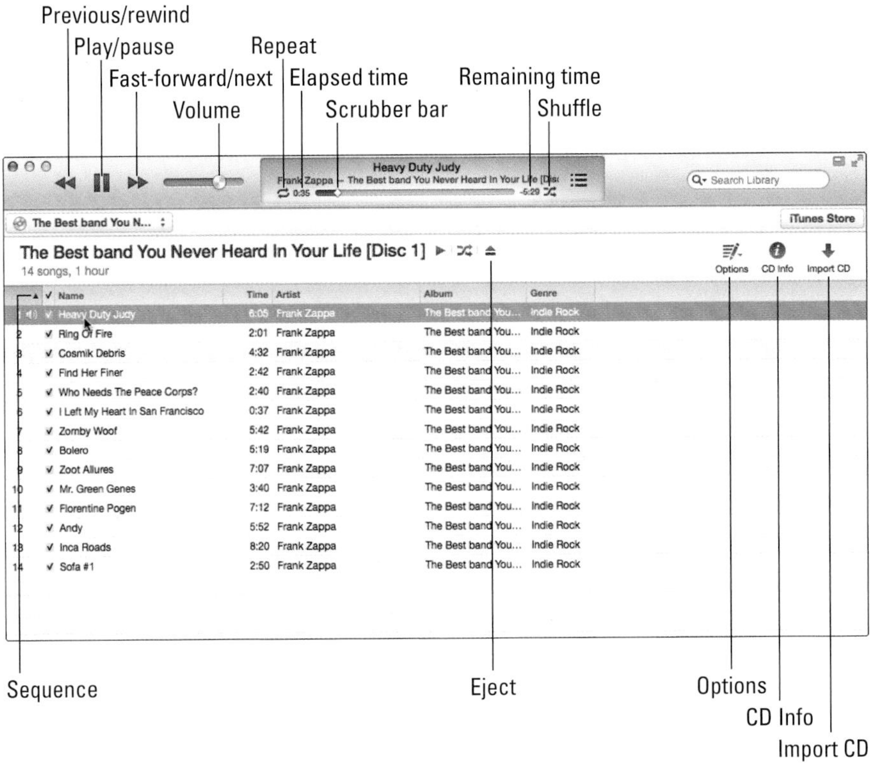

Previous/rewind
Play/pause | Repeat
Fast-forward/next | Elapsed time | Remaining time
Volume | Scrubber bar | Shuffle

Sequence | Eject | Options
| | CD Info
| | Import CD

Figure 5-8: Playing a CD in iTunes.

The playback status pane (refer to Figure 5-8) tells you the name of the artist and the song title as well as the elapsed time of the track. The pane also provides a scrubber bar showing the progress of the tune's playback, and you can drag the scrubber bar along the slider to move back and forth in the song. The time on the left of the slider in the pane is the elapsed time; the time on the right is the remaining time for the song. When you click the remaining time, it changes to the duration of the song; click it again to return to the song's remaining time.

You can repeat an entire CD by clicking the repeat button on the left side of the playback status pane (or choosing Controls⇨Repeat⇨All). When it's selected, the repeat button shows blue highlighting. Click the repeat button again to repeat the current song (or choose Controls⇨Repeat⇨One). The button changes to include a blue-highlighted numeral 1. Click it once more to return to normal playback (or choose Controls⇨Repeat⇨Off).

The shuffle button, located to the right of the slider in the playback status pane (refer to Figure 5-8), plays the songs on the CD in random order, which can be fun. You can then press the arrow keys on your keyboard or click the previous/rewind and fast-forward/next buttons to jump around in random order.

You can rearrange the order of the tracks to automatically play them in any sequence you want, similar to programming a CD player. When you click the sequence up arrow at the top of the first column (refer to Figure 5-8), it changes to a down arrow, and the tracks appear in reverse order. To change the order of tracks that you're playing in sequence, just click and hold the track number in the leftmost column for the song; then drag it up or down in the list.

To skip tracks so that they don't play in sequence, deselect the check box next to the song names. iTunes skips deselected songs when you play the entire sequence.

To eject a CD from the drive, click the eject button next to the CD name (refer to Figure 5-8) or by choosing Controls⇨Eject Disc.

Importing Audio CDs

Bringing music tracks from a CD into iTunes is called *ripping* a CD (audio programmers *do* have a sense of humor). *Ripping,* in technical terms, is extracting the song's digital information from an audio CD and encoding it in a compressed AAC or MP3 digital audio file format or wrapping it in a WAV or AIFF file format container, which I explain later in this chapter. The format and its settings affect the sound quality and the space occupied by the song file on the computer and the iPod. They also affect the song's compatibility with other types of players and computers.

How easy is it to rip a CD? Click the Import CD icon after inserting the CD (refer to Figure 5-8). After setting your import format and settings (or deciding to use the default format and its settings), click OK to rip your CD into iTunes and, without further ado, your CD tracks are absorbed into your iTunes library.

Deselect the check boxes next to any songs on the CD that you don't want to import. iTunes imports only the songs that have check marks next to them.

Changing import preferences and settings

After clicking the Import CD icon, the Import Settings dialog appears as shown in Figure 5-9, offering the following choices:

- ✓ **Import Using:** Set this pop-up menu to choose the import format. This choice is perhaps the most important, and I describe it in more detail later in this section.

- ✓ **Setting:** This offers different settings depending on your choice of format. For example, in Figure 5-9, I am about to change the format from the AAC Encoder to the MP3 Encoder in the Import Using menu. After changing the format, I can choose the quality setting for the encoder in the Settings menu. (For example, iTunes Plus is the quality setting for the AAC encoder and for music available in the iTunes Store.) Set this pop-up menu to the iTunes Plus or High Quality setting for most music, or choose Custom to choose a custom setting. The Spoken Podcast setting is for lower-quality voice recordings. See the following bulleted list for more information about encoders and settings, including how they affect quality and file size.

✓ **Use Error Correction When Reading Audio CDs:** Although it reduces importing speed, select this check box to use error correction if you have problems with audio quality or if the CD skips. (Not every skipping CD can be imported even with error correction, but it might help.)

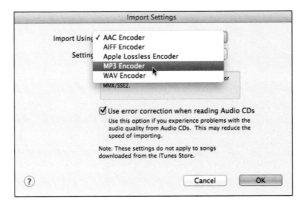

Figure 5-9: Change your import settings for ripping CDs.

For a quick and pain-free ripping session, choose from among the following formats in the Import Using pop-up menu, based on how you plan to use the music:

✓ **AAC Encoder:** I recommend encoding music into the AAC format for almost all uses except for burning another audio CD. (AIFF, Apple Lossless, or WAV is better if you plan to burn another audio CD at the highest quality with the songs you ripped, and MP3 is the only format to use for MP3 CDs.) For music, choose the High Quality or iTunes Plus settings from the Setting pop-up menu.

✓ **AIFF Encoder:** Use AIFF if you plan to burn the song to an audio CD using a Mac (use WAV for Windows) or use it with a GarageBand project. AIFF offers the highest possible quality, but it takes up a lot of space (about 10MB per minute). Choose the Automatic option from the Setting pop-up menu for best results. Don't use AIFF for songs that you intend to transfer to your iPod or to an MP3 CD.

You can rip a CD as many times as you want, and use a different format for each version, as long as you modify the album name or song title to identify each version. For example, you might rip *Sgt. Pepper's Lonely Hearts Club Band* with the AAC Encoder for use in your iPod. You might then rip it again after changing the encoder to the higher-quality Apple Lossless or AIFF Encoder, using a different album name (such as Sgt. Pepper-2), for burning onto an audio CD. After burning the CD, you can delete Sgt. Pepper-2 to reclaim the hard drive space.

✔ **Apple Lossless Encoder:** Use the Apple Lossless format for songs that you intend to burn onto audio CDs as well as for playing on an iPod. The music is imported at the highest quality, with compression that doesn't lose any information (which is why it is called *lossless*). The files are just small enough (about 45–70 percent of the size of the AIFF versions) that they don't hiccup on playback on the iPod.

✔ **MP3 Encoder:** Use the MP3 format for songs that you intend to burn on MP3 CDs, or that you intend to use with MP3 players or your iPod — it's universally supported. If you use MP3, I recommend choosing the Higher Quality option from the Setting pop-up menu.

✔ **WAV Encoder:** WAV is the high-quality sound format that's used on PCs (like AIFF on Macs), but it also takes up a lot of space (about 10MB per minute). Use WAV if you plan on burning the song to an audio CD or using WAV with PCs. Choose the Automatic option from the Setting pop-up menu for best results. Don't use WAV for songs that you intend to transfer to an MP3 player or to an MP3 CD; use MP3 instead.

To find out more about audio encoding formats, how to adjust custom settings to reduce space and increase audio quality, and how to convert songs from one format to another (and what problems to look out for when doing so), see Bonus Chapter 2 in the free tips section of the author's website (www.tonybove.com/tips).

To change the way iTunes rips — whether it rips right away, asks first, or automatically ejects afterward — follow these steps:

1. **Choose iTunes⟡Preferences⟡General on a Mac or Edit⟡Preferences⟡ General in Windows.**

   The iTunes Preferences dialog opens, showing the General preferences, including the When You Insert a CD pop-up menu and the Import Settings button, as shown in Figure 5-10.

2. **Choose what action iTunes should take for the When You Insert a CD option in the General preferences.**

   Choose one of the following actions on the pop-up menu for when you insert an audio CD:

   • *Show CD:* iTunes does nothing else. This preference is ideal if you're not sure whether you want to play the CD first or edit the song information before importing, as I describe in Chapter 11.

- *Begin Playing:* See the earlier section, "Playing Audio CD Tracks," for details on playing CDs. A good choice if you often play CD tracks.

- *Ask to Import CD:* iTunes displays the dialog that asks whether you want to import the CD. This preference is ideal if you are not sure if you want to import the CD every time you insert one.

- *Import CD:* iTunes uses the current import format and settings and automatically imports the CD. This preference is useful if you want to use the same import format and settings every time you insert a CD.

- *Import CD and Eject:* iTunes automatically imports and then ejects the CD, making way for the next one. This preference is useful for importing a batch of CDs (such as a box set), when you want to use the same import format and settings for the entire batch.

3. **Make sure that the Automatically Retrieve CD Track Names from Internet check box is selected (if not, click to check it).**

   This check box is selected by default. iTunes automatically grabs the song titles, artist names, album titles, and so on directly from the Internet, as I describe in Chapter 9.

4. **(Optional) Click the Import Settings button in the General preferences to change your import settings, and then click OK.**

   Refer to Figure 5-9 for the Import Settings dialog.

5. **Click OK to close the Preferences dialog.**

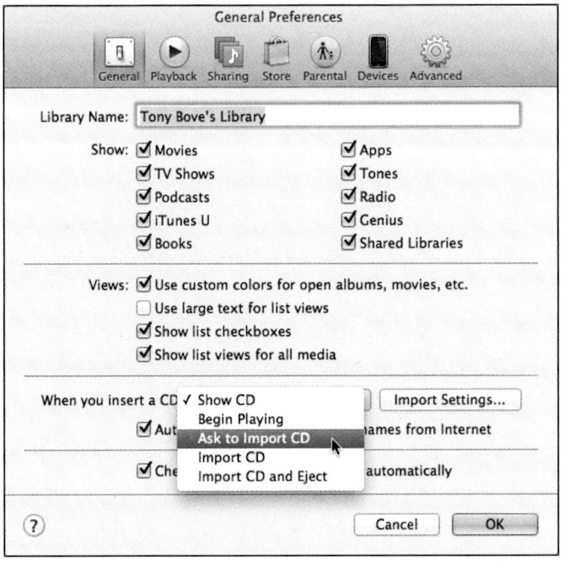

Figure 5-10: Set the appropriate action for iTunes after a CD is inserted.

Editing the CD info and joining tracks

Some CDs — particularly live concert albums, classical albums, rock operas (such as The Who's *Tommy*), and theme albums (such as *Sgt. Pepper's Lonely Hearts Club Band* by The Beatles) — are meant to be played straight through, with no fading between the songs. Fortunately, you can join tracks of a CD so that the tracks play seamlessly one to the next. You can also edit the CD information — the artist name, composer, album name, disc number, year, and genre.

To edit the CD information, click the CD Info button to the left of the Import CD icon (refer to Figure 5-8). The CD Info dialog opens, as shown in Figure 5-11. Edit the information fields as you wish and click OK.

To join multiple tracks on the CD into one track, first select the songs that you want to play continuously (such as the first two songs of *Sgt. Pepper* or all the songs of a live CD).

CD Info		
Artist		
Frank Zappa		
Composer		
Album	**Disc Number**	
The Best Band You Never Heard In Y	1	of 2
Genre	**Year**	
Indie Rock ▾	1991	
☐ Compilation CD		
(?)	Cancel	OK

Figure 5-11: Edit the CD information.

To select multiple songs, click the first one, press and hold ⌘ on a Mac or Ctrl in Windows, and click each subsequent song. To select consecutive songs, click the first one, hold down the Shift key, and click the last one.

After selecting the songs, click Options and choose Join CD Tracks, as shown in Figure 5-12. You can join tracks only before ripping a CD, not afterward.

Let it rip

After clicking the Import CD icon (refer to Figure 5-8) and clicking OK for the Import Settings dialog (refer to Figure 5-9), the ripping begins.

The playback status pane shows the progress of the operation, as shown in Figure 5-13. To cancel, click the small *x* next to the progress bar in the status display. iTunes displays an animated waveform icon next to the song that it's imporing. When iTunes finishes importing each song, it replaces the wave-form icon with a green check mark.

When all the songs are imported, you can eject the CD by clicking the Eject button (refer to Figure 5-8) or choosing Controls⇨Eject Disc.

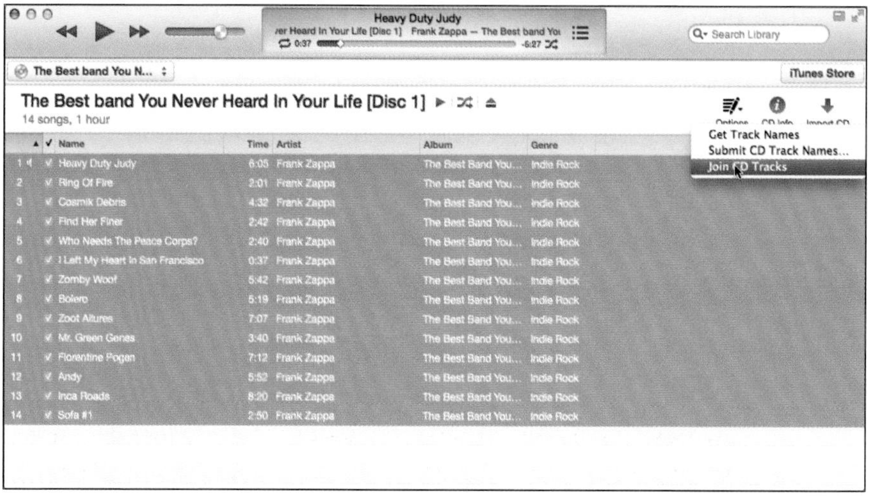

Figure 5-12: Join the selected songs.

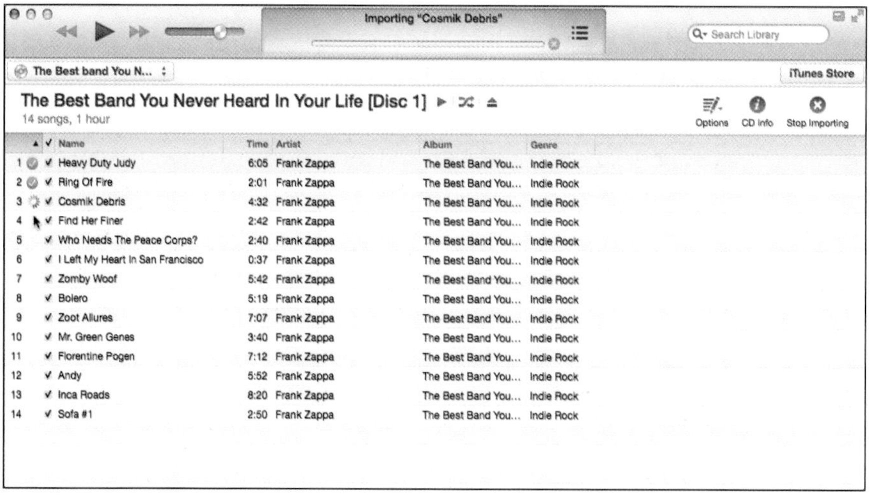

Figure 5-13: iTunes shows a check mark to indicate that it's done ripping the song.

Exploring the iTunes Store

The iTunes Store offers millions of songs — many for $0.69, $0.99, or $1.29, although album prices may vary. Some of these albums offer an immersive visual experience (called iTunes LP) that includes liner notes, pictures, video, animation, and lyrics. You can also buy audio books, e-books, TV episodes, and first-run movies, as well as rent movies and TV shows. On top of that, iTunes offers tons of free content in the form of *podcasts,* which are similar to syndicated radio and TV shows. You can download podcasts into iTunes and play them at your convenience on your computer and on your iPod. iTunes even offers free lectures, language lessons, and audio books with educational content in its iTunes U section.

The iTunes Store includes the App Store, which offers free and commercial iPod touch applications by the hundreds of thousands. You can find apps in just about every category you can think of, including gaming, social networking, sports, business, and more. The iTunes Store also includes the iBookstore, which provides e-books for the iBooks app.

You can download and organize your content and apps in your iTunes library on your computer, and then sync them to an iPod, as I describe in Chapter 7. You can also browse content from the iTunes Store and apps from the App Store and download them directly to an iPod touch. By setting your store preferences in iTunes as I describe in this chapter, you can automatically download to iTunes the music, apps, and e-books you downloaded to your iPod touch from Apple's online stores.

Setting Up an Account

One important task that you must do is set up your iTunes Store account. For most people who use an iPod touch, their iTunes Store account is the same as their iCloud account, which you can set up while setting up your iPod touch (as I show in Chapter 2). However, you may want to maintain more than one iTunes Store or iCloud account. You can do that by setting up another account using iTunes or using an iPod touch.

You need an account to purchase content or apps on your computer as well as to use the iTunes Store, App Store, and iBookstore on your iPod touch. You can create as many accounts as you need — perhaps one for each family member.

After creating an account or signing into an account using iTunes, you can sync your iPod touch as I describe in Chapter 7. Your account information carries over to the iPod touch, so that you don't have to set it up again. You can also set up or sign in to a different account using your iPod touch.

To create or sign in to an iTunes Store account using iTunes on your computer, follow these steps:

1. **In iTunes, click the iTunes Store button in the upper-right corner.**

   The iTunes Store home page appears, as shown in Figure 6-1.

2. **Click the Sign In tab in the upper-left area of the window (refer to Figure 6-1) to either create an account or sign in to an existing account.**

   When you're logged in to an iTunes account, the account name appears in place of the Sign In tab.

   After you click the Sign In tab, iTunes displays the account sign-in dialog.

   If you already set up an account with the iTunes Store or with iCloud, or with other Apple services that require a payment card (such as Apple's online store), you're halfway there. Type your ID and password and then click the Sign In button. Apple remembers the personal information that you put in previously, so you don't have to reenter it every time you visit the iTunes Store. If you forgot your password, click the Forgot Password? button; iTunes provides a dialog so that you can answer your test question. If you answer correctly, iTunes e-mails your password to you. After entering your password, skip to Step 8.

3. **To create a new account, click the Create Apple ID button.**

   iTunes displays a new page that welcomes you to the iTunes Store.

4. **Click Continue on the iTunes Store welcome page.**

Figure 6-1: The iTunes Store home page.

After you click Continue, the terms of use appear with the option at the end to agree to the terms. If you don't select the option to agree, iTunes continues to display the terms until you agree or click Cancel.

5. **Select the I Have Read and Agree to These Terms and Conditions option to agree with the legal terms. Then click Continue.**

   iTunes displays the next page of the setup procedure.

6. **Fill in your personal account information.**

   In addition to other personal information, you need to enter your e-mail address, password, and security questions and answers (in case you forget your password). *Don't forget your password* — you need it to access the store.

7. **Click the Continue button to go to the next page of the account setup procedure, and then enter your payment card information.**

   The entire procedure is secure, so you don't have to worry. The iTunes Store keeps your personal information (including your payment card information) on file, so you don't have to type it again.

8. **Click Continue to finish the procedure.**

   The account setup finishes and returns you to the iTunes Store home page. You can now use the iTunes Store to purchase and download content to play in iTunes and use on any iPod.

To sign in to or create an iTunes account directly on your iPod touch, follow these steps:

1. **Choose Settings⌤iTunes & App Stores from the Home screen.**

   The iTunes & App Stores screen appears.

   - If you haven't set up an iTunes Store or iCloud account, you see the screen in Figure 6-2, left side. Skip to Step 3.

   - If you have already set up an iTunes Store or iCloud account to sync with, you see the screen in Figure 6-2, right side.

2. **If you are already synced to an iTunes Store or iCloud account, tap the button with your Apple ID, and then tap Sign Out in order to switch to another account.**

3. **Tap Create New Apple ID to set up a new account, or fill in your Apple ID and password and tap Sign In to sign in to an existing account.**

   If you sign in to an existing account, you are done; skip the rest of these steps.

4. **Confirm your country or region for the new account and tap Next.**

5. **Tap Agree to the terms of service.**

6. **Enter the information on the New Account screen.**

7. **Tap Next to continue through the setup screens to finish setting up your account.**

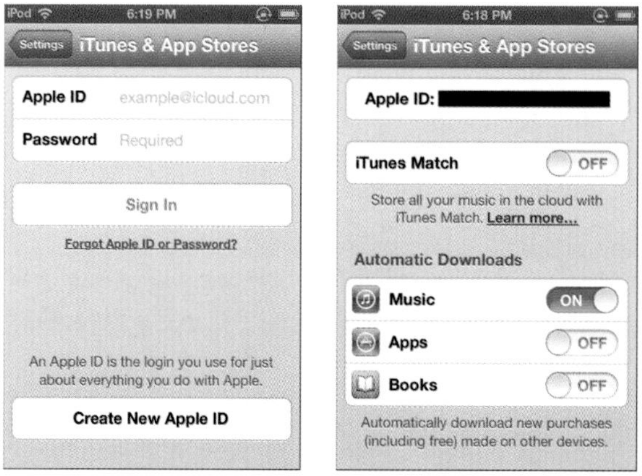

Figure 6-2: The iTunes & App Stores screen before setting up an account (left) and after setting up an account (right).

Shopping with iTunes

If you sign in to an iTunes Store account with iTunes (see the previous section), you can buy and download content immediately, including movies and TV shows for rent. I don't know of a faster way to purchase or rent content from the comfort of your home.

If you already have your iTunes program open, click the iTunes Store button in the upper-right corner of the iTunes window. The iTunes Store home page appears (refer to Figure 6-1).

Cruising in the multimedia mall

The iTunes Store home page is loaded with specials and ads to peruse. To look at music in more depth, click the Music tab (refer to Figure 6-1). You can also pick a music genre by clicking the down-arrow button that appears next to the Music tab when your pointer is over the tab, as shown in Figure 6-3.

Figure 6-3: The Music tab's menu.

Besides Music and other tabs, the iTunes Store offers other buttons along the top of the iTunes window (refer to Figure 6-1). The left and right triangle buttons work just like the back and forward buttons of a web browser, moving back a page or forward a page, respectively. The Home page button (a Home icon) takes you to the iTunes Store home page.

After you click an album or select an advertisement for an album, the album's page appears with a description and other links, as shown in Figure 6-4. You can then click the Buy button with the album price or the Buy buttons with song prices for individual songs, as I describe in the "Buying and downloading items" section, later in this chapter.

Figure 6-4: An iTunes Store page showing an iTunes LP album.

Want to tell a friend about a song, album, movie, TV show, or any other iTunes Store content? Click the arrow attached to the Buy button to see a menu of choices for telling the world at large:

✔ **Gift This or Add to Wish List:** You can e-mail a gift certificate from the iTunes Store for this item to someone, or just put it on your iTunes Store wish list, which you can visit later to buy your choices.

✔ **Tell a Friend:** E-mail a link to this content item.

✔ **Copy Link:** Copy the link to this content item to use in a document, e-mail message, or social media posting.

✔ **Share On Facebook or Share On Twitter:** Share a link to this content item on either Facebook or Twitter. For details about these social networks, see Chapter 18.

To browse the iTunes Store, choose View➪Column Browser➪Show Column Browser, or click the Browse link in the Quick Links column on the right side of the iTunes Store home page (Browse doesn't appear on other pages, just the home page). iTunes displays the store's offerings categorized by type of content (such as Music), and it displays music by genre and subgenre — and within each subgenre, by artist and album. Select a genre in the Genre column, then a subgenre in the Subgenre column, then an artist in the Artist column, and finally an album in the Album column, which takes you to the list of songs from that album that are available to preview or purchase, as shown in Figure 6-5.

You can play music in your iTunes library while shopping in the iTunes Store, as I do in Figure 6-5 — I'm playing Elvis in my library while browsing for more Elvis in the store.

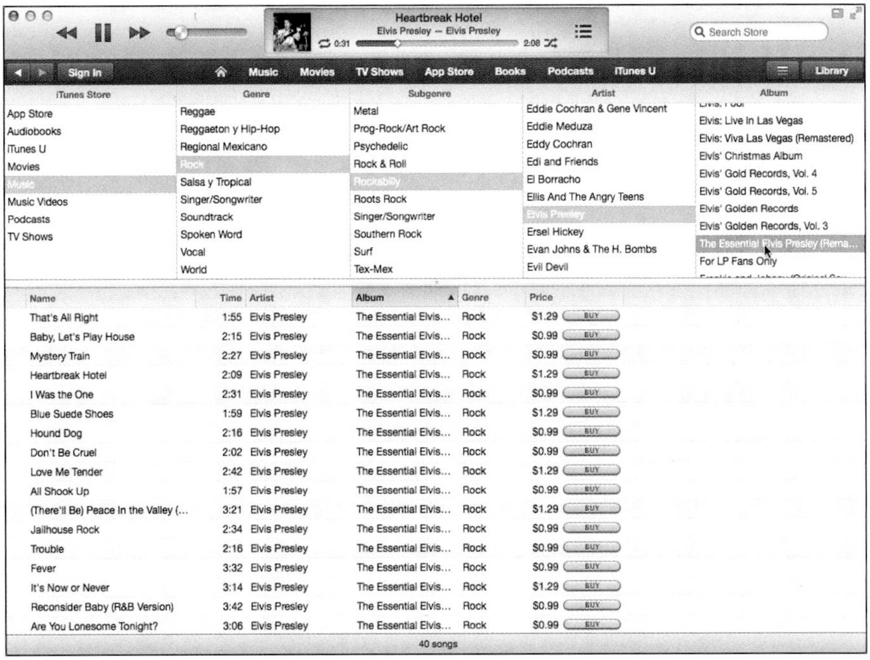

Figure 6-5: Browse the iTunes Store for music by genre, artist, and album.

If you're looking for "That Song That Jane Likes" by the Dave Matthews Band or know specifically what to search for, type it into the Search Store field in the upper-right corner of the iTunes window (refer to Figure 6-1); this lets you search the iTunes Store for just about anything. You can type part of a song title or artist name to quickly display suggestions in a drop-down list below the Search Store field –- click a suggestion to use it.

Browsing other content

To find TV shows, movies, music videos, or books, you can

- ✔ Click the Movies, TV Shows, or Books tab at the top of iTunes Store page. You can also click the down-arrow button next to each tab to browse by specific genres.

- ✔ For music videos, click the down-arrow button next to the Music tab and then select Music Videos from the pop-up menu. You can also select Music Movies in this menu.

- ✔ Use the column browser (refer to Figure 6-5). You can then select App Store, Audiobooks, iTunes U, Movies, Music, Music Videos, Podcasts, or TV Shows from the iTunes Store column, and then pick a genre.

You can preview content in the iTunes Store. Many song previews are nearly a minute and a half. Some movies offer 1-minute previews and movie trailers you can view free, and many TV shows and audio books offer previews from 30 to 90 seconds; some TV shows offer entirely free episodes. To preview a song, TV show, movie, or music video, click the title in the list, and then click the play button next to the title (or double-click the title). Click the iTunes player buttons to control playback and use the iTunes volume slider to control the volume. See Chapter 10 for content in iTunes.

To see all the selections you recently previewed, click the preview history button (refer to Figure 6-1). The items you previewed appear in a drop-down menu, and you can select any of them to return to the Store page for that item.

Browsing and subscribing to podcasts

Podcasting is a popular method of publishing audio and video shows to the Internet, enabling people to subscribe to a feed and receive the shows automatically. Similar to a tape of a radio broadcast, you can save a podcast episode and play it back at your convenience, both in iTunes on your computer and on your iPod. You can also burn an audio podcast episode to an audio CD or MP3 CD.

By *subscribing,* I mean listing the podcast in the Podcasts section of your iTunes library, so that new episodes download automatically. It's like a magazine subscription that's updated with a new issue every month or so. Your copy of iTunes automatically finds new podcast episodes and downloads them to your computer.

A podcast episode can be anything from a single song to a commentary-hosted radio show; a podcaster, like a broadcaster, provides a stream of episodes over time. Thousands of professional and amateur radio and video shows are offered as podcast episodes. Video podcasts are also called *video-casts* or *vodcasts.*

The iTunes Podcast page in the iTunes Store lets you browse, find, preview, and subscribe to podcasts, most of which are free. To find podcasts in the iTunes Store, do one of the following:

- ✔ **Click the Podcasts tab at the top of the iTunes Store page.** The iTunes Store displays the Podcast page, with advertisements for popular pod-casts. You can click the down-arrow button next to the Podcasts tab to choose specific categories.

  You can also get to the Podcast page by clicking Podcasts in the iTunes source list, clicking the List tab to see your podcasts, and then clicking Podcast Catalog at the bottom of the list.

- ✔ **Browse all podcasts in a particular category.** Use the column browser (refer to Figure 6-5) and select Podcasts in the iTunes Store column. Select options from the Category column and Subcategory column.

- ✔ **Search for a podcast by name or keyword.** You can type a search term into the Search Store field in the upper-right corner of the iTunes window to find any podcasts or other content items that match.

You can also find podcasts outside of the iTunes Store on the Internet. To find out how to add podcasts to iTunes manually from the Internet, see Bonus Chapter 3 in the free tips section of the author's website (www.tonybove.com/tips).

After you select a podcast, the iTunes Store displays the podcast's specific page in the iTunes Store, showing all available podcast episodes. To select, play, and subscribe to a podcast, follow these steps:

1. **Choose a podcast in the iTunes Store.**

   The iTunes Store offers a description and a Subscribe button to receive new podcasts. The page also lists the most recent podcast episodes. You can click the *i* icon on the far-right listing margin to display separate information about each podcast episode.

2. **To preview the podcast, click an episode title, and then click the play button next to the title.**

   You can play a preview of any episode in the list. iTunes plays the epi-sode for about 90 seconds, just like a web radio station streaming to your computer. To jump ahead or play the entire episode, you must first subscribe to the podcast. By subscribing, you enable automatic down-loading of episodes to your computer.

3. **Click the Subscribe button on the podcast page to subscribe to the podcast.**

   In typical Apple fashion, iTunes first displays an alert to confirm that you want to subscribe to the podcast.

4. **Click the OK button to confirm.**

   iTunes downloads the podcast. iTunes displays your newly subscribed podcast in the Podcasts section of your library. See Chapter 10 for details on playing podcasts in iTunes.

5. **(Optional) Get more episodes of the podcast.**

   When you subscribe to a podcast, you get the current episode. However, a podcast probably has past episodes still available. To download any free or commercial episodes, click the Free or Buy button at the far-right side of the episode.

You can play the podcast, incorporate it into playlists, and make copies and burn CDs as much as you like.

Updating podcasts

Many podcast feeds provide new material on a regular schedule. iTunes can check these feeds automatically and update your library with new podcast episodes. You can, for example, schedule iTunes to check for new podcast episodes — such as news, weather, traffic reports, and morning talk shows — before you wake up and automatically update your iPod.

To check for updates manually, select Podcasts in the Library section of the source list, and then click the round-circle refresh button in the lower-left corner of the view under the Unplayed or Podcasts tab, or the Refresh button in the lower-right corner of the view under the List tab. All subscribed podcast feeds are updated immediately when you refresh, and iTunes downloads the most recent (or all) episodes, depending on how you set your podcasts preferences to schedule podcast updates.

To change your podcast settings so that iTunes can check for new podcasts automatically, click the List tab, and then click the Settings button at the bottom of the List tab view to display the Podcast Settings dialog. You can change the settings for each podcast separately by choosing the podcast in the Settings For pop-up menu. The settings are as follows:

- **Check for New Episodes:** Choose to check for podcasts every hour, day, week, or manually — whenever you want.

- **Settings For:** Choose which podcast in your iTunes library you are scheduling updates for or choose Podcast Defaults to apply these settings to all podcasts in your library.

✔ **When New Episodes Are Available:** You can download the most recent one (useful for news podcasts), download all episodes (useful for podcasts you might want to keep), or do nothing so that you can use the Refresh button to update manually as you need.

✔ **Episodes to Keep:** Choose to keep all episodes, all unplayed episodes, the most recent episodes, or previous episodes.

Keeping unplayed episodes is a useful way to organize your news podcasts. If you've played an episode (or a portion of it), you likely don't need it anymore, but you probably do want to keep the ones you haven't played yet. With this setting, iTunes automatically deletes the ones you've played.

If you sync podcasts automatically to your iPod, as I describe in Chapter 7, don't set the Episodes to Keep pop-up to All Unplayed Episodes — use All Episodes instead. This is why: If you listen to part of a podcast episode on your iPod, and then sync the device, the podcast episode disappears from iTunes (because it is no longer unplayed). If the episodes are still out there on the Internet, you can recover them by choosing Download All for the When New Episodes Are Available option.

Buying and downloading items

While you browse content items in the iTunes Store, you can purchase and download them to your computer immediately. All you need to do is click the Buy button, which appears with the price on an album or movie page, or in the far-right column of the song or other content item in a list — you may have to scroll your iTunes Store window to see the far-right column (refer to Figure 6-4 for an album page showing a Buy button or to Figure 6-5 for the column browser showing items you can buy separately).

The iTunes Store may prompt you to log in to your account after you click the Buy button (unless you just recently logged in). Then a warning dialog displays to make sure that you want to buy the item; you can continue by clicking the Buy button or Cancel. After you click the Buy button, iTunes downloads the item, and after downloading, it appears in your iTunes library. You can continue buying items while downloading.

You can see the list of all the items that you purchased using iTunes, or purchased using each iPod touch you synced with iTunes, by selecting Music in the Library section of the source list, and then clicking the Playlists tab. Select one of the Purchased playlists that appear at the top. (For example, I have "Purchased" for iTunes purchases and "Purchased on TBone iPod" for iPod touch purchases.).

Each time you buy content, you get an e-mail from the iTunes Store with the purchase information. It's nice to know right away what you bought.

You can change iTunes Store preference settings by choosing iTunes⇨Preferences on the Mac or by choosing Edit⇨Preferences in Windows. In the Preferences window, click the Store tab. The Store preferences pane appears, and you can set the following features:

- **Always Check for Available Downloads:** Set this preference to automatically check for interrupted downloads from Apple's online stores and finish them (see the next section for details).

- **Download Pre-Orders When Available:** If you pre-order items or use iTunes Pass to access a suite of content related to one artist for a limited time for a fixed price, set this preference so that when the items become available, iTunes automatically downloads them.

- **When Downloading High Definition Videos, Prefer:** Choose the type of HD (high definition) videos you want, either 720p or the higher-resolution 1080p.

- **Automatic Downloads:** You can select Music, Apps, and Books to automatically download to iTunes the music, apps, and e-books you downloaded from Apple's online stores to your iPod touch or other iOS devices or other computers using your iTunes Store account.

- **Show iTunes in the Cloud Purchases:** View all the purchases you made in the iTunes Store.

- **Sync Playback Information across All Devices:** Turn on this option so that your iOS devices, such as an iPod touch, can start playing the content you were playing in iTunes at the same point where you left off.

- **Automatically Download Album Artwork:** Turn this option on to download iTunes Store cover art for albums in your library that don't have cover art. You must also turn on the Share Details option (next) to find cover art for albums you didn't purchase in the iTunes Store.

- **Share Details about Your Library with Apple:** Turn this option on to share your library information so that Apple can find cover art and make Genius suggestions based on the content you have in your library. See Chapter 10 for details about Genius suggestions.

Resuming interrupted downloads

All sales are final; you can't return the digital merchandise. However, the download must be successful — you have to receive it all — before the iTunes Store charges you for the purchase. If for any reason the download is interrupted or fails to complete, your order remains active until you connect to the iTunes Store again.

iTunes remembers to continue the download when you return to iTunes and connect to the Internet. If for some reason the download doesn't continue, choose Store⇨Check for Available Downloads to continue the interrupted download.

Your downloads are automatically transferred to one of the Purchased playlists, but during the downloading process, a download button (a down-arrow) appears in the upper-right corner of the iTunes window. Click the download button to see the Downloads window. You can click the Pause All button to pause downloads and later click Resume All to resume downloads. You can also click the Pause button at the right side of each item's row to pause the downloading of a single item; click it again to resume downloading that item. You can prioritize the order of downloading by dragging items into a different order in the Downloads window.

Appearing at the App Store

You can get loads of free and commercial apps that run on your iPod touch just like the built-in apps such as Map and Weather. (To no one's big surprise, many of the apps are games.) To find hundreds of thousands of apps, click the App Store tab at the top of the iTunes Store window (refer to Figure 6-1). The App Store page appears, as shown in Figure 6-6. Click the iPhone tab to see apps that run on the iPod touch and iPhone.

Figure 6-6: Find iPod touch apps in the iPhone section of the App Store.

Click an app's icon to go to the information page for that app, which may also contain reviews and a slide show depicting the app in all its glory. The information page offers the Buy button with its price (to purchase and download a commercial app) or the Free button (to download a free app). Click the Buy or Free button to download the app to your iTunes library.

Downloaded apps appear in the Apps section of your iTunes library — click Apps in the Library section of the source list to see their icons.

Shopping with Your iPod touch

The entire iTunes Store and App Store are available right at your fingertips on your iPod touch. You can search for, browse, and preview content; make purchases; and download content and apps directly to your iPod touch. You use the following apps:

- ✐ iTunes for music, movies, TV shows, tones, and audio books
- ✐ App Store for apps
- ✐ iBooks for e-books
- ✐ Podcasts for podcasts
- ✐ iTunes U for iTunes U lectures

Whatever you buy on your iPod touch is automatically copied to your iCloud account so that you can download it again, and also copied to your iTunes library the next time you synchronize it with your computer, as I describe in Chapter 7. If you set the Automatic Downloads option in iTunes, as I show in the earlier section, "Buying and downloading items," the music, apps, or books you buy are automatically downloaded to your iTunes library. You can also set your iPod touch to automatically download any purchases you made on your other iPad, iPod touch, or iPhone models by choosing Settings➪iTunes & App Stores and tapping the On/Off button next to the Music, Apps, or Books options to turn one or more of them On.

Be sure to set up an iTunes Store account first if you don't already have one, as I describe earlier in this chapter — and you'll need to remember your password. To download content and apps directly to your iPod touch, you can set up your iPod touch with iTunes, which basically means signing in to your iTunes Store account in iTunes on your computer, and then syncing your iPod touch to iTunes as I describe in Chapter 7. After doing that once, you shouldn't have to bother with it again, and you can download items from the iTunes Store and App Store on your iPod touch from then on. All you need to do is enter the password for your iTunes Store account when prompted.

You can sign in to one or more iTunes Store accounts directly from your iPod touch and view your account information by choosing Settings⇨iTunes & App Stores from the Home screen. To sign in to an existing account, enter your Apple ID and password and tap Sign In. If your iPod touch is already synced with your account, the button with your Apple ID appears at the top of the iTunes & App Stores screen — tap the button to see a pop-up menu offering View Apple ID to see your account information, Sign Out to sign out, or Cancel.

Browsing and downloading content

To browse and download music, movies, TV shows, tones, and audio books on an iPod touch, tap the iTunes icon on the Home screen. The iTunes Store screen appears with Music, Movies, TV Shows, Search, and More icons along the bottom. Here's the lowdown on the icons:

✔ **Tap the Music icon** to see music, new releases, and store recommen-dations, as shown in Figure 6-7. You can tap the Features tab to see new releases at the top, and you can swipe across the screen to see more of them. Scroll the page to see more albums, or tap Charts to see the top charting songs and albums. To search through genres, tap the Genres button in the top-left corner and choose a genre. Some albums offer bonus content, such as liner notes, which are downloaded to your iTunes library on your computer, but not to your iPod touch.

✔ **Tap the Movies or TV Shows icon**, and the screen displays Movies or TV Shows. Scroll either screen to see more movies and TV shows.

Figure 6-7: Browse the iTunes Store (left) and the App Store (right) on an iPod touch.

✔ **Tap the Search icon** to search the store, and then tap the entry field to bring up the onscreen keyboard. Type the search term and tap the Search button to search the store, or tap one of the suggestions that the store provides as you enter the search term.

✔ **Tap the More icon** for more choices, including Audiobooks, Tones, Genius, Purchased, and Downloads. Audiobooks takes you right to a section of the store dedicated to audio books. Tones shows you tones you can play in your iPod touch when you receive FaceTime calls or messages in the Messages app. Genius shows you selections related to the music you already own and store on your iPod touch or in iTunes Match. Purchased shows the content you've purchased from the iTunes Store, which is automatically stored in the iCloud service — tap Music, Movies, or TV Shows to see the content you've purchased. Downloads shows you the progress of your downloads from the store.

If this is your first time to the store on your iPod touch, the Music section appears. Tap any song to hear a preview. To buy and download a song, tap the price button, and then tap the Buy button (which replaces the price button). Enter your password and tap OK. Purchased and downloaded items are added to a Purchased playlist on your iPod touch.

You can similarly preview a video before buying it — tap the video to start the preview. To buy the item, tap the price button and then tap the Buy button that appears.

If you received a gift certificate for a content item by e-mail or some other method (such as an iTunes or App Store gift card), you can redeem the gift by scrolling to the bottom of the Music, Movies, or TV Shows screens and tap the Redeem button. You can then enter the redemption code in the certificate or gift card to download the content item.

If you lose your network connection or turn off your iPod touch while downloading, the download pauses and resumes when you reestablish Wi-Fi. If you go back to your computer, iTunes can complete the download operation to your iTunes library. To make sure you received all downloads to your iPod touch, use iTunes on your computer and choose Store⇨Check for Available Downloads.

Browsing and downloading apps

Tap the App Store icon on the Home screen to grab some apps, as shown in Figure 6-7, right side. The Store screen appears with Featured, Top Charts, Genius, Search, and Updates icons along the bottom of the screen. The following list tells you what's what when it comes to the icons:

✔ **Tap the Featured icon** for featured apps. You can scroll the screen to see new apps and "hot" apps (based on downloads).

- ✔ **Tap the Top Charts icon** and scroll the screen to see the top paid apps and free apps by popularity.

- ✔ **Tap Genius** to see App Store recommendations based on apps you already own. Tap Turn On Genius if it isn't already on, and then enter your account's password.

- ✔ **Tap the Search icon** to search the store, and then tap the entry field to bring up the onscreen keyboard. Type the search term and tap Search to search the store. Suggestions pop up right away; for example, if you search for *Tony's Tips* in the App Store, my app, Tony's Tips for iPhone Users Manual, appears in the list of suggestions.

- ✔ **Tap the Updates icon** . . . wait, forget I said that. I cover that icon in the next section, so check that out if you want details.

Tap the Categories button in the top-left corner (refer to Figure 6-7, right side) to browse by category, and then tap a category, such as Games, to see a list of all games by popularity.

To download an app, tap the price button (for a paid app) or Free button (for a free app). The price or Free button changes to the Install button. Tap Install, enter your password, and tap OK.

The iPod touch displays the Home screen with the icon for the new app as it loads. As soon as the Loading message is replaced by the name of the app, the icon is ready to be tapped.

If you already have the app on your iPod touch, the Open button appears in place of the price or Free button — tap Open to open the app on your iPod touch.

Updating Apps

You can find out from within iTunes if an app you downloaded is updated by its publisher. Choose Apps in the Library section of the source list and click the Check for Updates button in the bottom-right corner of the apps screen. iTunes checks to see which apps should be updated and takes you to the My Apps Update page in the iTunes Store, where you find icons of the apps to update. You can click the Get Update button next to each app's icon to download the update or click Download All Free Updates in the upper-right corner of the page to grab all the updates at once. iTunes may ask for a password first; enter your password and click the Buy button (even though the updates are mostly free). (iTunes may also ask for age confirmation if there are any items rated 17+ or adult.) After the downloads are completed, click the Done button on the My App Updates page. The updated apps automatically replace the previous versions of the apps.

The App Store on your iPod touch notifies you if any of your apps have been updated — a number appears in the App Store icon. You should update an app when an update is available because updates fix bugs and introduce new features you may want.

Tap the Updates icon at the bottom-right corner of the App Store screen to see the list of updated apps. You can then tap the Update All button in the top-right corner of the Updates screen to download all the available updates. To update a single app, tap the app in the list to see the app's information screen, and then tap the Update button. The Update button changes to the Install button. Tap Install, enter your password, and tap OK.

The updated versions replace the previous versions of the apps as they download into your iPod touch. As soon as the Loading message is replaced by the name of the app, the app is ready to be tapped.

You can also see all the app purchases you've made on your iTunes Store account by tapping Purchased at the top of the Updates screen on the iPod touch.

Getting in Sync with Your iTunes Library

In This Chapter

▶ Synchronizing your iPod with your iTunes library

▶ Synchronizing with iTunes Match

▶ Choosing what to sync

▶ Copying content directly to, or deleting from, your iPod

*i*Tunes is an all-knowing, all-powerful synchronizer that you can use to put content on your iPod and content and apps on your iPod touch.

Synchronizing your iPod means automatically copying content and apps, and any *changes* to the content and apps, to the device from your iTunes library. You can also sync an iPod touch with the iTunes Match library in your iCloud account.

If you make changes in iTunes to content you synced to the iPod, those changes are automatically carried over to the iPod when you sync it again. Your iPod mirrors the content of your iTunes library, or as much of the content as will fit or as you specify — and iTunes can make assumptions if the entire library won't fit or give you options to be more selective, as I describe in this chapter.

This chapter also shows how to copy songs and videos directly to your iPod using the manual method. You can even combine automatic syncing with manual methods to build your iPod library as you see fit.

If you store photos in an iPhoto library on a Mac, or in a program (such as Adobe Photoshop Elements) in Windows, you can set up your iPod with the option to copy your entire photo library. See Chapter 14 for details.

Syncing Differently

You can synchronize any iPod model with iTunes by connecting the device to a USB connection on your computer. With an iPod touch, you can also sync wirelessly with iTunes on your computer over your Wi-Fi network, as I describe in the "Syncing wirelessly or not at all" section, later in this chapter. You can also sync your music content with the iTunes Match library in your iCloud account.

When you first set up your iPod using iTunes, you can choose the option to sync your entire iTunes library automatically. From that point on, your iPod can synchronize with your entire library automatically. (See Chapter 2 for details on setting up your iPod.)

The full, everything-but-the-kitchen-sync approach works well if your combined iTunes library, apps, and photo library are small enough to fit in their entirety on your iPod. For example, if your apps, iTunes content, and photo libraries combined are less than 60GB and you have a 64GB iPod touch, you can sync everything (although you may not have enough room for shooting photos and videos). Syncing everything copies your entire library, and it's just as fast as copying individual items (if not faster) because you don't have to select the items to copy.

You can see the size of the music, movies, TV shows, and other sections of your iTunes library in GB, or *gigabytes,* by choosing View➪Show Status Bar. The status bar appears at the bottom of the iTunes window in the center and its information changes with each source you select (Music, Movies, TV Shows, and so on) and each tab you select for each source. The status bar shows the number of items (such as albums under the Albums tab), the time it would take to play everything shown under the selected tab, and the space it occupies in gigabytes. To hide the status bar, choose View➪Hide Status Bar.

If your iTunes library has more content than your iPod can hold, you can make decisions about which parts to sync. You can select options to synchronize music, TV shows, movies, and so on. For example, you can copy all your songs and audio books, but only some of your TV shows, none of your movies, and only the podcasts you haven't heard yet.

You can also sync an iPod touch with your songs stored in the iTunes Match library in your iCloud account, as I describe in the later section, "Making the iTunes Match." Your purchased content from the iTunes Store is automatically stored in iCloud so that you always have a backup; you can also store songs in iCloud from other sources (such as downloaded songs and music on CDs) by setting up the iTunes Match service, which I describe in Chapter 11.

Syncing everything

Follow these five easy steps to sync all the content and apps in your iTunes library to an iPod:

1. **Connect the iPod and click the iPod button as shown in Figure 7-1.**

   After connecting the iPod, iTunes adds the iPod button in the upper-right corner of the window, which includes the eject button on the right side, and either the X cancel button to cancel syncing (move your pointer over the animated sync icon to see the X if the iPod is syncing) or an iPod icon on the right side.

   After you click the iPod button, iTunes displays the sync options with tabs for each sync options page. iTunes automatically starts syncing your iPod, and the sync status pane tells you the progress. (If you're playing music while syncing, you can switch between the sync status and playback status by clicking the up or down arrows next to the status pane.)

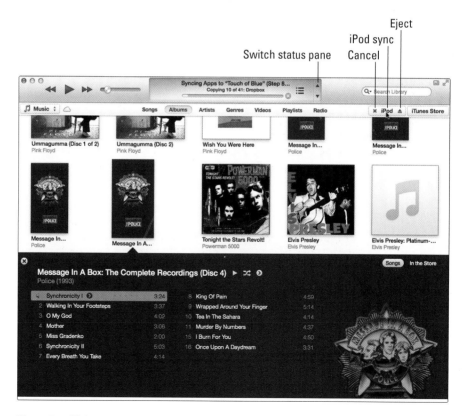

Figure 7-1: Click the iPod button that appears when you connect an iPod.

2. **Click the Summary tab to see the Summary page, if it is not already selected.**

The Summary tab displays the Summary page of sync options, and shows how much space on the device is occupied by content and how much is still free. You can also scroll the Summary page to change sync options in the Backup and Options sections. (See Figure 7-2 for the iPod touch Summary page and Figure 7-3 for the iPod nano Summary page.)

If you haven't made any sync selections, the default is to copy everything in your iTunes library that your iPod model can play. An iPod touch can play everything including apps, and show photos and videos from your photo library. An iPod classic can play everything but apps, and show photos and videos. An iPod nano can play music, music videos, audio books, iTunes U courses, and audio podcasts; it can also show photos. An iPod shuffle can play music, audio books, iTunes U courses, and audio podcasts.

After changing a sync option, the Revert and Apply buttons appear in the lower-right corner of the sync pages (refer to Figure 7-2). Click Apply to apply your sync option change or click Revert to revert back to the previous sync option setting. (If there are no changes to sync options, the Sync button appears in their place — click Sync to start syncing if syncing hasn't already started.)

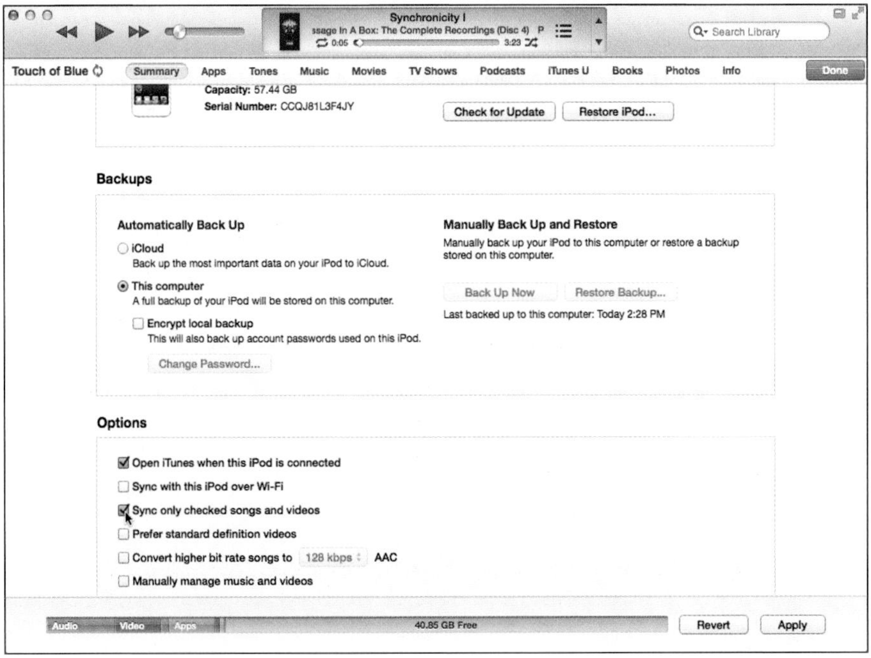

Figure 7-2: The Summary sync options page for an iPod touch named "Touch of Blue."

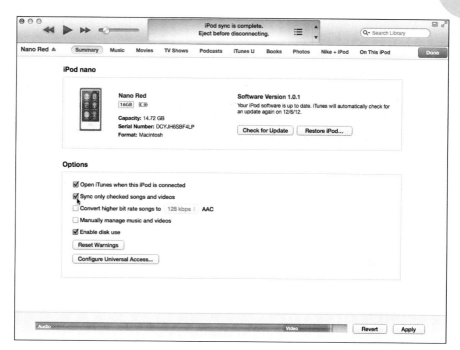

Figure 7-3: The Summary sync options page for an iPod nano named "Nano Red."

Even while syncing is going on, you can select or deselect content to sync, as I describe later in this chapter, and click Apply or Revert.

3. **Click Done in the upper-right corner of the sync pages (refer to Figure 7-2 or 7-3) to finish changing sync settings.**

   When you're done with the sync options, click Done to re-sync again with the new settings. iTunes displays whatever content section of the library you were viewing when the sync started.

4. **Wait for syncing to finish, and then click the eject button next to the "iPod" in the iPod button (refer to Figure 7-1).**

   You should always wait until the sync status pane (at the top) displays that the synchronization is complete, as shown in Figure 7-3.

5. **Disconnect your iPod from your computer.**

   That's it. Your iPod is now synchronized.

Photos from a photo library are also copied if you choose to automatically sync photos when you set up your iPod touch, iPod classic, or iPod nano (see Chapter 2 for details). See Chapter 14 for details on photo syncing.

If you make changes in your iTunes library after syncing the iPod, those changes are automatically copied over to the iPod when you sync again — unless you manually manage content, as I describe in the later section "Manually Managing Music and Videos." That means if you delete an album or video from your iTunes library, that album or video is also deleted from your iPod the next time you sync.

Sizing up your syncing

You probably don't need to know anything else in this chapter about synchronizing with content — unless your iTunes library and additional photo library are too large to fit, you want to sync an iPod touch with iTunes Match, or you want to be more selective about which content to synchronize.

iTunes backs up your synchronization settings for each iPad, iPod, and iPhone model that you connect from the last time when you synchronized the device. You can also enable backing up your iPod touch settings in iCloud, as I describe in Chapter 8.

Even if your iTunes library is larger than your iPod can hold, you can still sync everything as I describe in the previous section. If your iTunes library is too large to fit on your iPod, iTunes chooses which songs and albums to include by using the ratings that you set for each song. (To find out how to set ratings, see Chapter 9.) If your iPod already has photos on it, iTunes asks whether you want to delete them to gain more space. After clicking the Yes or No button, iTunes tries its best to fit everything. If it has to cut something, though, it skips copying new photos and displays the message Some photos were not copied.

You can squeeze more songs onto an iPod if you convert them to a lower-bit-rate format — and you can do this on the fly while syncing with iTunes (although it can dramatically increase sync time; large libraries might need to be synced overnight). Select the Convert Higher Bit Rate Songs to 128 kbps AAC option (refer to Figure 7-3). You can also click the 128 kbps setting to choose another bit rate. As a result, the songs take up less space on the iPod than they occupy in your iTunes library.

If you're still short of space even after skipping photos, iTunes displays a warning about the lack of free space, and it asks whether you want to disable podcast synchronization and let iTunes create a selection of songs in a playlist based on ratings and playback counts in iTunes. (See Chapter 10 for details on using playlists.)

✔ **If you click the Yes button,** iTunes creates a new playlist (titled "*Your device name* Selection," as in "My iPod touch Selection") and displays a message telling you so. Click the OK button, and iTunes synchronizes your iPod using the new playlist. iTunes also sets your iPod to synchronize music automatically by playlist, as I describe in the next section.

✔ **If you click the No button,** iTunes updates automatically until it fills your iPod without creating the playlist.

From that point on, your iPod synchronizes with your iTunes library automatically, right after you connect it to your computer.

Syncing wirelessly or not at all

You don't have to connect an iPod touch directly to your computer using a USB cable — you can instead connect wirelessly over your Wi-Fi network. After connecting your iPod touch by cable the first time to sync to iTunes, you can set iTunes to sync the device wirelessly from that point on.

To set iTunes to sync wirelessly with an iPod touch, click the Summary tab in the sync options to see the Summary page (refer to Figure 7-2). In the Options section of the page, choose Sync With This iPod over Wi-Fi. Click the Apply button in the lower-right corner of the iTunes window, and when you are finished changing other sync settings, click Done. When regular syncing is finished, click the eject button next to the "iPod" in the iPod button (refer to Figure 7-1).

To sync your iPod touch wirelessly, plug the device into power and make sure it is connected to the same Wi-Fi network as your computer (see Chapter 4 to learn how to turn on Wi-Fi). Choose Settings⇨General⇨iTunes Wi-Fi Sync, and then tap the Sync Now button. Your iPod touch syncs wirelessly with iTunes on your computer.

If you want to connect your iPod to your computer without automatically syncing it, connect it once and click to remove the check mark next to the Open iTunes when This iPod Is Connected option. The next time you connect your iPod, iTunes won't automatically open. However, if iTunes *is* open before you connect your iPod, it will start syncing the iPod.

To prevent an iPod from automatically synchronizing, choose Preferences from the iTunes menu on a Mac or the Edit menu in Windows, click the Devices tab, and then turn on the Prevent iPods, iPhones, and iPads from Syncing Automatically option — which prevents all these devices from syncing automatically with iTunes on that computer. If you forgot to do this, you can still keep an iPod from automatically synchronizing. Press ⌘-Option (Mac) or Ctrl-Alt (Windows) while you connect the device. You can then change the iPod sync setting to manually manage music and videos, as I describe later in this chapter.

If you connect an iPod previously linked to another computer to *your* computer (and the other computer's iTunes installation is connected to a different Apple ID or iTunes Store account), iTunes displays a message warning you that clicking the Yes button replaces its content with the content from your computer's library. If you don't want to change the content on the iPod, click No. If you click Yes, iTunes erases the device and synchronizes it with your computer's library. To avoid this warning, first set the iPod sync settings to manually manage music and videos, as I describe later in this chapter, on the same computer the device was previously synced with, and with iTunes logged in using the same Apple ID or iTunes Store account.

Enabling other sync options

The sync options are the same or similar for each iPod model, but some models offer additional options. For example, the iPod nano, iPod classic, and iPod shuffle offer an extra sync option called Enable Disk Use, which lets you use your iPod as a disk drive.

With the VoiceOver option, an iPod shuffle speaks song titles and artist names, a menu of playlists for you to choose from, and the status of your battery charge. (With a third-generation iPod shuffle, you need the Apple Earphones with Remote and Mic or the In-Ear Headphones with Remote and Mic to use VoiceOver to navigate playlists.) You can enable VoiceOver for an iPod shuffle in iTunes when you set it up (as I describe in Chapter 2) or enable it on the Summary sync options page when you synchronize your iPod shuffle.

To enable VoiceOver, sync your iPod shuffle to iTunes. The Summary page of sync options appears — you may have to scroll it to see all the options. Under Voice Feedback, select the Enable VoiceOver check box to turn it on (or deselect it to turn it off). With an iPod shuffle, you also have the option to choose the language you want from the Language pop-up menu. This sets the language for spoken messages and playlist names, as well as many of the song titles and artist names. Finally, click the Apply button to apply these settings. To find out how to use VoiceOver with an iPod shuffle, see Chapter 12.

You can also enable VoiceOver for an iPod nano by clicking the Configure Universal Access button at the bottom of the Summary sync options page, and then clicking the VoiceOver option.

The iPod touch offers VoiceOver as part of the accessibility features to make it easier to use for people with visual, auditory, or other physical disabilities. (You can turn the accessibility features on or off by choosing Settings⇨General⇨Accessibility from the Home screen.) It works by telling you about each element on the screen as you select it.

To discover how to enable your iPod as a disk drive, and how to use VoiceOver on an iPod touch, see "Tips on Using iPods and iPhones" in the free tips section of the author's website (www.tonybove.com/tips).

Making the iTunes Match

With an iPod touch, you can set up the iCloud service, as I describe in Chapter 2, so that you can back up your iPod touch settings and sync personal information to your iPod touch. You can also automatically keep a copy of everything you purchase in the iTunes Store, App Store, and iBookstore, as I describe in Chapter 6. In addition, you can subscribe to iTunes Match in iCloud to match most, if not all, of the songs in your iTunes library — even downloaded songs and commercial CDs you ripped — and keep a safe copy in iCloud, as I describe in Chapter 11.

To sync your iPod touch to your iTunes Match library, choose Settings⇨Music to display the Music settings screen, and click the On/Off button for the iTunes Match option to turn it On. (You can also choose Settings⇨iTunes & App Stores and turn on the iTunes Match option.)

Turning on iTunes Match removes previously synced music from your iPod touch.

To play songs in your iTunes Match library on your iPod touch, launch the Music app, as I describe in Chapter 11. As you select songs in your iTunes Match library, you can either play them over the Internet or download them directly to your iPod touch to store them for playback when your iPod touch is not connected to the Internet.

After turning on iTunes Match, the Show All Music option appears underneath it on the Music settings screen (turned on by default). Click the On switch to turn this option off if you want to show only the music you've downloaded from iTunes Match. Turn it back on if you want to show all the music and playlists that you have in your iTunes Match library.

Choosing What to Sync

If you have a massive content library that doesn't fit on your iPod, you can go the selective route, choosing which content to automatically sync with your iTunes library. By synchronizing selectively, you can still make your iPod match at least a subset of your iTunes library. If you make changes to that subset in iTunes, those changes are automatically made in the device when you synchronize again.

The "everything but the kitchen sync" method

You can decide which items you *don't* want to synchronize and simply not include them by first *deselecting* them one by one in your iTunes library. (If you have a large iTunes library, this may take some time — you may find it easier to synchronize by playlists, artists, and genres, as I show in the next section.)

By default, all content items are selected — a check mark appears in the check box next to the item. To deselect an item in your iTunes library, click the check box next to the item so that the check mark disappears. To select an item again, just click the check box.

You can quickly select (or deselect) an entire album by clicking the Songs tab to show the column browser (choose View➪Column Browser➪Show Column Browser if the column browser is hidden). You can then click the album in the Albums column to see all the songs. Press ⌘ (Mac) or Ctrl (Windows) while clicking the check box for a single song in the album to deselect all of the songs in the album.

After you deselect the items you don't want to transfer, connect your iPod to your computer and click the iPod button (refer to Figure 7-1). Then select the Sync Only Checked Songs and Videos check box on an iPod touch (refer to Figure 7-2), or Sync Only Checked Songs on an iPod nano or iPod shuffle (refer to Figure 7-3). Click the Apply button, and then click Done.

iTunes restarts synchronization and deletes from the iPod any items in the library that are deselected, to save space, before adding back in the items in the iTunes library that are selected. That means the items you deselected are now *gone* from your iPod — replaced by whatever items were selected. Of course, the items are still in your iTunes library. Wait for the synchronization to finish, and then click the eject button next to the iPod name in the source pane.

Getting picky about playlists, artists, and genres

You can include just the items that are defined in playlists, including Genius playlists, and/or just specific artists. Syncing by playlists, artists, and genres is a great way to sync vast amounts of music without syncing the entire library. (To find out how to create playlists, see Chapter 10.)

For example, you can create four playlists that contain all essential rock, folk, blues, and jazz albums, and then select all four, or just one, two, or three of these playlists to sync with your iPod, along with everything by specific artists (such as Frank Zappa, who doesn't fit into these categories).

After connecting your iPod to your computer, click the iPod button (refer to Figure 7-1). Then click the Music tab of the sync pages. The Music sync page appears, as shown in Figure 7-4.

If you have already turned on iTunes Match for an iPod touch as I describe in the earlier section, "Making the iTunes Match," the Music tab shows "iTunes Match is on" and provides only the Sync Voice Memos option for syncing voice memos from the Voice Memos app, in addition to your iTunes Match library.

Figure 7-4 depicts the iTunes Music sync options window.

The window shows:

Nano Red — Summary | Music | Movies | TV Shows | Podcasts | iTunes U | Books | Photos | Nike + iPod | On This iPod — Done

☑ Sync Music 1588 songs

○ Entire music library
⊙ Selected playlists, artists, albums, and genres

☑ Include music videos
☐ Automatically fill free space with songs

Playlists

- ☑ Music Videos
- ☑ My Top Rated
- ☑ Recently Added
- ☐ Recently Played
- ☐ Rented Movies
- ☐ Ringtones
- ☐ Top 25 Most Played
- ☐ AA-Gleeson playlist
- ☐ AAA_list
- ☐ Airplane_chrono
- ☐ Airplane_solo
- ☐ Allison_Mose
- ☐ Allman_Bros
- ☐ Americana_Roots
- ☐ Ballad Roots of CA Rock
- ☐ Band-chrono

Artists

- ☐ Troggs
- ☐ Troopers
- ☐ Doris Troy
- ☐ Frankie Trumbauer & His Orchestra
- ☐ KT Tunstall
- ☐ Big Joe Turner
- ☐ Ike & Tina Turner
- ☐ Tina Turner
- ☐ Turtles
- ☑ U2
- ☐ UB40
- ☐ Uncle Dave Macon
- ☐ Undisputed Truth
- ☐ Keith Urban
- ☐ Utopia
- ☐ Dave Van Ronk

Genres

Albums

Revert   Apply

Figure 7-4: Sync only the selected playlists, artists, and genres.

For details on using Voice Memos, see Bonus Chapter 4 in the free tips section of the author's website (www.tonybove.com/tips).

Click the Sync Music option at the top of the Music sync options page if it isn't already selected (refer to Figure 7-4). You can then click the Entire Music Library option in the Sync Music section to sync your entire music library, or choose the Selected Playlists, Artists, Albums, and Genres option in order to choose playlists, artists, genres, and albums.

If you were manually managing music before clicking the Sync Music option, a message appears asking whether you are sure that you now want to sync music, stating that all content already on your iPod will be replaced. Click the Sync Music button to go ahead (or Cancel if you changed your mind), which returns you to the Music sync options page.

After clicking the Selected Playlists, Artists, Albums, and Genres option, you can then select each playlist from the Playlists list, each artist from the Artists list, and (if you scroll the Music sync options page) each genre from the Genres list and each album from the Albums list. You can choose any number of playlists, artists, albums, and genres. (In Figure 7-4, I selected the Music Videos, My Top Rated, and Recently Added playlists in the Playlists column along with U2 in the Artists column.) Finally, click the Apply button in the lower-right corner of the page to apply changes (or Revert to cancel). Click Done when you are finished changing sync options.

iTunes copies only what you've selected in the Playlists, Artists, Genres, and Albums columns of the Music sync options page. If you also select the Include Music Videos check box (as I do in Figure 7-4), iTunes includes music videos listed in the playlists (except, of course, for an iPod shuffle, which doesn't play video).

You can also automatically fill up the rest of your iPod free space with random songs (after syncing your selected playlists, artists, and genres) by selecting the Automatically Fill Free Space with Songs option. iTunes randomly chooses the music, as I describe in the latter part of the "Syncing Everything" section, earlier in this chapter.

If you select the Sync Only Checked Songs and Videos check box on the Summary sync options page, only selected items are copied. iTunes ignores items that are not selected, even if they're listed in the chosen playlists, artists, and genres for synchronization.

Picking podcast episodes and books

You can get picky about which podcast episodes — and even which parts of audio books — should be copied during synchronization. When syncing an iPod touch that already has Apple's iBooks app installed, you can also choose which electronic books to sync and use with iBooks.

Clicking the Podcasts tab presents options for choosing podcast episodes to include. (You can include audio podcasts to sync with an iPod shuffle, but not video podcasts.)

Connect your iPod to your computer, and click the iPod button (refer to Figure 7-1). Then click the Podcasts tab of the sync pages. The Podcasts sync page appears, as shown in Figure 7-5. Click the Sync Podcasts option at the top.

The Podcast sync options let you choose unplayed or recently added episodes. Select the Automatically Include ____ Episodes Of ____ check box; choose a modifier from the first pop-up menu, such as All Unplayed or 3 Most Recent; and then choose All Podcasts or Selected Podcasts from the second pop-up menu. If you chose Selected Podcasts, you can select a podcast in the Podcasts column below these options, and then select specific episodes in the Episodes column (which may already be selected, depending on your choices in the pop-up menus).

Figure 7-5: Sync the three most recent episodes of selected podcasts and an extra episode of a selected podcast.

For example, in Figure 7-5, I automatically synchronized the three most recent episodes of selected podcasts — and two podcasts are selected (The Flying Other Brothers-Music Podcast and Rockument). This syncs the three most recent episodes of those two podcasts. I also manually selected one more episode of the Rockument podcast.

When you're set, click the Apply button to apply changes.

Clicking the Books tab of the sync pages presents options for choosing audio books. If you have the iBooks app installed on your iPod touch and you've downloaded books from the iBookstore (or other sources, such as Project Gutenberg), you also have options for choosing e-books. To sync books, follow these steps:

1. **Connect your iPod to your computer and click the iPod button (refer to Figure 7-1).**

   The sync pages appear.

2. **Click the Books tab.**

   The Books sync options page appears. You can sync e-books and audio books.

3. **To sync e-books for use with an iPod touch running iBooks, click the Sync Books option, and then click one of the following sync options:**

   - Choose All Books to sync all of them.

   - Choose Selected Books, and then select the books you want to sync, or deselect the books you don't want to sync. You can sort the list of books by title, author, or date in the Sort pop-up menu within the Books section, and select either Only Books (e-books designed for the iBooks app), Only PDF Files (documents in the Portable Document Format that can be viewed in iBooks), or Books and PDF Files.

4. **To sync audio books, scroll down the Books sync page and click the Sync Audiobooks option, and then click one of the following sync options:**

   - Choose All Audiobooks to sync all of them.

   - Choose Selected Audiobooks, and then choose entire audio books in the Audiobooks column on the left or select an audio book on the left and then choose specific parts of the audio book in the right column.

5. **After choosing sync options, click Apply to apply changes, and then click Done to finish changing sync options and start syncing.**

After syncing podcast episodes, audio books, or e-books, you can continue listening or reading from where you left off on your computer or other synchronized device. For example, if you were reading an e-book using the iBooks app on an iPod touch, synced the iPod touch with iTunes, and then synced your iPad with iTunes, you can continue reading with the iBooks app on your iPad from where you left off on the iPod touch.

Choosing movies and TV shows for an iPod touch

Movies and TV shows take up a lot of space, so if you limit the movies and TV episodes you synchronize with your iPod touch, you gain extra space for more music, audio books, podcasts, and photos.

To get choosy about movies, connect your iPod touch to your computer and click the iPod button (refer to Figure 7-1). Then click the Movies tab of the sync pages. The Movies sync page appears with the Sync Movies and Automatically Include options at the top.

Select the Sync Movies check box at the top of the page. You can then select the Automatically Include _____ Movies check box; choose a modifier from the pop-up menu, such as All, 1 Most Recent, 3 Most Recent, All Unwatched, or 10 Most Recent Unwatched. If you choose any option other than All, you can then select specific movies from the list below the option.

To pick only the TV episodes you want, click the TV Shows tab. The TV Shows sync options page appears, as shown in Figure 7-6.

Select the Automatically Include ____ Episodes Of ____ check box; choose a modifier from the first pop-up menu, such as All, All Unwatched, Newest, or 5 Most Recent; and then choose All Shows or Selected Shows from the second pop-up menu. If you choose Selected Shows or deselect the Automatically Include option, you can select shows in the Shows column below these options, and then select specific episodes in the Episodes column.

For example, in Figure 7-6, I automatically included the newest episode of the selected shows — *Bones, Boston Legal,* and *Star Trek: The Original Series.* I also added a second *Star Trek* episode to the sync mix (the "newest" episode — the episode most recently purchased, in this case — is already selected).

After choosing sync options, click the Apply button to apply changes, and then click Done if you are finished changing sync options.

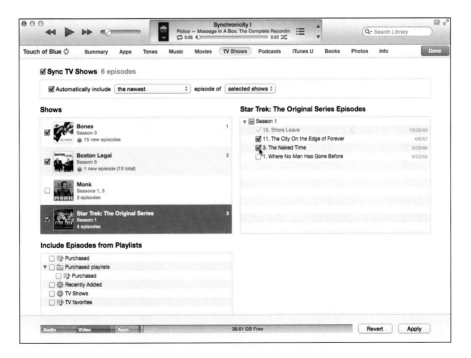

Figure 7-6: Sync only selected TV show episodes.

Syncing and arranging apps for an iPod touch

Your iPod touch is set by default to sync all the apps in your iTunes library that can run on an iPod touch (including just about all iPhone apps). iTunes automatically skips any app that doesn't belong on the device (such as an iPad app) and displays a warning about any other app it skips for other reasons (such as not having a proper authorization code). I recommend simply letting iTunes do its thing and sync all the apps that belong on the device.

However, you can selectively choose apps to synchronize. Follow these steps:

1. **Connect your iPod touch to your computer and click the iPod button (refer to Figure 7-1).**

2. **Click the Apps tab.**

   The Apps sync options page appears, as shown in Figure 7-7. By default, all apps that work on the iPod touch are automatically synced.

3. **From the list box on the left (see Figure 7-7), click the Install or Remove button for each app that you want to install or remove from the iPod touch.**

   You can scroll the list box to see all your apps — and you can click the Sort button at the top to toggle sorting the list by Name, Kind, Category, Date, or Size. For example, in Figure 7-7, I am switching from Sort by Kind to Sort by Category.

You can set iTunes to automatically sync to your iPod touch all new apps that you acquire from the App Store using iTunes, without having to selectively choose them. Scroll the Apps sync options page to the bottom and select the Automatically Sync New Apps option. Deselect this option to prevent iTunes from automatically syncing all new apps.

Although you can rearrange and delete apps on your iPod touch Home screens directly, as I describe in meticulous detail in Chapter 3, you can also do this in iTunes while syncing. Click the thumbnail image of any Home screen on the far right side of the Apps sync options page to view the app icons on that Home screen, and then click and drag the app icons to the positions you want. You can drag an app icon to another Home screen by dragging it over the Home screen's thumbnail. You can also do two things that you can't do on the iPod touch — you can reorder the home screens by dragging them into different positions, and you can drag an app from the list box to its precise position on any Home screen to sync that app. To delete the app from the iPod touch, select the app icon and click the circled X in the upper-left corner. (The app is still available in your iTunes library.)

Figure 7-7: Sort the list of apps and then select apps to remove.

To organize apps into folders, drag an app icon on top of another in the Home screen on the right side of the Apps sync options page. For example, in Figure 7-8, I dragged the Magic Guitar app over the LeafTLite app to create a new folder, which I renamed to Musical.

If you use apps that can share files between your computer and your iPod touch — such as Stanza with its library of electronic books or Pages for word processing — scroll the Apps sync options page all the way down to the bottom to see the File Sharing section. Select the app in the Apps column on the left. You can then save a document or file on your computer by selecting it in the right column, clicking the Save To button, and then browsing for a location on your hard drive to save it. You can also copy a document or file onto your iPod touch by selecting the app in the Apps column, clicking the Add button, browsing for the file, and clicking Open. The file is automatically copied to the iPod touch to use with the app.

After choosing sync options, click the Apply button to apply changes.

Figure 7-8: Organize apps into folders on Home screens.

Syncing tones for an iPod touch

You can purchase ringtones and text tones from the iTunes Store using iTunes on your computer, or make your own using various Windows and Mac audio apps or GarageBand on a Mac, and then synchronize them with your iPod touch to use with FaceTime calls and Messages texts.

To selectively choose tones for your iPod touch, follow these steps:

1. **Connect your iPod touch to your computer, and click the iPod button (refer to Figure 7-1).**

2. **Click the Tones tab of the sync options page.**

   The Tones sync options page appears.

3. **Click Sync Tones at the top of the page if the option is not already turned on.**

4. **Click the All Tones option, or click the Selected Tones option, and then select each tone to synchronize in the Tones box.**

   You can scroll the list box to see all your tones. Click the check box to select one.

5. **Click Apply to apply changes, and then click Done if you are finished changing sync options.**

iTunes erases any previous tones in the iPod touch and copies only the tones you selected in Step 4.

Manually Managing Music and Videos

If your entire library is too big for your iPod, you may want to copy individual items manually. By setting your iPod to manually manage music and videos, you can add content to the device directly via iTunes. You can even copy some songs or videos from another computer's iTunes library without deleting any content from your iPod.

To set your iPod to manually manage music and videos, first connect it to your computer. Then follow these steps:

1. **Click the iPod button (refer to Figure 7-1).**

   The Summary sync page appears, displaying sync options (refer to Figure 7-2 for an iPod touch and to Figure 7-3 for an iPod nano, which offers similar settings as an iPod classic).

2. **Select the Manually Manage Music and Videos check box (on an iPod shuffle, select Manually Manage Music; if the iPod touch is synced to iTunes Match, select Manually Manage Videos).**

   iTunes displays a message for iPod nano and iPod classic models (and older models), warning you that manually managing music and videos also requires manually ejecting the iPod before each disconnect.

3. **Click the OK button for the warning and click the Apply button to apply the change.**

Autofilling it up

After setting your iPod to manually manage music and videos, you can automatically fill your iPod without syncing. Autofill either randomly picks songs from your entire iTunes library or picks songs from a playlist you specify.

Autofill is especially useful for copying random songs to an iPod shuffle every time you connect it to your computer. Eventually, you can shuffle through everything in your library if you so wish by randomly autofilling your iPod shuffle every time you sync.

To autofill your iPod, connect it to your computer, click the iPod button, and set the option to manage music and videos (or to manually manage music on the iPod shuffle) on the Summary sync page, as I explain in the previous section — if you haven't done this already. Then follow these steps:

1. **Click the On This iPod tab.**

   The music on your iPod appears, along with the Autofill From pop-up menu at the bottom, as shown in Figure 7-9.

2. **Choose your source of music from the Autofill From pop-up menu.**

   Choose either one of your playlists, or choose Purchased (for all purchased music) or Music for the entire music library. If you choose a playlist, Autofill uses only the playlist as the source to pick random songs. After choosing your source of music, iTunes creates a playlist and displays it (see Figure 7-9).

Add to iPod

Autofill iPod from a source

Figure 7-9: Autofill an iPod shuffle from an iTunes playlist.

3. **(Optional) Click the Settings button to set options, and then click the OK button.**

   After clicking the Settings button, the Autofill Settings dialog appears. You can choose to replace all the items on the iPod, to choose items randomly, or to choose higher rated items more often.

4. **Click the Autofill button to start copying songs.**

   iTunes copies the contents of the Autofill playlist to your iPod.

5. **Wait for the copy operation to finish, and then click Done.**

   Always wait until the iTunes status pane tells you that the copying is finished.

Copying items manually to your iPod

To copy items manually to your iPod, connect the iPod to your computer, click the iPod button, and set the option to manage music and videos (or to manually manage music on the iPod shuffle) on the Summary sync page — if you haven't done this already. Then follow these steps:

1. **Click the On This iPod tab.**

   The music on your iPod appears (refer to Figure 7-9).

2. **Click the Add To button in the upper-right corner of the view under the Done button.**

   Your iTunes library shifts over to the left to make room for the iPod column showing the content types and playlists on the iPod, as shown in Figure 7-10.

3. **Drag items (such as one or more songs or an album) directly from your iTunes library to the iPod column.**

   You can drag individually selected songs or selected albums (see Figure 7-10) — the number of items you are copying appears over the pointer as you drag the items. When you drag an album cover or album title, all the songs in the album are copied. If you drag a playlist name from your library to the iPod column, all the songs associated with the playlist copy along with the playlist itself. You can also copy albums *into* a playlist on the iPod, as I do in Figure 7-10, by dragging them over the playlist name in the iPod column.

4. **Wait for the copying to finish and then click Done.**

5. **Click the eject button (refer to Figure 7-1) and disconnect your iPod from your computer.**

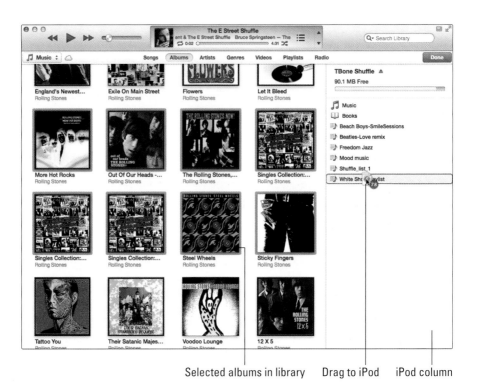

Selected albums in library   Drag to iPod   iPod column

Figure 7-10: Drag albums to a playlist on the iPod shuffle (TBone Shuffle).

Syncing Your Day in the Life

In This Chapter

- Using iTunes to sync calendars and contacts with an iPod
- Using iTunes to sync e-mail accounts, notes, and bookmarks
- Synchronizing over the Internet with iCloud
- Setting up e-mail accounts on your iPod touch

*Y*ou may choose an iPod classic to play music and videos on the road, but you may also find it useful for viewing the personal information — contacts, appointments, and events — that you manage on your home or office computer. The iPod classic offers *one-way* synchronization of personal information from your computer to the iPod. (The iPod shuffle and sixth-generation iPod nano don't hold personal information, so this chapter isn't relevant for them.)

The iPod touch can take care of all aspects of your digital life: It can send and receive e-mail, save your notes, keep track of your calendar, sort your contacts, and save bookmarks to all your favorite websites as you browse them. You can also add personal info directly to your iPod touch and synchronize that information back with your computer, which is *two-way* synchronization.

If you're a road warrior, you may want to fill your iPod with your personal information. This chapter shows you how.

Organizing Your Personal Info

You already manage your contacts, calendars, e-mail, and web bookmarks with applications on your computer. Now you can use iTunes to synchronize your iPod classic with these calendars and contacts, or use your iPod touch with these calendars, contacts, e-mail accounts, notes, and bookmarks.

The iPod touch can send and receive e-mail using the Mail application (as I describe in Chapter 16). It also offers the Contacts app to store contact info, the Calendar app to store events (see Chapter 18), the Notes app to take notes (see Chapter 3), and the Safari app to surf the web with your bookmarks (see Chapter 15).

You can use iTunes to synchronize your iPod touch apps with the calendars, contacts, notes, e-mail accounts, and bookmarks you've already organized on your computer. With a little help from these apps, you'll soon have your schedule whipped into such shape that it will be humming along like a finely tuned German automobile.

If you're a Mac user, you have it easy: You can use the free applications that come with the Mountain Lion version of the OS X operating system — Calendar and Contacts to manage your calendars and contacts, Mail to manage e-mail and notes, and the Safari web browser to manage your bookmarks. You can also sync contacts from Yahoo! Address Book, and Google Address Book.

If you're a Windows user, you can sync your contacts and e-mail accounts with Microsoft Outlook, Yahoo! Address Book and Yahoo! Mail, Google Address Book and Gmail, Windows Address Book (Outlook Express), AOL (e-mail only), or Vista Contacts. You can sync calendars and notes with Outlook and use Microsoft Internet Explorer or Apple Safari to manage bookmarks. The iPod touch can also use the Exchange ActiveSync protocol to sync e-mail, calendars, and contacts with Microsoft Exchange Server 2003 Service Pack 2 or Exchange Server 2007 Service Pack 1. For many e-mail accounts, the settings automatically appear, like magic.

If you signed up for Apple's iCloud service, you can automatically keep your iPod touch synchronized along with several computers, iPads, and iPhones, all at once, with the latest iTunes purchases, e-mail, bookmarks, calendar entries, and contacts, as I describe in the "Syncing your iPod touch with iCloud" section, later in this chapter.

What's cool about cloud computing web services like iCloud, Microsoft Exchange, and Yahoo! Mail is that their e-mail services *push* e-mail messages to your computer and your iPod touch so that they arrive immediately and automatically. Other types of e-mail account services let you *fetch* e-mail from the server — you must first select the account in Mail on your iPod touch before your iPod touch can actually retrieve the e-mail. I show you how to use your push and fetch settings in Chapter 16.

You probably already know how to manage your calendar activities and your contacts on your computer. In fact, you're probably knee-deep in contacts, and your calendars look like they were drawn up in the West Wing. If not, see "Tips on Managing Contacts and Calendars" in the free tips section of the author's website (www.tonybove.com/tips) for advice on adding and editing contacts and calendar information on your Mac (with the Contacts and Calendars applications) or Windows computer (with Outlook).

Syncing Your Personal Info Using iTunes

You use iTunes to synchronize an iPod classic with calendars and contacts on your computer.

With an iPod touch, you can sync your personal information using iTunes, or a push service such as iCloud or Microsoft Exchange. You can switch between iTunes and the push service anytime you want. iCloud and Microsoft Exchange get their write-ups in the next section, and this section tackles the iTunes method.

To sync your iPod with contacts, calendars, e-mail accounts, notes, and bookmarks on your computer by using iTunes, follow these steps:

1. **Connect the iPod and click the iPod button in the upper-right corner of the iTunes window.**

   iTunes displays the Summary sync page (under the Summary tab). For details on syncing an iPod and accessing sync options, see Chapter 7.

2. **Click the Info tab.**

   The Info sync page appears, as shown in Figure 8-1 for an iPod classic, offering the Sync Contacts and Sync Calendars sections. An iPod touch Info sync page also includes the Mail Accounts, Other (bookmarks and notes), and Advanced sections, which you have to scroll the page to see.

3. **Select the option to sync contacts:**

   • *On a Mac:* Select the Sync Contacts check box. With an iPod touch, you can also sync with Yahoo! Address Book and Google Contacts — click the Configure button to enter your login information.

   • *On a Windows PC:* Select the Sync Contents From option (refer to Figure 8-1) and choose Yahoo! Address Book, Windows Address Book, Google Contacts, or Microsoft Outlook from the pop-up menu.

4. **Select the All Contacts option or select the Selected Groups option and choose which groups to sync.**

   You can synchronize all contacts or just selected groups of contacts. To choose groups, select the check box next to each group in the list; scroll the list to see more groups.

   If you select groups for an iPod touch, you can also select the Add Contacts Created Outside of Groups on This iPod To option and choose a group for the new contacts you create on your iPod touch.

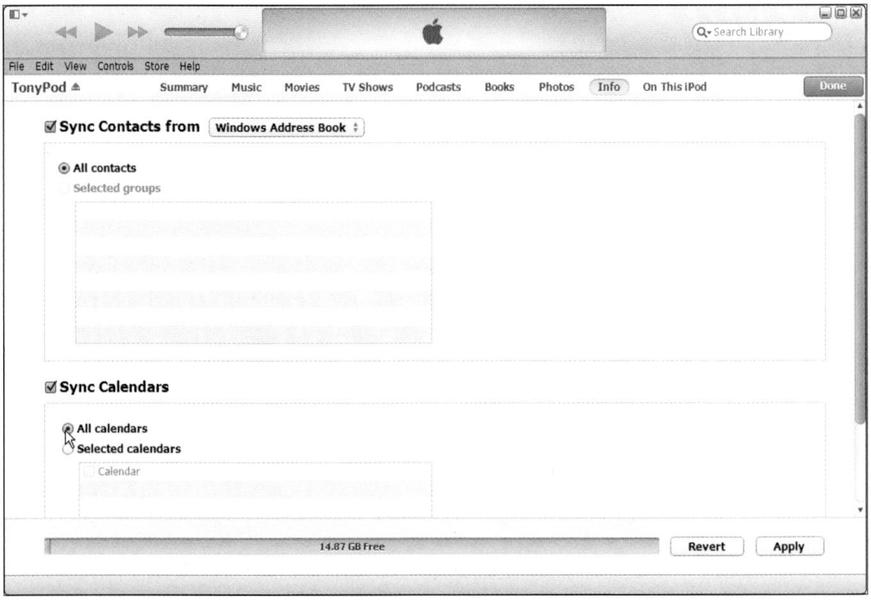

Figure 8-1: Sync contacts and calendars using iTunes.

5. **Scroll the page and select the option to sync calendars.**

   • *On a Mac:* Select the Sync Calendars check box.

   • *On a Windows PC:* Select the Sync Calendars From option and choose Microsoft Outlook from the pop-up menu. If Microsoft Outlook is the only choice you have on your Windows PC, the option is Sync Calendars From Microsoft Outlook without a pop-up menu.

6. **Select the All Calendars option. (Alternatively, if you're using Calendar with OS X, select the Selected Calendars option and choose the calendars to synchronize.)**

   In Windows, you can synchronize all calendars with Outlook, but not selected calendars. With Calendars on OS X, you can synchronize all calendars or just those you select. To choose specific calendars, select the check box next to each calendar in the list.

   With an iPod touch, you can also set the Do Not Sync Events Older Than *xx* Days option, in which you can set the number of days.

   If you're syncing an iPod classic, you can skip to Step 11.

7. **To sync e-mail accounts with an iPod touch, scroll down to the Mail Accounts section and select the Sync Mail Accounts option.**

   Mail Accounts appears below the Calendars section on the Info sync options page. On a Mac, select the Sync Mail Accounts option. On a

Windows PC, choose Microsoft Outlook or Outlook Express from the pop-up menu for the Sync Mail Accounts From option. After you select the sync option, a list of e-mail accounts appears in the box below the option.

8. **Choose the e-mail accounts you want to sync with your iPod touch.**

   To choose accounts, select the check box next to each account in the list; scroll the list to see more e-mail accounts.

9. **To sync web bookmarks with an iPod touch, scroll down to the Other section and select the Sync Bookmarks With option.**

   On a Mac running OS X, the option is Sync Safari Bookmarks; on a Windows PC, iTunes offers a pop-up menu to choose Internet Explorer or Safari.

10. **To sync notes with an iPod touch, select the Sync Notes With option in the Other section.**

    You can sync the notes you create in the Notes app (see Chapter 3) with the Notes application on a Mac running Mountain Lion or with Outlook on a Windows PC. On a Mac, select the Sync Notes option; on a Windows PC, choose Outlook from the pop-up menu for the Sync Notes From option.

11. **Click the Apply button to apply the changes. (Alternatively, click Revert to revert to the original settings.)**

12. **Click Done if you are finished changing sync options.**

    See Chapter 7 for details about the other sync options. After you click Done, iTunes returns to the library display and starts to synchronize your iPod.

13. **After the sync is done, eject the iPod by clicking the eject button next to the "iPod" in the iPod button.**

    Wait until the sync status pane (at the top) displays the message `Sync is Complete` before clicking the eject button.

After you set the sync options, every time you connect your iPod, iTunes automatically synchronizes it with these settings. Synchronizing an e-mail account to your iPod touch copies *only* the e-mail account setup information; the messages are retrieved by the iPod touch over the Internet.

If you select a calendar or a group of contacts to be synchronized and later want to remove that particular calendar or group of contacts, deselect the calendar (see the preceding Step 6) or the group (see the preceding Step 4), and then click Apply to resynchronize. iTunes synchronizes only the group of contacts and calendars selected, removing from the iPod any that aren't selected.

iTunes also offers Advanced options at the bottom of the iPod touch Info page for syncing your iPod touch from scratch to replace all contacts, calendars, notes, or mail accounts. You can choose which ones you want to replace by selecting the check box next to each option. iTunes replaces the information once, during the next sync operation. After that operation, these Advanced options are automatically turned off.

When You Sync Upon iCloud

iCloud synchronizes your iTunes purchases, apps, and iBookstore purchases as well as e-mail, contacts, calendars, bookmarks, and documents on a web server on the Internet — also known as *the cloud.* You can even include music you didn't purchase through iTunes; Apple offers the iTunes Match service for $24.99 a year that lets you store music you've ripped from CDs or purchased elsewhere. (For details on iCloud and iTunes Match, see Chapters 7 and 11.)

With iCloud, you can keep your iPod touch synchronized to everything you have in the cloud wirelessly, without having to connect it to your computer (that is, from any Wi-Fi location). iCloud stores your stuff and wirelessly syncs with all your Macs, iPod touches, iPhones, and iPads. Of course, your iPod touch must be awake to sync (meaning that the screen is on).

Apple provides 5GB of free storage in your iCloud account, but iTunes purchases — including music, apps, books, and TV shows — don't count against the 5GB. (Neither do your photos in Photo Stream, which I describe in Chapter 14.) That means you can use the 5GB for other stuff, like documents, calendars, contacts, and e-mail.

iCloud first makes its appearance when you set up your iPod touch: the Set Up iCloud screen appears, as I show in Chapter 2. After setting up your iCloud account on your iPod touch, you can set it up on your Mac or Windows PC, as described in the next sections.

Setting up on a Mac

iCloud requires Lion (OS X version 10.7) or Mountain Lion (OS X version 10.8). Setting up iCloud is easy: Open System Preferences, click iCloud, and then click Add account. Sign in with your Apple ID or create a new Apple ID (for details on setting up an Apple ID account, see Chapter 6).

When you sign in to iCloud for the first time, the service automatically configures Mac OS X Mail on your Mac to send and receive e-mail from your iCloud account and to synchronize contacts from the Contacts application and calendars from the Calendars application. If you already set up your iPod touch with iCloud, as I describe in Chapter 2, automatic synchronization should already be set up on that Mac.

To specify which iCloud services to use with your Mac, choose System Preferences➪iCloud, and then enable or disable each service by turning them on or off.

Setting up on Windows

iCloud (including iTunes Match) requires Windows 7 or newer, or Windows Vista; the service is not available for Windows XP users as of this writing. You need to use Outlook 2007 or Outlook 2010 to sync calendars and contacts with iCloud. Download and install on your PC the latest version of iCloud Control Panel for Windows, available from Apple at `www.apple.com/icloud`. iCloud Control Panel for Windows is required to set up and manage iCloud services with Windows 7 or newer, or Windows Vista.

To set up a Windows PC to sync with iCloud or to check or change your services, open Control Panel from the Windows Start menu and choose iCloud Control Panel. Sign in with your Apple ID or create a new Apple ID (for details on setting up an Apple ID account, see Chapter 6). You can then enable or disable each service by turning them on or off.

Syncing your iPod touch with iCloud

You already set up your iPod touch with iCloud in Chapter 2. To automatically download content you purchased on the iTunes Store with your account — on your computer, or on any iPod touch, iPhone, or iPad wirelessly (that is, from any Wi-Fi location) — tap Settings➪iTunes & App Stores. The iTunes & App Stores screen appears. (I show this screen in Chapter 6.) You can then turn on or off the Music, Apps, or Books options in the Automatic Downloads section. When turned on, all iTunes purchases you make of music, apps, or books from the iBookstore on any other iCloud-synced device are automatically downloaded to your iPod touch.

To set up or change iCloud options on your iPod touch, choose Settings➪iCloud. The iCloud settings screen appears with on/off switches for each service, as shown in Figure 8-2 (left side). The Accounts button (with your account's e-mail address) appears above the Mail service (not shown in Figure 8-2).

You can turn the iCloud services on or off, such as Mail, Contacts, Calendars, Reminders, and Safari (for bookmarks). iCloud stores the most current version of this information from all your other iCloud-enabled devices — including your Mac or Windows PC, and any other iPod touches, iPhones, or iPads you've set up with iCloud. Your iPod touch syncs automatically with the information in your iCloud account.

You can turn the Photo Stream service on to sync the photos you recently took with your iPod touch when using iCloud — see Chapter 14 for details.

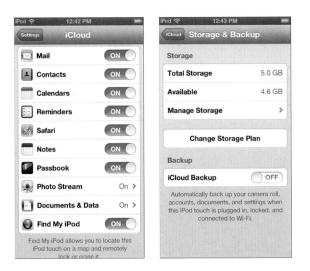

Figure 8-2: Turn on iCloud sync services (left) and manage your storage (right).

To see how much storage and backup space you have on iCloud, and to buy more, scroll to the very bottom of the iCloud settings screen and tap Storage & Backup. The Storage & Backup screen appears, as shown in Figure 8-2 (right side). The Storage section shows the total storage you have and the amount still available. You can choose to turn on iCloud Backup, which automatically keeps a backup of your Camera Roll, account settings, documents, and other settings. The backup occurs when your iPod touch is plugged in, locked, and connected to Wi-Fi — so that the backup operation doesn't run down your battery.

To buy more storage space from Apple for your iPod touch backup, tap Manage Storage on the Storage & Backup screen, and then tap the Buy More Storage button on the Manage Storage screen — the Buy More Storage screen appears with selections for 10GB ($20/year), 20GB ($40/year), and 50GB ($100/year). Choose one and follow the instructions to finish the purchase. You don't need more storage for music — use iTunes Match for storing your music in iCloud (see Chapter 11 for details).

To see your account and payment information, tap the account button (the button with your e-mail address) at the top of the iCloud settings screen. You can then see your account information and your storage plan, and you can tap the Payment Information button to see your payment information.

Finding a lost iPod touch

One of the most valuable features of iCloud is the Find My iPhone feature, which also works with iPod touch, iPhone, and iPad models, as well as Macs running Mountain Lion. If you have lost your iPod touch or you think it may have been stolen, and have already enabled the Find My iPod touch feature as described in Chapter 2, and have turned on Wi-Fi and location services for the iPod touch, you can:

- ✒ Find its approximate location on iCloud (www.icloud.com) using any Mac or PC with a web browser, or using the free Find My iPhone app on another iPhone, iPad, or iPod touch.
- ✒ Play an alert sound on your lost iPod touch.
- ✒ Remotely erase everything on it, in case it was stolen.
- ✒ Set the iPod touch to Lost Mode, which lets you change its passcode.

To find your iPod touch, sign into iCloud (at www.icloud.com) and click Find My iPhone. Click the Devices button in the upper-left corner to choose your iPod touch, and iCloud locates your iPod touch on a map. You can then click:

- ✒ **Play Sound:** Play an alert sound on your iPod touch. This is useful if you've just misplaced it and can't find it. When my iPod touch was lost somewhere in my home (it had fallen under the couch), this sound made it easy to find.
- ✒ **Lost Mode:** Lock your iPod touch with a new passcode.
- ✒ **Erase iPod touch:** Erase all of your content and settings on the iPod touch. After doing this, you can't use Find My iPhone to find it again.

Setting Up Mail Accounts on Your iPod touch

To set up a Mail account on your iPod touch — including an iCloud e-mail account (with contacts, calendars, and bookmarks) or a Microsoft Exchange account — follow these steps:

1. **Choose Settings⬚Mail, Contacts, Calendars from the Home screen.**

   The Mail, Contacts, Calendars settings screen appears with the Accounts section at the top, as shown in Figure 8-3 (left side).

2. **Tap the Add Account button and then tap the account type from the list of account types that appears.**

   As shown in Figure 8-3 (right side), your choice is iCloud, Microsoft Exchange, Gmail, Yahoo! Mail, AOL, Microsoft Hotmail, or Other (not shown). After you tap the account type, the New Account screen appears for iCloud, Exchange, Gmail, Yahoo! Mail, and AOL accounts; the Other screen appears for Other accounts.

3. **Enter your account information as follows:**

   - *iCloud, Gmail, Yahoo! Mail, or AOL:* Enter your name, username, password, and optional description in the New Account screen, and then tap Save in the upper-right corner. If the account is verified, you're done for a Gmail, Yahoo! Mail, or AOL account, and you can skip the rest of these steps — the Mail, Contacts, Calendars settings screen appears with the new account listed in the Accounts section. For iCloud, your iPod touch displays the account's settings screen. (If your account doesn't verify, try Steps 2 and 3 again.)

   - *Exchange:* Enter your name, username, domain (optional), password, and optional description in the New Account screen, and then tap Next in the upper-right corner to move on to the Exchange account's settings screen. Microsoft's Autodiscovery service kicks in to check your username and password to determine the address of the Exchange server. If it can't find the server's address, a dialog appears for you to enter it — enter the complete address in the Server field and tap Save.

   - *Other:* Tap Add Mail Account on the Other screen for an IMAP (Internet Message Access Protocol) or POP (Post Office Protocol) account. The New Account screen appears; enter your name, username, password, and an optional description, and then tap Save in the upper-right corner to save account information. The iPod touch searches for the account on the Internet and displays the New Account settings screen.

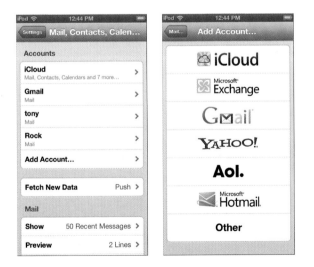

Figure 8-3: Tap Add Account (left) to see the list of account types (right).

4. Set your mail account settings in the New Account settings screen as follows:

- *iCloud or Exchange:* Turn on any or all the items you want to sync: Mail, Contacts, Calendars, and Safari for bookmarks (iCloud only). If you sync these items using your iCloud or Exchange account, syncing them in iTunes is turned off, and they are replaced by the iCloud or Exchange account versions in your iPod touch. You can always return to the account setting's screen to turn them off in order to enable syncing with iTunes. For Exchange, you can set how many days of e-mail you want to sync. Tap Save in the upper-right corner to finish and save your settings.

- *Other:* Tap IMAP or POP on the New Account settings screen, depending on the type of e-mail account you have — ask your e-mail service provider if you don't know. Then enter or edit the existing account information (also get this information from your service provider if you don't know). Tap Save in the upper-right corner to finish and save your settings. The Mail, Contacts, Calendars settings screen appears with the new account listed in the Accounts section.

5. When the Sync or Cancel warning appears for iCloud or Exchange accounts, tap Sync (or Cancel).

When you tap the Sync button, iCloud or Exchange overwrites any existing contacts, calendars, and bookmarks on your iPod touch (or the subset of these that you chose in Step 4). After you finish syncing, the Mail, Contacts, Calendars settings screen appears with the new account listed in the Accounts section.

6. Tap Fetch New Data on the Mail, Contacts, Calendars settings screen (refer to Figure 8-3, left side), and tap Off for the Push option to turn it on (if it isn't already on).

That's it! Your iPod touch syncs automatically from this point on, with data pushed or fetched from the e-mail account depending on your Push and Fetch settings (see Chapter 16 for details on Push and Fetch).

Whether the messages in your inbox appear on your iPod touch *and* on your computer depends on the type of e-mail account you have and how you've configured it. For example, if you delete on your computer an e-mail message from a push account (such as Exchange) or from an account set up to delete messages on the server as soon as you delete them on your computer, the message also disappears from your iPod touch.

Explaining all the e-mail account and advanced options is way beyond the scope of this book. Grab your network administrator or Internet service provider and offer free coffee in exchange for help. If you don't have anyone to turn to, see "Tips on Using iPods and iPhones" in the free tips section of the author's website (www.tonybove.com/tips).

Changing and Deleting Mail Accounts

You can temporarily turn off a Mail account on your iPod touch, as well as change its settings or delete it. To turn off a Mail account in your iPod touch temporarily or change account settings, choose Settings⟷Mail, Contacts, Calendars from the Home screen, and then tap the account in the Accounts section to see that account's settings screen. You can then change your account's settings, including the items that are synced with an iCloud or Exchange account.

To delete the account, scroll down and tap Delete Account. Deleting a Mail account from iPod touch doesn't affect the e-mail account or its settings on your computer.

Changes you make to accounts are *not* transferred back to your computer when you synchronize, so it's safe to make changes without affecting e-mail account settings on your computer.

9

Putting iTunes to Work

In This Chapter

▶ Retrieving information online

▶ Editing information for each content item

▶ Sorting columns of content by view options

▶ Searching for content in the library

▶ Adding information, cover art, comments, and ratings

*O*rganization depends on information. You expect your computer to do a lot more for you than just store a song with *Track 01* as the only identifier. Not only can iTunes retrieve an album's track information from the Internet, but it can also find the cover art for you.

Adding all the information for your iTunes content seems like a lot of trouble, but you can get most of the information automatically from the Internet. Adding track information is important because you certainly don't want to mistakenly play Frank Zappa's "My Guitar Wants to Kill Your Mama" when trying to impress your classical music teacher with the third movement of Tchaikovsky's *Pathétique Symphony,* do you?

iTunes retrieves information from a database of albums — you must be ripping a CD for iTunes to retrieve the proper information. Of course, the information may not be exactly what you want (it may even contain misspellings). And because iTunes can't find information on videos you make yourself or convert from other sources, you have to enter *some* description to tell them apart.

If your content collection is getting large, organize it to make finding content items easier. After all, finding U2's "I Still Haven't Found What I'm Looking For" is a challenge, even in a library that fits on an iPod nano.

This chapter shows you how to add information to your content library in iTunes and edit it for better viewing so that you can organize your content by artist, album name, genre, composer, and ratings. You can then use this information to sort your content by clicking the column headings under the List tab. You can also change the viewing options to make your library's display more useful, such as displaying songs sorted by artist, album, genre, or other attributes, or sorting TV shows by season or episode. This chapter also describes how to add cover art for the albums and songs you rip or import yourself, as I show in Chapter 5.

Retrieving Song Information from the Internet

You can easily get information about most music CDs from the Internet. The online database available for iTunes users holds information for millions of songs on commercial CDs and even some bootleg CDs. When you pop a commercial music CD into your computer running iTunes, iTunes automatically looks up the track information for that CD on the Internet and fills in the information fields (name, artist, album, and so on). You can also edit the information after iTunes fills in the fields.

If your computer doesn't access the Internet automatically, you might want to turn off automatic information retrieval. To turn off the retrieval of track information, choose iTunes➪Preferences (Mac) or Edit➪Preferences (Windows), and then click the General tab (if it's not already selected). Deselect the Automatically Retrieve CD Track Names from Internet option near the bottom of the dialog and click OK. You can turn it back on by reselecting the option.

Editing Content Information

Retrieving ready-made song information from the Internet is a great help, but you might not always like the format it comes in. Maybe you want to edit artist and band names or other information. Some facts — such as composer credits — might not be included. Adding composer credits is usually worth your effort because you can then search and sort by composer and create playlists based on the composer. You might also want to change the information that is supplied by the iTunes Store for the content you download. And if you obtain your content from other sources, you might need to add information for the first time. You have to enter the information for certain media, including CDs that aren't known by the database, custom CD-Rs, and some of the audio files, videos, and audio books that you bring into iTunes from sources other than the iTunes Store.

Editing fields for a single item

You can edit content information for a single item by directly editing the item's fields (such as title, album name, artist, and so on). You may find it easier to do this under the Songs tab when changing songs, as shown in Figure 9-1, or the List tab when changing other items such as movies, e-books, audio books, and podcasts. Choose a source from the source list (refer to Figure 9-1), and then click the Songs tab for Music, or the List tab for Movies, TV Shows, Podcasts, iTunes U, or Books. (Tones offers only a list view.) You can't change the content fields for Apps.

If you want to change the fields for multiple songs, jump ahead to the "Editing multiple items at once" section. If you just want to change a single item's information, follow these steps:

1. **Click directly in a field (such as Name for a song, as shown in Figure 9-1).**

2. **Click again so that the mouse pointer toggles to an editing cursor and the text in the field is highlighted — but not so quickly that the track starts playing.**

3. **Type text directly into the field.**

While typing, you can select the existing text and type over it — or use the Copy, Cut, and Paste commands on the Edit menu — to move tiny bits of text around within the field.

Editing more than one field for a single item is easier if you select the item and then choose File➪Get Info (or press ⌘-I on a Mac or Ctrl-I in Windows). The item's information dialog appears with the following tabs:

✔ **Summary:** Offers useful information about the media file format and location on your hard drive, the file size, and the digital compression method (along with bit rate, sample rate, and other settings).

✔ **Info:** Allows you to change the name, artist, composer, album, genre, year, and other information. You can also add comments, as shown in Figure 9-2.

✔ **Video:** Lets you enter information to describe a video. The information fields are set up for TV shows, including the title of the show, episode number and ID, and season number, but you can just add a description. You can also edit the description of a podcast, which appears in the Video tab's Description field.

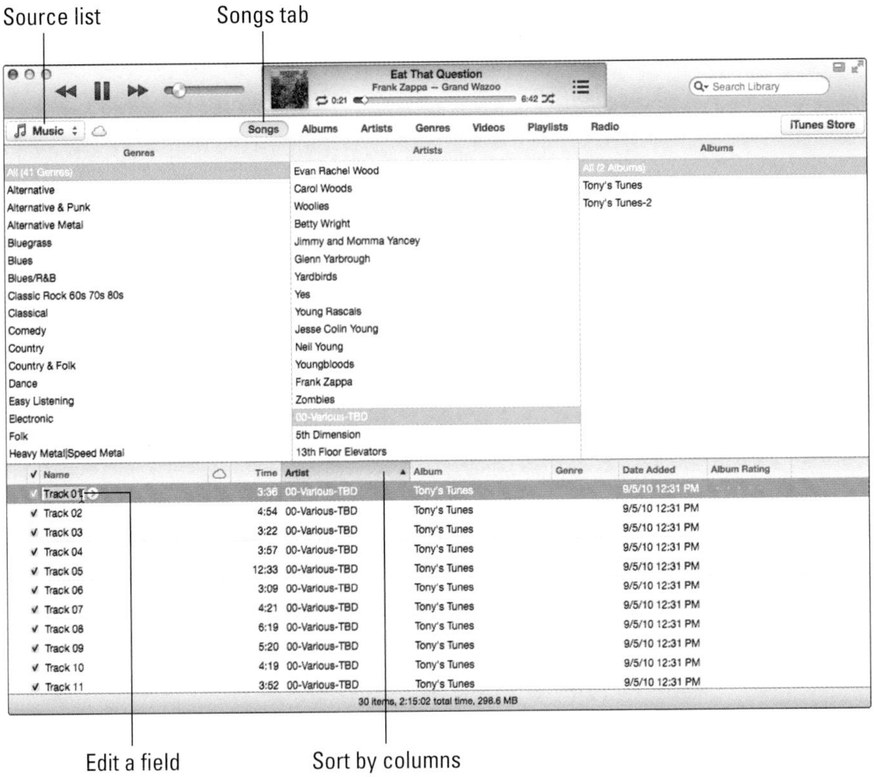

Source list   Songs tab

Edit a field   Sort by columns

Figure 9-1: Edit a single field.

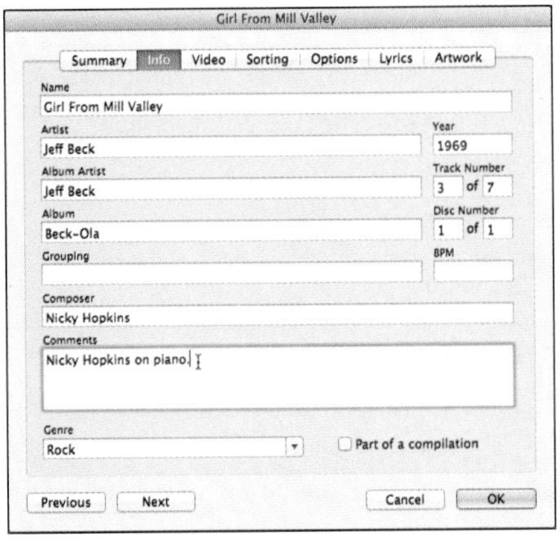

Figure 9-2: View and edit information under the Info tab.

✔ **Sorting:** Allows you to add information to sort fields that affect how your library content appears in sorted lists. For example, you can add a different name for the artist in the Sort Artist field to the right of the Artist field, such as *Dylan, Bob* for *Bob Dylan*, so that Dylan appears in the D section of the artists when sorted alphabetically. Information from the Info tab appears on the left side, and you can add the alternative sort field on the right side.

✔ **Options:** Offers the following, as shown in Figure 9-3:

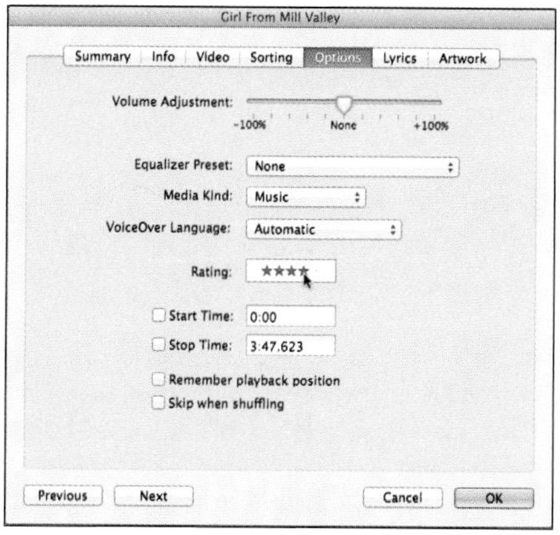

Figure 9-3: Add a rating to a song under the Options tab.

- *Volume Adjustment:* You can set the volume for a song, video, podcast, or audio book in advance so that it always plays at that volume (or lower, if your overall iTunes or iPod volume is set lower). Drag the slider to the right to increase the volume adjustment up to 100 percent (twice the usual volume); drag the slider to the left to decrease the volume adjustment to –100 percent (half the usual volume).

- *Equalizer Preset:* Choose an equalizer preset for an item.

For more details on adjusting the volume in advance and using the equalizer in iTunes, see Bonus Chapter 3 in the free tips section of the author's website (www.tonybove.com/tips). You also see how to use an equalizer preset to control how an item sounds on your iPod.

- *Media Kind:* Set (or change) the type of media. For example, after importing a video, you can change its Media Kind to movie, TV show, or music video. See the upcoming section, "Changing the media type," for details.

- *Rating:* Assign up to five stars to an item as a rating. (See how in the next section.)

- *Start Time and Stop Time:* Set the start and stop times for an item. You can use these options to cut unwanted intros and outros of a song (such as announcers, audience applause, and tuning up), or to skip opening credits or commercials of movies. You can also use it in conjunction with the Convert feature to split an item (or, in the parlance of record label executives and artists, split a track) into multiple items (tracks).

  For details on setting start and stop times, see Bonus Chapter 3 in the free tips section of the author's website (`www.tonybove.com/tips`).

- *Remember Playback Position:* Set this option for an item so that when you select and play the item, iTunes resumes playing it from where you left off. This option is usually turned on for audio books, movies, and TV shows.

- *Skip When Shuffling:* Set this option for an item to be skipped from Party Shuffle.

✓ **Lyrics:** Offers a text field for typing or pasting lyrics (or any text). Some songs in the iTunes Store are supplied with lyrics — you can find them here.

You can view lyrics on an iPod touch by starting a song and then, while the song is playing, tapping the song's album cover. To see lyrics on an iPod classic, start playing a song and then press the Select button several times until you see the lyrics. On an iPod nano, tap the Now Playing icon, tap the Now Playing display, and then swipe twice to see the lyrics. If you press the Select button or swipe too many times, the iPod classic or iPod nano returns to the Now Playing display.

✓ **Artwork:** Allows you to add or delete artwork for the item. See the upcoming section, "Adding Cover Art."

To move through an album one item at a time when using Get Info (without closing and reopening the information dialog), click the Previous or Next buttons in the lower-left corner of the dialog.

Adding a rating

iTunes allows you to rate your content. The cool thing about ratings is that they're *yours.* You can use ratings to mean anything you want. For example, you can rate songs based on how much you like them, whether your mother would listen to them, or how they blend into a work environment. You can also rate videos based on your watching habits, as well as audio books and podcasts.

To add a rating to a content item, click the Options tab (refer to Figure 9-3) and drag inside the My Rating field to add stars. If you added a Ratings column to the list view by changing the view options, as I describe in the later section, "Displaying and Sorting Content," you can drag inside the Ratings column to add stars. The upper limit is five stars (for the best). You can also select the item and choose File⇨Rating to assign a rating to an item, or display a Ratings column in List view to assign ratings.

Changing the media type

If an audio book file imports as a song into your iTunes library, or a video file of a TV show imports as a movie, or you want to change podcast episodes so that they show up as audio books or songs, you can change the media type for the content item.

To change the media type, first select the content item, choose File⇨Get Info (or press ⌘-I on a Mac or Ctrl-I in Windows), and then click the Options tab (refer to Figure 9-3). You can then choose the option you want in the Media Kind pop-up menu. The options for the Media Kind menu change depending on the content item selected. You can change the selected song to Podcast, iTunes U lesson, Audiobook, or Voice Memo; the selected podcast episode to a song (Music), iTunes U lesson, Audiobook, or Voice Memo; the selected video podcast to a Movie; the selected video to a Music Video, Movie, TV Show, Podcast, or iTunes U lesson; and so on.

If you are changing a song to a podcast, use the episode title for Name (song title), the podcast publisher for Artist, and the podcast name for Album in the information dialog. Then click the Video tab in the information dialog and enter the podcast's description in the Description field.

Editing multiple items at once

Typically, you need to edit multiple items at once, such as changing all the tracks of an album. Changing all the information in one fell swoop is fast and clean, but like most powerful shortcuts, you need to be careful because it can be dangerous.

Follow these steps to change a group of items at once:

1. **Select an album, or select a group of content items by clicking the first item and then pressing Shift while you click the last item.**

   All the items between the first and last are highlighted. You can extend a selection by Shift-clicking other items or add to a selection by ⌘-clicking (Mac) or Ctrl-clicking (Windows). You can also remove items already selected by ⌘-clicking (Mac) or Ctrl-clicking (Windows).

2. **Choose File⇨Get Info or press ⌘-I (Mac) or Ctrl-I (Windows).**

   A warning message displays: `Are you sure you want to edit information for multiple items?`

   Speed-editing the information in multiple items at once can be dangerous for your library organization. If, for example, you change an informational snippet for one item in a selected group (the song or movie title, for example), the corresponding snippet for all items in the selected group is going to change as well! Be careful about what you edit when using this method.

3. **Click the Yes button to edit information for multiple items.**

   The Multiple Item Information dialog appears with the Info, Video, Sorting, and Options tabs.

4. **Click the tab for the type of information you want to edit (Info, Video, Sorting, or Options).**

5. **Edit the field or fields you want to change.**

   When you edit a field, a check mark appears automatically in the check box next to the field, as shown in Figure 9-4. iTunes assumes that you want that field changed in *all* of the selected items. Make sure that no other check box is selected except the ones for the fields that you want to change.

6. **Click the OK button to make the change.**

   iTunes changes the field for the entire selection of items.

One of my routine multiple-item edits is to change the Sort Artist field for the artist under the Sorting tab. You can add the artist name the way you want it to be sorted, as I do with "Hartford, John" in the Sort Artist field in Figure 9-4. That way the John Hartford songs show up in the *H* artists (as if the artist is "Hartford, John") rather than in the *J* artists when sorted alphabetically, but the artist name still appears as "John Hartford."

You may want to change the Album Artist field under the Info tab and the Sort Album Artist field under the Sorting tab, or fill them in if they're blank, for certain songs on compilation albums or music from box sets. iTunes offers both Artist and Album Artist fields for a song so that you can include the album artist name if it's different — such as the artist name for a compilation album that features songs by different artists (for example, a duet album by an artist who brings in other guest artists).

You can also change the view options for the list pane (as I describe in the next section) to include the Album Artist field as a column for sorting the song list.

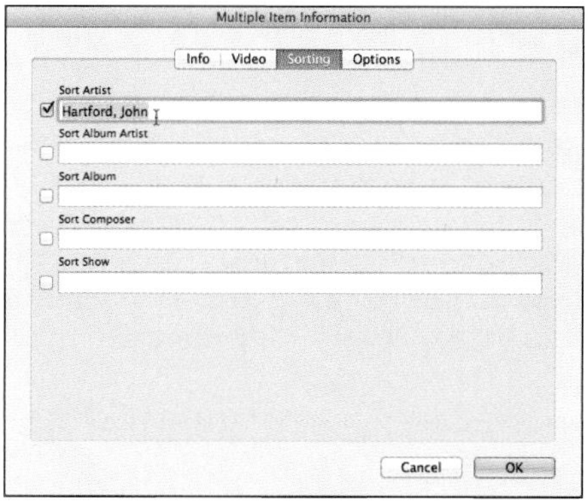

Multiple Item Information

Info   Video   Sorting   Options

Sort Artist
☑ Hartford, John

Sort Album Artist
☐

Sort Album
☐

Sort Composer
☐

Sort Show
☐

Cancel   OK

Figure 9-4: Change the Sort Artist field to the list artist by last name.

Displaying and Sorting Content

You can display your music under the Songs tab (refer to Figure 9-1) and other content under the List tab. With just a little know-how, you can use the view options for the Songs tab or List tab to sort the listing of content items by column heading. You can sort items not only by headings for the name or album fields but also by composer, the date the items were added to the library, or other information that you can add to an item.

You can change the order of columns by clicking a column heading and dragging the entire column to the left or right.

At the very least, you can sort the content by the column headings you now use, such as Artist and Album (refer to Figure 9-1), which correspond to the fields you can edit (as I describe in the "Editing Content Information" section, earlier in this chapter). For example, click the Artist heading to sort the items in the list by artist name in A–Z alphabetical order — indicated by the little arrow in the heading pointing up. Click the Artist heading again to sort the list in reverse Z–A alphabetical order — indicated by the arrow pointing down. Clicking the Time column heading reorders the items by their duration in ascending order, from shortest to longest (arrow pointing up). If you click the Time heading again, the sort is in descending order, which is reversed, starting with the longest item (arrow pointing down).

iTunes also lets you sort the song list using the Album column. Click the Album column heading to switch it to Album by Artist — you can then click the heading arrow to sort in ascending or descending order. Click the Album by Artist heading to switch it to Album by Artist/Year. Click the heading one more time to switch back to Album, which sorts by album title.

TIP

You can make a column wider or narrower. While you move your cursor over the divider between two column headings, the cursor changes to a vertical bar with opposing arrows extending left and right. You click and drag the divider to change the column's width.

You can also change which columns are visible by Control-clicking (on a Mac) or right-clicking (in Windows or on a Mac) any column heading under the Songs tab for music or the List tab for other content. The contextual pop-up menu appears, as shown in Figure 9-5, with choices for column headings that can also be used to sort the content.

You might have to drag the horizontal scroll bar along the bottom of the iTunes window to see all these columns. You can display more, fewer, or different columns.

You can more easily see your choices for column headings by first selecting the type of content in the Library section of the source list and choosing View➪View Options. Then select the columns that you want to appear in the list from the View Options dialog (as shown in Figure 9-6, left side, for Music, and right side for TV Shows). Deselect the columns that you don't want to appear.

Figure 9-5: Add or change column headings.

To help you identify which songs were uploaded to iTunes Match in iCloud versus which songs were matched with songs in the iTunes Library, add the iCloud Status column in the View Options dialog (refer to Figure 9-6, left side). For details on using iTunes Match, see Chapter 11.

Enabling the Kind column in the View Options dialog can help you keep track of different kinds of files, such as songs encoded in the AIFF, AAC, WAV, Apple Lossless, or MP3 formats, or videos encoded in the QuickTime or MPEG formats.

iTunes keeps track of the songs, books, TV shows, and podcasts you skip — not to be polite, just to be useful. You can use this feature to sort the Music, TV Shows, and Books lists of your library, thereby making it easier to select and delete the items you skip. Add the Skips column in the View Options dialog (refer to Figure 9-6), and then click the column's heading to sort the list by the number of skips.

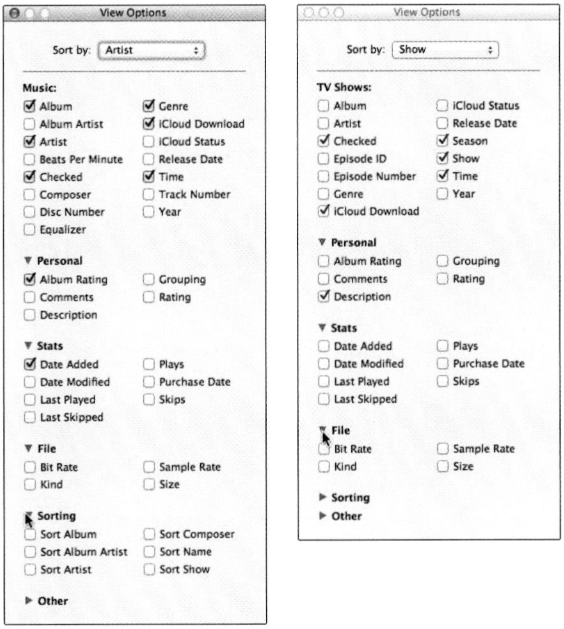

Figure 9-6: Change the view options for music (left) and TV shows (right).

Searching for Content

Because your iTunes library will most likely grow, you might find the usual browsing and scrolling methods too time-consuming. Let iTunes find your content for you!

Locate the Search field — the oval field in the upper-right corner — and follow these steps:

1. **Click in the Search field and enter several characters of your search term.**

   As you type, suggestions appear in a drop-down list. Use these tips for successful searching:

   - *Specify your search* with a specific title, artist, or album.

   - *Narrow your search* by typing more characters. Using fewer characters results in a longer list of possible items.

   - *Pick a specific content type or playlist first* by choosing Music, Movies, TV Shows, Podcasts, iTunes U, Books, Apps, or Tones in the source list, or if searching in a music playlist, select the playlist first under the playlist tab of the Music section.

   - *Case doesn't matter, nor do whole words.* The search feature ignores case. For example, when I search for *miles,* iTunes finds a long list that includes "Eight Miles High," "Forty Miles of Bad Road," and "She Smiles like a River," as well as everything by Miles Davis.

2. **Look through the results in the drop-down list, which appear as you type.**

   The search operation works immediately, displaying any matches in artists, albums, and content types.

3. **Scroll through the search results and click an item to select it, or click the very top Show In choice.**

   The Show In choice takes you directly to that particular section of the library with all items that match the search term; for example, Show in Music takes you to the Music section with all songs, artists, and albums matching the search term.

To back out of a search so that the full list appears again, click the circled *X* in the Search field or delete what you typed.

Deleting Content

Deleting content might seem counterproductive when you're trying to build your iTunes library, but sometimes you just have to do it — for example, if you ripped a CD twice (in AAC format for an iPod and again in Apple Lossless format for burning a CD), and you want to delete the duplicates, or if you simply need to remove content and store it elsewhere.

After selecting a media category (such as Music, Movies, TV Shows, and so on) in the Library section of the source list, you can select any content item and delete it by pressing Delete/Backspace (or choosing Edit⊃Delete). To delete an album, select the album and press Delete/Backspace (or choose Edit⊃Delete). You can delete all episodes of a TV Show or podcast by selecting the TV show or podcast first.

You can delete multiple items in one clean sweep. Press Shift while you click a range of items. Alternatively, press ⌘ (Mac) or Ctrl (Windows) when you click individual items to add them to the selection. Then press Delete/Backspace (or choose Edit⊃Delete).

If you subscribe to iTunes Match in iCloud (see Chapter 11 for details), you can delete a song from your iTunes library and automatically keep a copy in your iTunes Match library in iCloud. To delete the song from the iTunes Match library in iCloud, see Chapter 11.

Deleting a content item from the iTunes library removes the item from your library, but it doesn't remove it from your hard drive until you agree. In the first warning dialog that appears, click the Remove button to remove the selected items from the library or click the Cancel button. iTunes then displays a second warning about moving the files that are still in the iTunes Music folder to the Trash (Mac) or Recycle Bin (Windows). You can click the Move to Trash button on a Mac, or the Move to Recycle Bin button in Windows, to trash the item. Click Keep File to keep it in your music folder, or click Cancel to cancel the operation.

If you choose to move the content to the Trash or Recycle Bin, the content is not yet deleted from your hard drive — you can recover the files by copying them out of the Trash or Recycle Bin, or you can empty them to delete them permanently.

Adding Cover Art

iTunes displays the cover art for your albums, videos, movies, TV shows, podcasts, books, audio books, and apps. All current iPod models (except the iPod shuffle) display the cover art. Therefore, it makes sense to get the art, especially because it's free!

Items that you buy from the iTunes Store typically include an image of the album, book, or box cover art or a photo of the artist and apps from the App Store use a larger version of the app icon as the cover art.

To fill your library automatically with cover art for the CDs you ripped, get yourself an iTunes Store account if you don't already have one. iTunes grabs the cover art not only for iTunes Store purchases but also for CDs you ripped — provided that the albums are also available in the iTunes Store.

To download cover art for ripped CDs automatically, choose iTunes⇨ Preferences on a Mac or Edit⇨Preferences in Windows, click the General tab if it is not already selected, and select the Automatically Download Missing Album Artwork option.

You can also get your cover art from other places that sell CDs, such as Amazon.com, or you can even scan them from the actual CDs. The optimal size for cover art is 300 x 300 pixels. Save it in a graphics format that iTunes (and its underlying graphics technology, *QuickTime*) understands — JPEG, GIF, PNG, TIFF, or Photoshop. With a web browser, you can visit web pages to scout for suitable art; just Control-click (Mac) or right-click (Mac or Windows) an image to download and save the image on your hard drive.

To add artwork to one or more items, select it (or them) in your iTunes library and do one of the following:

✔ **Add artwork to a single item through the information window.**

Choose File⇨Get Info and click the Artwork tab in the information dialog. Click the Add button, browse your hard drive or network for the image file, select the file, and click the OK button.

✔ **Add artwork for multiple items in the Multiple Item Information dialog.**

Choose File⇨Get Info after selecting the items, enable the Artwork field (select its check box), and then drag a graphics file for the cover art from a Desktop folder to the Artwork well. Click the Yes button for the warning message to change the artwork.

See the earlier section, "Editing multiple items at once," to find out more about using the Multiple Item Information dialog.

To remove the artwork from an item, view the artwork in a larger window or resize the artwork, choose File⇨Get Info, and then click the Artwork tab. You can add a different image with the Add button, delete images with the Delete button, or resize images with the size slider.

Playing Content in iTunes

In This Chapter

⟩ Playing songs, podcasts, and audio books in iTunes

⟩ Creating a playlist of songs and albums

⟩ Creating a Genius playlist

⟩ Playing videos in iTunes

*I*f you like to entertain folks by spinning tunes and playing videos at home or at parties, iTunes could easily become your media jockey console. With iTunes, your computer is a mean multimedia machine that can mix sounds, photos, and videos. In this chapter, you discover how to play music, videos, audio books, and podcasts with iTunes. You also get some advice on playlists from Apple's Genius feature, and you discover the iTunes DJ feature, and possibly also discover the DJ in yourself.

The ability to play any set of songs in a specific order is one of the joys of using iTunes. A *playlist* is a list of the items that you want, organized in the sequence that you want to play them. For example, you can make a playlist of love songs from different albums for a romantic mood or surf songs for a trip to the beach. You can also organize playlists for different operations, such as burning a CD or syncing content to your iPod. You can even create a *smart playlist,* which automatically includes items in the playlist based on the criteria you set up and removes items that don't match the criteria.

The Beatles (White Alb... The Beatles

Beatles For Sale The Beatles

A Hard D The Beatl

Let It Be The Beatles

Magical Mystery Tour The Beatles

Past Mas The Beatle

 ON THE WEB

To discover more advanced iTunes playback tricks including how to create smart playlists, see "Tips on Using iTunes" in the free tips section of the author's website (www.tonybove. com/tips).

Playing Songs

When you find a song you want to play (see Chapter 5 for browsing and searching details), simply double-click it, or select it and then click the play button. The play button toggles to a pause button while the song plays, as shown in Figure 10-1. When the song finishes, iTunes continues playing the songs in the list or album in sequence until you click the pause button (which then toggles back into the play button) or until the song list or album ends.

Press the spacebar to perform the same function as the play button; press the spacebar again to pause.

You also have these controls:

- **Player buttons — forward and back:** Use these buttons to control the playback of content in iTunes. You can skip to the next song by clicking the forward button or pressing the right-arrow key. From the middle of a song you can skip to the beginning of the song by clicking the back button or pressing the left-arrow key. To skip to the previous song from the beginning of the current song, click the back button or press the left-arrow key once; from the middle of a song, double-click the back button or press the left-arrow key twice.

- **Scrubber bar:** The scrubber bar shows the progress of the tune's playback, and you can drag the scrubber bar along the slider to move back and forth in the song.

- **Elapsed and remaining time:** The time on the left of the scrubber bar slider is the elapsed time; the time on the right is the remaining time for the song. When you click the remaining time, it changes to the duration of the song; click it again to return to the song's remaining time.

- **Volume control:** You can change the volume level in iTunes by dragging the volume control slider in the upper-left section of the iTunes window to the right to increase the volume or to the left to decrease it. The maximum volume of the iTunes volume slider is the maximum set for the computer's sound, which you set separately.

  To discover how to set volume levels and tweak the sound, see "Tony's iTunes Tips" in the free tips section of the author's website (www.tonybove.com/tips).

- **Up Next menu:** The Up Next menu (see Figure 10-1) shows an Up Next section with the songs that will play in sequence after the song you are currently playing. If you are playing an album or a playlist, the songs that are "up next" are the rest of the songs of the album or playlist. You can scroll the menu to see more songs, including songs you played previously in the Back section. Double-click any song to start playing it. You can also remove songs from the Up Next list by clicking the tiny *x* that appears when you hover your pointer over a song in the menu.

Figure 10-1: Player controls and what's up next.

> ✔ **Shuffle:** The shuffle button that appears next to the artist name plays all the songs by that artist in random order. The shuffle button that appears when you move your pointer over the album or playlist title plays the songs on the album or in the playlist in random order.

You can repeat an entire album or playlist by starting to play the album or playlist and then choosing Controls➪Repeat➪All. To repeat the current song, choose Controls➪Repeat➪One. To return to normal playback, choose Controls➪Repeat➪Off.

The Play iTunes LP button appears for albums that provide videos and animated liner notes, as shown in Figure 10-2 — click the Play iTunes LP button to show a full-screen menu of the album's contents.

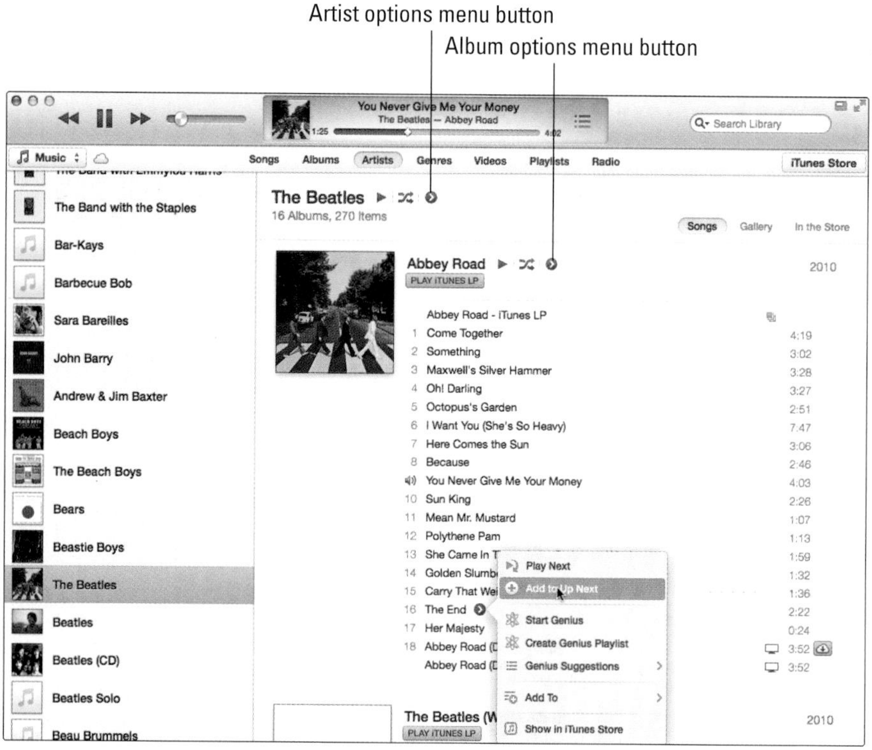

Artist options menu button

Album options menu button

Figure 10-2: The options menu lets you add to the Up Next list.

The options menu button (shown in Figure 10-2) appears next to each song as you move your pointer over the song — click it to see the options menu for songs. The options menu button also appears next to the album title for options that apply to the entire album, and the artist options menu button appears next to the artist name for options that apply to all of the artist's songs.

The options menu for songs, albums, or artists gives you the following playback options:

  ✔ **Play Next:** Set this song, album, or artist as the next one to play. If you use the album options menu, iTunes sets the first song of the album as the next one to play. If you use the artist options menu, iTunes sets the first song of the first album by the artist as the next one to play.

  ✔ **Add to Up Next:** Add this song, album, or artist to the end of the Up Next list. You can see the Up Next list in the Up Next menu (refer to Figure 10-1). All tracks are added for an album, and all albums are added for an artist.

✔ **Start Genius, Create a Genius Playlist, and Genius Suggestions:** I impart my wisdom about the Genius feature in the "Adding a touch of Genius" section, later in this chapter.

✔ **Add To:** Add this song, album, or artist to a playlist. See the section, "Creating your own playlists," later in this chapter.

✔ **Go to:** This option appears with the album name if you're browsing songs or albums under tabs other than the Albums tab, and takes you to the album under the Albums tab. This option appears with the artist name if you're browsing songs or albums under tabs other than the Artists tab, and takes you to the artist under the Artists tab. Under tabs other than Albums and Artists, both Go To an album and Go To an artist appear.

✔ **Show in iTunes Store:** View this song, album, or artist in the iTunes Store (Internet connection required).

If you use iTunes Match to store songs in iCloud (see Chapter 11 for details), you can see and play the songs stored in iTunes Match as well as the songs in your iTunes library. To hide the iTunes Match songs, choose View⊏>Hide Music in the Cloud. To show the iTunes Match songs, choose View⊏>Show Music in the Cloud. To find out more about playing and downloading iTunes Match songs, see Chapter 11.

Using the MiniPlayer and AirPlay

If you want to see the rest of your computer screen while playing music, you can switch to the MiniPlayer, shown in Figure 10-3 (left and right sides), which offers playback controls and other options, including controlling AirPlay-compatible speakers or Apple TV.

To display *only* the MiniPlayer on a Mac, choose Window⊏>Switch to MiniPlayer or press ⌘-Option-M (or click the MiniPlayer icon in the upper-right corner of the iTunes window next to the full-screen button). On a Mac, you can also display the MiniPlayer *in addition* to the iTunes window by choosing Window⊏>MiniPlayer or pressing ⌘-Option-3. To switch back to iTunes, click the tiny iTunes button on the MiniPlayer (see Figure 10-3, left side) or press ⌘-Option-M; to close MiniPlayer if iTunes is already open, click the tiny *x* in the upper-left corner.

On a Windows PC, choose Switch to MiniPlayer from the shortcut menu in the upper-left corner of the iTunes window, or press Ctrl-Shift-M. To switch back to iTunes, click the tiny iTunes button on the MiniPlayer (see Figure 10-3, left side), or press Ctrl-Shift-M.

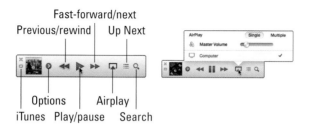

Figure 10-3: The MiniPlayer (left) controlling AirPlay speakers (right).

The MiniPlayer gives you a lot of control in a tiny package. You get not only the usual play/pause, previous/rewind, and fast-forward/next buttons but also the options menu (refer to Figure 10-2), the search field, the album cover (click it to see the cover in a large window), the Up Next list (refer to Figure 10-1), and the AirPlay menu.

AirPlay lets you play music and video wirelessly to speakers and a television. The AirPlay menu (refer to Figure 10-3, right side) lets you control the volume for AirPlay devices such as AirPlay-compatible speakers and Apple TV. The Single button assigns the audio and/or video to a single device. Each device appears below the active Computer option; click a device to make it active. The Multiple button lets you assign the audio and video to more than one device at the same time. You can control the volume for each device and the master volume (for all devices).

Cross-fading song playback

DJs in clubs and on the radio often make a smooth transition from the ending of one song to the beginning of the next one. This is called a *cross-fade*. Ordinarily, iTunes is set to have a short cross-fade of one second (the time after the fade-out of the first song to the fade-in of the second), but you can adjust that if you like.

You can change the cross-fade by choosing iTunes⇨Preferences on a Mac or Edit⇨Preferences in Windows and clicking the Playback icon. The Playback preferences appear, as shown in Figure 10-4.

Select the Crossfade Songs preference and then increase or decrease the cross-fade by dragging the slider. Each notch in the slider represents 1 second. The maximum amount of cross-fade is 12 seconds. With a longer cross-fade, you get more overlap from one song to the next; that is, the second song starts before the first one ends. To turn off the cross-fade, deselect Crossfade Songs.

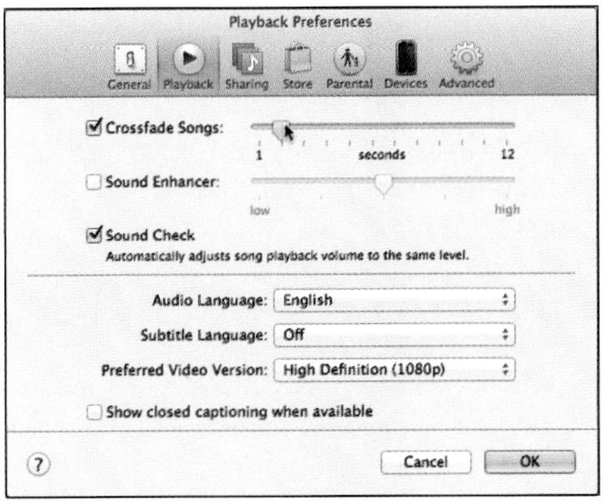

Figure 10-4: Set the cross-fade between songs and other playback options.

Creating your own playlists

In addition to providing the convenience of arranging songs in a certain play order in advance, playlists are also important for managing your content library. They can also make it easier to find items you like without searching the entire library for them. You can create playlists of individual songs or entire albums. You can also include audio books, TV shows, videos, podcast episodes, and web radio stations in playlists.

To create a music playlist from scratch, follow these steps:

1. **Choose Music from the source list and browse for music under any of the tabs (Songs, Albums, Artists, and so on).**

   See Chapter 5 for more information about browsing content.

2. **Choose File⇨New⇨Playlist (or press ⌘-N).**

   This step creates a new, untitled playlist. The library content you were browsing appears in the wider left column, and the empty playlist appears in the right column, as shown in Figure 10-5.

   If you're browsing playlists under the Playlists tab, you can create a new untitled playlist by clicking the Add (+ sign) button in the lower-left corner under the playlists and choose New Playlist.

3. **Give the playlist a descriptive name.**

   You can click the playlist name if it isn't already selected, and begin typing a new name and press Return (or just click somewhere else) to save the name.

Figure 10-5: Drag an album to the new playlist.

4. **Drag items such as an album or selected songs from the library to the playlist, as shown in Figure 10-5.**

   Drag one item at a time or drag a group of items into the playlist column. The initial order of items in the playlist is based on the order in which you drag them to the list. You can add an entire album to a playlist with the songs in album order by dragging the album (or album name), or you can drag separate songs to the playlist in any order you want.

5. **(Optional) Rearrange items in the playlist.**

   You can change the sorting of items in the playlist by clicking the Sort by Manual Order link at the top of the playlist (refer to Figure 10-5). You can sort by Name, Time, Artist, Album, Genre, Rating, or Plays (number of plays). Switching back to Sort by Manual Order lets you drag items up or down the list to rearrange them.

6. **Click Done to finish adding to the playlist.**

You can view and select the playlist by clicking the Playlists tab. The Playlists screen appears showing a selected playlist (the first playlist if this is your first visit), and a list of playlists in the left column, as shown in Figure 10-6.

Your new playlist appears in the alphabetical list of playlists. Select the playlist and the items in the playlist appear on the right. Select any item in the playlist to start playing from that item to the end of the playlist and click the play button. You can switch the Playlists tab view by clicking the View button in the upper-right corner — your choices are List, Grid (shown in Figure 10-6), and Artist List.

Adding an album or a song to an existing playlist is simple. If you're already browsing under the Playlists tab, select a playlist and click the Add To button in the upper-right corner. The display switches so that library content appears in the wider left column and the playlist in the right column, in the same layout as Figure 10-5. You can then drag items to the playlist.

To add an album or a song to an existing playlist while browsing in another tab, click the options menu button for a song, album, or artist to see the options menu (refer to Figure 10-2), and click Add To. A pop-up menu of playlists appears, as shown in Figure 10-7.

Figure 10-6: Switching the view of the Playlists tab.

Figure 10-7: Add an album to a playlist.

Creating a playlist *starting* with an album or set of songs is also simple. Select the album or songs and then choose File➪New➪Playlist from Selection. iTunes automatically creates a new playlist named after the album and artist. You can create a playlist with all of a podcast's episodes the same way.

To add other content items to a playlist, choose the content type in the source list (Movies, TV Shows, and so on), and Control-click or right-click a selected item. A contextual menu appears. Choose Add to Playlist, and then choose a playlist from the submenu. You can also create playlists from content such as movies, TV shows, and podcasts by selecting the items and choosing File➪New➪Playlist from Selection.

You can delete items from playlists as you wish. When you delete an item from a playlist, the item is simply deleted from the list — not from the library. To delete an item from a playlist, select the playlist in the Playlists tab view, and then select the item. Press Delete/Backspace or choose Edit➪Delete. In the warning dialog that appears, click the Remove button to remove the selected item from the list.

You can also delete entire playlists without harming the content in the library. *Note:* You need to switch to the Songs, Albums, Artists, Genres, or Videos tab to delete music content from your library. You can also delete items from the other content types (Movies, TV Shows, and so on).

The one way you can completely delete an item from your library from within a playlist is by selecting the item and pressing ⌘-Option-Delete (Mac) or Ctrl-Alt-Backspace (Windows).

To delete a whole playlist, select the playlist in the left column of the Playlists tab view and then press Delete/Backspace or choose Edit⇨Delete.

Adding a touch of Genius

The Genius feature works with Apple's iTunes Store content to match your tastes to other iTunes users using a technique called *collaborative filtering*. The Genius feature analyzes the music in other people's iTunes libraries — people who also have the same song you selected (if they also turn on the Genius feature in iTunes). All this information is shared anonymously. The only music Genius knows, however, is music in the iTunes Store.

For the Genius feature to work, you need an iTunes Store account (see Chapter 6), and you need to select the Share Details about Your Library with Apple check box — either when you first start using iTunes, as I show in Chapter 5, or by choosing Preferences from the iTunes menu on a Mac or from the Edit menu on a Windows PC, clicking the Store tab, and selecting the Share Details About Your Library With Apple check box. When you add new music, you can tell iTunes to immediately update the Genius feature with new information by choosing Store⇨Update Genius.

To use the Genius feature, click the option menu button next to a song, album, or artist to see the option menu (refer to Figure 10-2). Choose one of the following:

- ✔ **Start Genius:** Start the Genius feature if it is not turned on yet and add Genius selections to the Up Next list.

- ✔ **Create a Genius Playlist:** Create a Genius playlist starting with this song, album, or artist, with songs suggested by the Genius.

- ✔ **Genius Suggestions:** View a list of Genius suggestions in your library based on the song, album, or artist.

The Genius creates a special Genius playlist with the name of the song, as shown in Figure 10-8. You can refresh the Genius playlist with a new batch of songs based on the selected song by clicking the Refresh button in the upper-right corner of the Genius playlist (see Figure 10-8). When you refresh a Genius playlist, you lose the previous version of that playlist.

You can also rearrange the songs in the Genius playlist by dragging them. To sort the songs, click the column headers in the list pane — just like other playlists.

Figure 10-8: Playing a Genius playlist.

You can sync your saved Genius playlists with your iPod (see Chapter 7 for sync details). Synchronized Genius playlists on the iPod contain the same songs that appeared in the iTunes version of the playlist. See Chapter 12 for details on creating Genius playlists right on your iPod.

The genius of iTunes is that it can take into consideration everything in your library and, comparing your library to other libraries, come up with an interesting mix of songs.

To give you a taste of what's possible with the Genius feature, check out Genius Mixes — select Genius Mixes in the Playlists tab. iTunes compiles a set of Genius mixes based on your library. Each square represents a separate mix. As you hover over a square, a play button appears; click the play button to play the mix.

Playing Podcasts and Audio Books

A podcast automatically transfers audio or audio/video episodes, such as weekly broadcasts, to your iTunes library from the Internet or through the iTunes Store (as I describe in episodic detail in Chapter 6).

To find your podcasts, select Podcasts in the Library section of the source list. The Podcasts screen offers three tabs for viewing podcasts:

- **Unplayed:** Shows only the podcasts with unplayed episodes.

- **Podcasts:** Shows all podcasts with cover art, with the All Episodes and Unplayed buttons to filter the view.

- **List:** Shows all podcasts in a list, as shown in Figure 10-9. Click the triangle next to a podcast to see its episodes. The triangle rotates, and a list of episodes appears beneath the podcast.

To play a specific podcast episode, double-click its title or select the title and click the Play button. You can use the iTunes playback controls to fast-forward or rewind the podcast, or play it from any point. The blue dot next to a podcast means that you haven't yet played it. After you listen to a portion of the episode, the dot turns into a half-moon until you play it to the end.

Figure 10-9: Open a podcast to see its episodes.

When you play a podcast, iTunes remembers your place when you stop listening to it, just like it remembers when you place a bookmark in an audio book or pause during a movie — even after quitting and restarting iTunes. iTunes resumes playing from that playback position when you return to the podcast to play it.

Some podcasts are enhanced to include chapter marks and photos. When you play an enhanced podcast in iTunes, a Chapters menu appears on the iTunes menu bar. Choose this menu to display the podcast's chapter marks, artwork, and chapter start times.

You can store and play audio books, articles, and spoken-word titles just like songs in iTunes, and you can download titles from the iTunes Store (as I describe prolifically in Chapter 6). Choose Books in the Library section of the Source pane to see them. (To change the media type of audio books imported as songs into iTunes so that they appear in the Books section of your library, see Chapter 9.)

To play an audio book, select it just like you would a song and click the play button. You can use the iTunes playback controls to fast-forward or rewind the audio book or play it from any point. Audio books from the iTunes Store are enhanced to include chapter marks. When you play any of these audio books in iTunes, the Chapters menu appears on the iTunes menu bar, just like it does for a podcast with chapters. Choose the Chapters menu to display and select the audio book's chapter marks.

Playing Videos

iTunes is versatile when it comes to playing videos — the TV shows, movies, video podcasts, and music videos you downloaded from the iTunes Store (see Chapter 6) as well as the video files you imported into iTunes from other sources (see Chapter 5).

To watch a video in iTunes, select it in your library (see details on browsing and listing movies, TV shows, and videos in Chapter 5), and then click the play button. The video appears in a separate window that includes a transparent control pane with buttons for controlling video playback, as shown in Figure 10-10. Click the play button at the center of the pane to play or pause, and then drag the scrubber to move forward or backward through the video. Click the previous button to play the previous video, the rewind and fast-forward buttons on either side of the play button to move backward or forward through a video, or the next button to play the next video. Click the close button to close the window just as you would close a window with Mac OS X or Windows.

Close   Rewind   Fast-forward

Play/pause

Scrubber   Previous Next Full-screen

Volume

Figure 10-10: Use the video player controls.

The semitransparent control pane disappears while the video plays, but you can make it reappear by moving the cursor to the bottom center of the video window. The controls pane also offers a volume slider to set the audio volume and the full-screen button to change the video display to full-screen with a black border. When you're playing a video in full-screen view, the following controls are available:

- ✔ **Esc (Escape):** Press to stop full-screen playback and return to the iTunes window.

- ✔ **Spacebar:** Press to pause playback. (Pressing the spacebar again resumes playback.)

- ✔ **Your mouse or pointing device:** Simply move these to display the semitransparent control pane and click the full-screen button to stop full-screen playback and return to the iTunes window.

Songs, videos, podcast episodes, and audio books can vary greatly from loud to soft. To remedy these problems, you can set the volume in advance for these items. You can also sound-check your entire music library to bring it in line, volume-wise. See "Tips on Using iTunes" in the free tips section of the author's website (www.tonybove.com/tips).

You can use any computer with iTunes to play its library content (audio *and* video) through Apple TV to your home entertainment system. That way, if you invite a friend over, you can quickly play any tune or video in her laptop's library. You can also stream music from iTunes to an iPad, iPod touch, or iPhone that is connected to the same Wi-Fi network as your computer. See "Tips on Using iTunes" in the free tips section of the author's website (www.tonybove.com/tips).

Gimme Shelter for My Media

In This Chapter

▶ Choosing the format and settings for burning a disc

▶ Burning an audio CD or an MP3 CD

▶ Subscribing to iTunes Match

▶ Locating and backing up files in the iTunes library

▶ Backing up your entire iTunes library

*Y*ou might think that your digital content is safe, stored as-is, on your iPod, in your iCloud, and on your hard drive. However, demons in the night are working overtime to render your hard drive useless — and at the same time, someone left your iPod with the cake out in the rain, and iCloud is somewhere over the rainbow, unreachable through a faulty Internet connection.

Copyright law and common sense prohibit you from using copyrighted content and then selling it to someone else. However, with iTunes, you're allowed to make copies of the content and apps that you own for personal use, including copies for backup purposes.

This chapter boils down everything you need to know about keeping your library backed up and burning discs to make copies of some of your content. For example, I burn audio CDs or MP3 CDs to make safety copies of songs I buy from the iTunes Store. I also like to custom-mix songs from different artists and albums onto an audio or MP3 CD.

I also copy my entire iTunes library to another hard drive as a backup, as I describe in this chapter. This operation is very important, especially if you've ripped CDs that you don't have any more except on your computer. You can also use an automatic backup system, such as

Apple's Time Machine for Macs. That way, even if your hard drive fails, you still have your iTunes library. You can also purchase the iTunes Match service that can match the music you ripped from CDs and store the matched copies in iCloud, as I describe in the "Subscribing to iTunes Match" section, later in this chapter.

To find out how to consolidate media files into one library, how to manage multiple iTunes libraries for easier synchronization with multiple devices, and how to move a library from one computer to another (such as a PC to a Mac or vice versa), see Bonus Chapter 3 in the free tips section of the author's website (`www.tonybove.com/tips`).

You should not rely on your iPod as your sole music storage device or as a backup for your iTunes library. Although purchases you make with your iPod touch *are* copied back to your iTunes library and to the iCloud, you can't copy any other content from your iPod to your computer via iTunes. It's a one-way trip from iTunes or iCloud *to* your iPod because record labels and video distributors don't want indiscriminate copying, and Apple has complied with these requests. You can, however, use *third-party utility programs* (not supported by Apple) to copy content from an iPod back to iTunes.

To find out more about third-party utility programs for managing your iPod or iPhone, see "Tips on Using iPods and iPhones" in the free tips section of the author's website (`www.tonybove.com/tips`).

The iTunes Store uses Apple FairPlay technology for some content (such as commercial movies and TV Shows), which protects the rights of copyright holders while also giving you some leeway in using the copyrighted content. But you can still copy the media files freely so that backup is easy and straightforward on either a Mac or a PC.

Do not violate copyright law. You're allowed to copy content for your own use, but you cannot legally copy content for any other purpose. Consult a lawyer if you're in doubt.

Burning Your Own Discs

Once upon a time, when vinyl records were popular, rock radio disk jockeys (who didn't like disco) held disco-meltdown parties. People were encouraged to throw their disco records onto a pile to be burned or steamrolled into a vinyl glob. I admit that I shamelessly participated in one such meltdown. However, this section isn't about that. Rather, *burning* a disc is the process in which the CD or DVD drive recorder's laser heats up points on an interior layer of the disc to record information.

Using recordable CDs and DVDs

If you have a CD-R, CD-RW, or DVD-R drive (such as the Apple SuperDrive that comes with some Macs) and a blank CD-R (*R* stands for recordable), you can burn music, audio books, and audio podcast episodes on audio CDs that play in most CD and DVD players. You can fit up to 74 minutes of music on a high-quality audio-format CD-R; most can go as high as 80 minutes. Blank audio CD-Rs (I'm talking discs now and not drives) are available in stores that carry consumer electronics.

You can also burn an audio CD-R of song files in the MP3 format, which is useful for backing up a music library or making discs for use in MP3 CD players. You can play MP3 files burned on a CD-R in MP3 format on any MP3 disc player, on combination CD/MP3 players, on many DVD players, and (of course) on computers that recognize MP3-formatted CDs (including computers with iTunes). An MP3-formatted CD-R can hold more than 12 hours of music. You read that right — *12 hours on one disc.* This is why *MP3 discs* are popular: They are essentially CD-Rs with MP3 files stored on them.

If you have a DVD burner, such as an Apple SuperDrive, you can burn *data discs* in the DVD-R or DVD-RW format to use with other computers. This approach is suitable for making backup copies of media files (or any data files). A DVD-R can hold about 4,700,000,000 bytes (more than 4GB), and a DVD-R DL can hold about 8.5GB.

Creating a disc burn playlist

To burn a CD (actually a CD-R, but most people refer to recordable CD-R discs as *CDs*), you must first create a playlist for the CD. (See Chapter 10 for a play-by-play on how to create a playlist.) You can use songs encoded in any format that iTunes supports; however, you get higher-quality music with the uncompressed AIFF and WAV formats or with the Apple Lossless format, which I describe in Chapter 5.

Calculating how much music to use

When you create an audio CD playlist, you can calculate how many songs can fit on the CD by totaling the durations of the songs. You can see the size of a playlist by selecting it and choosing View⇨Show Status Bar; the status bar at the bottom of the iTunes window shows the number of songs, the duration of the songs, and the amount in megabytes for the selected playlist, as shown in Figure 11-1.

In Figure 11-1, the selected playlist takes about 1.1 hours (1:08:54, to be precise) to play, so it fits on a standard audio CD. (The 15 songs take up only 94.5MB of hard drive space; they were purchased from the iTunes Store.)

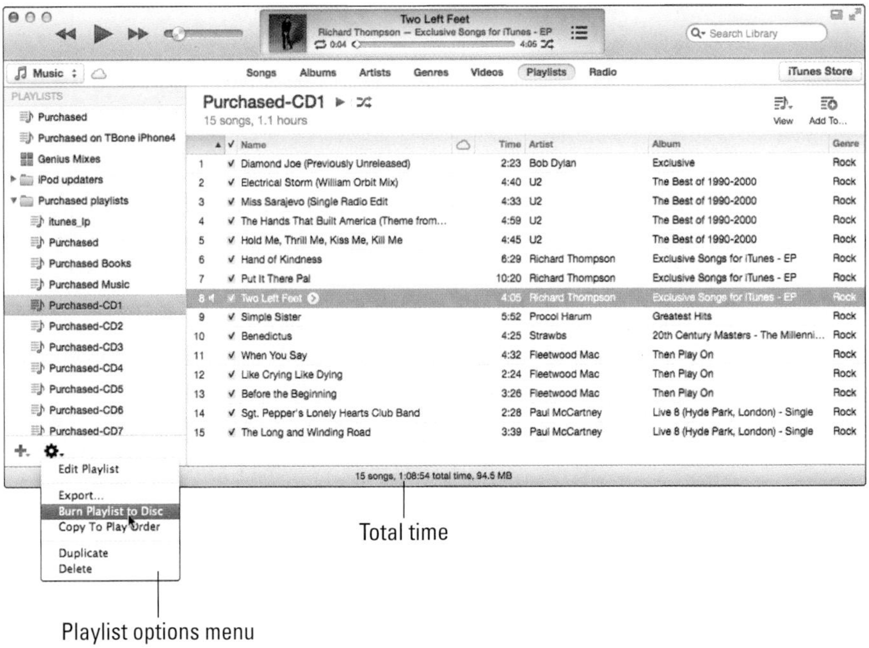

Figure 11-1: The duration of the playlist in the status bar.

A one-hour playlist of AIFF-formatted music, which occupies more than 600MB of hard drive space, also fits on a standard audio CD. You calculate the amount you can fit on a standard audio CD using the duration, not the hard drive space occupied by the music files. Although a CD holds between 650MB and 700MB (depending on the disc), the music is encoded in a special format known as CD-DA (Compact Disc-Digital Audio, or Red Book) that fills byte sectors without error-correction and checksum information. Thus, you can fit about 90MB more — 740MB total — of AIFF-formatted music on a 650MB disc. I typically put 1.1 hours (about 66 minutes) of music on a 74-minute or an 80-minute CD-R, leaving minutes to spare.

Always use the actual duration in hours, minutes, and seconds to calculate how much music you can fit on an audio CD — either 74 or 80 minutes for blank CD-Rs. I recommend leaving at least 1 extra minute to account for the gaps between songs.

You do the *opposite* for an MP3 CD or a data DVD. Use the actual megabytes to calculate how many song files can fit on a disc — up to 700MB for a blank CD-R. You can fit lots more music on an MP3 CD-R because you use MP3-formatted songs rather than uncompressed AIFF (or WAV) songs.

If you have too many songs in the playlist to fit on a CD, iTunes gives you the option to cancel the burn operation or to burn as many songs in the playlist as will fit on the CD (either audio or MP3). Then it asks you to insert another CD to continue burning the remaining songs in the playlist.

Importing music for an audio CD-R

Before you rip an audio CD of songs that you want to burn to an audio CD-R, you might want to change the import settings (as I describe in Chapter 5). Use the AIFF, WAV, or Apple Lossless formats for songs from audio CDs if you want to burn your own audio CDs with music at its highest quality. You can also burn MP3-formatted songs to an audio CD, but the quality is not as good as with AIFF, WAV, or Apple Lossless.

AIFF is the standard digital format for uncompressed sound on a Mac, and you can't go wrong with it. *WAV* is basically the same thing for Windows. Apple Lossless provides CD-quality sound in a file size that's about 55 to 60 percent of the size of an AIFF or WAV file. Both AIFF and WAV offer the same custom settings for sample rate, sample size, and channels (to see how to customize your settings before ripping audio CDs, see Chapter 5). You can choose the automatic settings, and iTunes detects the proper sample rate, size, and channels from the source. Apple Lossless is always set to automatic.

The songs you purchase from the iTunes Store are supplied in the unprotected iTunes Plus AAC format that carries no restrictions. However, you may still have songs in the older protected AAC format that was used until 2009. You can't convert the protected format to anything else, but you can still burn the songs onto CDs, and the quality of the result on CD is acceptable. Audio books also come in a protected format that can't be converted by iTunes, but you can burn them onto CDs with acceptable quality.

The AAC format is similar in audio quality to the MP3 format but takes up less space; both are acceptable to most CD listeners. I think AAC offers a decent trade-off of space and quality and is suitable (although not as good as AIFF or Apple Lossless) for burning to an audio CD.

For a complete description of these formats, see Bonus Chapter 2 in the free tips section of the author's website (`www.tonybove.com/tips`).

Switching import formats for MP3 CD-Rs

MP3 discs are essentially CD-Rs with MP3 files stored on them. Consumer MP3 CD players are readily available in consumer electronics stores, including hybrid models that play both audio CDs and MP3 CDs.

You can fit 8–12 hours of stereo music on an MP3 CD with the MP3 format — the amount varies depending on the encoding options and settings you choose. For example, you might be able to fit up to 20 hours of mono (monaural) recordings because they use only one channel and carry less information. On the other hand, if you choose the setting to encode stereo recordings at a high bit rate (above 192 bits per second), you can fit only 9 hours.

Only MP3-formatted songs can be burned on an MP3 CD-R. Any songs not formatted in MP3 are skipped and not burned.

Burning a disc

Burning a CD is a simple process, and getting it right the first time is a good idea because when you burn a CD-R, it's done — right or wrong. You can't erase content and reuse a CD-R. Fortunately, CD-Rs are inexpensive, so you won't be out more than a few cents if you burn a bad one. (Besides, they're good as coasters for coffee tables.)

Follow these steps to burn a disc:

1. **Select the playlist under the Playlists tab.**

2. **Choose Burn Playlist to Disc from the playlist options menu (refer to Figure 11-1) or choose File⇨Burn Playlist to Disc.**

   After choosing Burn Playlist to Disc, the Burn Settings dialog appears, as shown in Figure 11-2.

3. **Select options in the Burn Settings dialog and click the Burn button.**

   See the following section for instructions on selecting these important options.

4. **Insert a blank disc.**

   iTunes immediately checks the media and begins the burn process, displaying a progress bar and the names of the songs burning to the disc.

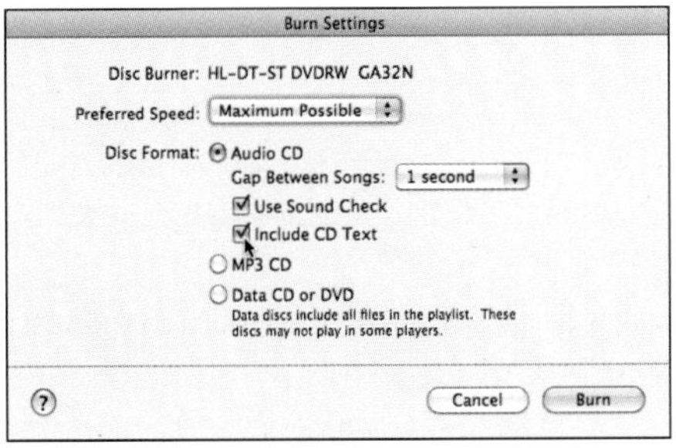

Figure 11-2: Choose burn settings before burning the disc.

If you chose the MP3 CD format, iTunes skips over any songs in the play-list that aren't in this format.

When iTunes finishes burning the disc, iTunes chimes, and the disc is mounted on the Desktop.

5. Eject the newly burned disc from your drive and then test it.

You can cancel the burn operation at any time by clicking the *X* next to the progress bar, but canceling the operation isn't like undoing the burn. If the burn has already started, you can't use that CD-R or DVD-R again.

If the playlist has more music than can fit on the disc using the chosen format, iTunes asks whether you want to create multiple audio CDs with the playlist. If you choose to create multiple audio CDs, iTunes burns as many full songs as possible from the beginning of the playlist and then asks you to insert another disc to burn the rest. To calculate the amount of music in a playlist, see the earlier section, "Calculating how much music to use."

Choosing your burn settings

Set the following options in the Burn Settings dialog to ensure that you burn your CD right the first time (refer to Figure 11-2):

- **Preferred Speed:** Choose a specific recording speed or the Maximum Possible option from the Preferred Speed pop-up menu. iTunes typi-cally detects the rating of a blank CD-R and adjusts the recording speed to fit. However, if your blank CD-Rs are rated for a slower speed than your burner or if you have problems creating CD-Rs, you can change the recording speed setting to match the CD's rating.

- **Disc Format:** The disc format is perhaps the most important choice you have to make. Decide whether you're burning an audio CD (CD-R), an MP3 CD (CD-R), or a Data CD (CD-R) or DVD (DVD-R or DVD-RW). Your choice depends on what type of player you're using or whether you're making a data backup of files rather than a disc that plays in a player. Choose one of the following:

  - *Audio CD:* Burn a normal audio CD of up to 74 or 80 minutes (depending on the type of blank CD-R) using any iTunes-supported music files, including songs bought from the iTunes Store. Although connoisseurs of music might use Apple Lossless, AIFF, or WAV for songs to be burned on an audio CD, you can also use the AAC and MP3 formats.

  - *MP3 CD:* Burn an MP3 CD with MP3-formatted songs. No other for-mats are supported for MP3 CDs.

  - *Data CD or DVD:* Burn a data CD-R, CD-RW, DVD-R, or DVD-RW with audio files. You can use any encoding formats for the songs. *Important:* Data discs won't play on most consumer CD players:

They're meant for use with computers. However, data discs are good choices for storing backup copies of songs bought from the iTunes Store.

✔ **Gap between Songs:** You can add an appropriate gap between songs, just like commercial CDs. With this option enabled, you can set the gap time as well. You can choose from a gap of 0 to 5 seconds or None. I recommend leaving the menu set to the default setting of 1 second for playlists of studio-recorded songs and None for concerts and songs recorded live.

✔ **Use Sound Check:** Musicians do a sound check before every performance to check the volume of microphones and instruments and their effect on the listening environment. The aptly named Use Sound Check option in the Burning preferences dialog turns on the Sound Check feature to balance your tunes, volume-wise.

✔ **Include CD Text:** Selecting this option adds the artist and track name text to the CD for certain CD players (often, in-car players) that can display the artist and track name while playing a CD.

Subscribing to iTunes Match

Apple's iCloud Internet service already keeps a copy of everything you purchase in the iTunes Store, App Store, and iBookstore. However, what about those songs you downloaded from someplace else or those CDs you ripped?

The iTunes Match service ($24.99/year) can match most, if not all, of the songs in your iTunes library and keep a safe copy in iCloud. iTunes matches the songs with versions from the iTunes Store encoded in the AAC format at 256 Kbps (iTunes Plus setting), which may be a higher-quality format than the version you have on your computer. If iTunes Match doesn't find a song, it automatically uploads the song as is, directly from your iTunes library to iCloud (as long as the song meets "certain quality criteria," according to Apple, and is not over 200MB). Songs encoded as ALAC, WAV, or AIFF are transcoded in iTunes to the 256 Kbps AAC format when uploaded to iCloud.

To subscribe to iTunes Match, click iTunes Match at the top of the right column of links on the Store home page (or choose Store⟡Turn On iTunes Match) and click Add This Computer. Follow the instructions to enter your Apple ID and password (for details on setting up an iTunes Store account, see Chapter 6), and click to agree to the iTunes Match Terms and Conditions. The matchmaking begins.

While the matching part of the service only takes a few minutes as it locates versions of your songs in the iTunes Store, uploading the songs that don't match (that are not available in the iTunes Store) can take hours. The benefit is that your songs are always available to download — you can access your iTunes Match library on your iPod touch, or on an iPhone, iPad, or iTunes libraries on up to five computers.

After turning on iTunes Match, iTunes automatically updates the iTunes Match library whenever you add new songs. You can turn off this feature by choosing Store➪Turn Off iTunes Match. To turn it back on, choose Store➪Turn On iTunes Match. To update your iTunes Match library with new music at any moment, choose Store➪Update iTunes Match.

After storing your music with iTunes Match, you can play the music the same way as playing music in your iTunes library — click the play button. The music streams from iCloud into your computer. By default, the songs in your iTunes Match library appear along with the songs in your iTunes library. You can hide the iTunes Match songs by choosing View➪Hide Music in the Cloud. To show the iTunes Match songs again, choose View➪Show Music in the Cloud.

You can also download a song to your iTunes library by browsing under the Songs tab and clicking the iCloud icon next to each song in the iCloud Download column, as shown in Figure 11-3 — the column with the iCloud icon as the heading. If you don't see this column, choose View➪View Options, and then select the columns that you want to appear from the View Options dialog — select iCloud Download, and while you're at it, select iCloud Status. Both columns appear in Figure 11-3. (For more tips about using viewing options, see Chapter 9.)

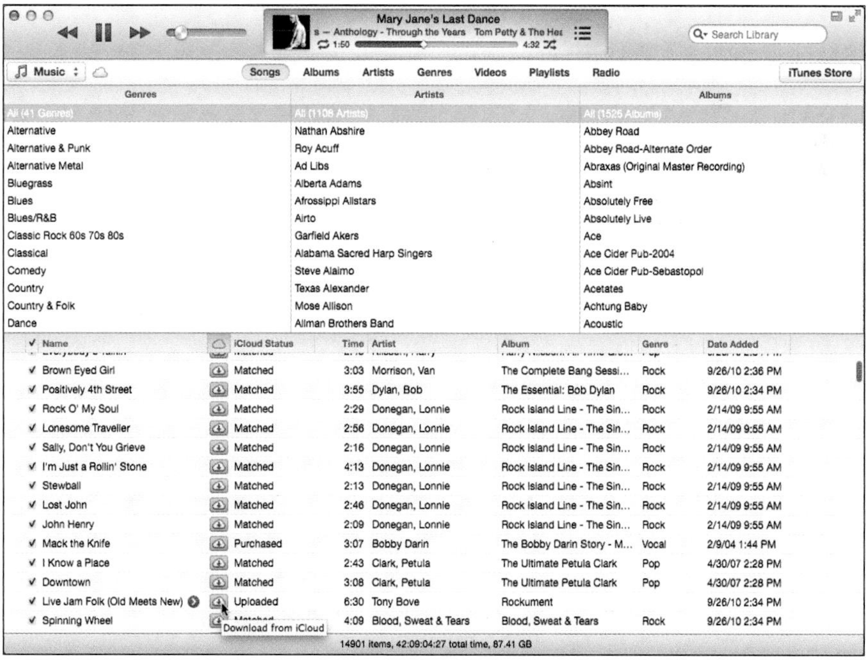

Figure 11-3: Download a song from your iTunes Match library in iCloud.

The iCloud Download column shows the following icons:

- **Cloud with down-arrow:** You can download the song to your iTunes library.

- **Cloud with a slash:** The song can't be uploaded. This icon can appear with songs that are larger than 200MB or encoded at 96 Kbps or less.

- **Two overlapping clouds with a slash:** The song is a duplicate of a song that has already been matched or uploaded.

- **Cloud with an X:** The song was removed from iCloud (but is still stored in your computer's iTunes library).

- **Cloud with an exclamation point:** There is some kind of error with the uploading operation, or the song file has been corrupted. Choose Store⇨ Update iTunes Match to try to resolve the issue.

- **Empty cloud:** iTunes is in the process of matching the song and hasn't finished yet.

- **No icon:** The song is in your iTunes Library.

The iCloud Status column shows the following:

- **Purchased:** The song was purchased from the iTunes Store and automatically copied to your iTunes Match library in iCloud.

- **Matched:** The song was matched by a copy in the iTunes Store, encoded in the AAC format at 256 Kbps (iTunes Plus setting).

- **Uploaded:** The song was uploaded as is. Songs encoded as ALAC, WAV, or AIFF are transcoded in iTunes to the 256 Kbps AAC format when uploaded.

- **Ineligible:** The song could not be matched or uploaded. This status can occur with songs purchased outside the United States (at the iTunes Store for another country), songs bought with a different Apple ID, or songs bought on another computer or iPod touch and not authorized to be played on your computer. (To authorize your computer, choose Store⇨Authorize This Computer and enter your account and password.)

To delete songs from your iTunes Match library, make sure iTunes Match is turned on, and then Control-click (or right-click) the song to see a pop-up menu and choose Delete (or select the song and choose Edit⇨Delete). The delete confirmation dialog appears. If the song is also stored in your iTunes library, the Also Delete This Song from iCloud option appears in the dialog — select this option to delete the song from both iTunes Match and your library. Finally, click OK to confirm the deletion. This is a nonrecoverable operation — the song disappears from iTunes Match. The song is also removed from your iPod when you sync it to your iTunes library or turn on iTunes Match.

To access iTunes Match from your iPod touch, see Chapter 7.

Studying Files in an iTunes Library

If you like to keep your records properly filed, you'll love iTunes and its nice, neat file-storage methods. For all content items, iTunes creates a folder named for the artist and subfolders within the artist folder named for each album. These folders are stored in the iTunes Media folder (unless you change your storage preferences). Note, however, that if you updated a previous version of iTunes that used the iTunes Music folder, iTunes continues to use the self-same iTunes Music folder.

Finding the iTunes library

The default method of storing content in the iTunes library is to store all media files — including music, videos, podcasts, and audio books — in the iTunes Media folder (or iTunes Music folder if you updated from a previous version of iTunes), which is inside the iTunes folder. With this method, media files that you drag to the iTunes window are copied into the iTunes Media folder (without deleting the original files). The iTunes folder also has folders for mobile applications and album artwork. So that's easy — everything is inside the iTunes folder.

On a Mac, iTunes stores your content library in your home folder's Music folder by default. The path to this folder's default location is

    your home folder/Music/iTunes/iTunes Media

On a Windows PC, iTunes stores your content library in your user folder. The path to this folder's default location is

    your user folder/My Documents/My Music/iTunes/iTunes Media

iTunes maintains a separate iTunes folder (with a separate iTunes Media folder) in each home folder (Mac) or user folder (PC). If you share your computer with other users who have home folders, each user can have a separate iTunes library on the same computer (and, of course, separate iPads, iPods, or iPhones that sync with it). You need only one copy of the iTunes program.

If you want to add content to the iTunes library without copying the files to the `iTunes Media` folder, you can copy a link to the original files without copying the files by doing the following:

1. **Choose iTunes➪Preferences (Mac) or Edit➪Preferences (Windows).**

2. **Click the Advanced tab in the iTunes Preferences dialog.**

3. **Deselect the Copy Files to iTunes Media Folder When Adding to Library option.**

However, if a content file is only linked to the `iTunes Media` folder and not copied to it, you can't change the file's name or move it to another folder (or rename the folder, either).

Locating a media file

You can find the location of any media file by selecting the item (such as a song or video), choosing File➪Get Info, and then clicking the Summary tab of the information dialog that appears. You can see the file type next to the Kind heading of the Summary pane. The Where section tells you where the song is — either the pathname to the folder and file on your hard drive, or iCloud if it's a song stored in iTunes Match.

You can also open the folder that contains the media file for any item. Select the item in List, Grid, or Cover Flow view. Then, on a Mac, choose File➪Show in Finder (or press ⌘-Shift-R); in Windows, choose File➪Show in Windows Explorer (or press Ctrl-Shift-R). iTunes gives control to the operating system, which displays the folder that contains the media file. This File menu choice is grayed out if the item is a song that is stored not in your iTunes library but in iTunes Match.

Copying media files

You can copy media files to other hard drives and computers without any restrictions on copying — just keep in mind that protected items, such as movies and TV shows you purchased from the iTunes Store, have some play-back restrictions (see Chapter 6 for iTunes Store details).

To copy the media file for an item to another hard drive or folder (such as a song or video), you can drag the item directly from the iTunes window to the other hard drive or folder.

You can also copy the files and folders from the `iTunes Media` folder to other hard drives or other computers using the operating system's copying function. For example, on a Mac, you can use the Finder to copy content files. Windows PCs offer several methods, including using Windows Explorer, to copy files. For example, copying an entire album or every song by a specific artist is easy — just drag the folder to its new home folder on another hard drive.

Backing Up an iTunes Library to Another Hard Drive

Backups? You don't need no stinkin' backups!

Yes, you do, so think twice about not making them! I know: Backing up your files can be inconvenient and can eat up the capacity of all your external hard drives. Still, it must be done. And fortunately, it's easy to do, either manually as described in this section or automatically with a system backup utility such as Apple's Time Machine. You can also keep a backup of your songs in iCloud — see the "Subscribing to iTunes Match" section, earlier in this chapter.

To copy your entire iTunes library to another hard drive, locate the iTunes folder on your computer (see the section, "Finding the iTunes library," earlier in this chapter). Drag this folder to another hard drive or backup device, and you're all set. This action copies everything, including the playlists in your library.

The copy operation might take some time if your library is huge. Although you can interrupt the operation any time, the newly copied library might not be complete. Finishing the copy operation is always best.

If you restore the backup copy to the same computer with the same name for the hard drive that holds the iTunes library, the backup copy's playlists work fine. Playlists are essentially lists of songs with pathnames to the song files. If the hard drive name is different, the pathnames won't work. However, if you export individual playlists, or all of your playlists, in the XML (eXtensible Markup Language) format beforehand, you can then import them back into iTunes when you restore your backup to realign the playlist pathnames to the new hard drive.

To export a playlist, select the playlist in the Playlists section of the iTunes source pane, choose File⇨Library⇨Export Playlist, and then choose a location on your hard drive. To export all of your playlists at once, choose File⇨Library⇨Export Library.

To import a playlist into iTunes, choose File⇨Library⇨Import Playlist, and then browse for and select the playlist's XML file on your hard drive. To import all the playlists at once, choose File⇨Library⇨Import Playlist and choose the iTunes Media Library.xml file (or iTunes Music Library.xml file for previous versions of iTunes).

Part III
Playing It Back with Interest

The 5th Wave   By Rich Tennant

©RICHTENNANT

"I build bookshelves and Bernice starts buying audiobooks for her iPod."

*H*ere's the big playback for your efforts. This part shows you how to play music, TV shows, movies, podcasts, audio books, and slide-shows on your iPod.

Chapter 12 is all about playing songs. I show you how to find songs, download them from iTunes Match, control the playback, make them shuffle, and repeat playlists and albums. I also show you how to control an iPod shuffle.

Next, Chapter 13 shows you to how to locate and play videos, including movies and TV shows. You can skip forward or backward, scale the picture to fit the display, and bookmark your favorite sec-tions. I also show you how to play podcasts, iTunes U courses, and audio books.

Then, in Chapter 14, you find out all about syn-chronizing photo albums with your iPod, taking pictures and videos with your iPod touch, zoom-ing into photos, sharing pictures with friends, and putting on a slideshow.

The Songs Remain the Same

*E*ven though the iPod and iTunes have irrevocably changed the entertainment industry and how you enjoy music, one thing remains the same: You still play songs. You just play them with more *panache* on your iPod.

You can pick any song that you want to hear at any time. You can also shuffle through songs to get an idea of how wide your music choices are or to surprise yourself or others. Browse by artist and album, select a playlist, and even create playlists on the fly — this chapter explains it all.

Locating "A Song for You"

With thousands of songs on your iPod, finding a particular song by its title may turn your finger into a scrolling stone. It may be faster to locate albums by cover art or to find songs by searching for artist (or composer), genre, album, or playlist. You can browse your music any number of ways without interrupting the music you're playing.

Going with the Cover Flow

Cover Flow (also called the *cover browser*) lets you flip through your cover art to select music alphabetically by artist. You can flip through cover art on an iPod touch or iPod classic.

On an iPod touch, choose Music from the Home screen and then rotate the iPod touch to view it horizontally. This movement changes the display to landscape mode and displays the cover browser, as shown in Figure 12-1.

Slide your finger across the album covers to scroll swiftly through the music library, or tap to the right or left of the cover art in the foreground to move forward or backward one album cover at a time. Tap the play button in the lower-left corner (shown in Figure 12-1) to start playing the first song in the foreground album; the play button turns to a pause button so that you can tap it again to stop playback. Tap the *i* button in the lower-right corner (or tap the foreground cover art) to list the songs in that album. Then you can tap a song to start playing it.

The Cover Flow browser is also available on the iPod classic. Choose Music from the main menu, and then choose Cover Flow from the Music menu.

To browse by cover art on an iPod classic, scroll the click wheel clockwise to move forward or counterclockwise to move backward through album covers. You can also press the Fast Forward or Rewind buttons to step forward or backward in your library one cover at a time. Press the Select button in the middle of the click wheel to select the album in the foreground; a list of songs appears. Use the click wheel to scroll the list of songs, and then press the Select button to select a highlighted song.

Figure 12-1: Cover Flow: The cover browser.

Browsing music on an iPod touch

You can quickly and easily locate a song by looking up either the song's artist or its album. To browse music on an iPod touch, tap the Music icon on the Home screen if the Music app is not already running.

If you store your music on iTunes Match in iCloud, as I describe in Chapter 11, you can choose whether to show all the music on your iPod touch, or just the music downloaded from iTunes Match and stored on the iPod touch. After syncing to iTunes Match, as I describe in Chapter 7, choose Settings⇨Music on your iPod touch to display the Music settings screen. The Show All Music option appears underneath the iTunes Match option on the Music settings screen (turned on by default if you turn on iTunes Match). Click the On switch to turn this option off if you want to show only the music you've downloaded from iTunes Match. Turn it back on if you want to show all the music and playlists that you have in your iTunes Match library.

To browse music by artist, tap the Music icon on the Home screen and tap the Artists icon along the bottom row of the Music screen. A scrollable list of artists appears, with an alphabet listed vertically along the right side, as shown in Figure 12-2 (left side) — flick your finger down to see the very top, which shows the search field.

Tap any letter in the alphabet shown on the right to scroll the list directly to that letter. Tap an artist name to see a list of albums or songs by that artist. (You see multiple albums if more than one album is available.) Tap an album title or its cover art to see a list of songs in the album. Tap a song title to start playing the song.

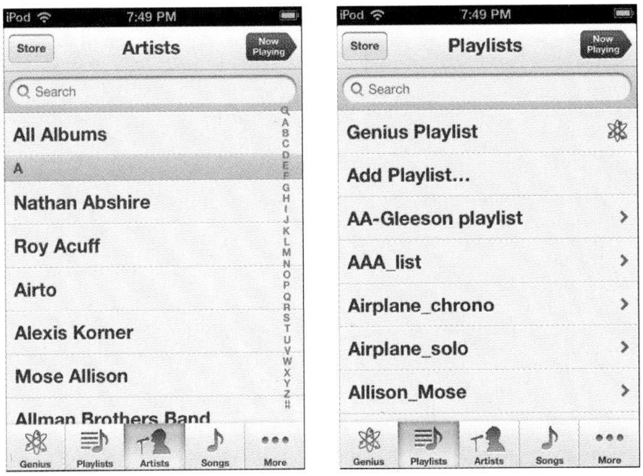

Figure 12-2: Locate an artist (left) or a playlist (right).

To search, tap inside the search field and start typing on the onscreen keyboard that appears. Suggestions appear below matching what you type — tap a suggestion to go to it.

To browse music by album title, tap Albums in the bottom row of icons. To locate songs by title, tap Songs in the bottom row of icons. In either case, a scrollable list appears — after tapping Albums, album titles appear in a scrollable list with the album cover on the left side and an alphabet along the right side. Just like the artists list, you can slide to scroll the list, tap a letter to go directly to that letter, and use the search field at the top.

If you sync Genius mixes (along with other music) to your iPod touch, or if you sync your entire music library (which includes Genius mixes), the Genius button appears in the lower-left corner of the Music screen, shifting the other buttons to the right (Albums moves to the More menu). In that case, in order to browse by albums on an iPod touch, tap More, and then tap Albums. To discover more about Genius mixes, see the "Selecting Genius Mixes" section, later in this chapter).

You can also find music by composer or genre by tapping the More icon along the bottom row of the Music screen, and then tapping either Composers or Genres.

When you sync your iPod touch with your entire iTunes library, your iTunes playlists are included (along with any Genius playlists and Genius mixes). Well, that makes sense, doesn't it?

To browse music by playlist on your iPod touch, tap the Playlists icon along the bottom row of icons. A scrollable list of playlists appears, as shown in Figure 12-2 (right side). Tap a playlist title to see a list of songs in the playlist and tap a song title to start playing the song.

The songs in the playlist are in the order defined for the playlist in iTunes. But don't despair for lack of something new — not only can you edit your playlist to change the song order and add and delete songs, but also you can create entirely new playlists — right in your iPod touch.

As you can see in Figure 12-2 (right side), the Playlists screen includes the Add Playlist choice. To find out how to create playlists on your iPod touch, see "Tips on Using iPods and iPhones" in the free tips section of the author's website (www.tonybove.com/tips).

Browsing music on an iPod nano or iPod classic

To browse music on an iPad nano, tap the Music icon on the Home screen. You can then scroll the Music screen and tap Genius Mixes, Playlists, Artists, Albums, Songs, Genres, Composers, Compilations, or Audiobooks (and also Podcasts and iTunes U, which I leave for Chapter 13). You can flick to browse lists and tap the menu bar at the top of any list to return to the top. Swipe right to return to the previous menu (and continue swiping right to return to the Home screen).

To choose a playlist on an iPod nano, tap Playlists on the Music screen, and then tap a playlist title in the list of playlists to see a list of songs in the playlist. Tap a song title to start playing the song.

Follow these steps with an iPod classic to locate a song by artist and then by album:

1. **Choose Music from the iPod main menu.**

2. **From the Music menu that appears, choose Artists.**

3. **Select an artist from the Artists menu.**

    The artist names are listed in alphabetical order by last name or the first word of a group. Scroll the Artists menu until the artist name is highlighted, and then press the Select button. The artist's menu of albums appears. (You can also select All Albums at the top of the Artists menu to go directly to the Albums menu.)

4. **Choose All Songs or the name of an album from the artist's menu.**

    You can find All Songs at the top of the artist's menu. Press the Select button to choose it or scroll until an album name is highlighted; then press the Select button. A song list appears after you choose either an album or All Songs.

5. **Select a song from the list.**

    The songs in the album list are in *album order* (the order that they appear on the album); in the All Songs list, songs are listed in album order for each album.

To choose an album directly on an iPod classic, choose Albums from the Music menu. The Albums menu appears, displaying albums in alphabetical order. Choose an album from the Albums menu. Then select a song from the list.

To locate a song on an iPod classic, choose Songs from the Music menu, and then select a song from the Songs menu. To choose a playlist, choose Playlists from the Music menu, select a playlist from the list, and then select a song to start playing the playlist from that song forward. The songs in the playlist are in *playlist order* (the order defined for the playlist when you created it in iTunes or on your iPod).

To find out how to create playlists on your iPod classic or iPod nano, see "Tips on Using iPods and iPhones" in the free tips section of the author's website (www.tonybove.com/tips).

In search of the lost chord

If you don't like the music, go out and make some yourself! You can look for the chord the guitar player is playing in a song, and you can try to play it yourself on your iPod touch. The App Store is loaded with musical gear and instruments, but you can't go wrong with Apple's very own GarageBand ($4.99), an app that turns your iPod touch into a virtual instrument and a recording studio. You can play and record guitar, bass, drums, and keyboard with your fingers on the iPod touch screen. (See the following figures.) GarageBand even offers classic amps and stompbox effects. And the music doesn't have to sound like it came from a garage — you can conduct a large string orchestra with your finger using its Smart Strings feature.

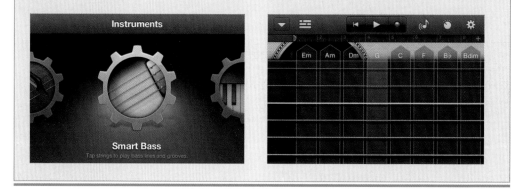

Controlling Song Playback on an iPod touch

To play a song on an iPod touch, tap the song title or the Play button in Cover Flow. When the song finishes, the iPod plays the next song in the sequence that appeared in the list you chose it from. For example, if you chose a song in the Songs screen, the next song would be the next one in sequence in the Songs screen. If you chose the last song on an album in the Albums screen, the iPod stops after playing it. If you chose a song from a playlist on the Playlists screen, the next song would be the next one in the playlist, and after playing the last song, it also stops playing, as with an album. (See the "Repeating songs" section, later in this chapter, to find out how to repeat albums and playlists.)

Whenever you play a song, you see the album cover associated with the song on the Now Playing screen, along with buttons for playback control — previous/rewind, play/pause, and next/fast-forward. (See Figure 12-3, left and right sides.) Slide your finger along the volume slider at the bottom of the display to change the volume. You also see more buttons and the scrubber bar for navigating through the song. (On a fourth-generation iPod touch, tap the cover art or anyplace under the album title while a song is playing to show more buttons and lyrics.)

You can tap the cover art to see lyrics, if lyrics are available in the iTunes information (to discover how to add lyrics to your song information, read about editing the song information in Chapter 9). The option to show lyrics is turned on by default. If you want to turn off the display of lyrics, choose Settings⇨Music from the Home screen, and tap the On button for the Lyrics & Podcast Info option to turn it off.

Tap the next/fast-forward button once to play the next song in sequence, and tap the previous/rewind button once at the beginning of a song, or twice during the song, to play the previous song. You can fast-forward through a song by touching and holding down the next/fast-forward button, and you can rewind a song by touching and holding down the previous/rewind button.

You can tap the list button in the upper-right corner if you want to display a list of the album's contents. You can then tap the title of another song on the album to start playing that song.

To return to menus and make other selections when playing a song, tap the left-arrow button in the upper-left corner of the display.

Figure 12-3: The Now Playing screen (left); tap the cover to show lyrics (right).

To skip to any point in a song, drag the playhead along the scrubber bar. To start a song over from the beginning, drag the playhead on the scrubber bar all the way to the left or tap the previous/rewind button once.

If you're viewing another content menu on the iPod touch, tap Now Playing at the top-right corner of the display to go directly to the Now Playing display.

You can control music playback while the iPod touch is locked — double-click the physical Home button to see the playback controls on the screen. You can also control music playback while using another app — double-click the physical Home button, and then flick left to right along the bottom row to see the Music app's music controls. Tap the Music icon to go back to the Music app. See Chapter 3 to find out more about using the Home button double-click to multitask your apps and lock the display orientation to portrait.

If you have on your Wi-Fi network an AirPlay speaker system or Apple TV (which supports AirPlay), you can play music wirelessly from your iPod touch over AirPlay.

For details on playing content on AirPlay speakers or Apple TV, see "Tips on Using iPods and iPhones" in the free tips section of the author's website (www.tonybove.com/tips).

Downloading songs from iTunes Match

While you can play any song in your iTunes Match library while connected to the Internet, what about when you aren't connected? You can download the songs from iTunes Match first, before disconnecting from the Internet.

Choose a playlist or an album as I describe in the earlier section, "Browsing music on an iPod touch." For a playlist, scroll the screen to the bottom to see the download button, which is a cloud icon with a down-arrow, as shown in Figure 12-4 (left side). Tap the download button to download the entire playlist. For an album, tap the download button that appears at the top of the album list, as shown in Figure 12-4 (right side). As the songs download, a progress circle appears next to each song. When the progress circle completes for a song, it disappears — the song is now on your iPod touch.

Repeating songs

If you want to drive yourself crazy repeating the same song over and over, your iPod touch is happy to oblige. (You might want to try repeating "They're Coming to Take Me Away, Ha-Haaa" by Napoleon XIV, a favorite from the old *The Dr. Demento Show* radio broadcasts — and perhaps they will come to take you away.) More than likely, you'll want to repeat a playlist or album, which you can easily do.

Download   Download

Figure 12-4: Tap the download button for a playlist (left) and for an album (right).

Tap underneath the left-arrow button or the album title while a song is play-ing. The repeat and shuffle buttons appear, along with the scrubber bar and lyrics, directly below the top row of buttons. (Refer to Figure 12-3, right side.)

Ordinarily when a song finishes, the iPod touch plays the next song in the sequence that appeared in the list on the screen you chose it from. When it reaches the end of that list, it stops — if you chose the last song on an album in the Albums screen, the iPod touch stops after playing it. But if you tap the repeat button once while the songs are playing, the entire sequence repeats. If you chose an album, the album repeats; if you chose a playlist, the playlist repeats.

After you tap the repeat button once to repeat the sequence of songs, the repeat button is highlighted. Tap the repeat button again to repeat only the current song — the highlighted button changes to include the numeral 1. Tap it once more to return to normal playback.

Shuffling song order

Maybe you want your song selections to be surprising and unpredictable, or you just want your iPod touch to mess with your mind. You can *shuffle* song playback to play songs in random order, just like an automated radio station without a disk jockey or program guide.

You can just shake your iPod touch, and it shuffles the songs in the album you are playing. By default, your iPod touch is set to shuffle when shaken (not stirred). To turn this off, choose Settings➪Music from the Home screen, and touch On for the Shake to Shuffle option to turn it off. You pretty much have to do this if you want to listen to your iPod when you work out.

You can also set your iPod touch to shuffle songs across your library. The shuffle algorithm is as random as it gets (not taking into account a fundamental tenet of chaos theory that says a pattern will emerge). When an iPod touch creates a shuffle, it reorders the songs (like shuffling a deck of cards) and plays them in the new order.

To turn your iPod touch into a random song player, choose Music from the Home screen and tap the Songs icon at the bottom of the display. The song list appears, with Shuffle at the top of the list. Tap Shuffle to turn on Shuffle.

You can set an iPod touch to shuffle any album or playlist *before* playing it. First, select the playlist or album; then tap Shuffle at the top of the list of songs for that playlist or album.

You can also shuffle songs within an album or playlist, which gives you some control over random playback. For example, you can create a playlist for all jazz songs and shuffle the songs within that jazz playlist. To shuffle songs in an album or playlist, start playing a song in the album or playlist, and then tap the cover art or anyplace under the album title while a song is playing. The repeat and shuffle buttons appear, along with the scrubber bar, directly below the top row of buttons (refer to Figure 12-3, right side). Tap the shuffle button to shuffle songs within the currently playing album or playlist.

Are your songs shuffling (or repeating) against your wishes? You may have tapped the repeat and/or shuffle buttons by mistake (it's easy to do, just by brushing your finger across the screen). The repeat and shuffle buttons are directly below the top row of buttons (refer to Figure 12-3, right side). If either (or both) buttons are highlighted, tap them to turn them off.

Want to repeat an entire album or playlist but still shuffle the playing order each time you hear it? Start playing a song in the album or playlist, and then set your iPod touch to repeat all the songs in the album or playlist, as described in the preceding section, "Repeating songs." Then set the iPod touch to shuffle the songs, as described in this section.

Controlling Song Playback on an iPod nano

Playback on the iPod nano is slick and easy. Browse music, as I describe in the "Browsing music on an iPod nano or iPod classic" section, earlier in this chapter, and tap a song title. The Now Playing screen appears. If you're already playing or have paused a song, you can reach the Now Playing screen by tapping Music on the Home screen, and then tapping Now Playing at the top of the Music screen.

The album artwork for the current song appears on the Now Playing screen — tap the artwork to show the play/pause, previous/rewind, and fast-forward/next song controls, as shown in Figure 12-5, along with the Repeat, Genius, and Shuffle icons and the scrubber bar. Lyrics appear below the controls (if you added them in iTunes).

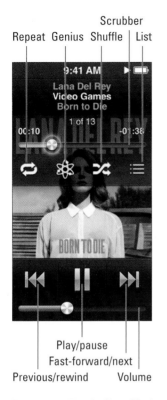

Repeat Genius Shuffle | List

Scrubber

Play/pause |
Fast-forward/next |
Previous/rewind   Volume

Figure 12-5: Tap the Now Playing artwork to see controls.

To pause playback, tap the play/pause control (or disconnect your earphones). To start playing again, tap the play/pause control again. Tap the fast-forward/next control once to play the next song in sequence, and tap the previous/rewind control once at the beginning of a song, or twice during the song, to play the previous song. You can fast-forward through a song by touching and holding down the fast-forward/next control, and you can rewind a song by touching and holding down the previous/rewind control.

You can tap the list button on the first Now Playing screen (refer to Figure 12-5) to display a list of the album's contents. You can then tap the title of another song on the album to start playing that song. To return to menus and make other selections when playing a song, swipe right.

To skip to any point in a song, drag the playhead along the scrubber bar on the Now Playing screen. See the earlier sections, "Repeating songs" and "Shuffling song order," to find out more about the Repeat and Shuffle icons, and see the later section, "Consulting the iTunes Genius," to discover more about using the Genius icon.

You can cross-fade songs on an iPod nano, just like in iTunes (as I describe in Chapter 10). A *cross-fade* creates a smooth transition from the ending of one song to the beginning of the next one. To set your iPod nano to cross-fade songs, tap Settings⇨Music from the second Home screen, and tap the Off button next to Audio Crossfade in the list to turn it on. (Tap On to turn it off.)

Controlling Song Playback on an iPod classic

To play a song on an iPod classic, browse for music and scroll the list to high-light the song title, and then press either the select button or the play/pause button to play the selected song.

While a song is playing, the artist name and song name appear on the Now Playing screen, along with the album cover and a progress bar. To pause playback, press the play/pause button while a song is playing. To stop play-ing a song, press the play/pause button again (the same button).

To skip to any point in a song, press the select button to reveal the scrubber bar. Scroll the click wheel to move the playhead across the scrubber bar for-ward (to the right) or backward (to the left) in the song.

Press the select button multiple times to cycle through the options: scrub-ber bar, Genius start button, rating bullets, shuffle settings, and lyrics (if you typed them in for the song, as I explain in Chapter 9, or if they were included with a downloaded song). After the rating bullets appear, scroll the click wheel to add a rating to the song. For details on the Genius feature, see the later section "Consulting the iTunes Genius," and to find out how to shuffle, see the earlier section "Shuffling song order."

Press the fast-forward/next button once to play the next song in sequence, and press the previous/rewind button once at the beginning of a song, or twice during the song, to play the previous song. You can fast-forward through a song by pressing and holding down the fast-forward/next button, and rewind a song by pressing and holding down the previous/rewind button.

To start a song over from the beginning, press the previous/rewind button once.

While playing a song, you can browse the album or its artist, as well as assign the song to an On-The-Go playlist or Genius playlist. Press and hold the select button, and a menu appears with the following choices: Start Genius, Add to On-The-Go, Browse Album, Browse Artist, and Cancel. Scroll the click wheel to choose an option.

To return to the menus and make other selections when playing a song, press the Menu button or press and hold the select button until a menu appears on top of the cover art.

You can cross-fade songs on an iPod classic, just like in iTunes (as I describe in Chapter 10). A *cross-fade* creates a smooth transition from the ending of one song to the beginning of the next one. To set your iPod classic to cross-fade songs, choose Settings⇨Playback⇨Audio Crossfade from the main menu and press Select to turn it on. (Press select again to turn it off.)

Repeating iPod classic songs

You can set your iPod classic to repeat a single song, or to repeat all the songs in the selected album or playlist, by following these steps:

1. **Locate and play a song.**

2. **While the song plays, press the Menu button repeatedly to return to the main menu, and then choose the Settings menu.**

3. **Scroll the Settings menu until Repeat is highlighted.**

    The Repeat setting displays Off, One, or All next to it.

4. **Press the select button until the setting changes to One to repeat one song or All to repeat all the songs in the album or playlist (or Off to turn Repeat off).**

    If you press the button more than you need to, keep pressing until the setting you want reappears. The button cycles among the Off, One, and All settings.

You can also press the previous/rewind button to repeat a song.

Shuffling the iPod classic

To turn your iPod classic into a random song player, choose Shuffle Songs from the main menu.

To shuffle songs in an album or a playlist, or to shuffle albums, follow these steps:

1. **Choose Settings from the main menu and scroll to Shuffle.**

    The Shuffle setting displays Off next to it.

2. **Press the select button once (Off changes to Songs) to shuffle the songs in the next album or playlist you play. Press select again (Songs changes to Albums) to shuffle the albums without shuffling the songs within each album.**

When you set Shuffle to Songs, the iPod classic shuffles songs within the currently playing playlist or album, or if nothing is playing, the next album or playlist you choose to play. When you set Shuffle to Albums, it plays all the songs on the currently playing album (or the next album you play) in order, and then randomly selects another album in the list and plays through it in order.

If you press the select button more than you need to, keep pressing until the setting you want reappears. The button cycles among the Off, Songs, or Albums settings.

Playing an iPod shuffle

Speaking of shuffling, the *iPod shuffle* is a special iPod designed with song shuffling foremost in mind — it offers no display or menus for selecting specific songs or albums by title. The idea is to use iTunes to sync songs, audio books, and podcasts — as well as playlists of these elements — on the iPod shuffle (as I describe in Chapter 7), clip it to your clothes or something, put earbuds or headphones in your ears, and listen.

You can use the front-panel controls on a fourth-generation iPod shuffle to control playback, or use the Apple-supplied earbud's remote controller with third-generation models. The VoiceOver button on the top of the fourth-generation iPod shuffle tells you the name of the song you're playing (as well as your battery status) and lets you choose from a spoken menu of playlists — VoiceOver also works with the earbud's remote controller for third-generation models.

Starting playback

The iPod shuffle has a three-position switch on the top for playing songs in playlist order, for shuffling songs randomly, and for turning it off. To start playing songs, plug in the earbuds into the iPod shuffle and place them in your ears, and slide the three-position switch from Off to Play in Order (the icon with arrows chasing each other in a closed loop) or Shuffle (the icon showing arrows crossed).

Playback starts as soon as you turn the three-way switch away from Off — to indicate this, the iPod shuffle status light blinks green once. However, if the iPod shuffle is already playing before you plug in your earbuds, playback may stop. To start playback, press the play button (the center button) on the iPod shuffle, or press the play button on the remote controller (or toggle the three-way switch to Off and back to Play in Order or Shuffle).

Controlling playback

To pause playback, press the play/pause button in the center (or the earbud remote controller's center button) once. The iPod shuffle status light blinks green for 30 seconds.

To go forward to the next track, press the fast-forward/next button, which is to the right of the play button, once — the status light blinks green once. (With an earbud remote controller, press the center button twice quickly.) To fast-forward through the current track to the next track, press and hold the fast-forward/next button.

To go back to the previous track, press the previous/rewind button on the left of the play button once (or press the center button of the earbud remote controller three times) — the status light blinks green once. To rewind through the current track to its beginning and then to the previous track, press and hold the previous/rewind button.

If you set the three-position switch to Play in Order, going backward or forward navigates in the order the songs were copied to the iPod shuffle or the order within each playlist. However, if you set the position switch to Shuffle, the playing order is randomized first. Then going backward skips backward within the shuffle order, and going forward skips forward within the shuffle order. For example, suppose your iPod shuffle plays the 14th song, then the 5th song, and then the 20th song. In that case, pressing the previous/rewind button within the first 6 seconds of the 20th song takes you back to the 5th song, and pressing it again takes you back to the 14th song. From there, pressing the fast-forward/next button skips through the songs in the same order again: the 14th song, the 5th song, and then the 20th song.

Using VoiceOver

If you enabled VoiceOver for your iPod shuffle in iTunes when you set it up (as I describe in Chapter 2) or enable it now as you synchronize your iPod shuffle (as I describe in this section), you can hear the iPod shuffle speak song titles and artist names, a menu of playlists for you to choose from, and the status of your battery charge. (With a third-generation iPod shuffle, you need the Apple Earphones with Remote and Mic or the In-Ear Headphones with Remote and Mic to use VoiceOver to navigate playlists.)

The iPod touch also offers VoiceOver as part of the accessibility features to make it easier to use for people with visual, auditory, or other physical disabilities. (You can turn the accessibility features on or off by choosing Settings⇨General⇨Accessibility from the Home screen.) To discover all about VoiceOver and the gestures you need to use to operate the feature on your iPod touch, see "Tips on Using iPods and iPhones" in the free tips section of the author's website (www.tonybove.com/tips).

To enable VoiceOver, sync your iPod shuffle to iTunes. The Summary page of sync options appears — you may have to scroll it to see all the options. Under Voice Feedback, as shown in Figure 12-6, select the Enable VoiceOver check box to turn it on (or deselect it to turn it off). With an iPod shuffle, you have the option to choose the language you want from the Language pop-up menu. This sets the language for spoken messages and playlist names, as well as many of the song titles and artist names. You can also limit the maximum volume of your iPod shuffle by selecting the Limit Maximum Volume option and dragging the volume setting underneath the option (and you can then lock this maximum volume by clicking the lock icon). Finally, click the Apply button to apply these settings.

To hear the title and artist of the song, press the VoiceOver button on the top of the fourth-generation iPod shuffle (or press and hold the center button of the earbud's remote controller for a third-generation iPod shuffle — and if you press the center button twice quickly to go to the next track, the next message plays as well).

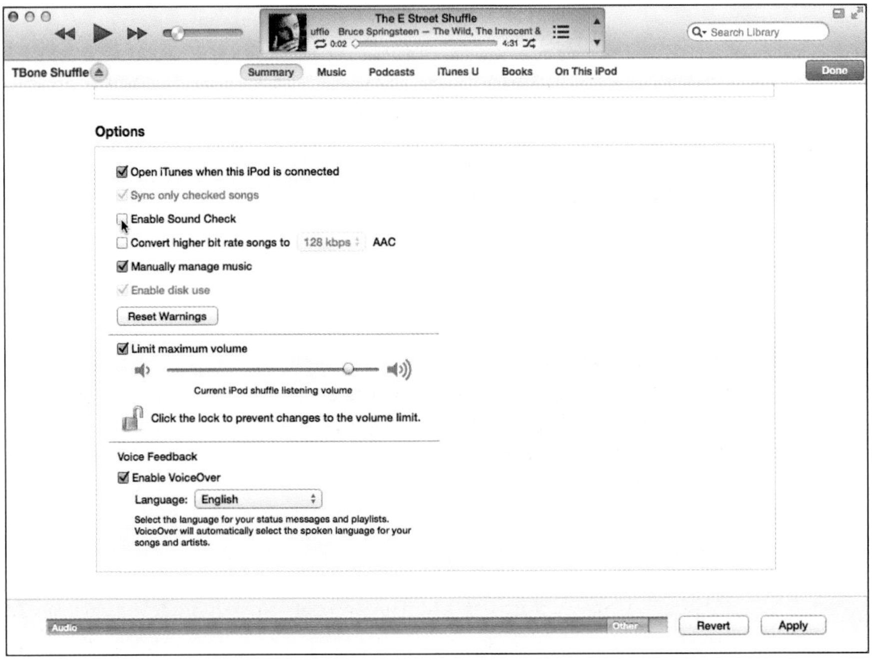

Figure 12-6: iPod shuffle sync settings.

On a fourth-generation iPod shuffle, you can navigate after pressing the VoiceOver button to hear the info about the next or previous track. While a track is playing, press fast-forward/next to skip to the next track and hear its info; press previous/rewind to move to the previous track and hear its info. If the iPod shuffle is paused when you do this, you can immediately press the VoiceOver button or play/pause button to play the track you navigated to.

To hear the playlist menu, press and hold the VoiceOver button (or the center button of the earbud's remote controller for a third-generation iPod shuffle) until you hear the names of playlists. The playlist menu announces the current playlist (if one is playing), All Songs, other playlists in alphabetical order, Genius Mixes, podcasts, iTunes U collections, and finally audio book titles. As you listen to the playlist menu, you can press the fast-forward/next or previous/rewind button to move forward or backward in the playlist menu. After hearing the item you want, press the VoiceOver or play/pause button (or the center button of the earbud's remote controller once) to select it. If you don't want to choose anything from the playlist menu, you can exit by pressing and holding the VoiceOver button (or center button of the earbud controller).

 If you've synced an iPod shuffle with the VoiceOver option turned on, iTunes adds a new option to the Options tab of the Get Info dialog: VoiceOver Language. You can use it to pick a different language for specific songs. After selecting the songs in iTunes, choose File⇨Get Info, click the Options tab, and then choose a language from the VoiceOver Language pop-up menu. Click the OK button to finish.

Consulting the iTunes Genius

Your iPod can also be a "genius" about picking songs. If you don't want to go through the process of selecting songs, just select one song and tap the Genius button. If you've already given Genius a lesson in your tastes, as I describe in this section, your iPod takes a look at whatever song you select and creates a playlist of songs already on the device that go along with it.

Giving Genius a lesson in your tastes

With an Internet connection, the Genius feature in iTunes works with the iTunes Store to match up your tastes to other iTunes users using a technique called *collaborative filtering*. The Genius software working behind the scenes in the store analyzes the music and video in other people's iTunes libraries — people who also have the same song or video you selected (if they also turn on the Genius feature in iTunes). The Genius feature informs the online store about the items you select in your iTunes library. You can then use the options menu next to a song or video, described in Chapter 10, to show music and video that other listeners purchased when they purchased the items you're playing. All this information is shared anonymously.

You can use the Genius feature in your iPod touch if you have an Internet connection and set it up to share information, as I describe in Chapter 2. For the Genius feature to work in your iPod, you must first give iTunes permission to scan your music library and catalog your iTunes collection, and then you need to sync your iPod (as I describe in Chapter 7). The scanning process may take a few minutes or (for very large collections) a few hours, but you can continue using iTunes while it scans your music. To allow the Genius feature to work, choose Preferences (from the iTunes menu on a Mac or the Edit menu on a Windows PC), click the Store tab, and make sure that the Share Details About Your Library with Apple option is selected.

If you don't have an iTunes Store account yet, select the Create a New iTunes Store Account option and see Chapter 6 for further instructions on creating an account.

If you add new music to your iTunes library, you can tell iTunes to immediately update the Genius feature with new information by choosing Store⇨Update Genius.

In your iPod, the Genius feature recognizes the song or video you selected, but you must have enough songs or videos on your iPod that are in the same genre, so that the Genius collaborative filtering technique has a large enough sample to match them.

Creating a Genius playlist on an iPod touch

To create a Genius playlist on your iPod touch, choose Music from the Home screen and follow these steps:

1. **Locate and start playing a song to base the Genius playlist on.**

   The Now Playing screen appears when the song is playing.

2. **Tap the Now Playing screen to see the control buttons.**

   Tap underneath the left-arrow button or the album title while a song is playing. The repeat, Genius, and shuffle buttons appear underneath the scrubber bar directly below the top row of buttons. (Refer to Figure 12-3, right side.) The Genius button is the one in the center sporting the atom icon.

3. **Tap the Genius button.**

   The Genius Playlist screen appears with New, Refresh, and Save buttons at the top. You can flick your finger to scroll the list. Tap any song to start playing the playlist from that song. If you navigate to other screens, you can return to the Genius playlist by tapping Genius Playlist in the Playlists menu.

4. **(Optional) Refresh the Genius playlist by tapping Refresh.**

   Refreshing a playlist changes it to include different songs based on the same song you played (depending on how many similar songs you have in your iPod touch).

5. **Save the Genius playlist by tapping Save.**

   The playlist is saved in the Playlists section of your iPod touch using the title of the song it is based on. The playlist is copied back to your iTunes library when you sync your iPod touch. That's all you need to do — the next steps are optional.

   If you subsequently refresh a saved Genius playlist before syncing, the saved playlist is refreshed and you lose the previous version of it.

6. **(Optional) Create a new Genius playlist by tapping New and selecting a new song to base it on.**

   After you tap New, the song list appears for selecting a song. Choose a song, and your iPod touch creates a new Genius playlist and starts playing the song, displaying the Now Playing screen.

7. **(Optional) After Step 6, return to the Genius playlist by tapping the left-arrow button in the top-left corner of the Now Playing screen.**

You can refresh any Genius playlist, whether you created it in iTunes and synced to your iPod touch or you created it directly on your iPod touch. Select the playlist and tap Refresh at the top of the list (or tap Delete to delete the list).

You can set an iPod touch to create a Genius playlist based on a song *before* you actually start playing the song itself. Just choose Music from the Home screen, tap Playlists, and then tap Genius Playlist at the top of the list of playlists, and a list of songs appears. Your iPod touch creates a Genius playlist based on it and starts playing the song you selected. To return to the Genius playlist, tap the left-arrow button on the Now Playing screen.

Creating a Genius playlist on an iPod nano

To create a Genius playlist on an iPod nano, follow these steps:

1. **Locate and start playing a song to base the Genius playlist on.**

   The Now Playing screen appears when the song is playing.

2. **Tap the Now Playing screen to see the control buttons (refer to Figure 12-5).**

   The repeat, Genius, and shuffle buttons appear. The Genius button is the one in the center sporting the atom icon.

3. **Tap the Genius button.**

   The Genius playlist appears based on the song you were playing, with Refresh and Save buttons at the top. You can flick your finger to scroll the list. Tap any song to start playing the playlist from that song.

4. **(Optional) Refresh the Genius playlist by tapping Refresh.**

   Refreshing a playlist changes it to include different songs based on the same song you played (depending on how many similar songs you have in your iPod nano).

5. **Save the Genius playlist by tapping Save.**

   The playlist is saved in the Playlists list using the title of the song it is based on. The playlist is copied back to your iTunes library when you sync your iPod nano.

If you subsequently refresh a saved Genius playlist before syncing, the saved playlist is refreshed and you lose the previous version of it.

To delete an existing Genius playlist already saved by name, select the playlist, flick down, and then tap Delete at the top of the list.

Creating a Genius playlist on an iPod classic

To create a Genius playlist on an iPod classic, follow these steps:

1. **Locate and start playing a song to base the Genius playlist on.**

   The Now Playing screen appears when the song is playing.

2. **Press and hold the select button until a menu appears on top of the Now Playing screen.**

3. **Choose Start Genius and press the select button.**

   The new Genius playlist appears, with Refresh and Save Playlist at the top of the list. Scroll the list to see all the songs, and then select any song to start playing the playlist associated with that song.

4. **(Optional) Refresh the Genius playlist by selecting Refresh at the top of the Genius playlist.**

   Refreshing a playlist changes it to include different songs based on the same song you played (depending on how many similar songs you have in your iPod).

5. **(Optional) Save the Genius playlist by selecting Save Playlist (under Refresh at the top of the Genius playlist).**

   The playlist is saved in the playlists section of your iPod using the title of the song it is based on. The playlist syncs automatically with your iTunes library the next time you connect your iPod and sync it (as I describe in Chapter 7).

If you subsequently refresh a saved Genius playlist, the saved playlist is refreshed and you lose the previous version of it.

Selecting Genius Mixes

Genius Mixes are generated by iTunes from songs in your library that go great together. Genius Mixes are synced automatically if you sync every-thing to your iPod, or you can sync specific Genius Mixes as playlists — see Chapter 7 to find out how to sync by playlist.

To play your Genius Mixes on your iPod touch, choose Music from the Home screen and tap the Genius icon in the lower-left corner. On an iPod nano, choose Music from the Home screen and tap Genius Mixes at the top of the Music screen.

On an iPod touch or iPod nano, you can flick with your finger left or right to browse the Genius Mixes — the dots at the bottom of the Genius Mixes screen indicate how many Genius Mixes are synced to your iPod touch or iPod nano. To start playing a Genius Mix, tap the play arrow in the middle of the screen for a Genius Mix.

Find out all about adjusting and limiting the volume of your iPod and tweak-ing the sound with the iPod equalizer and other sound options in "Tips on Using iPods and iPhones" in the free tips section of the author's website (www.tonybove.com/tips).

13

Bring Videos, Books, and Podcasts

In This Chapter

▷ Playing movies and TV shows

▷ Listening to the iPod nano's FM radio

▷ Playing podcasts and audio books

*T*he Buggles sang "Video Killed the Radio Star," but both videos and music coexist quite nicely on your iPod touch or iPod classic, which is not only a fantastic music player but also a terrific video player, with crisp, clear picture quality. Video can appear horizontally on an iPod touch screen (in what's known as *landscape mode*), and if you rotate it 180 degrees to the opposite horizontal position, the video adjusts accordingly. All the controls you expect in a DVD player are right on the screen at the touch of a finger.

You can also play audio books and podcasts on this multimedia machine, and the iPod nano can even play FM radio. The iTunes Store offers an amazing selection of TV shows, movies, audio books, iTunes U courses, and podcasts. (See Chapter 6.) This chapter shows you how to control video playback, skip forward or backward, and scale the picture to fit your screen.

Everything's Coming Up Videos

Movies, TV shows, and music videos are easy to locate and play on an iPod touch with the supplied Videos app. Videos you purchase from the iTunes Store are ready to use, but videos you bring in from other sources may have to be converted first for use on your iPod touch. You can tell if a video needs to be converted by selecting the video in iTunes and checking the Advanced menu: The Create iPod or iPhone version option is grayed out.

To convert a video using iTunes, select the video and choose Advanced⇨Create iPod or iPhone Version.

You can use a variety of applications to convert your video, such as Handbrake (`http://handbrake.fr`) for Mac or Windows, which converts formats not supported by iTunes and can even convert video from a DVD.

To find out more about why videos need to be converted and how to prepare your own videos and convert imported videos for use with an iPod touch, see Bonus Chapter 2 in the free tips section of the author's website (`www.tonybove.com/tips`).

Playback at your fingertips on an iPod touch

To locate and play a video on your iPod touch, follow these steps:

1. **Tap the Videos app on the iPod touch Home screen.**

2. **Scroll the Videos screen to see the sections for Movies, TV Shows, and Music Videos.**

   The video titles are listed in alphabetical order within these sections.

3. **Tap the title of an item to play it.**

Tap the screen to show video controls (as shown in Figure 13-1). You can tap again to hide them. Tap the play/pause button while a video is playing to pause the playback. To raise or lower the volume, drag the volume slider along the bottom of the screen. (See Figure 13-1.)

Figure 13-1: Tap the screen to use playback controls.

You can fast-forward through a video by touching and holding down the fast-forward/next button, and you can rewind a video by touching and holding down the previous/rewind button. To skip to any point in a video, drag the playhead along the scrubber bar. To start a video over from the beginning, drag the playhead on the scrubber bar all the way to the left or tap the previous/rewind button (if the video doesn't contain chapters).

If the video contains chapters, you can skip to the previous or next chapter by tapping the previous/rewind or fast-forward/next button. To start playing at a specific chapter, tap the bullet-list button that appears in the top-right corner — but remember, this trick works only if the original video was set up to contain chapters.

If you have an AirPlay-compatible speaker system (such as the Denon Cocoon speaker docks [http://airplayspeakers.com/denon-cocoon-speaker-docks] or the Marantz NR1602 AV Receiver [http://airplay speakers.com/marantz-nr1602-av-receiver]), you can play the sound wirelessly from your iPod touch. If you have an Apple TV, you can also play video wirelessly. To discover how, see "Tips on Using iPods and iPhones" in the free tips section of the author's website (www.tonybove.com/tips).

To stop watching a video before it finishes playing, tap the Done button in the upper-left corner of the display or press the Home button on the device.

If a video offers an alternative audio language or subtitles, a Subtitles button appears. Tap the Subtitles button and choose a language from the Audio list or a language from the Subtitles list, or tap On to turn off subtitles.

Videos are automatically set to remember the playback position when you pause. This feature lets you pause a video or TV episode in iTunes while you synchronize your iPod touch. After syncing, you can continue playing the video or episode on your iPod touch from where you paused. This feature also works in reverse: If you start playing a video on your iPod touch and pause it, and then you sync it with iTunes, the video retains the playback position so that you can continue playing it in iTunes from where you paused.

You can delete a video directly from your iPod touch by flicking left or right across the video selection in the Videos menu and tapping the Delete button that appears. If your video is still in your iTunes library, you can sync the video with the iPod touch again or copy the video back to it manually (as I explain in Chapter 7). If you delete a *rented* movie from the iPod touch, it's deleted permanently.

Scaling the picture on an iPod touch

Videos can be displayed in either portrait or landscape mode on your iPod touch, and in widescreen format if they were released as widescreen format. You can also scale the video picture to fill the screen or to fit entirely within the screen. Tap the scale button in the upper-right corner of the screen (refer to Figure 13-1) or double-tap the video picture to switch from one to the other. The scale button shows two arrows facing away from each other (as in Figure 13-1) when the picture fits entirely within the screen. The two arrows face toward each other when the picture fills the screen edge-to-edge.

All you have to do is stream

If you're a stream lover (like I am), you can find streaming web radio stations and video streams using iPod touch apps such as ABC Player and Hulu (TV shows), Netflix (TV shows and movies), Pandora and Spotify (streaming music), CBS Sports (live games), and Truveo (TV stations). Your iPod touch needs to be connected to Wi-Fi and the Internet to stream video — see Chapter 4 to get set up.

The ABC Player (see the following figures) streams TV shows featured on the ABC television network, gives you a list of the most popular shows, and also provides information about shows playing on the network (including a schedule).

Pandora lets you type the name of an artist, song, or composer, and it creates a custom station that streams to your iPod touch the music you chose — and more music like it. You can tap the thumbs-up or thumbs-down buttons to let Pandora know your musical tastes.

CBS Sports NCAA March Madness on Demand streams live video of every game from the NCAA Division I Men's Basketball Championship.

And with Truveo, it's easy to search for streaming video across sites that include NBC, CNN, The Disney Channel, HBO, Discovery Channel, Comedy Central, PBS, MTV, The Wall Street Journal, YouTube, and Dailymotion; and to browse featured videos, top searches, channels, or categories.

Filling the screen may crop the sides or the top and bottom of the picture to give you a larger view of the center of the picture. Fitting entirely within the screen assures that the entire picture is shown, but you may see black bars on the sides (pillarboxing) or top and bottom (letterboxing).

Playback under your thumb on an iPod classic

The video playback controls on an iPod classic work the same way as with songs — you use precisely the same buttons, in other words. Scroll the click wheel to adjust the volume as you would for a song (as I describe in Chapter 12).

To pause playback, press the play/pause button while a video is playing. To start again, press play/pause again.

To skip to any point in a video, press the select button to reveal the scrubber bar. Scroll the click wheel to move the playhead across the scrubber bar forward (to the right) or backward (to the left) in the video.

Press the fast-forward/next button once to play the next video in sequence (such as the next episode of a TV show), and press the previous/rewind button once at the beginning of a video, or twice during the video, to play the previous video in sequence. You can fast-forward through a video by pressing and holding down the fast-forward/next button, and rewind a video by pressing and holding down the previous/rewind button.

If the video contains chapters, you can skip to the previous or next chapter by pressing the previous/rewind or fast-forward/next button — but remember, this trick works only if the original video was set up to contain chapters.

To start a video over from the beginning, move the playhead on the scrubber bar all the way to the left, as previously described, or press the previous/rewind button once. To return to menus and make other selections on an iPod classic, press the Menu button.

One Chapter at a Time: Audio Books, iTunes U, and Podcasts

Audio books are, naturally, organized into chapters or parts. Podcasts and iTunes U courses are also organized into parts, called *episodes,* and they all play the same way. The audio book, course, or podcast title and episode appear on your iPod touch or iPod nano display along with its cover — similar to a book or album cover.

After syncing your audio books, courses, and podcast episodes along with the rest of your content (as I describe in glorious detail in Chapter 7), you can play them on your iPod. While podcasts and audio books play on an iPod classic, iTunes U courses play only on the iPod touch and iPod nano.

Audio books, courses, and podcasts are set to remember the playback position when you pause. If you pause your iPod and sync with iTunes, you can resume playback at that position on the iPod or in iTunes.

Playing on an iPod touch

You can find audio books on the iPod touch by tapping Music on the Home screen, and then tapping the More icon at the lower-right corner of the Music screen to see the More screen. You can then select Audiobooks on the More screen. Tap an audio book on the Audiobooks screen that appears, and then tap a chapter or part to play starting from that point. The audio book chapters or course parts are listed in proper order for each book or course.

Apple offers the Podcasts app for playing podcasts, and the iTunes U app to play iTunes U courses. To get these app, visit the App Store on your iPod touch (see Chapter 6 for details). If you don't already have these apps installed, the App Store displays a pop-up menu for installing them. You can also find them in the Apps Starter Kit section.

To play podcasts, tap the Podcasts app; to play iTunes U courses, tap the iTunes U app. If this is the first time running either app, the Sync Podcasts or Sync iTunes Courses dialog appears — tap Sync to use your Apple ID to sync podcasts or courses on your iPod touch with other iOS devices that are signed into iCloud with your Apple ID, such as an iPhone or iPad (or tap Don't Sync to skip this step).

Your synced podcasts from other iOS devices and from your iTunes library appear on the Podcasts app screen represented by their cover art. (To find out how to sync podcasts to your iPod touch using iTunes, see Chapter 7.)

Tap a podcast's cover art to see the Episodes screen, as shown in Figure 13-2 (left side). Podcast episodes are listed within each podcast in the order that they were released (by date). A blue dot appears next to any unplayed episodes; the dot is half filled in if you've played only part of an episode.

You can share a link to the podcast by tapping the options button between the Episodes screen title and the Now Playing button in the title bar (refer to Figure 13-2, left side). A sheet appears with icons for Mail (to e-mail the link), Message (to send a message with the link), Twitter (to tweet the link), Facebook (to post a status message with the link), and Copy (to copy the link so that you can paste it in another app).

Tap an episode to play it, and the playing screen appears, as shown in Figure 13-2 (center). The playing screen provides previous/rewind, play/pause, and next/fast-forward buttons for controlling playback. The screen also includes a 30-second fast-rewind button to the left of the play/pause button and a 30-second fast-forward button to the right of the play/pause button.

Figure 13-2: Tap a podcast episode (left) to play an episode (center), or search for podcasts (right).

You control the playback of an podcast episode exactly the same way as a song (see Chapter 12) — you can pause playback by tapping the play/pause button, and so on. You can control video podcasts the same way you control videos. (See the "Everything's Coming Up Videos" section, earlier in this chapter.)

To find more podcasts to play, tap Top Stations on the Episodes screen, and then drag the wheel at the top of the screen (see Figure 13-2, right side) to see podcasts in different genres.

Your synced iTunes U courses from other iOS devices and from your iTunes library appear on the iTunes U app screen represented by cover art on a bookshelf. (To discover how to sync iTunes U courses to your iPod touch using iTunes, see Chapter 7.)

Tap a course's cover art to see the course episodes. A blue dot appears next to any unplayed episodes; the dot is half filled in if you've played only part of an episode. Tap an episode to play it, and the playing screen appears with previous/rewind, play/pause, and next/fast-forward buttons for controlling playback. The screen also includes a 30-second fast-rewind button to the left of the play/pause button. You control the playback of an episode exactly the same way as a song (see Chapter 12) — you can pause playback by tapping the play/pause button, and so on.

You can control playback of podcasts in the Podcasts app, or courses in the iTunes app, while the iPod touch is locked — double-click the physical Home button to see the playback controls on the screen. You can also control playback while using another app — double-click the physical Home button, and then flick left to right along the bottom row to see the app's playback controls. Tap the Podcasts or iTunes U icon to go back to the Podcasts or iTunes U app. See Chapter 3 to find out more about using the Home button double-click to multitask your apps and lock the display orientation to portrait.

Audio books, courses, and podcasts are automatically set to remember the playback position when you pause. If you pause playback on your iPod touch and then sync with iTunes, you can resume playback at that position on either the iPod touch or in iTunes.

Playing on an iPod nano

To play audio books, podcasts, or iTunes U courses on an iPad nano, tap the Audiobooks, Podcasts, or iTunes U icons on the Home screens; tap the audio book, podcast, or iTunes U course; and then tap the chapter or episode. You can also tap Music on the Home screen and then scroll down and tap Audiobooks, Podcasts, or iTunes U on the Music screen.

You control the playback of an audio book, course, or podcast episode the same way as a song (see Chapter 12) — you can pause playback by tapping the play/pause button, and so on. You can control video podcasts the same way you control videos. (See the "Everything's Coming Up Videos" section, earlier in this chapter.)

Audio books, courses, and podcasts are automatically set to remember the playback position when you pause. If you pause playback on your iPod nano and then sync with iTunes, you can resume playback at that position on either the iPod nano or in iTunes.

Playing on an iPod classic

Podcasts, naturally, have their own menu on an iPod classic. They're organized by podcast name (which is like an album name), and podcast episodes are listed within each podcast in the order that they were released (by date).

To play a podcast episode, choose Podcasts from the iPod classic main menu. Scroll the Podcasts menu until the podcast name is highlighted and press the select button; then scroll and select an episode. A blue dot appears next to any podcast that has unplayed episodes.

To play an audio book, choose Music from the iPod classic main menu, and then Audiobooks from the Music menu. The audio book episodes (collections of chapters) are listed in the proper order for each book. Scroll the list of audio book episodes until the one you want is highlighted, and then press the select button to play it.

Playing the FM Radio in an iPod nano

The iPod nano includes an FM radio that displays station and song information for radio stations that support RDS (*R*adio *D*ata *S*ystem). If the station supports iTunes Tagging, you can tag any songs you hear for later purchase from the iTunes Store. You can also use the Live Pause feature to pause a radio broadcast and resume playing it from the same point up to 15 minutes later.

Connect your earbuds or headphones to your iPod nano first because the iPod nano uses the earbud or headphone cord as the FM radio antenna.

To hear the radio, tap Radio on the iPod nano Home screen. The radio's Now Playing screen appears with a station already selected and a radio tuner underneath the station's number, as shown in Figure 13-3. Tap the play button to hear the station. To see the Live Pause controls and radio menu button shown in Figure 13-3, tap the radio station number.

To tune the radio, you can scroll the radio tuner "dial" by flicking your finger left or right while you listen for a signal, or tap the right or left arrow buttons to jump from station to station. Tap and hold these buttons to scan stations and hear a 5-second preview of each station. To stop scanning and listen to the current station, tap either right or left arrow.

To fast-tune to local stations, tap the radio menu button (refer to Figure 13-3) to show the Radio menu, and then tap Local Stations. Your iPod nano scans the available frequencies and lists the local stations. You can then tap the tiny Play button next to a station to listen to the station without leaving the menu, or tap the station to tune to that station and return to the Now Playing screen with the live pause controls.

If you hear something you like, save a station as a favorite — tap the star icon next to the radio station number. After saving one or more favorite stations, tapping the arrow buttons while tuning takes you to the next or previous favorite station. You can also tap the radio menu button to see the Radio menu, and then tap Favorites.

Figure 13-3: Tap the radio station number on the Now Playing screen to see live pause controls.

After you tune to a station, tap the station number to see the Live Pause controls, as shown in Figure 13-3. The Live Pause progress bar appears, filling up as you continue to listen to the station. To pause the broadcast while the radio is playing, tap the play/pause button in the center. The actual time you paused appears above the progress bar. As Live Pause continues, a yellow triangle appears for your pause point in the progress bar, and the progress bar continues to fill up — showing the time that's passed since you paused. Tap play/pause again to resume the broadcast from the point you paused.

This radio is different from normal radios — with the Live Pause feature, it lets you navigate back and forth along the progress bar so that you can hear up to 15 minutes into the past. Tap the rewind 30 second button to skip back by 30 seconds, or tap the fast-forward button to move forward by 30 seconds. Drag the progress bar slider to move more freely backward and forward. To catch up to the live broadcast, drag the progress bar slider all the way to the right.

The progress bar displays as completely filled when Live Pause reaches the 15-minute limit. You can still navigate back and forth through the 15 most recent minutes, as long as your pause isn't cleared. Anything older than 15 minutes is cleared to make room for the continuing broadcast. If you pause without resuming for 15 minutes, your iPod nano goes to sleep and clears your paused radio. Changing stations or playing other media content also clears paused radio.

You may want to disable Live Pause to conserve battery power. To disable Live Pause, tap Settings on the iPod nano Home screen, tap Radio, and then tap the On button next to Live Pause to turn it off. To enable Live Pause again, tap Off to turn it back on.

Tagging a song that strikes your fancy for later purchase from the iTunes Store works great with stations that support iTunes Tagging. To tag a song you hear, tap the tag icon (refer to Figure 13-3) that appears in the upper-left corner for stations that support iTunes Tagging. Tagged songs are marked with a tag icon next to the song title, and they appear in the Radio menu under Tagged Songs (tap the radio menu button to see the Radio menu).

The next time you sync your iPod nano to iTunes, your tagged songs are synced to iTunes and removed from the iPod nano. You can preview and purchase these tagged songs by clicking Tagged in the Store section of the iTunes source pane, and then click the View button for the song you want. To preview the song, double-click it or click the Preview button. To buy the song, click the Buy button.

To turn off the FM Radio and clear paused radio, tap the square button in the center (which appears only if the radio is on). You can also display the most recently played songs on a station that supports RDS by tapping the radio menu button and choosing Recent Songs from the Radio menu.

Pocketing Your Pictures

14

The world is awash in pictures, from photos and video stills to cartoons, images, and famous paintings. For simplicity in this chapter, I refer to everything you can see as a picture — whether it be a photo, graphic image, or video clip (a moving picture).

If you like to carry pictures around with you, you're going to love the iPod nano, iPod classic, or iPod touch as a player for viewing pictures. You can also use your iPod touch to share pictures synced from your computer, and to take pictures as well. This chapter shows you how.

Syncing with Photo Albums and Folders

After you import pictures taken with a camera or your iPod touch into your computer, you can organize them into albums or collections that sync through iTunes. On a Mac, you can sync photos and videos with iPhoto (provided free as part of the iLife suite) or photos with Aperture. iPhoto lets you organize pictures by events, places, and faces as well as in albums — you can assign pictures to an event, assign locations to pictures, and assign faces to pictures; you can then browse by events, places, or faces. On a Windows PC, you can sync photos with Adobe Photoshop Elements (version 8.0 or newer).

You can then set up your iPod touch, iPod nano, or iPod classic to sync with your entire photo library or with specific photo albums in your library so that any changes you make to the library or to those photo albums are copied to the device. Additionally, any pictures you collect from e-mails on an iPod touch are synced to the photo library on your computer.

You don't have to use these applications — you can use any other photo-editing or photo-organizing software and store your photos in their own folder on your hard drive (such as the Pictures folder in your user folder on a Mac, or the My Pictures folder in your My Documents folder in Windows). You can then use iTunes to sync pictures from this folder, treating the folder as a single photo album.

If you want to organize pictures into photo albums on your iPod (without using iPhoto or Adobe Photoshop Elements), use the Finder (on a Mac) or Windows Explorer (in Windows) to create subfolders inside the folder and organize your picture files inside these subfolders. iTunes syncs the subfolder assignments as though they were album assignments. This technique is useful for Adobe Photoshop users who set up Adobe Bridge to organize images.

To find out more about organizing photos into albums, see Bonus Chapter 2 in the free tips section of the author's website (www.tonybove.com/tips).

If you turn on Photo Stream, as I describe in "Syncing photos with Photo Stream," later in this chapter, you can automatically sync photos you've just taken with your iPod touch over a wireless Internet connection with your computer and other iPads, iPod touches, and iPhones.

Transferring pictures to your iPod

You can take pictures with an iPod touch (as I show in the "Shooting Photos and Videos on an iPod touch" section, later in this chapter), but most folks already have pictures organized on their computers. To copy the pictures from your computer to your iPod using iTunes, follow these steps:

1. **Connect your iPod to your computer and click the iPod button (see Chapter 7 for details).**

   iTunes displays the Summary page (under the Summary tab of the sync pages).

2. **Click the Photos tab of the sync pages.**

   The Photos sync options appear, as shown in Figure 14-1 (on a Mac, with Sync Photos from iPhoto selected).

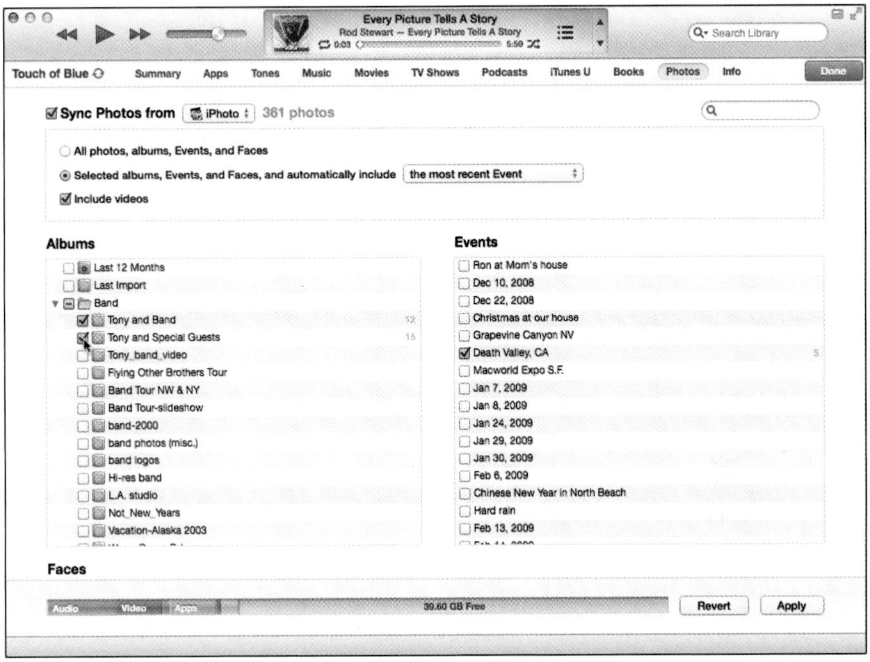

Figure 14-1: Sync photos from an iPhoto library.

3. **Select the Sync Photos From check box, and then pick the source of your photos from the pop-up menu: a photo application, the Pictures (Mac) or My Pictures (Windows) folder, or the Choose Folder option.**

   Pick your photo application (such as iPhoto on a Mac or Adobe Photoshop Elements in Windows) from the pop-up menu. If you don't use these applications, pick the Pictures folder on a Mac or the My Pictures folder on a Windows PC. If you don't use those folders for your pictures, pick Choose Folder to browse your hard drive or other storage media for the folder containing your pictures. After you select the folder, click Choose (Mac) or OK (Windows).

4. **Select all the pictures, or choose pictures organized in folders or photo albums, or select by events or faces.**

   If you're syncing photos from the Pictures (Mac) or My Pictures (Windows) folder, choose the All Photos option to copy all the pictures in the folder; or choose Selected Folders and choose subfolders in the Pictures or My Pictures folder, which are treated as photo albums by the Photos app on your iPod touch.

If you're syncing photos with an Adobe Photoshop Elements library, Aperture, or a version of iPhoto older than version 8, choose the All Photos (or All Photos and Albums) option to copy all the pictures in the library, or choose Selected Albums and choose albums.

If you're syncing with iPhoto version 8 or newer, which organizes pictures by album, events, faces, and places, select one of the following options below the Sync Photos From check box:

- *All Photos, Albums, Events, and Faces:* Select this option to copy all pictures from the library (or folder) selected in Step 3, including albums in iPhoto (or Adobe Photoshop Elements), and events and face assignments in iPhoto.

- *Selected Albums, Events, and Faces, and Automatically Include:* Select this option to be more specific about which albums, events, and/or faces to sync, and to include recent events automatically. You can choose how many recent events (or events from the last month or several months) from the pop-up menu, or choose All Events or No Events. After you select this option, you can make selections in the Albums, Events, and Faces columns.

- *Albums column:* Click the check box next to each photo album you want to sync. (In Figure 14-1, I chose the "Tony and Band" and "Tony and Special Guests" albums from the Band folder in my iPhoto library.)

- *Events column:* Click the check box next to each name or date of an event to sync the event's pictures. (In Figure 14-1, I select the Death Valley, CA event.)

- *Faces column:* Click the check box next to each face's name to sync all photos for that face.

5. **(Optional) Select the Include Videos option.**

   Select the Include Videos option to sync video clips from your iPhoto library or from your Picture or My Picture folder (iTunes doesn't sync video clips from Adobe Photoshop Elements).

6. **Click the Apply button to apply changes.**

   iTunes copies the pictures you selected to your iPod. In the process, it also deletes all other pictures from the iPod — except those saved in Camera Roll or Photo Stream on an iPod touch, as I show in the next section and in the "Using Photo Stream" section.

Syncing iPod touch pictures with your computer

The Photos app on the iPod touch stores all recently saved pictures — the pictures (photos and video clips) you take with your iPod touch, pictures that you receive via e-mail on your iPod touch, images that you tap on web pages in Safari to save, images you save from other apps, and screen images of the iPod touch screen — in a special photo album on your iPod touch called Camera Roll (or Saved Photos on previous iPod touch models without cameras).

To synchronize these new pictures with your computer's photo library, you can connect your iPod touch to your computer and use whatever application you selected in the iTunes Photos sync options described in the previous section (such as iPhoto, Adobe Photoshop Elements, or a folder). If you turn on Photo Stream, as I describe in the next section, you can synchronize new pictures with your computer wirelessly with iCloud. This section describes syncing without Photo Stream turned on.

On a Mac, if you selected iPhoto for syncing pictures, iPhoto pops up automatically. (You can set a different application, such as Aperture, to pop up for cameras in the Image Capture application's preferences). Click the Import All button, or select the pictures you want and click the Import Selected button. After you import the pictures into the iPhoto library, iPhoto asks whether you want to delete the original pictures from the iPod touch. Click Delete Photos to delete them from the iPod touch (they're safe in the photo library on your computer now) or click Keep Photos to save them on your iPod touch — in case you want to use them as wallpaper, sync them with another computer, e-mail them, or upload them to social networks from your iPod touch. (If you use Aperture rather than iPhoto, you can select the project or folder you want to put the pictures in before syncing.)

On a Windows PC, follow the instructions that came with your photo application to import the pictures from a digital camera, or use the Microsoft Scanner and Camera Wizard, which saves the pictures to a folder of your choice. (The iPod touch can trick your PC into thinking it's a digital camera.) Most applications also provide an option to delete the pictures from the camera (the iPod touch) after you import the pictures.

Using Photo Stream

With the Photo Stream feature of iCloud, the photos you take with your iPod touch are copied wirelessly to your other iOS devices (iPads, iPod touches, and iPhones) automatically. Your photo stream holds the 1,000 most recent photos for all of your devices running iOS 6 or newer, without you having to lift your shutter finger. iPhoto on a Mac (running Mountain Lion or a newer operating system) can also tap into your photo stream so that you can copy the photos to your iPhoto albums, and copy images from your iPhoto library to your iPod touch and other iOS 6 devices. iPhoto on a Mac can keep all your photo stream photos permanently.

In addition, you can create photo streams to share with other people who use devices running iOS 6 or newer, or Macs running Lion or newer. They can subscribe to the shared photo streams to see them on their devices or computers. You can also post shared photo streams in iCloud to enable others to see them on the web with a browser.

To enable Photo Stream, choose Settings⇨iCloud from the Home screen and tap the Photo Stream option to switch from Off to On. (Or choose Settings⇨Photos & Camera and tap the My Photo Stream option to switch from Off to On.) From that point on, the next 1,000 photos you take with your iPod touch are copied to the photo stream named My Photo Stream. The Shared Photo Streams option is turned on by default; to turn it off, choose Settings⇨Photos & Camera and tap the Shared Photo Streams option to switch from On to Off.

If you take a photo (or save an image) on your iPod touch, you can open My Photo Stream in the Photos app to see the photos and images from your other devices running iOS 6 or newer (and from a Mac running Lion or newer and iPhoto). On *another* iPod touch (or another device running iOS 6 or newer), you can open My Photo Stream in the Photos app and save the photos to the Camera Roll or other album in your device.

Follow these steps to open Photo Stream and save or share photos:

1. **Tap Photos from the Home screen, and then tap the Photo Stream icon in the bottom row of icons.**

   The Photo Stream screen appears with a list of shared photo streams (if any) and My Photo Stream.

2. **Tap My Photo Stream.**

   The My Photo Stream screen appears, as shown in Figure 14-2 (left side).

Figure 14-2: Open My Photo Stream (left), select photos (center), and share them (right).

3. **Tap the Edit button in the upper-right corner.**

   The Select Photos screen appears.

4. **Tap each thumbnail on the Select Photos screen, as shown in Figure 14-2 (center), to select each image you want to save or share.**

   As you tap each thumbnail, a check mark appears in the thumbnail to indicate that it is part of the selection. The Share, Save, and Delete buttons appear at the bottom of the iPod touch screen as you make a selection.

5. **Tap one of the following:**

   - *Save:* Add the selected photos to a new album. After tapping Save, tap Save to New Album or tap Cancel.

   - *Share:* Share, copy, or print the selected photos, as shown in Figure 14-2 (right side). Tap Facebook or Twitter to share over those social networks, or tap Photo Stream to create a shared photo stream. You can tap Mail or Message to send the photos by e-mail or message. You can also tap Print to print the photos wirelessly to a printer on your Wi-Fi network, Copy to copy the photos to another app or to an e-mail message, or Save to Camera Roll to save the photos to the Camera Roll on your iPod touch.

   - *Delete:* Delete the selected photos from My Photo Stream.

If you tap Share and then Photo Stream, a screen appears with a To: field for entering e-mail addresses. Enter the addresses of those who should receive an e-mail with a link to open the shared photo stream. You can tap the Name field to enter a name for the shared photo stream. You can also turn on the Public Website option (tap the Off button to turn it on) to post the photo stream in iCloud for viewing on the web. Finally, tap Create to create the shared photo stream.

If you use iPhoto on a Mac and you activate Photo Stream, you don't have to sync your iPod touch photos as I describe in the previous section — you can use iPhoto to open My Photo Stream and copy the photos to albums. If you sync your iPod touch to the computer, as I describe in the previous section, the photos already in My Photo Stream show up in iPhoto as "Already Imported" and, because they're already in your iPhoto library, you can click the Remove Photos from iPod button to remove them from your iPod touch.

Viewing Pictures and Slide Shows

You might remember the old days when you carried fading, wallet-sized photo prints, or worse, a deck of slides that required a light box or projector to show them to others. You can now dispense with all that because all you need is your iPod.

Slide shows are an especially entertaining way of showing pictures because you can include music as well as transitions between them. With an iPod touch, you can use Apple TV to show off your creation on a high-def TV. With an iPod nano or iPod classic, you can use the Composite AV Cable from Apple (available in the Apple Store).

To find out how to use Apple TV with your iPod touch, see "Tips on Using iPods and iPhones," and for details on connecting an iPod classic or iPod nano to televisions, see Bonus Chapter 4 — both are in the free tips section of the author's website (www.tonybove.com/tips).

Viewing pictures on an iPod touch

To view pictures on your iPod touch, tap Photos on the Home screen. The Photos app displays the last screen you viewed when you used the app before. If this is the first time, the Albums screen appears, as shown in Figure 14-3 (left side).

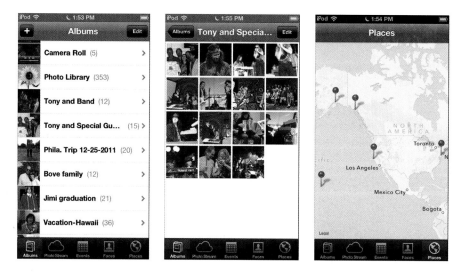

Figure 14-3: Tap a photo album (left), tap a thumbnail to see a photo (center), tap a place (right).

You can tap the Albums, Photo Stream, Events, Faces, and Places buttons to browse pictures:

- **Albums:** Albums include Camera Roll for saved pictures from e-mails and for new photos and video clips shot with the Camera app, as well as albums organized in your photo app or folders. Tap a photo album to see its pictures, or tap Photo Library to see all pictures. Thumbnail images appear, as shown in Figure 14-3 (center). Scroll the thumbnails up or down to see more of them. Tap one to view the picture.

✔ **Photo Stream:** (Appears only if Photo Stream is turned on.) This choice shows My Photo Stream and any shared photo streams you created or subscribed to. See the "Using Photo Stream" section, earlier in this chapter, for details.

✔ **Events:** Shows a list of event titles or dates with thumbnails of the first picture of each event (based on the date of pictures in iPhoto). Tap a thumbnail or the event title or date to display thumbnails of pictures from that event.

✔ **Faces:** Shows a list of faces if you've assigned faces to pictures in iPhoto. Tap a face to display thumbnails of pictures with that face, and then tap a thumbnail to view its picture.

✔ **Places:** Shows a world map, as shown in Figure 14-3 (right side) with pins of locations associated with pictures (organized by iPhoto). Tap a map pin to see a label showing how many pictures were taken at that location, and tap the label to see thumbnails of those pictures. Tap a thumbnail to view its picture.

To show the options, play buttons, and top menu, as shown in Figure 14-4 (left side), tap the photo once.

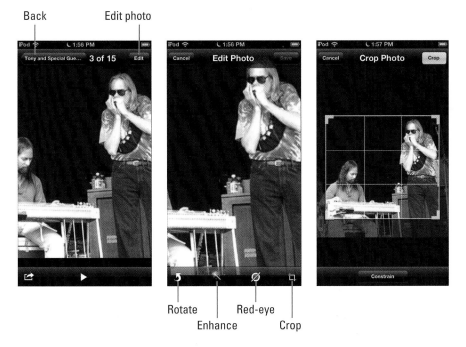

Back   Edit photo

Rotate   Red-eye

Enhance   Crop

Figure 14-4: View the option and play buttons (left), choose an edit tool (center), and crop the photo (right).

To zoom into a photo or image to see more detail, double-tap the area you want to zoom into. Double-tap again to zoom out. You can also zoom into a photo or image by unpinching with two fingers, and zoom out by pinching. To pan around a photo or image, drag it with your finger.

To view a picture in landscape orientation, rotate the iPod touch sideways. The picture automatically changes to fit the new orientation and expands to fit the screen. To move to the next picture in the album or collection, flick horizontally across the picture with your finger. You can flick across to go backward or forward through the album or collection of pictures.

If the picture is a video clip, it appears with a circled play button in the center of the picture; tap the circled play button to view the clip.

While playing the clip, you can tap the picture to see the previous and next buttons at the bottom of the picture, along with a frame viewer at the top that shows thumbnails of frames in the video clip and a scrubber bar. You can drag the scrubber bar with your finger (or tap a tiny thumbnail) to go to another position in the video clip.

Editing photos on an iPod touch

You can enhance your photos and create amazing effects using Apple's iPhoto app on an iPod touch ($4.99 at the App Store). However, you can also perform simple editing chores right in the Photos app.

To edit a photo, tap the Edit button in the upper-right corner. An editing toolbar appears under the photo, as shown in Figure 14-4 (center). You can tap the following editing tools:

- **Rotate:** Rotate the image 90 degrees counterclockwise. Keep tapping the rotate tool to continue rotating the image if you need to.

- **Enhance:** Enhance the image by increasing bright areas and sharpening dark areas.

- **Red-eye:** Tap this editing tool, and then tap an area in the image to reduce the red-eye effect that appears in eyes when a flash goes off.

- **Crop:** Tap this editing tool, and then drag the corners of the grid in the cropping screen, as shown in Figure 14-4 (right side), to limit the visible image to a rectangle that shows exactly what you want to show. To finish, tap the yellow Crop button in the top-right corner of the cropping screen.

To save the newly edited version of your photo in the Camera Roll, after you edit the photo, tap the Save button in the upper-right corner of the screen.

Setting up a slide show on an iPod touch

To set up a slide show, follow these steps:

1. **Choose Settings⟳Photos & Camera from the Home screen.**

   The Photos & Camera screen appears.

2. **Tap the Play Each Slide For option to set the duration of each slide.**

   You can select ranges from 2 to 20 seconds.

3. **Select the other options as appropriate for your slide show:**

   - *Repeat:* Repeats the slide show.
   - *Shuffle:* Shuffles photos in the slide show in a random order.

4. **Tap the Settings button to return to the Settings screen or press the physical Home button to return to the Home screen.**

To play a slide show, follow these steps:

1. **Tap Photos on the Home screen.**

2. **Choose a picture as described previously, and tap it to show the buttons and top menu.**

3. **Tap the play slide show button at the bottom of the picture. (Refer to Figure 14-4, left side.)**

   The Slideshow Options screen appears.

4. **(Optional) Tap the Transitions option to pick a transition to use between pictures in the slide show.**

   The Wipe Across transition is my favorite, but you can select Cube, Dissolve, Ripple, or Wipe Down.

5. **(Optional) To turn on music for the slide show, tap the On/Off switch for the Play Music button so that it is set to On.**

   The Music option appears.

6. **(Optional) Tap the Music option and select a song from your iPod touch music library.**

   After you select a song, the Slideshow Options screen appears again.

7. **Tap the Start Slideshow button to start the slide show (or tap Cancel to cancel the slide show).**

   The slide show starts to play. You can swipe any picture left or right to move to the next or previous picture.

8. **Tap a picture or press the Home button to stop the slide show.**

   The Home button returns you to the Home screen. You can also stop a slide show while remaining in the Photos app by tapping the picture.

Viewing pictures on an iPod nano or iPod classic

To view pictures (photos and images, but not video clips) on your iPod nano or iPod classic, follow these steps:

1. **Choose Photos from the iPod nano's Home screen or the iPod classic main menu.**

   The Photo Albums menu appears on an iPod nano with All Photos at the top, and the Photos menu appears on an iPod classic with All Photos and Settings choices at the top. Both menus offer a list of photo albums in alphabetical order. The iPod nano includes Events, Faces, and Places if you synced collections of those types from iPhoto.

2. **Choose All Photos or an album or event name.**

   The All Photos choice displays thumbnail images of all the pictures in your iPod. Selecting an album or event displays thumbnail images of only the pictures assigned to that album or event.

3. **Flick the iPod nano thumbnails to see more thumbnails, or scroll the click wheel of the iPod classic to highlight the thumbnail you want.**

   You can flick the iPod nano thumbnail screen up or down to see more thumbnails. On an iPod classic, you may have several screens of thumb-nails — scroll the click wheel to scroll through them. As you scroll, each thumbnail is highlighted.

4. **Tap a thumbnail on the iPod nano screen, or press the select button on the iPod classic (after highlighting a thumbnail) to open the picture.**

   When you select a thumbnail, your iPod displays the picture.

On an iPod nano, you can swipe left or right to scroll through all the photos. Tap a photo to see controls, and then tap the thumbnails icon in upper-left corner to return to the thumbnail view. To view a picture in horizontal (landscape) orientation on an iPod nano, rotate the iPod nano to a horizontal position.

You can also double-tap to quickly zoom in on a photo to see more detail, and then drag the image to see different parts in the center of the screen. If you sync a collection of Faces from iPhoto, double-tapping zooms in on the subject's face. Double-tap again to zoom back out to full size.

When viewing a photo on an iPod nano, tap it to see controls; you can then tap the previous/rewind button to see the previous picture in the album or library, or the fast-forward/next button to see the next picture. Tap the play/pause button to start a slide show.

On an iPod classic, you can use the previous/rewind and fast-forward/next buttons to move backward or forward through photos, and press the play/pause button to start a slide show. Press Menu to return to the thumbnails, and press Menu again to return to the Photos menu.

To set up a slide show on an iPod nano or iPod classic, follow these steps:

1. **Tap Settings⇨Photos from the iPod nano's Home screen, or choose Photos⇨Settings from the iPod classic main menu.**

2. **Choose Times per Slide to set the duration of each slide.**

   You can select ranges from 2 to 20 seconds. On an iPod classic, you can also select Manual to set the slide show to advance to the next slide when you press the fast-forward/next button.

3. **iPod classic only: Choose Transitions to select a transition to use between photos in the slide show.**

   You can select Cross Fade, Fade to Black, Zoom Out, Wipe Across, or Wipe Center, or choose Off for no transition.

4. **iPod classic only: Pick your music by choosing Music from the Settings menu and then choose a playlist.**

   You can choose any playlist in your iPod classic for your slide show, including On-The-Go and Now Playing. (On an iPod nano, it is easy to quickly start a song in an album or playlist, and then switch to Photos to start a slide show.)

5. **iPod classic only: Set the iPod to display the slide show by choosing TV Out from the Settings menu.**

   You have three choices for TV Out:

   • *On* displays the slide show on a television. While the slide show plays on your TV, you can also see the slides as large thumbnails on your iPod, along with the photo number within the album or library, and the Next and Previous icons.

   • *Ask* displays a screen requesting that you select TV Off or TV On; you make the choice each time you play a slide show.

   • *Off* displays the slide show with full-size images on the iPod.

6. **(Optional) Select other preferences for the iPod nano or iPod classic slide show:**

   • *Repeat:* Repeats the slide show. Tap Off next to Repeat on an iPod nano to turn it on; on an iPod classic, scroll the menu to highlight Repeat and press the Select button.

   • *Shuffle Photos:* Shuffles photos in the slide show in a random order. Tap Off next to Shuffle Photos on an iPod nano to turn it on; on an iPod classic, scroll the menu to highlight Shuffle Photos and press the Select button.

- *TV Signal* (iPod classic only): Changes your television signal to a standard for another country (such as PAL for the U.K.). Choose NTSC (also referred to humorously as "never the same color") for the United States.

To play a slide show on an iPod nano or iPod classic, follow these steps:

1. **Choose Photos from the home screen of the iPod nano or the iPod classic main menu.**

2. **Choose an album, another collection, or All Photos.**

3. **iPod nano only: Tap the thumbnail of the first photo and tap the picture to see the controls.**

4. **To start the show on an iPod nano, tap the play/pause icon; on an iPod classic, press the play/pause button.**

   You can also start a slide show when viewing a single picture on an iPod classic by pressing the select button.

5. **iPod classic only: If you previously set TV Out to Ask (as described in the previous step list), choose TV On or TV Off for your slide show.**

   - *TV On* displays the slide show on a television (through the video-out connection). You can also see the slides as large thumbnails on the iPod.

   - *TV Off* displays the slide show with full-size images on the iPod.

6. **iPod classic only: To navigate the slide show, press the playback buttons.**

   If you set Time per Slide to Manual on an iPod classic, press fast-forward/next to move to the next picture and press previous/rewind to return to the previous picture. If you set Time per Slide to a specific duration, use play/pause to pause and play the slide show.

7. **To stop the slide show on an iPod nano, tap any picture to see the controls, and then tap the thumbnails icon in the upper-left corner; on an iPod classic, press the Menu button.**

Shooting Photos and Videos on an iPod touch

The iPod touch has a 5-megapixel iSight photo camera and HD (1080p) 30 frame-per-second video camera on the back. The lens is on the back so that you can see the picture you are about to take on the display. The back camera offers 5x digital zoom and the ability to tap the picture to adjust the exposure for lighting conditions.

The iPod touch also has a 1.2-megapixel front camera that can take photos and record HD (720p) videos at up to 30 frames per second as well as show FaceTime video calls.

You can use the Camera app to shoot photos and video clips in portrait or landscape orientation with either back or front camera. You can record video clips that are suitable for sharing on Facebook, Twitter, or YouTube; you can copy them to your computer for further editing or edit them with Apple's iMovie app (available in the App Store for $4.99).

To take a picture, choose Camera from the Home screen. If this is the first time you are using Camera or if you've turned Location Services off (see Chapter 4 for details), the Camera app asks if you want to turn Location Services on (if it is not already on), and if you want Camera to use your current location. You don't have to let Camera use Location Services to take pictures. But if you *do* turn it on and give Camera permission by tapping OK, Camera can then tag photos and videos with location information — which is useful for posting photos and videos on social networks like Facebook; for navigating your photo library using the Places screen (as I show in the "Viewing pictures on an iPod touch" section, earlier in this chapter); or just for tracking the locations of your shots and clips. Camera photos are tagged with location data that includes your current geographical coordinates.

After awakening but before unlocking your iPod touch, you can quickly take a picture with the iPod touch camera by sliding the camera icon up to reveal the Camera app.

After you choose Camera, the view through the lens appears in the iPod touch display, as shown in Figure 14-5. You can hold the iPod touch vertically (for portrait mode) or horizontally (for landscape mode, as in Figure 14-5) to snap a photo. The photo/video switch is set to photo at first (or the last setting you used); if not, tap or slide the switch to set it to photo. The switch cameras icon (circular arrow) lets you switch from the back camera to the front camera.

When using the back camera, which is the main camera (higher in resolution and more suitable for most photos), you can pinch the picture to show the 5x digital zoom slider (see Figure 14-5). You can zoom in or out by dragging the slider (this is a digital zoom, which magnifies pixels, not an optical zoom, which changes the focal length of the camera by adjusting the lens and produces a higher-quality result).

If you tap the picture before taking the picture, a light blue exposure rectangle appears briefly near the center of the view through the lens (refer to Figure 14-5). This rectangle shows the area where the Camera app is sensing the lighting conditions for adjusting the exposure and focus. Change the area by tapping the photo once in the spot in the picture where you want to focus. The Camera app automatically adjusts the exposure and focus of the shot based on the lighting conditions for that area of the photo. Tap and hold (a long tap) until the exposure rectangle pulses in order to lock the exposure and focus (AE/AF Lock appears at the bottom of the screen, indicating that they are locked).

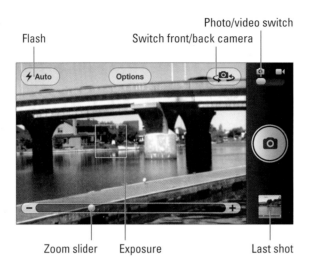

Flash

Switch front/back camera

Photo/video switch

Zoom slider   Exposure

Last shot

Figure 14-5: Pinch to show the zoom slider and tap the shutter to take a photo.

Tapping the picture also displays the Options button at the top of the screen (camera mode only). Tap Options, and then tap the on/off switch for the Grid option in the Options pop-up menu to turn Grid to On, which shows a grid for positioning the image in the frame of the shot so that you get the best quality. Tap Done above the Options menu to close the menu.

You can also turn high dynamic range (HDR) for photos on or off. HDR increases the dynamic range by combining three separate exposures into a single shot. HDR works best with photos of stationary objects. Tap Options, and then tap the on/off switch for the HDR option in the Options pop-up menu to turn HDR to On or Off. If you turn HDR on, you may also want to keep a normal version of the photo in addition to the HDR version — choose Settings➪Photos & Camera from the Home screen, and tap the on/off switch for the Keep Normal Photo option to turn it to On or Off.

You can tap the shutter button to take the photo, or if you have the time, you can hold your finger on the shutter button until you're ready, and then lift your finger to take the shot — to avoid shaking the device and thereby shifting the focus. As an alternative, you can press the volume button on the side of the iPod touch. An image of a shutter closing appears on the display to indicate a photo was taken. The iPod touch makes a shutter sound unless you set the Ringer and Alerts volume all the way down by choosing Settings➪Sounds (see Chapter 4 for details on sound effects).

The photo is stored in the Camera Roll of the Photos app. A thumbnail of your last shot appears in the corner of the Camera screen (refer to Figure 14-5). Tap this thumbnail to see your last shot.

Panoramas are unbroken views of an entire area. You can snap a panoramic photo with your iPod touch. You get better results taking the panoramic shot with your iPod touch in horizontal orientation. Tap Options, and then tap Panorama to enter Panorama mode. An arrow and horizontal lines appear on the screen with the message `Move iPod continuously when taking a Panorama`. Focus on one end of the panoramic area, and tap the shutter. The shutter turns into a Done button. Move your iPod touch in a continuous motion in a single direction — as you move the iPod touch, the arrow moves across the screen. For best results, keep the arrow on the center line as you move the iPod touch. Tap the Done button to finish the panorama, and then tap the Done button in the upper-right corner of the screen to exit Panorama mode.

If you turn HDR on, you may also want to keep a normal version of the photo in addition to the HDR version — choose Settings➪Photos & Camera from the Home screen, and tap the on/off switch for the Keep Normal Photo option to turn it to On or Off. To shoot video, hold the iPod touch vertically (for portrait mode) or horizontally (for landscape mode), and tap or slide the photo/video switch to set it to video, as shown in Figure 14-6. The shutter button turns into a red record button. Tap the record button to start recording — it blinks while recording. Tap the blinking record button again to stop recording.

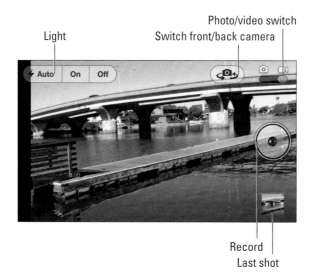

Figure 14-6: Tap the red record button to shoot video.

You can get better results when shooting pictures if you find out more about photography and video recording, and a great place to start is *iPhone Photography & Video For Dummies,* by Angelo Micheletti (Wiley).

To see the pictures (photos and video clips) you've just taken, tap the last shot button (refer to Figure 14-5 when taking a photo and Figure 14-6 when shooting a video). You can then delete that picture if you don't want to include it with the pictures to be synced to your computer and other devices. To delete the picture, tap the trash icon in the lower-right corner, and then tap the Delete Photo or Delete Video button (or Cancel to cancel).

If you're not in Camera, or you want to see more of your pictures, you can also choose Photos from the Home screen. The Photos app displays the Camera Roll choice at the top, followed by Photo Library and a list of photo albums (refer to Figure 14-3, left side). After you choose Camera Roll, thumbnail images appear for all the pictures in your Camera Roll.

To learn more about organizing and managing photos and video clips, see "Tips on Importing and Managing Media Content" in the free tips section of the author's website (www.tonybove.com/tips).

Sharing Photos and Videos

What good is it to take pictures — photos and video clips — without sharing them with other people? You can share pictures stored in your iPod touch by attaching them to e-mail messages and uploading them to social networks.

Sending a picture by e-mail

To send a photo or video clip in an e-mail, select a photo as I describe in the "Viewing pictures on an iPod touch" section, earlier in this chapter. Tap the picture to see the options button (refer to Figure 14-4, left side). Tap the options button to see the sharing sheet, as shown in Figure 14-7 (left side), and then tap the Mail icon to e-mail the picture.

The New Message screen appears with the photo or video clip embedded in the message. You can tap in the message field to enter text. Then fill in the To and Subject fields as described in Chapter 16.

You can also tap the Contacts icon to assign the picture to a contact in your Contacts list (see Chapter 18 for details) and tap the Use as Wallpaper icon to use the picture as the iPod touch wallpaper (see Chapter 4).

Figure 14-7: Share a picture (left) and select multiple pictures to share (right).

Sharing pictures over social networks and messages

If you've set up Twitter on your iPod touch (as I describe in Chapter 18) to tweet messages with others on Twitter, you can include photos from your iPod touch in your Twitter stream so that others can immediately see them. Tap the options button when viewing a photo as described in the previous section, and then tap the Twitter icon (refer to Figure 14-7, left side).

If you've set up Facebook on your iPod touch (as I describe in Chapter 18), you can do the same thing: Share the pictures with your Facebook friends by tapping the Facebook icon (refer to Figure 14-7, left side).

To share a photo by instant messaging, tap the Message icon. The Messages app launches with a new message containing the photo (see Chapter 18 for details on using the Message app). You can also print a photo to a printer on your Wi-Fi network by tapping the Print icon.

If you have an account on YouTube, you can upload a video clip to the account. Tap the options button when viewing a video, and then tap the YouTube icon. You can then sign in to your YouTube account (if you're not already signed in), edit the video clip's description, set it to Standard Definition or HD format, select a specific YouTube category and tags, and tap the Publish button in the top-right corner to publish it.

See Chapter 18 for a more sociable description of Twitter and Facebook.

Selecting and copying multiple pictures

To select more than one photo or video clip to copy and paste into another app or to share by e-mail, tap Camera Roll, Photo Library, or a photo album in the Photos app (refer to Figure 14-3, left side), and then tap the Edit button in the top-right corner of the thumbnail images (refer to Figure 14-3, center). The Select Items screen appears with thumbnails for both photos and video clips; otherwise, the screen's title is Select Photos (for thumbnails of only photos) or Select Videos (for thumbnails of only video clips). Tap each thumbnail in the Select Items, Select Photos, or Select Videos screen to select it for copying. When you tap each thumbnail, a check mark appears in the thumbnail, as shown in Figure 14-7 (right side), to indicate that it is part of the selection, and the Share and Add To buttons appear at the bottom of the screen; if you choose from Camera Roll, a Delete button also appears.

To e-mail selected pictures, tap the Share button, and then tap the Mail icon on the sharing sheet. The Mail app launches and starts a new e-mail message that includes all the selected pictures (see Chapter 16 for details on sending e-mails).

Note that if you select too many photos or a selected video is too long, the Mail icon doesn't appear in the sharing sheet because the e-mail attachment would be too large. If you still want to share them by e-mail, you should *copy* them. Tap the Copy icon. You can then paste the photos into any app that accepts pasted images — such as Pages. Touch and hold to mark an insertion point (which brings up the keyboard), and the Select/Select All/Paste bubble appears (see Chapter 3 for details on copying and pasting). Tap Paste to paste the images.

Saving Pictures Attached to Messages on an iPod touch

You probably receive photos and short video clips from others by e-mail. Now that you can get your e-mail on your iPod touch (see Chapter 16 for details on how to check your e-mail), you may also want to save the pictures you receive directly on your iPod touch so that you can view them with the Photos app or include them in a slide show.

A down-arrow button appears within a message that contains an attached picture. Tap the down-arrow button to download the picture to your iPod touch. After the download completes, tap the picture itself in the e-mail message, and the Save Image and Cancel buttons appear. Tap the Save Image button to save the picture for the Photos app (in Camera Roll) or tap Cancel to cancel. If the message has more than one picture (such as three), you can tap a button to save them all (such as the Save 3 Images).

Part IV
Touching the Online World

The iPod was always in a class by itself as a media player. But the iPod touch takes the concept of playing media to an entirely new level by providing access to the world of online content. Now you can visit websites around the world, download songs, stream videos, check your e-mail, and even monitor your stock portfolio.

Chapter 15 spins the Web and shows you how to surf web pages with Safari. You discover how to search with Google, Bing, or Yahoo! and interact with web services to do everything from checking live news feeds to making travel reservations.

Next, in Chapter 16, you find out how to turn your iPod touch into a lean, clean, e-mail machine. You can check e-mails from multiple e-mail accounts, send messages, and manage your e-mail settings.

Then, in Chapter 17, the weather becomes more predictable, your stocks proudly show their charts, your boarding pass displays conveniently when you need it, and the Earth itself reveals its secrets in satellite and map views — all on your iPod touch.

Surfin' Safari

In This Chapter

▷ Browsing the web with your iPod touch

▷ Saving and using web page bookmarks

▷ Navigating, scrolling, and zooming into web pages

▷ Saving website icons to your Home screen

The World Wide Web makes the world go 'round a whole lot faster than ever before. I browse the web for many different kinds of content and services. It's gotten to the point where I now make travel, restaurant, and entertainment reservations, and I purchase everything on the web from music, videos, books, and clothing to electronics equipment, garden supplies, groceries, and furniture. I get to track my shipments and purchases, review the latest news, check up on the blogs of my friends and associates, read novels, view slide shows and movies posted on the Internet, and even scan text messages from cellphones — all thanks to the Internet.

You can do all this on your iPod touch, using the Safari app after you connect to the Internet, as I describe in Chapter 4. You can also search using Google, Bing, or Yahoo! — all three services are built into Safari, and you can always browse any other search site.

Safari offers privacy settings for secure browsing, including private browsing, a fraud warning, the ability to accept or block cookies and pop-ups, and a button for clearing your browsing history and cookies. To change your privacy settings, tap Settings⇨Safari. To dig into these settings (such as finding out why you don't need cache for cookies!) and general privacy settings, see Chapter 20.

Take a Walk on the Web Side with Safari

Safari on the iPod touch not only lets you browse through websites, but also lets you add bookmarks and icons to your Home screen for convenient access. (You can also synchronize those bookmarks with your computer's web browser, as I describe in Chapter 8.)

Go URL own way

It's a snap to browse any website. Just tap out the site's address on the onscreen keyboard. (For instructions on using the onscreen keyboard, see Chapter 3.)

The full protocol designator (`http://`) and website address (`www.apple.com` or `www.tonybove.com/tips`) is known as a URL (Uniform Resource Locator). However, you can leave off the `http://` part and just go with the rest of the characters of the URL. In many cases you can even skip the `www.` part and just type **apple.com**.

For the blow-by-blow account, check out the following steps:

1. **Tap the Safari icon on the Home screen.**

   The iPod touch displays either the last web page you visited, or a blank page, as shown in Figure 15-1 (left side), with the rectangular URL entry field at the top-left corner and an oval search entry field in the top-right corner. (If you don't see these two entry fields side by side, tap the status bar at the top of the screen to jump to the top of the web page.)

2. **Tap the URL field.**

   The onscreen keyboard appears, as shown in Figure 15-1 (right side). Above that is an entry field for typing the URL.

3. **If the entry field already has a URL, tap the circled _X_ in the right corner of the field to clear its contents.**

4. **Tap out the URL for the web page using the onscreen keyboard.**

   Immediately as you start typing the characters of the URL, you see a list of suggested websites that match the characters you typed so far (see Figure 15-1, right side). You can scroll the suggested list by dragging up and down. If the website you want appears, tap it to go directly to the site without further ado. Otherwise, keep typing the URL, including the extension — the keyboard includes a .com button next to the Go button, and if you touch and hold the .com button, you can drag upward slightly to select .net, .edu, .org, or .us.

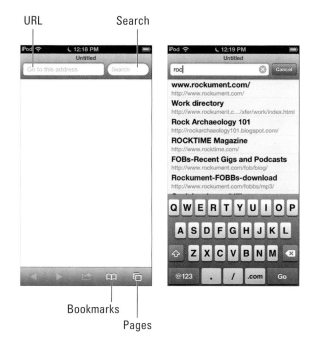

URL   Search

Bookmarks

Pages

Figure 15-1: Open Safari (left) and enter the web page URL (right).

5. Tap the Go button on the keyboard (or tap Cancel to cancel).

When you tap the Go button, your iPod touch closes the keyboard, displays Loading in the status bar, and loads the web page from the Internet, if the page exists. If you mistyped the URL or the page doesn't exist, you get a `server doesn't exist` or `can't open the page` message. Tap OK and start again from Step 2.

To cancel entering a URL, tap the Cancel button in the top-right corner of the screen (refer to Figure 15-1, right side).

To stop a web page from loading if you change your mind, tap the *X* on the right side of the URL entry field (refer to Figure 15-1, right side). This *X* turns into a circular arrow after the page is loaded, as shown in Figure 15-2 (left side). To reload an already-loaded web page to refresh its contents, tap the circular arrow.

Reading and bookmarking as you go

If the text on a web page is difficult to read on the iPod touch, tap the Reader button that appears inside the URL entry field (see Figure 15-2, left side). The Reader button appears if the web page offers a sufficient amount of text. Tap the Reader button to see the text from the page more clearly, as shown in Figure 15-2, right side.

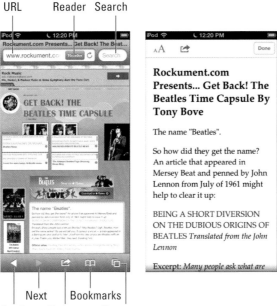

URL　　Reader　Search

Next　Bookmarks
Previous　Options　Pages

Figure 15-2: View a web page (left) and use the Reader to view the page (right).

Scroll the Reader screen vertically to read the text, which is presented as a continuous scrollable page with page breaks for any "go to next page" links, so that you can read all the text easily. The Reader screen offers the text-size button in the upper-left corner that enables you to change the size of the characters from small to large. Tap the Done button in the upper-right corner to return to the Safari main screen.

You can keep a reading list of web pages that you want to read later on your iPod touch. The reading list syncs wirelessly to your computer and to devices running the current version of iOS. You can either tap the options button to the right of the text-size button in the Reader screen, or tap the options button in the Safari main screen, and then tap the Add to Reading List button. The Add to Reading List option adds the text of the website to your reading list, which you can view by choosing Reading List in the Bookmarks screen (which I describe next). Tap the Done button in the upper-right corner to return to the web page.

The best way to keep track of web pages you've visited and want to visit again is to create bookmarks for the pages. You can then quickly go back to that page by selecting the bookmark. The bookmarks you create in your iPod touch synchronize with your Safari bookmarks on your Mac, or with your Safari or Internet Explorer bookmarks on your PC, as well as wirelessly with iOS devices, as I describe in Chapter 8.

Follow these steps to save a bookmark:

1. **Browse to the web page you want.**

2. **Tap the options button (refer to Figure 15-1, left side).**

   The options sheet appears, as shown in Figure 15-3 (left side), with buttons for different options.

3. **Tap the Bookmark button to add a bookmark.**

   The Add Bookmark screen appears with the name of the website in the title field, ready for editing, along with the onscreen keyboard, as shown in Figure 15-3 (right side). Below that is the actual URL for the web page, and below that is the Bookmarks folder.

Figure 15-3: Tap the Bookmarks button on the option sheet (left) to add a bookmark (right).

4. **(Optional) Edit the bookmark's title.**

Before saving a bookmark, you can edit its title with the onscreen keyboard. Tap the circled X on the right side of the title field to clear its contents or use the backspace key (the left-arrow with an X on the right side of the keyboard) to erase backward from the end of the title, and type the new title.

5. **(Optional) Tap a bookmark folder.**

Before saving a bookmark, you can choose a bookmark folder in which to save the bookmark; otherwise, Safari saves the bookmark in the top-most level of bookmarks. Tap Bookmarks to see the list of bookmark folders — you can flick to scroll the list quickly, or drag the list slowly, and tap one to choose it.

6. **Tap the Save button to save the bookmark or tap Cancel to cancel.**

The Save button appears in the upper-right corner of the display (refer to Figure 15-3, right side), and the Cancel button appears in the upper-left corner.

You can also add bookmarks to your iPod touch by syncing bookmarks from your computer's web browser, as described in Chapter 8.

After saving or adding bookmarks, you can go directly to a bookmarked page on the web by selecting the bookmark. Follow these steps:

1. **Tap the Safari icon on the Home screen (if it is not already running).**

Your iPod touch displays the last web page you visited or a blank page, with a navigation bar that includes the Bookmarks button along the bottom (refer to Figure 15-2, left side).

2. **Tap the Bookmarks button — the one that looks like an open book.**

The Bookmarks menu appears with a scrollable list of folders, including the Reading List with the names of web pages you added, the History folder that records your page visits, the iCloud Tabs folder that keeps track of the Safari tabs on your Mac and other iOS devices (if you turn on iCloud, as I describe in Chapter 8), and other Bookmark-related folders (such as Bookmarks Bar and Bookmarks Menu, provided with the Safari application on computers and the iPad). You can scroll this list by dragging up and down.

3. **Tap a bookmark folder to access its bookmarks.**

For example, tapping Bookmarks Menu opens the folders and bookmarks from the Bookmarks Menu section of Safari on your Mac or PC, or your other iOS devices synced to iCloud. Tapping Bookmarks Bar opens the folders and bookmarks in the Bookmarks Bar section. Tapping History opens the history of the web pages you've visited.

4. **Tap a bookmark to load the web page.**

   Folders have a folder icon to the left of their names, and actual book-marks have an open-page icon next to their web page names. Tap a folder to reveal its contents and tap a bookmark to load a web page.

You can edit your bookmarks and bookmark folders. Tap the Bookmarks button in the navigation bar (refer to Figure 15-2, left side), and then choose the folder to edit or the folder that has the bookmark you want to edit. Then tap the Edit button in the lower-left corner of the Bookmarks menu. The Edit Bookmarks display appears, with circled minus (–) signs next to the book-mark folders.

You can then do any of the following:

- ✔ To make a new folder within the selected folder, tap the New Folder button. If you want to create a new folder at the topmost level, tap the Bookmarks button in the upper-left corner to go back to the topmost Bookmarks list, tap the Edit button, and then tap New Folder.

- ✔ To delete a bookmark or folder, tap the circled minus (–) sign next to the bookmark or folder and then tap Delete.

- ✔ To reposition a bookmark or folder, drag the move icon on the right side of each bookmark or folder to a new position in the list.

- ✔ To edit the name of a bookmark or folder, tap the bookmark or folder and use the onscreen keyboard to type the new title. (Tap the circled X in the title field to clear its contents first, if you want.)

- ✔ To change where a bookmark or folder is stored, tap the Bookmark Folder field for the selected bookmark or folder, and then tap a new folder to hold the bookmark or folder chosen for editing.

Tap the Done button in the bottom-left corner of the Edit Bookmarks display to finish editing.

Sharing a web link

You just found a web page that you want to share with your friends, your acquaintances, or an entire social network such as Facebook or Twitter. Sharing a web link is much easier to do from your iPod touch than from your computer because it involves only a few taps and you can do it from any-where, as long as you're connected to a Wi-Fi network and the Internet.

Not only can you share the link with people on social networks, but also with anyone whose e-mail address you know. As I describe in Chapter 16, your iPod touch can send e-mail as well as receive it.

To share a web link, the steps are simple:

1. **Browse to the web page and tap the options button. (Refer to Figure 15-2, left side.)**

   The options sheet appears (refer to Figure 15-3, left side).

2. **Tap the medium for sharing the link, such as Facebook, Twitter, Mail, or Message, tap Print to print the web page, or tap Copy to copy the web link.**

   If you already set up your Facebook or Twitter account, as I describe in Chapter 18, tapping Facebook or Twitter brings up a screen for typing a message to go along with the web link and the Add Location option to add your physical location along with the message. You can then tap Send to send the message and web link.

   If you have already set up an e-mail account on your iPod touch, as I describe in Chapter 8, tapping Mail brings up an e-mail message ready for you to finish composing. The Subject field is already filled in with the web page name, and the link itself is already inserted in the body of the message. See Chapter 16 for details on addressing the e-mail and sending it.

   Tapping Print sends the web page to a printer on your Wi-Fi network, and tapping Copy copies the web link so that you can paste the link in other app that accepts pasted text (such as Pages or Notes). See Chapter 3 for details on how to paste.

Pearl diving with Google, Yahoo!, or Bing

If you've done any web surfing at all, you've already used one of the popular search engines. They're simply *the* tool for finding websites. The three most popular — Google, Yahoo!, and Bing — are built in to Safari on your iPod touch.

Google is set up to be your default web search engine, but you can quickly change that. To choose Yahoo! or Bing (or to go back to Google), tap Settings➪Safari➪Search Engine, and then tap Yahoo!, Bing, or Google. Turning on one search engine turns off whichever search engine was active before.

Follow these steps to search from within Safari:

1. **Tap the Safari icon on the Home screen.**

   The iPod touch displays the last web page you visited or a blank page. You can find the search field, with Google, Yahoo!, or Bing in gray, in the top-right corner (you can see Search in gray in the search field in Figure 15-1, left side). (If you don't see the URL entry and search fields side by side, tap the status bar at the top of the screen to jump to the top of the web page.)

2. **Tap the search field.**

   The onscreen keyboard appears. Above that is the search field (with a magnifying glass icon).

3. **Tap out the search term using the keyboard.**

   Immediately as you start typing characters, you see a list of suggested bookmarks in your bookmarks folder or history list. You can scroll this list by dragging up and down.

4. **Tap a suggestion or tap the Search button on the keyboard.**

   If a suggestion appears that satisfies your search, tap it to go directly to the web page without further ado. Otherwise, keep typing as much of the search term as you think necessary and tap Search. The keyboard disappears and displays the search results. (***Note:*** The Search button replaces the Go button on the keyboard when searching.)

Let Your Fingers Do the Surfing

After you've found the web page you want, you can use your fingers to navigate its links and play any media it has to offer. You can also bounce around from previous to next pages in your browsing session, open multiple pages, zoom into pages to see them clearly, and scroll around the page to see all of its sections while zooming.

Scrolling and zooming

To zoom into a web page in Safari, spread two fingers apart on the screen (unpinch). To zoom back out, bring your fingers together (pinch).

Double-tap the display to zoom into any part of the page. You can also double-tap a column to automatically zoom in so that the column fills the iPod touch display. Double-tap again to zoom back out.

To scroll around the page, touch and drag the page. (If you happen to touch a link and you don't want to go there, drag the link before letting go.) You can drag up, down, or sideways to see the entire web page; or flick your finger up or down to quickly scroll the page. Use two fingers to scroll within a frame on a web page or one finger to scroll the entire page.

To jump to the top of a web page, tap the status bar at the top of the iPod touch screen.

All these gestures work the same way in either portrait or landscape orientation. To view a web page in landscape orientation, rotate the iPod touch sideways. Safari automatically reorients and expands the page (unless you locked your iPod touch in portrait mode — see Chapter 3 for details). To set it back to portrait, rotate the iPod touch again.

It's all touch and go

To follow a link on a web page, tap the link. Text links are usually underlined (sometimes in blue). Many images are also links you can tap to navigate to another page or use to play media content.

If a link leads to a sound or movie file supported by the iPod touch, Safari plays the sound or movie. (See Chapter 12 for sounds and Chapter 13 for videos.) Tap an e-mail link, and your iPod touch launches Mail.

You can see the link's destination — without following it — by touching and holding the link until the destination address appears (next to your finger). You can touch and hold an image to see whether it has a link.

To move to the previous page in your browsing sequence, tap the left-arrow button in the left side of the navigation bar at the bottom of the screen. (Refer to Figure 15-2, left side.) Safari replaces the current page with the previous one. If you've just started browsing and this is the first page you've opened, the left-arrow button is grayed out.

To move to the next page, tap the right-arrow button (to the right of the left-arrow button) in the navigation bar at the bottom of the screen. (Refer to Figure 15-2, left side.) Safari replaces the current page with the next one in the browsing sequence. This button is grayed out unless you've navigated backward to some previous page.

You can always go back to any of the pages you visited by tapping the bookmarks button and tapping History. To clear your History list on your iPod touch, tap Clear.

Surfing multiple pages

Although you can open web pages one at a time and switch back and forth between them, you can also open several pages and start a new browsing sequence with each page, just like opening separate browser windows or tabs.

Some links automatically open a new page instead of replacing the current one, leaving you with multiple pages open. Safari displays the number of open pages inside the pages button's icon in the bottom-right corner of the screen. The pages button without a number means only the currently viewed page is open (as in Figure 15-2, left side).

To open a separate page, tap the pages button to display the page's thumbnail image (as shown in Figure 15-4), and then tap the New Page button in the bottom-left corner of the screen. Safari brushes aside the existing page to display a new one. You can then use your bookmarks, enter a web page URL, or search for a web page. (If you change your mind and don't want to open a new page, tap the Done button to cancel.)

Figure 15-4: Switch among open web pages.

To switch among open pages, tap the pages button to display the page thumbnail images (refer to Figure 15-4), and flick left or right to scroll the images. When you get to the thumbnail image of the page you want, tap it!

To close a separate page, tap the pages button to display the page thumbnail images, and then tap the red circled *X* in the top-left corner of the web page thumbnail (refer to Figure 15-4) for the page you want to close.

Interacting with pages

Many web pages have pop-up menus for making choices. For example, Craigslist (www.craigslist.org) offers a pop-up menu for searching through its classified listings. To make choices from a pop-up menu, tap the menu. Safari displays a list of possible choices for that pop-up menu (for example, Craigslist offers the Search Craigslist pop-up menu with choices for Housing, Jobs, Personals, Services, For Sale, and so on). Choose one by tapping it; you can also flick to scroll the list of choices, or start typing to scroll directly to the first match.

After choosing an option, tap the Done button to finish with that pop-up menu. You can also tap the Previous or Next button to move to the previous or next pop-up menu.

Entering text into a website — such as reservation information, passwords, credit card numbers, search terms, and so on — is as easy as tapping inside the text field. Safari brings up the keyboard, as shown in Figure 15-5, and you can type the text. You may want to rotate the iPod touch sideways to view web pages in landscape (horizontal) orientation to make the keyboard wider and easier to use.

You can move to the next or previous text field by tapping the Next or Previous button or by tapping inside another text field. To finish typing with the keyboard, tap the Done button. If you don't like what you typed, use the delete key to delete it before tapping Done.

Figure 15-5: Entering text for a field on a web page.

After you finish filling out all the required text fields on the page, tap Go on the keyboard (or tap Search, which some pages use rather than Go). If the web page is a form, tapping Go automatically submits the form. Some web pages offer a link for submitting the form, which you must tap in order to finish entering information.

The AutoFill button (refer to Figure 15-5) can help you fill out web forms. To activate AutoFill, choose Settings➪Safari and tap the AutoFill button. To use information from the Contacts app for autofilling (such as your name, phone number, e-mail, and address), turn on the Use Contact Info option, tap My Info, and then select the contact. Safari uses information from this contact to fill in fields on web forms. To use information from names and passwords, turn on the Names & Passwords option so that Safari remembers names and passwords of websites you visit and automatically fills in the information when you revisit them. To remove all AutoFill information, tap Clear All.

Copying text

You may want to copy one or more paragraphs of text from a web page to paste into another app (such as Notes or Pages) or into an e-mail. Although you can e-mail a link to a web page (as I show you in the "Sharing a web link" section, earlier in this chapter), you may want to copy a section of text and paste the section into the message.

To copy a section of text from a web page, touch and hold somewhere within the section (also known as a *long tap*). Safari automatically highlights the section with selection handles on either end and displays the Copy bubble (see Figure 15-6). Tap Copy to copy the selection.

If you zoom into the web page and use a long tap to select only a single word, you see a larger bubble with Copy and Define — tap Define to see a definition of the word.

You can also make a more precise selection after a long tap by dragging one of the handles. A rectangular magnifier appears for dragging the handle precisely. After you remove your finger to stop dragging, the Copy bubble appears.

For details on pasting the selected text into apps such as Notes or into an e-mail, see Chapter 3.

Figure 15-6: Copy a selected section of text on a web page.

Bringing It All Back Home

Got some favorite web pages? You can add web thumbnail icons for them to the Home screen so that you can access each page with one touch. Web page icons appear on the Home screen along with the icons of other apps. (Discover how to rearrange the icons and add multiple screens to the Home screen in Chapter 3.)

Follow these steps to add a web page to your Home screen:

1. **Browse to the web page you want.**

2. **Tap the options button (refer to Figure 15-2, left side).**

   The options sheet appears (refer to Figure 15-3, left side).

3. **Tap the Add to Home Screen button.**

   The Add to Home screen appears with the title of the web page in the title field, ready for editing, along with the keyboard. The icon to be added to the Home screen — a thumbnail image of the site or a graphic image defined by the site for this purpose (usually a logo) — appears to the left of the title field.

4. **(Optional) Edit the web page title.**

   Before saving a web icon to the Home screen, you can edit its title with the keyboard. Tap the circled X on the right side of the title field to clear its contents, or you can use the delete key on the keyboard to erase backward from the end of the title and type the new title.

5. **Tap the Add button to add the web page icon or tap Cancel to cancel.**

   The Add button appears in the upper-right corner of the display, and the Cancel button appears in the upper-left corner.

The Postman Always Rings Once

In This Chapter

▶ Checking and sending e-mail with an iPod touch

▶ Changing message settings and sending options

▶ Setting the Push and Fetch features for optimal e-mail retrieval

*Y*our e-mail is just a touch away. The Mail app on your iPod touch can display richly formatted messages with attachments, and you can send as well as receive photos and graphics, which are displayed in your message along with the text. You can even receive files as attachments and open them on your iPod touch if the files are compatible with any of your apps, such as Portable Document Format (PDF) files, documents from Apple's apps (Pages, Numbers, and Keynote), Microsoft Word documents, Microsoft Excel spreadsheets, and so on.

The Mail app on your iPod touch can work in the background to retrieve your e-mail when you're online (see Chapter 4 for instructions about getting online). If you signed up for Apple's iCloud service, as I describe in illustrious detail in Chapter 8, your iPod touch can receive e-mail the instant it arrives in the mailbox on the service. You hear a single ding sound when your mail has arrived (unless you turned off the New Mail sound, as I describe in Chapter 4). Services such as iCloud, Microsoft Exchange, and Yahoo! Mail can *push* e-mail messages to your iPod touch so that they arrive immediately, automatically (unless you turn off the push option, as I describe in the later section, "If Not Push, Then Fetch").

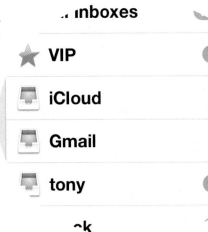

These and other types of e-mail account services also let you *fetch* e-mail from the server — when you select the account in Mail on your iPod touch, Mail automatically starts fetching the e-mail. You can

browse your e-mail accounts or even use other apps while Mail fetches messages. You can tell Mail to fetch more messages by swiping down the Mail, Mailboxes, or message screens — a spinning circle appears indicating that Mail is fetching. Some e-mail accounts don't offer push, so fetch is the only way your iPod touch receives messages from them.

For push-type accounts, you can balance pushing and fetching to save battery power, as I describe in the later section, "If Not Push, Then Fetch."

You need to set up your e-mail accounts on your iPod touch in order to use Mail with them. See Chapter 8 for details on syncing, setting up, deleting, and changing settings for e-mail accounts.

Checking E-Mail

You know that you have unread e-mail if the Mail icon on the iPod touch Home screen shows a number — this is the number of unread messages in your inboxes (you can turn this off by turning off the Badge App Icon setting in Settings⬆Notifications and tapping Mail near the bottom of the Notifications screen (see Chapter 4 for more details about notifications). As e-mail is pushed (or fetched) to your iPod touch, this number increases until you read the messages. Tap the Mail icon to start the Mail app.

Mail starts out by displaying the Mailboxes screen, which gives you quick access to your account's inbox and other mailboxes, as shown in Figure 16-1 (left side). If your iPod touch is set up with multiple e-mail accounts, the Mailboxes screen lists all your inboxes, followed by the e-mail accounts, as shown in Figure 16-2 (right side). Tap the inbox for your single e-mail account, or tap All Inboxes if you have multiple accounts, to see incoming message headers. A list of incoming message headers appears, as shown in Figure 16-2 (left side), with the sender's name, subject, and the first sentence or two of each message, along with a blue dot or blue VIP star if the message hasn't been read yet. (The blue VIP stars appear for messages in the VIP mailbox for your account — I describe how to add VIPs in the "Setting up your VIPs" section, later in this chapter.)

Messages are organized by conversation thread, so that related messages appear as a single message header in the mailbox (I show you how to change that setting in the "What you see is what you got" section, later in this chapter). Message header threads have a number next to the right arrow, showing the number of messages in the thread — as in the 5 in the header for the top message in Figure 16-2 (left side). The message header displayed for the thread is for the oldest unread message in the thread, or the most recent message if all the messages are read. A blue dot or VIP star appears for any message in the thread you haven't read.

To see the messages in a thread, tap the thread in the mailbox. The message headers in the thread appear, as shown in Figure 16-2 (right side).

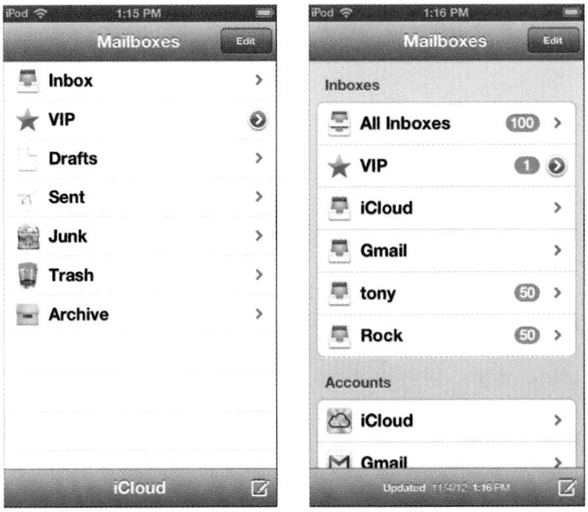

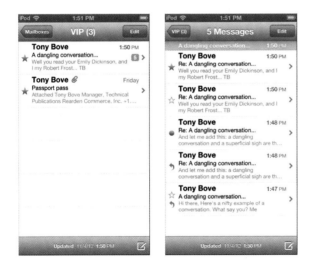

Figure 16-1: A single e-mail account (left); multiple e-mail accounts (right).

Figure 16-2: Tap a message header thread (left) to see its message headers (right).

The message is the medium

To read a message, tap its message header in a mailbox or in a thread. Within a message, tap the up or down arrows to see the next or previous message in the mailbox or the thread.

After you tap a message header to read the message, you can scroll the message by flicking or dragging your finger, and zoom into and out of the message by unpinching and pinching with your fingers. You can also zoom directly into a column in the message by double-tapping the message and zoom out by double-tapping it again.

If the e-mail includes an attachment, a button appears within the message showing the icon of an attached file and a right arrow — to view the attachment, just tap the button. If the format of the attached file is one of the supported formats (which include files that have the extensions `.doc`, `.docx`, `.htm`, `.html`, `.pdf`, `.txt`, `.xls`, or `.xlsx`), Mail downloads and opens the attachment; if not, Mail displays a document icon with the name of the file — but you can't open it.

You can see all the recipients of a message (except Bcc, or *blind carbon copy,* recipients) by opening the message and tapping Details, shown in blue in the top-right corner of the message. Tap a name or e-mail address that appears to see the recipient's contact information. Tap Hide to hide the recipients.

You can add the sender or recipient to your Contacts list on your iPod touch by tapping the name or e-mail address. A menu appears with the contact's e-mail address and the Create New Contact, Add to Existing Contact, and Add to VIP buttons. Tap Create New Contact to create a new contact or tap Add to Existing Contact if you want to add the information to an existing contact. Tap the e-mail address to send an e-mail to that recipient's address. (See the "Sending E-Mail" section, later in this chapter.) Tap Add to VIP to add the contact to your VIP list, which I describe in the "Setting up your VIPs" section, later in this chapter.

Links appear in a message underlined in blue, and images embedded in the message may also have links. Tapping a link can take you to a web page in Safari, open a map in Maps, or open a new pre-addressed e-mail message in Mail. To return to your e-mail, press the Home button on your device and tap the Mail icon.

You can mark a message as unread so that the blue dot or blue VIP star appears for it: Open the message, tap the flag icon in the bottom-left corner (refer to Figure 16-3, left side), and tap Mark as Unread. The message is marked as unread — the blue dot or blue VIP star appears next to the message header in the mailbox list until you open it again.

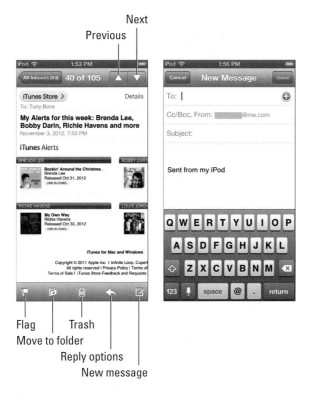

Flag

Move to folder

Trash

Reply options

New message

Figure 16-3: An e-mail message (left) and the new message screen (right).

Deleting a message

To delete an open message, tap the Trash icon in the center of the bottom row of buttons in the message display. Mail deletes the message from your iPod touch. If your account is a push-type account (such as iCloud), your message is also deleted from your cloud mailbox. If your account is a fetch-only account (see more details about accounts in Chapter 8), the message still shows up in your computer's e-mail program and is not deleted from the mail server (unless it's set up that way — see Chapter 8).

After deleting the message, Mail displays the next message in sequence. You can also move to the previous or next message by tapping the up and down arrows in the top-right corner.

You can also delete a message without opening it. In the list of message headers, drag your finger across a message header and tap the Delete button that appears.

To delete a list of messages quickly, choose the mailbox (such as Inbox) and tap the Edit button in the top-right corner of the screen. The messages appear with empty circles next to them. Tap each message so that a check mark appears in the empty circle. After checking off the messages to delete, tap the Delete button in the bottom-left corner.

Setting up your VIPs

If you get a lot of e-mail (and who doesn't?), you may want to designate some of your contacts — such as friends, relatives, your boss, your spouse, and so on — as VIPs (very important persons), so that their e-mails show up in the VIP mailbox (refer to Figure 16-1, left or right). You can then tap VIP in the Mailboxes screen to see only those e-mails.

To set up your VIPs, tap VIP in the Mailboxes screen, and then tap Add VIP. Your contacts appear, and you can navigate through your contacts, tap each contact to see the VIP List screen, and tap Add VIP on the VIP List screen. E-mail from these contacts will appear in the VIP mailbox.

You can also set custom alerts for VIP e-mails. After tapping VIP in the Mailboxes screen, tap VIP Alert to go directly to the VIP section of the Notifications settings. You can also get to these settings by tapping Settings⇨Notifications⇨Mail⇨VIP. For details on notification settings, see Chapter 4.

Sending E-Mail

You can use the Mail app to reply to any message instantly and send e-mail to any e-mail address in the world. You can even send a message to a group of people without having to select each person's e-mail address.

To send an e-mail, follow these steps:

1. **Tap the Mail icon on the Home screen.**

   The Mailboxes screen appears. If you've set up more than one e-mail account, go to Step 2; otherwise, skip to Step 3.

2. **(Optional) Scroll the Mailboxes screen if necessary to see your accounts, and then choose an account for sending the e-mail.**

   You can skip this step if you synced only one e-mail account. If you have several e-mail accounts on your iPod touch, you can select one of them, or you can use the default account for sending e-mail. (See the section, "Message Settings and Sending Options," later in this chapter, to set the default account.) You can also defer this decision until Step 6.

3. **Tap the new message icon (pencil in a document) in the lower-right corner of the Mail screen (refer to Figure 16-1, left side).**

   The New Message screen appears, as shown in Figure 16-3 (right side), along with the onscreen keyboard. If you have multiple accounts set up on your iPod touch, the default account for sending e-mail appears in the Cc/Bcc, From field (grayed out in Figure 16-3 for privacy).

4. **Enter the recipient's e-mail address in the To field.**

   If your recipient is listed in your Contacts on your iPod touch, tap the circled addition symbol (+) on the right side of the To field (refer to Figure 16-3, right side) and choose a contact to add the contact's e-mail address to the To field. You can repeat this process to add multiple e-mail addresses to the To field from your contacts.

   If your recipient isn't listed in your Contacts or if you don't know whether the recipient is listed, tap the To field entry and use the keyboard to type one or more e-mail addresses (and use a comma to separate each address). As you type an e-mail address, e-mail addresses that match from your Contacts list appear below. Tap one to add it to the To field.

5. **(Optional) Add more addresses to the Cc or Bcc field.**

   You can add e-mail addresses to the Cc (carbon copy) and Bcc (blind carbon copy) fields to copy others. While Cc addresses appear on messages received by recipients indicating that they were copied on the message, Bcc addresses don't appear on messages received by recipients — they're like stealth readers. Tap the Cc/Bcc letters to expand the message to include the Cc and Bcc fields; then enter addresses the same way you do in Step 4.

   You can drag e-mail addresses from the To field to the Cc or Bcc field, and vice versa. You can also drag e-mail addresses within a field to reorder them.

6. **(Optional) Change the From address.**

   You can change the e-mail address for the sender to one of your other e-mail accounts. The default e-mail account for sending e-mail is already selected; tap the From letters to display a pop-up menu of e-mail accounts, and then tap an e-mail account to use as the sender's account.

7. **Enter the e-mail subject.**

   Tap the Subject entry field (refer to Figure 16-3, right side) to type a subject with the keyboard.

8. **Tap underneath the Subject field to type a message and press Return on the keyboard when you're finished.**

9. **(Optional) Select the text and change the formatting.**

   Tap and hold on a word (a long tap), and then tap the Select or Select All bubbles, as I describe in Chapter 3; a bubble appears with Cut, Copy, Paste, and a right-arrow. Tap the right-arrow, tap the BIU button, and then tap the Bold, Italics, and/or Underline bubbles to change the text style.

10. **Tap Send in the upper-right corner of the display (refer to Figure 16-3, right side) to send the message.**

You can also forward and reply to any message you receive. Open the message and tap the reply options button — the curled left-arrow that appears in the bottom-left side of the message display (refer to Figure 16-3, left side). Then tap Reply to reply to the sender of the message, Reply All (which appears only if there are other recipients) to reply to all the recipients as well as the sender, or Forward to forward the message to someone else (or Cancel to go back to the message). The New Message screen appears with the onscreen keyboard so that you can type your reply or add a message to the one you're forwarding. Tap Send to send the reply or forwarded message.

You can also print the e-mail message to a printer on your Wi-Fi network by tapping the reply options button and choosing Print.

When you reply to a message, files or images attached to the initial message aren't sent with the reply. When you tap Forward to forward a message, a pop-up menu with the Include or Don't Include buttons appears for a message with an attachment. Tap Include to include the attachment in the forwarded message, or Don't Include to forward the message without the attachment.

To save a message as a draft so you can work on it later, start typing the message as described in the preceding steps, but before tapping Send, tap Cancel in the upper-left corner of the display (refer to Figure 16-3, right side). Then, from the menu that appears, tap Save to save the message in the Drafts mailbox of the account or tap Don't Save to discard the message (or Cancel to go back to typing the message). You can find the saved message in the Drafts mailbox of the same e-mail account. Tap the message to add to it or change it, and then send it.

To send a photo in a message, tap the Photos icon on the Home screen and choose a photo for viewing, as described in Chapter 14. As I show in that chapter, you can either start a new e-mail message with the photo, or copy the photo and then paste it into a draft message or reply.

Message Settings and Sending Options

To change your e-mail message settings and sending options, choose Settings⊅Mail, Contacts, Calendars from the Home screen. In the Mail, Contacts, Calendars settings screen that appears, use your finger to scroll down to the Mail section to change your e-mail message settings and sending options, as shown in Figure 16-4 (the upper part on the left side and the lower part on the right).

In the Mail section, you can change global settings for messages in all accounts. To set the number of messages you can see at once in a mailbox, tap Show and choose a setting. You can choose to see the most recent 50, 100, 200, 500, or 1,000 messages. (To download additional messages when you're in Mail, scroll to the bottom of your inbox and tap Download More.)

If you think you have shaky fingers and might delete a message by mistake, you can set Mail to confirm that you want to delete a message first before deleting. Tap the Off button to turn on the Ask Before Deleting option. (Tap it again to turn it off.) If Ask Before Deleting is on, Mail warns you before you delete a message, and you have to tap Delete to confirm the deletion.

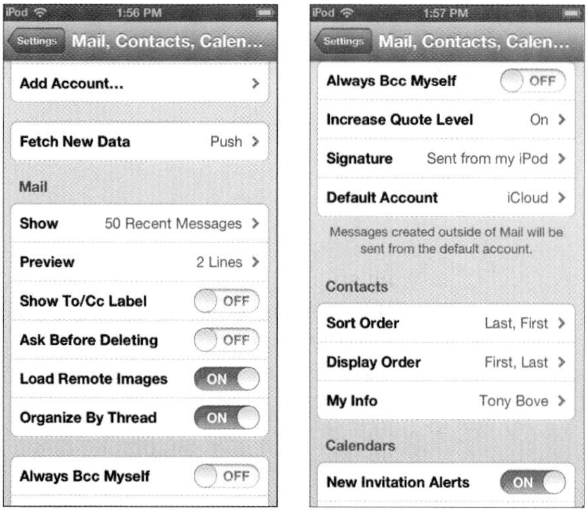

Figure 16-4: The upper (left) and lower (right) parts of the Mail section of Mail, Contacts, and Calendars settings.

What you see is what you got

You can also set how many lines of each message are previewed in the message list headers. Choose Preview (refer to Figure 16-4, left side) and then choose to see any amount from zero to five lines of each message.

If you want to see the Internet images linked to your e-mails, turn on the Load Remote Images option. However, images downloaded from the Internet can also be used by spammers to collect information, or may even harbor malicious code. If you leave Load Remote Images off, your messages appear faster, but you have to touch each image icon to download and see it.

If you care about whether a message was sent directly to you or whether you were sent it as a Cc copy (which still might make it important, but at least you know), you can set whether Mail shows the To and Cc labels in message lists. Tap the Off button for the Show To/Cc Label option to turn it on. (Tap On to turn it off.) If Show To/Cc Label is on, you see To or Cc in the list next to each message.

If you don't want messages to be organized into conversation threads, turn off the Organize By Thread option (tap On to turn it off). All messages appear as single messages.

Return to sender, address unknown

Mail can send you a copy of every message you send, which is useful for ensuring the e-mail was sent and for keeping threaded conversation threads intact (otherwise, your replies would not be included in the thread). Scroll the Mail, Contacts, Calendars settings screen down to the bottom of the Mail section below the Organize By Thread option (refer to Figure 16-4, right side), and tap the Always Bcc Myself on/off button to turn it On. The Bcc refers to *blind carbon copy,* and it means that your message is sent and copied back to you without your e-mail address appearing in the recipient's list.

If you want Mail to automatically indent messages that you're forwarding, or indent the original message when replying, tap Increase Quote Level (refer to Figure 16-4, right side), and tap the on/off button to turn it On.

You can add a *signature* to your messages that can include any text to personalize your e-mails — not your real, handwritten scrawl but rather a listing of your name, title, phone number, favorite quote, or all of these. Tap Signature (refer to Figure 16-4, right side) and type a signature with the onscreen keyboard. The signature remains in effect for all future e-mails sent from your iPod touch.

To set the default e-mail account for sending messages, tap Default Account (refer to Figure 16-4, right side) and choose an e-mail account. Your iPod touch will use this account whenever you start the process of sending a message from another application, such as sending a photo from Photos or tapping the e-mail address of a business in Maps.

For details on synchronizing e-mail accounts automatically from iTunes or iCloud, as well as for setting up an account, changing account settings, and deleting accounts manually on your iPod touch, see Chapter 8.

If Not Push, Then Fetch

The Push and Fetch options control how your iPod touch receives e-mail. You can set these options for each account and for all accounts.

iCloud, Microsoft Exchange, Gmail, and Yahoo! Mail are examples of e-mail accounts that can *push* messages *to* your iPod touch so that they arrive immediately after arriving at the account's e-mail server. Other types of accounts *fetch* messages *from* the account's e-mail server — either on a time schedule or manually. (If manually, you select the account before your iPod touch retrieves the e-mail.) Push accounts (such as an iCloud account) can be set to either push or fetch.

You can turn the Push feature on or off as you please. Keeping it on uses more battery power because the iPod touch receives messages immediately — whenever it's connected to Wi-Fi. When you turn the Push feature off, push accounts fetch the e-mail instead, and you can set the timetable for fetching or set fetching to manual.

For optimal battery life, turn Push off and set Fetch to Manually so that fetching occurs only when you tap the e-mail account or drag down on a mailbox view to read e-mail (or send an e-mail). Pushing e-mail as it arrives, or fetching e-mail often, uses up a considerable amount of battery power; doing both drains the battery even more quickly.

To turn Push on or off, choose Settings⇨Mail, Contacts, Calendars from the Home screen, scroll to the Mail section (refer to Figure 16-4, left side), and tap Fetch New Data. The Fetch New Data screen appears. Tap the On button for Push to turn it off (and vice versa).

Don't fret over whether you will remember to check your e-mail. You can set a timetable for fetching e-mail automatically. Choose a time interval in the Fetch New Data screen — tap Every 15 Minutes, Every 30 Minutes, or Hourly; tap Manually so that the iPod touch fetches only when you tap the e-mail account to read or send e-mail.

You can also set Push or Fetch settings for individual accounts. Scroll the Fetch New Data screen to the bottom and touch Advanced. The Advanced screen appears, showing each account. Tap the account to change its push and fetch settings separately.

Setting Push to Off or setting Fetch to Manually in the Fetch New Data screen overrides the individual account settings.

1,216 miles
CONTINUE ON I-35 N

UNITED STATES

17

5 miles
ON I-35 N

UNITED STATES

1,2
CONTIN

Earth, Wind, and Finance

In This Chapter

▶ Using the Maps app to find locations

▶ Getting step-by-step directions to locations

▶ Checking the weather in various cities

▶ Pricing stocks and mutual funds

▶ Keeping track of your tickets and coupons

*Y*our iPod touch can find almost anything on Earth, even itself, and show the location on a map or satellite picture. And although you can't harness the forces of nature, or even the influences that drive Wall Street, you can use your iPod touch to make better guesses about the weather and the stock market.

This chapter describes how to use the Maps app to find nearly any location on Earth and obtain driving directions — without having to ask someone out on the street. Your iPod touch offers Location Services to nail down the unit's physical location, and it offers that information to the Maps app and any other app that needs it so that you can instantly find out where you are in the world.

This chapter also shows you where the winds are blowing and what the climate is like in different cities around the world. Using the Weather app, you can get real-time information about the weather as you travel.

I also describe how to use the Stocks and Passbook apps. You can personalize the Stocks app to reflect your exact portfolio, and you can add electronic tickets, boarding passes, coupons, and store cards to Passbook to keep track of them.

0.2 mile
MAKE A U-TURN AT
MARLIN AVE

Your iPod touch needs to be connected to the Internet over Wi-Fi for these apps to gather new information for you — see Chapter 4 for details on getting online.

Tapping Your Maps

I once had to find my way to a meeting on a university campus that I was already late for, and after driving endlessly around the campus looking for the proper entranceway, I tapped the Maps icon on my iPod touch and was able to immediately look up the location, see a map of it, and get directions. The Maps app is that good — most paper maps aren't even accurate for city streets, let alone campus driveways. (And, yes, I pulled over to the curb first for safety.)

The Maps app provides street maps, satellite photos, and hybrid street-satellite views of locations all over the world. It also offers detailed driving (or walking, or public transportation) directions from any location to just about any other location — unless you can't get there from here.

Where are you?

To use Maps, tap the Maps icon on the Home screen. The Maps app appears, as shown in Figure 17-1 (left side), ready for zooming, scrolling, or searching specific locations. The blue dot shows your (actually *my*) location.

How does Maps already know where I am? I tapped the location button in the lower-left corner of the map screen. When you do this, a dialog appears, asking whether Maps can use your current location; tap OK to use it. The map then changes to show your general location with a blue dot representing your approximate physical location, as shown in Figure 17-1 (right side).

You can zoom in to the map by double-tapping the map with one finger or unpinching with your fingers. To zoom out, pinch with your fingers or double-tap with two fingers. You can also drag the map to pan around it and see more areas.

Searching locations

To find a location and see a map, tap the Maps icon on the Home screen, and then tap the search field at the top of the Maps screen that appears. The onscreen keyboard appears, which you use to enter information.

You can find any location by its address or closest landmark, or you can find the physical address of a friend: Type the name of someone in your contacts list, or an address, an intersection, the name of a landmark or of a general area, or a zip code.

Directions   Bookmarks

3D view   Options

Location

Figure 17-1: Tap the location button (left) to show your location closely (right).

For example, to search for a friend, start typing the person's name. If the letters you type match names with street addresses in your contacts list, Maps offers them up as suggestions. Tap a suggested name to look up that person's home or business address.

You can also use the Contacts app to view your contacts list and then tap a contact's address to see that person's address in Maps.

To search for a landmark, an intersection, a zip code, or a type of business, enter as much as you know into the search field — such as *94111 pizza* for a pizza shop in the 94111 zip code. If the landmark is well known (such as Elvis Presley's Graceland in Memphis, TN), start typing its name. Then tap a suggestion that appears, or finish typing its name, as I do in Figure 17-2 (left side), and tap the Search key on the onscreen keyboard. A red pin appears to mark the location you've searched for on the map, with a label showing the name of the location or the address (see Figure 17-2, right side, for Graceland).

To clear the entry from the search field quickly, tap the *x* on the right side of the field. You can then type a new search term.

Figure 17-2: Type a search term and tap a suggestion or the search button (left) to see the location (right).

If you search for the name of a business or type of business *after* searching for your own location, as I do in Figure 17-3 (left side) for the nearest Starbucks, Maps is smart enough to locate the closest ones. Multiple red pins appear on the map, showing the location of each business, as shown in Figure 17-3 (right side).

Figure 17-3: Type the name of a popular business (left) to see its nearest locations (right).

Pinpointing the spot

Red pins mark the locations you've searched for on the map (refer to Figure 17-2 and Figure 17-3, right side), and each has a label (such as Graceland and Starbucks). You can also drop your own pin on the map to pinpoint an exact spot so that you can bookmark it. The pin you drop is purple until you bookmark it and give it a name. (See the "Bookmarking the spot" section, later in this chapter.)

To drop your own pin, follow these steps:

1. **Locate the area around the point you want the pin to drop on.**

   Drag the map to pan around and see more areas and zoom in to the location you want to pinpoint by double-tapping the map with one finger or unpinching with your fingers.

2. **Tap the options button — the curled page icon in the bottom-right corner (refer to Figure 17-1, left side).**

   You see a menu underneath the map, as shown in Figure 17-4 (left side).

3. **Tap the Drop Pin button in the menu.**

   A purple pin appears on the map with the label Dropped Pin (see Figure 17-4, center).

4. **Touch and hold the pin and drag it on the map to put it where you want it.**

   You can unpinch the map to zoom in farther; drag the pin to a precise point, such as an intersection; pinch to zoom out; and drag to pan the map to see other areas, as shown in Figure 17-4 (right side).

Figure 17-4: The options menu (left), a dropped pin (center), and dragging the pin's location (right).

To remove the pin, tap the circled right arrow on the right side of the pin's label to see the Info screen, and then tap Remove Pin.

To see a list of all pinpointed places on your map, tap the options button and tap List Results. You can then tap any location in the list to select that specific pin and its label.

Bookmarking the spot

Do you want to save these locations? You can add as many pins as you want to your map and save them as bookmarks. It makes sense to bookmark your home, your zip code (to make it easy to find businesses in your area), your office, and any other locations you visit often. After you've saved bookmarks, you can go back to any location by tapping the bookmarks button in the search field (refer to Figure 17-1, left side) to bring up a list of bookmarked locations and then tapping a location.

To bookmark a location after searching for it or dropping a pin, tap the circled right arrow on the right side of the pin's label to see the Location screen, as shown in Figure 17-5 (left side). You can then mark the spot with a bookmark that includes a name and description, or do other things such as get directions. (See the "Getting directions" section, later in this chapter.)

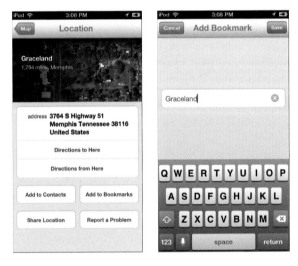

Figure 17-5: The Location screen for the location (left) for saving a bookmark (right).

Scroll the Location screen to find and tap the Add to Bookmarks button, which brings up the onscreen keyboard so that you can type a name for the location, as shown in Figure 17-5 (right side). Tap Save in the upper-right corner of the Add Bookmark screen to save the bookmark (or Cancel to cancel the bookmark). Tap Map in the upper-left corner of the Info screen to go back to the map. After you add a pin to your bookmarks, it changes from purple to red.

You can also touch the pin or its label and tap Directions To Here or Directions From Here (refer to Figure 17-5, left side) to get directions. (See the later section, "Getting directions.")

To go directly to a bookmarked location, tap the bookmarks icon in the search field (refer to Figure 17-1, left side) and then tap a location, or tap the Done button in the upper-right corner to return to the map.

The bookmarks icon in the search field also offers a list of the recently searched locations as well as access to your Contacts list. Tap the bookmarks icon, and then tap the Recents button at the bottom of the screen to see a list of recent locations found on the map. Tap the Contacts button next to Recents to view your Contacts and select one to see that person's address on the map. Tap the Done button in the upper-right corner to return to the map.

A bird's-eye view

Do you want to see what the location looks like? You can change the view of the location to show a satellite image (if available), a hybrid of the standard street view and satellite, or a list of bookmarked locations. Tap the options button — the curled page icon in the bottom-right corner (refer to Figure 17-1, left side) — to see the options menu underneath the map (refer to Figure 17-4, left side). Then tap Satellite to view a satellite image of the site, as shown in Figure 17-6 (left). You can zoom in to the image the same way you zoom in to the map.

You can also view a hybrid of the satellite image and standard street map, as shown in Figure 17-6 (center) — tap Hybrid in the menu underneath the map. In any of these views — Standard, Hybrid, or Satellite — you can tap the 3D or flyover (3D buildings) button in the lower-left corner to see a 3D or flyover version of that view. Figure 17-6 (right side) shows 3D with Satellite view. The flyover button appears if you use two fingers to drag up (vertically) on the screen, and lets you navigate in a 3D view of buildings and zoom in to see the buildings up close.

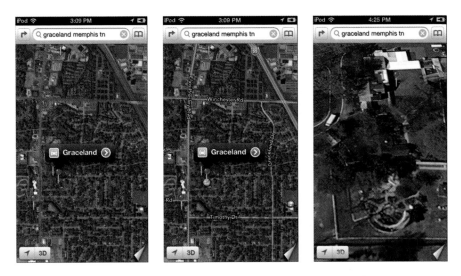

Figure 17-6: Try Satellite view (left) or Hybrid view (center), and go 3D (right).

Getting directions

The easiest way to get driving, walking, or transit directions is to ask Siri. (As of this writing, transit directions require an app such as Waze, available in the App Store.) Hold down the physical Home button until the Siri microphone appears on the screen and say something like "Do you know the way to San Jose?" Siri launches Maps and provides the route from your current location — you can tap the Start button in the upper-right corner, and Siri voices turn-by-turn directions.

If you don't like to ask anyone for directions, you can use Maps with your fingers. To get directions from one location to another, tap a pin on a map to see the Location screen for one of the locations (refer to Figure 17-5, left side), and then tap Directions To Here or Directions From Here to get directions. A screen appears with the first location selected as either the Start or the End. For example, after tapping the Graceland pin to show the Location screen in Figure 17-5 (left side), I tapped Directions To Here, which automatically placed the location in the End field, as shown in Figure 17-7 (left side), and "Current Location" in the Start field.

As you enter the Start and End locations for directions (refer to Figure 17-7, left side), you can tap the walking man icon to see walking directions; by default, Maps is set to give you driving directions. You can also tap the bus icon to see a list of apps (such as Waze) that can plot the route and provide public transit directions. The Maps app can also give you traffic information — see Chapter 20 for details.

Figure 17-7: Set the Start and End fields and tap Route (left) to see the route on the Directions map (right).

Another way to start getting directions is to search for or pinpoint a location, as described in the previous section, and then tap the directions button at the top-left corner of the map screen (refer to Figure 17-1, left side). For example, if you want to get directions from your current location to a bookmarked location, follow these steps:

1. **Tap the location button to find your physical location on the map.**

   The location button is in the lower-left corner of the map screen (refer to Figure 17-1, left side).

2. **Tap the directions button.**

   As a result, "Current Location" is already filled in for the Start field, as shown in Figure 17-7 (left side). A list of recent and bookmarked locations appears underneath the Start and End fields (the list is empty in Figure 17-7, left side).

3. **Tap a recent or bookmarked location in the list for the End field.**

You can also type entries or select bookmarks for both the Start and End fields by tapping those fields and using the onscreen keyboard.

TIP

Are you taking a round trip? You can switch the entry for Start to End (or vice versa) by tapping the switch button to the left of the Start and End fields (refer to Figure 17-7, left side). Using this button, you can get directions one way; tap the button to reverse the Start and End fields to get directions for the way back.

After setting your Start and End locations, tap Route (either at the top-right corner of the screen or in the bottom-right corner of the onscreen keyboard — refer to Figure 17-7, left side) to mark the route on the map, as shown in Figure 17-7 (right side). The route on the map is blue, with pins marking the start and end locations. Alternatively, you can tap Cancel in the upper-right corner (refer to Figure 17-7, left side) to cancel getting directions.

To see turn-by-turn directions on the map and hear Siri's voice tell you the directions, tap Start in the upper-right corner of the map (refer to Figure 17-7, right side). The Maps application graciously walks you turn-by-turn through your entire journey. A signpost showing directions and mileage appears at the top of the map, as shown in Figure 17-8 (left side). Swipe the signpost right-to-left to see the next stretch, and keep swiping through each stretch, as shown in Figure 17-8 (center) all the way to the end (see Figure 17-8, right side). You can swipe the signpost left-to-right in any of the turn-by-turn directions to go back a step and rap the Overview button in the top-right corner to see the entire route.

Figure 17-8: Get turn-by-turn directions from beginning (left), through the journey (center), and to the end (right).

Digging into Google Earth

With the Google Earth app for the iPod touch (shown in the first figure), you can take a peek in your neighbor's backyard or on the streets where you live (the second figure shows my current location), or find the source of the Nile River and follow it all the way to the Great Pyramids in Egypt (which you can see in the third figure in this sidebar). Google Earth, available for free for desktop computers, lets you fly anywhere on Earth to view satellite imagery, maps, terrain, 3D buildings, from galaxies in outer space to the canyons and mystery spots of the ocean.

The Google Earth app for the iPod touch displays the same imagery and offers the same navigational capabilities as the desktop version, and it includes layers with geo-located Wikipedia articles and Panoramio photos (as shown in the fourth figure), as well as map labels and borders. With the Search Near Me function, query results are not only geo-located within Google Earth, but also are automatically relevant to your location — search for *pizza* while in San Francisco, and it shows a collection of San Francisco pizza restaurants (the second figure shows the pizza parlors near my location). The Auto tilt feature uses the iPod touch built-in accelerometer to change your view in Google Earth when you tilt the iPod touch — you can tilt at an angle, as shown in the third figure, to see a skyline view of a location or tilt it all the way to see the sky itself.

To view all the legs of your journey in a list, tap the list icon at the bottom of the map (refer to Figure 17-7, right side) to see step-by-step driving directions and the approximate driving time for each step. You can tap any location in the list to see a map showing that leg of the trip.

To see your most recent set of directions, tap the bookmarks icon in the search field and tap Recents in the Bookmarks screen to change it to the Recents screen. If you close Maps and return to it later, your directions appear automatically. Tap the Done button in the upper-right corner to return to the map.

Checking for Stormy Weather

The Weather app provided with your iPod touch looks up the current temperature and weather conditions, and it provides a 6-day forecast for any city of your choice. Weather isn't the only app that does this — you can try other apps such as The Weather Channel, WeatherBug, or WeatherHD.

To use Weather, tap the Weather icon on the Home screen. If this is the first time you started Weather, or if you had previously turned off location services (as I describe in Chapter 4), Weather asks to use your current location. If you tap OK to use your current location, Weather starts off with a screen showing the weather in your local area (the closest city). In daytime, the Weather screen is light blue, and at night it's dark purple.

What makes Weather useful is your ability to add your own cities — as many as you need — so that you can look up the weather in multiple locations instantly.

To add a city, follow these steps:

1. **Tap the *i* button in the lower-right corner of the weather display, as shown in Figure 17-9 (left side).**

2. **Tap the add (+) button in the upper-left corner of the Weather screen (Figure 17-9, center).**

   A location field appears with the onscreen keyboard (Figure 17-9, right side).

3. **Enter the city's name or zip code — as you type, suggestions appear below in a list.**

4. **Choose one of the suggestions or continue typing the city name or zip code, and then tap Search.**

   The city you chose appears in the list of cities in the Weather screen, with a circled minus (–) sign next to it on the left and the move icon (three horizontal gray bars) on the right, as shown in Figure 17-10 (left side).

Figure 17-9: Tap the *i* button in Weather (left) to view the list of cities (center) and to add another city (right).

 At this point, you can add more cities by tapping the add (+) button in the upper-left corner again. You can also reorder the list of cities by dragging the move icon next to a city to a new place in the list, as shown in Figure 17-10 (right side).

To delete a city, tap the circled minus sign next to the city name to show the Delete button (see Figure 17-10, left side) and then tap the Delete button (or tap the circled minus sign again to leave it alone).

 The local weather appears as the first screen automatically, based on your location, and also appears in the Notifications Center that you can drag down from the top of the Home screen status bar (for more about the Notification Center, see Chapter 4).

Tap the Done button in the top-right corner of the Weather screen to finish adding cities and see the weather display for your city.

To switch from one city to the next, swipe right-to-left to move down the list or left-to-right to move up the list. You can also tap the tiny white buttons at the bottom of the city weather display (refer to Figure 17-9, left side). To see the hourly weather data, tap a single day in any Weather screen; to go back to the daily view, tap any hour.

Figure 17-10: Delete a city in Weather (left); reorder the city in the list (right).

Shaking Your Money-Maker

You can check your stocks, funds, and indexes with the Stocks app. (Whether the news is good or bad, you can quickly make a FaceTime call to your broker — see Chapter 18.) Tap the Stocks icon on the Home screen. The Stocks app displays a few stocks and indexes you may be interested in (such as Apple, of course). Scroll the Stocks list by dragging or flicking it with your finger.

Swipe the lower section of the Stocks screen to see a summary, a graph (as shown in Figure 17-11, left side), or the latest news. To see a current graph of the stock, swipe the lower section to the center, and then tap the 1d (1 day), 1w (1 week), 1m (1 month), 3m (3 months), 6m (6 months), 1y (1 year), or 2y (2 years) buttons above the graph in the stock reader. Tap the change number next to each stock to switch to show the percentage change, the market cap, or the change in price.

Of course, you'll want to add your portfolio to Stocks. To add a stock, index, or fund to watch, here's what you do:

1. **Tap the *i* button in the lower-right corner of the stock reader, as shown in Figure 17-11 (left side).**

2. **Tap the add (+) button in the upper-left corner of the Stocks screen (Figure 17-11, center).**

   The Add Stock field appears with the onscreen keyboard (Figure 17-11, right side).

3. **Enter the stock symbol or company name (or index or fund name).**

   As you type, suggestions appear below in a list.

4. **Choose one of the suggestions or continue typing the symbol or name and then touch Search.**

Figure 17-11: Touch the *i* button in Stocks (left) to view the list (center) and to add another stock, fund, or index (right).

The stock, fund, or index you chose appears in the list in the Stocks screen, with a circled minus (–) sign next to it on the left and the move icon (three horizontal gray bars) on the right (refer to Figure 17-11, center).

At this point, if you want to add more stocks, funds, or indexes, tap the add (+) button in the upper-left corner again. To reorder a list of stocks, drag the move icon next to a stock to a new place in the list, in the same way that you can reorder cities in the Weather app (refer to Figure 17-10, right side).

To delete a stock, tap the circled minus sign next to the stock name to show the Delete button (refer to Figure 17-11, center), and then tap the Delete button (or tap the circled minus sign again to leave it alone).

Tap the Done button in the top-right corner of the Stocks screen to finish adding stocks and see the stock reader.

Opening Your Passbook

Now that you can book your travel using an iPod touch app for your airline or travel service, or just using the Safari browser to access their web services, you can also store the electronic boarding pass for a flight in the Passbook app. You can then use the Passbook app to display your boarding pass at the gate. If you collect store cards or coupons, you can also store them in your Passbook app and display their bar codes at the checkout counter.

Passbook can store all the temporary passes and tickets you need while traveling and shopping, from loyalty cards, gift cards, and coupons to movie and sports tickets and boarding passes. Many of these electronic items include electronic bar codes, so you can use Passbook to display them in order to check in for a flight, get into a movie, or redeem a coupon. You can see when coupons expire, pinpoint where your concert seats are, or check the balance of a coffee loyalty card. If you're close to a movie theater or store, the app uses location services to serve up a ticket or relevant coupon on the lock screen.

To add these items (let's call them all *passes*) to Passbook, you need to use apps or services that offer them. You also have to be signed into your iCloud account to add passes to Passbook (see Chapter 8 for details on setting up your iCloud account).

Passbook service in iCloud is on by default, so that passes are pushed to your other iOS devices that are signed in to your iCloud account. If you have turned off some iCloud services, including Passbook, you can turn them back on by choosing Settings⊅iCloud, and then tapping the Passbook On/Off switch to turn Passbook service on or off.

Tap the Add to Passbook button on a merchant's app, website, or confirmation e-mail message. For example, you can tap the Manage button for your cards in the Starbucks app to see the menu in Figure 17-12 (left side), and then tap Add Card to Passbook. The Passbook pass for the card appears on the screen, and you can tap Add to add it to Passbook (or Cancel).

Launch Passbook, and the pass for the card appears, as shown in Figure 17-12 (center), along with other passes that appear as banners. You can see the banner for a Studio Botan pass from Deem Offers under the Starbucks pass in Figure 17-12 (center). Tap a banner to view the pass. You can then point the bar code at the bar code reader or scanner at the checkout counter or boarding gate.

You don't have to launch Passbook to show your passes in some stores, theaters, and airports — if you turn on Location Services (as described in Chapter 4); your pass appears on the lock screen when you arrive at the store, theater, or boarding gate. You can then point the bar code at the bar code reader or scanner without unlocking your iPod touch.

To prevent passes from appearing on your lock screen, choose Settings➪ General➪Passcode Lock from the Home screen, tap the Turn Passcode On button and enter a passcode if a passcode is not already active, and tap the On switch for Passbook to turn it off. To find out more about passcodes, see Chapter 4.

Figure 17-12: Add a Starbucks card to Passbook (left); view the pass (center) and change its settings (right).

To view more information about the pass, change its settings, or delete it, tap the *i* (information) button in the lower-right corner of the pass (refer to Figure 17-12, center). The information screen appears with any settings the pass offers (such as Automatic Updates for the Starbucks pass), as shown in Figure 17-12 (right side). To delete the pass, tap the trash icon in the upper-left corner. To view the pass again, tap Done in the upper-right corner.

Passes associated with apps, such as the Starbucks pass in Figure 17-12 (right side), typically include an Open button on the information screen for opening the app — in this case, the Starbucks app.

Part V
Staying in Touch and Up-to-Date

The 5th Wave   By Rich Tennant

"I'd respond to this person's comment on Twitter, but I'm a former Marine, Bernard, and a Marine never retweets."

*B*y now you should be accustomed to using your iPod touch like a small computer — and that's just what it is, a computer in your pocket that runs apps from the App Store. Some of these apps are just as powerful as the ones on your computer, especially ones that connect you to your social world. And the iPod classic can help you keep track of your contacts and your calendar events.

Chapter 18 puts you in contact with your contacts, and helps you manage your calendar. With an iPod touch you can also ask Siri to help manage your life, send free instant messages to your friends, and connect to your contacts with FaceTime video calls — using your iPod touch like a videophone. You can also connect with your friends and followers on the most popular social networks on the planet — Facebook and Twitter. And don't forget, you also get to play in the Game Center.

I saved the unfun stuff for Chapter 19: how to keep your iPod software up-to-date, how to reset the software and your settings, and how to restore your iPod to pristine factory condition.

18

A Day in the Social Life

In This Chapter

▶ Checking your calendar and entering events

▶ Entering and sorting your contacts

▶ Using Facebook, Twitter, and the Game Center

▶ Making FaceTime video calls

As John Lennon once sang, "Life is what happens to you when you're busy making other plans." And while life happens to you in real time, you can consult your iPod calendar and contacts to view your appointments and look up friends. You can go further with an iPod touch and change them, and make new ones. One of the major benefits of using an iPod touch is the onscreen keyboard, which you can use to enter text, such as calendar entries and new contacts, as I describe in this chapter. You can also ask Siri on an iPod touch to look up contacts, search the Internet, and schedule appointments for you.

In this chapter, I also demonstrate how to look up contact names, addresses, and phone numbers with your iPod, and also change contact information and add new contacts with an iPod touch. Any changes you make to calendars and contacts on your iPod touch are synchronized with your desktop applications (as I describe in Chapter 8).

To socialize and stay in contact with friends, relatives, and associates, you can use an iPod touch with social networks, such as Twitter and Facebook, to share photos, thoughts, links, and profile information. You can also make FaceTime video calls with people you know who are using an iPod touch, an iPhone 4 or 5, or a Mac (running OS X 10.6.6 or later).

The iPod classic offers extras (in the Extras menu) such as Calendars, Contacts, and Voice Memos, as well as click wheel games. The iPod touch, on the other hand, can run many hundreds of thousands of apps available in the App Store. (See Chapter 6 for details on downloading from the iTunes Store and App Store.) This chapter shows you how to use the Calendars and Contacts extras on an iPod classic, as well as how to use the social apps supplied with your iPod touch.

To find out how to sync and play click wheel games on an iPod classic, or record Voice Memos on an iPod classic, iPod nano, or iPod touch, see Bonus Chapter 4 in the free tips section of the author's website (www.tonybove. com/tips).

Checking Your Calendar

The calendar in your iPod isn't just for looking up dates (though it's quite good at that). You can synchronize your iPod with your calendar files from iCal or Calendar (Mac) or Outlook (Windows), or from iCloud, as I describe in Chapter 8. Rather than seeing a blank calendar, you see your calendar view filled with events.

Viewing your iPod classic calendar

To view your calendar on an iPod classic, choose Extras⇨Calendars. If you've synchronized multiple calendars, a list of calendars appears with All Calendars at the top. Press the Select button to select All Calendars for a merged view of all your calendars, or scroll the click wheel and press the Select button to select a specific calendar.

You can then scroll the click wheel to go through the days of the calendar. Select an event to see its details. Press the Next and Previous buttons to skip to the next or previous month. To see your To-Do list, choose Extras⇨Calendars⇨To Do's.

Using Calendar on an iPod touch

To see the calendar on your iPod touch, tap the Calendar app. A monthly calendar appears with events synced from your computer or iCloud, as shown in Figure 18-1 (left side).

If you've synced multiple calendars to your iPod touch, you can select individual calendars by tapping the Calendars button in the upper-left corner of the calendar view (refer to Figure 18-1, left side) to see the list of calendars, as shown in Figure 18-1 (right side). You can scroll the list of calendars to see all of them.

If only a few calendars (or no calendars) are selected, the Show All Calendars button appears at the top — tap it to show all the calendars in the calendar view. You can then tap a specific calendar to remove it from the calendar view.

If you set up your Facebook account on your iPod touch and enabled access to your calendar, as I describe in the "You've got a Facebook friend" section, later in this chapter, Facebook Events and Birthdays appear as calendars on the Calendars screen, and you can tap them to either add or remove them from the calendar view.

If all your calendars are already selected, the Hide All Calendars button appears at the top — tap it to hide all your calendars. You can then tap specific calendars to add them to the calendar view.

Tap any day to see the events on that day, which are displayed below the calendar view in a list (see Figure 18-1, left side); tap the event to see the event's information.

Tap the List, Day, or Month buttons (refer to Figure 18-1, left side) to change the calendar view to a list of events, a full day of scheduled events, or a month view, respectively. In Day or Month view, tap the left or right arrow at the top of the calendar to switch days or months. If you roam around from day to day or month to month, tap the Today button in the lower-left corner of the display to see the calendar for today.

Figure 18-1: The calendar view (left) and list of calendars (right).

A change is gonna come

Change happens, and you'll want to change your schedule or even add new events as you learn about them. You can enter events on your computer and sync them with your iPod classic or iPod touch, as I show in Chapter 8. You can also enter and change events directly in your iPod touch and keep changes and additions synced with your computer and with other devices using iCloud.

To add an event to your iPod touch calendar, follow these steps:

1. **Open the Calendar app as described earlier.**

   The Calendar app opens (refer to Figure 18-1, left side).

2. **Tap the add (+) button in the upper-right corner of the Calendar screen.**

   The Add Event screen appears.

3. **Tap the Title/Location button and enter the event's title and location using the onscreen keyboard, as shown in Figure 18-2 (left side).**

4. **Tap Done in the upper-right corner to save the entry (or Cancel in the upper-left corner to cancel the entry).**

5. **Tap the Starts/Ends/Time Zone button to enter the starting and ending times and dates and time zone.**

   The Start & End screen appears, as shown in Figure 18-2 (center), with a slot-machine-style number wheel to select the date and time, and an option to change the time zone for the event.

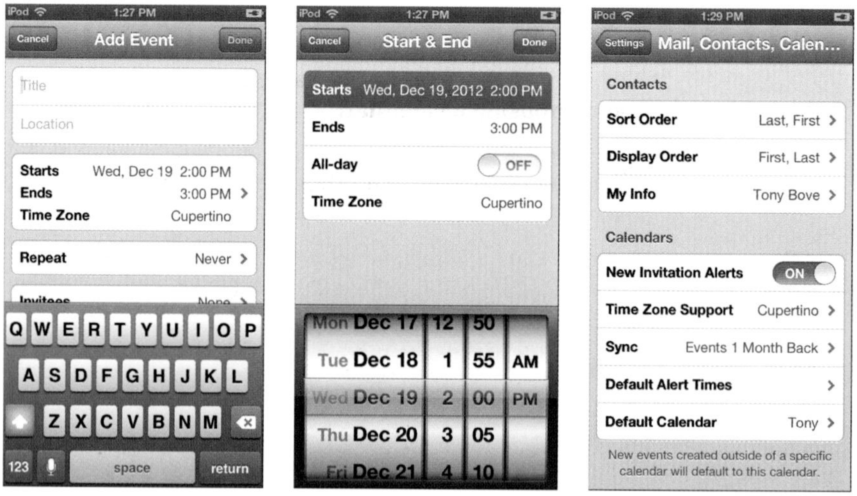

Figure 18-2: Add an event in Calendar (left) and set the start time (center); change calendar settings (right).

6. **Tap the Starts button and select the date and time, or tap the Off switch for All-Day to turn on the All-Day option.**

   Slide your finger up and down the slot-machine-style number wheel to select the date and time. If you turn on the All-Day option, the number wheel changes to show only dates; select a date for the all-day event and skip the next step.

7. **Tap the Ends button and select the date and time as you did in Step 6.**

8. **Tap Done in the upper-right corner to save the entry (or Cancel in the upper-left corner to cancel the entry).**

   The Add Event screen appears again, and you can scroll the screen to see more options.

9. **(Optional) Set the event to repeat by tapping Repeat and selecting a repeat frequency; tap Done (or Cancel).**

   You can set the event to repeat every day, every week, every two weeks, every month, or every year (or none, to not repeat).

10. **(Optional) Invite others to the event by tapping Invitees, entering or choosing a contact's e-mail address, and tapping Done (or Cancel).**

    You can send an invitation by e-mail to any contact by tapping the plus (+) icon and choosing the contact. You can also enter an e-mail address in the To field.

11. **(Optional) Set an alert for a time before the event by tapping Alert and choosing an alert time; tap Done (or Cancel).**

    You can set the alert to occur from five minutes to two days before the event. You can also set a second alert time in case you miss the first one or need two alerts.

12. **(Optional) If you have multiple calendars synced with your iPod touch, you can change the calendar for the event by tapping Calendar and choosing a calendar.**

    The Calendars screen appears with a list of your calendars. Tap a calendar's name to choose it. After you tap Done (or Cancel), the Add Event screen appears again.

13. **(Optional) Tap Availability and choose Busy or Free.**

    The Calendars screen shows whether you are busy or free for this event.

14. **(Optional) Add a URL for the event by tapping URL and using the onscreen keyboard to type the URL.**

    The URL field appears along with the keyboard for typing the web page URL (web address). Tap Done or Cancel to return to the Add Event screen.

15. **(Optional) Enter notes about the event by tapping Notes and using the onscreen keyboard to type notes.**

    The Notes field appears along with the keyboard for typing your notes. Tap Done (or Cancel).

16. **Tap Done in the upper-right corner of the Add Event screen to save the event (or Cancel in the upper-left corner to cancel the event).**

    The new event now appears in your calendar in the lower portion of the calendar view when you select the day.

You can edit the events you created, but not the events that appear in your Facebook Events calendar. To edit an event, tap the event in the lower portion of the calendar view, and then tap Edit in the upper-right corner of the Event Details screen. The Edit screen appears with event information ready for editing. To edit the event information, follow Steps 3–16 in this section. To delete the event, scroll the Edit screen all the way to the bottom to see the Delete Event button (which appears only when you're editing an event). After you tap Delete Event, a warning appears to confirm the deletion — tap Delete Event again or tap Cancel. The calendar view appears again.

Yesterday's settings (and today's)

If the calendar events you synced from your computer include alarms, you can turn on your iPod classic calendar alarm so that it beeps for those events. Choose Extras➪Calendars➪Alarms. Select Alarms once to set the alarm to Beep, select Alarms twice to set it to None (so that only the message for the alarm appears), or select it a third time to set it to Off. (The Alarms choices cycle from Beep to None to Off and then back to Beep.) For details on setting alarms, see Chapter 4.

On an iPod touch, you can set alerts for meeting invitations and choose how many weeks of events to sync back to (to clear out old events). Choose Settings➪Mail, Contacts, Calendars from the Home screen, and then scroll the Mail, Contacts, Calendars settings screen to the Calendars section, as shown in Figure 18-2 (right side).

To set the option for how far back in time to sync your calendar events, tap Sync and choose a period of time (such as Events 1 Month Back).

If you have an iCloud or Microsoft Exchange account set up with Calendars enabled, you can receive and respond to meeting invitations from others in your organization that also use Exchange. To set a sound as an alert for receiving a meeting invitation, tap the On/Off button for New Invitation Alerts to turn it on.

You can also turn time zone support on or off. When time zone support is on, event dates and times are displayed in the time zone of the city you selected. When time zone support is off, events are displayed in the time zone of your current location as determined by the network time. You might want to turn it on and select your home city so that dates and times are displayed as if you were in your home city, rather than where you actually are. For example, if you live in San Francisco and you're visiting New York, turning on Time Zone Support and selecting San Francisco keeps the dates and times in your calendars on San Francisco time. Otherwise, they switch to New York time.

To turn on Time Zone Support, tap Time Zone Support, and on the Time Zone Support screen, tap Off to turn on Time Zone Support (or tap On to turn it off). Then tap Time Zone and enter the name of a major city. As you type, city names are suggested based on what you've typed. Select the city to return to the Time Zone Support screen, and then tap the Mail button in the upper-left corner to return to the settings screen — or if you're finished making changes, press the Home button to leave settings altogether and return to the Home screen.

You can set your iPod touch to play an alert tone for your calendar. Choose Settings↪Sounds↪Calendar Alerts, and then select an alert tone or select None for no alert sound.

Using Your Contacts

The bits of information that you're most likely to need on the road are people's names, addresses, and phone numbers. You can use your iPod to store this information and keep it all in sync with your computer. (For sync info, see Chapter 8.)

To view contacts on an iPod touch, tap the Contacts app in the Utilities folder on the second Home screen. The All Contacts screen appears. If you've organized contacts into groups, you can tap the Groups button in the upper-left corner of the screen to show the Groups screen, and then tap a group to see just that group, or tap All Contacts to return to the All Contacts screen.

The contact list is sorted at first in alphabetical order by last name (in bold) but displayed so that the first name comes first, as shown in Figure 18-3, left side. (You can change contact sorting and displaying, as I show in the next section.) Scroll the list of contacts with your finger or tap a letter of the alphabet along the right side to go directly to names that begin with that letter. Then tap a contact to see that person's Info screen. If the contact appears in more than one group, you see all of the contact's information in both contact records on the Unified Info screen.

Figure 18-3: Viewing all contacts (left), adding a new contact (center), and entering the phone number (right).

The contact's info screen shows all the information about reaching that contact. Tap an e-mail address to bring up the Mail app and send an e-mail to that contact. Tap a website address to load that page into Safari. Tap a physical address (with a street address) to bring up the Maps app and locate the contact on the map.

To view a contact on an iPod classic, choose Extras➪Contacts from the main menu. If you've organized contacts into groups, a list of groups appears, with All Contacts at the top. Press the Select button to select All Contacts, or scroll the click wheel and press the Select button to select a group. You can then scroll the list of contacts and select a contact. The contact list is sorted automatically in alphabetical order by first name and then last name, or by last name followed by first name.

Orders to sort and display

You can change which way the contacts sort so that you can look up people by their first names (which can be time-consuming with so many friends named Elvis).

On an iPod touch, choose Settings➪Mail, Contacts, Calendars, and then scroll the Mail, Contacts, Calendars settings screen to the Contacts section (refer to Figure 18-2, right side). Tap Sort Order and then tap one of these options:

- ✔ **First, Last:** Sorts the contact list by first name, followed by the last name, so that *Brian Jones* sorts under the letter *B* for *Brian* (after *Brian Auger* but before *Brian Wilson*).

- ✔ **Last, First:** Sorts the contacts by last name, followed by the first name, so that *Brian Jones* sorts under the letter *J* for *Jones*. (*Jones, Brian* appears after *Jones, Alice* but before *Jones, Norah.*)

On an iPod classic, choose Settings➪General➪Sort Contacts, and then press the Select button in the scrolling pad for each option:

- ✔ **First:** Sorts the contact list by first name, followed by the last name.

- ✔ **Last:** Sorts the contacts by last name, followed by the first name.

You can also display contacts on an iPod touch with their first names followed by their last names, or last names followed by first names, regardless of how you sort them. Choose Settings➪Mail, Contacts, Calendars, and then scroll the Mail, Contacts, Calendars settings screen to the Contacts section. Tap Display Order and tap one of these options:

- ✔ **First, Last:** Displays the contacts list by first name and then last name, as in *Paul McCartney*.

- ✔ **Last, First:** Displays the contacts list by last name followed by a comma and the first name, as in *McCartney, Paul*.

You can also choose the default account for syncing your contacts by tapping Default Account and choosing the account (such as iCloud) — any contact you add without first choosing an account is synced with the default account.

Tap the My Info option to choose the contact information for yourself.

Soul searchin' on an iPod touch

Can't remember the person's full name or last name? You can search for any part of a person's name in Contacts by tapping the Search entry field at the very top of the list of contacts (refer to Figure 18-3, left side). The Search entry field appears with the onscreen keyboard and suggestions appear as you type.

Tap a suggested name to open the Contacts record for that person. You can then edit or delete the contact information.

Adding, editing, and deleting contacts on an iPod touch

You meet people all the time, so why not enter their information immediately? You can enter new contacts, edit existing contacts, and even delete contacts directly on your iPod touch, and keep your contacts in sync with your computer and with other devices using iCloud. (For sync info, see Chapter 8.)

To add a contact, follow these steps:

1. **Tap the Contacts app in the Utilities folder on the second Home screen.**

2. **Tap the add (+) button in the upper-right corner of the Contacts display.**

   The New Contact screen appears, as shown in Figure 18-3, center.

3. **Tap the First/Last/Company button and enter the contact's first and last name, as well as the company name, into each field using the onscreen keyboard.**

   The First, Last, and Company fields are ready for you to enter text with the keyboard. If you're entering a company name, use only the Company button.

4. **Scroll the screen and tap the Phone button next to the mobile label to enter a phone number.**

   After you tap Phone, as shown in Figure 18-3 (right side), it enables you to type the number. (After you type a number, another Phone button appears below it, enabling you to type more numbers.)

5. **(Optional) Tap the Mobile label to change the phone number's label.**

   Tap the number's label to select a different label for the type of phone (Mobile, iPhone, Home, Work, and so on).

   To enter a pause in a phone number (sometimes required for extensions or code numbers), tap the +*# button and tap Pause, which inserts a comma representing the pause. Each pause lasts 2 seconds; you can enter as many as you need.

6. **(Optional) Scroll down and tap the next Phone button to add more phone numbers, following the instructions in Steps 4 and 5 for each phone number.**

   After you type a number, another Phone button appears below it, enabling you to type more numbers — scroll the screen to see the button.

7. **Tap the Email button to add an e-mail address using the onscreen keyboard; tap the Home label to change the label for the type of e-mail address.**

   After you tap Email, the onscreen keyboard appears under the field to enter the e-mail address. Tap the Home label to change the label describing the e-mail address. After you type an e-mail address, another Email button appears below it, so that you can type more e-mail addresses — scroll the screen to see the button.

8. **(Optional) Scroll down and tap the next Email button to add more e-mail addresses, following the instructions in Step 7 for each e-mail address.**

9. **(Optional) Tap Default next to the ringtone label to set a specific ringtone for this contact to use in FaceTime.**

   The ringtone you choose will play whenever that contact makes a FaceTime call to you. See the later section, "Communicating with FaceTime," for details on making and receiving FaceTime video calls.

10. **(Optional) Tap Default next to the text tone label to set a unique text tone for messages in the Messages app.**

    The text tone you choose will play whenever you get an instant message. See the later section, "Messaging with Your iPod touch," for details on texting and receiving messages.

11. **(Optional) Tap the URL button to add a web page URL for the contact, and tap the home page label to change the label for the type of web page.**

    After you type a web page URL, another URL button appears below it, enabling you to type more web page URLs — scroll the screen to see the button.

12. **Scroll the New Contact screen and tap Add New Address to add the address information; then tap the home label to change the label for the type of address.**

    The keyboard appears with two entry fields for Street and one each for City, State, and ZIP. Tap the country button to set the country and the label button (set to Home) for the type of address. After you type the address, another Add New Address button appears below it, enabling you to type more addresses — scroll the screen to see the button.

13. **(Optional) Tap Add Field to add more fields to the contact.**

    You can add a prefix, middle name, suffix, phonetic first and last names, nickname, job title, department, birthday, date, or note. As you tap each field, the New Contact screen appears with the keyboard so that you can type the information.

14. **(Optional) Add a photo.**

To add a photo, tap Add Photo in the upper-left corner of the New Contact screen (refer to Figure 18-3, center). A pop-up menu appears with Take Photo, Choose Photo, or Cancel. The Take Photo option takes you to the Take Picture screen, where you can tap the camera shutter button to take a picture (or tap Cancel to cancel). The Choose Photo option takes you to the Photos app, where you can tap a photo album and tap a photo. Finally, tap Set Photo (or Cancel).

15. **Tap Done in the upper-right corner of the New Contact screen to save the contact information (or Cancel in the upper-left corner to cancel the contact information).**

To edit a contact, tap the contact to see the contact's Info or Unified Info screen, and then tap Edit in the upper-right corner of the Info screen to show the circled minus (–) sign and add (+) button.

If your contact appears in a Unified Info screen, it means that there are multiple contact records in different groups on your iPod touch — your editing changes all of them. If you want to edit them separately, go back to the contacts screen and tap Groups, as I describe at the beginning of this section, hide all the groups, and then select the group with the contact information you want to edit.

You can edit or delete any information for a contact while leaving the rest of the information intact. Tap any field to edit the information in that field. Tap the circled minus (–) sign next to the information to reveal a Delete button; tap the Delete button to delete the information, or tap the circled minus sign again to leave it alone.

To change a photo, tap the existing photo in the upper-left corner of the Info screen. A pop-up menu appears for you to tap Take Photo, Choose Photo, Edit Photo, Delete Photo, or Cancel. Tap Take Photo or Choose Photo as described in Step 14 earlier. To move or scale the photo, tap Edit Photo to show the Move and Scale screen. Then pinch the image with your fingers to zoom out or unpinch to zoom in, and drag the image with your finger to show only a portion of it. Tap the Set Photo button in the bottom-right corner of the Move and Scale screen to save the edited image (or tap Cancel). You return again to the Info screen.

Tap Done in the upper-right corner of the Info screen to finish editing and return to the contact information.

To delete a contact entirely, tap Edit, scroll down to the bottom, and then tap Delete Contact. Remember, if you do this, the contact will also be deleted from your contact list on your computer and in the iCloud if you sync your iPod touch.

Siri, Can You Hear Me?

Like the perfect genie, the Siri intelligent personal assistant, included with the newest iPod touch, responds to your command and tries to understand your requests. You can ask for directions, look up contacts, search the Internet, schedule appointments, look up baseball scores, and take dictation with apps that offer Siri in the online keyboard, such as Notes (as I show in Chapter 3).

To turn Siri on or off, choose Settings⇨General⇨Siri from the iPod touch home screen, and tap the on/off switch on the Siri settings screen. You can also tell Siri who you are by tapping My Info and then choosing your name in the Contacts app. Siri not only uses your current location but also uses your contact information (such as your home and work addresses, phone numbers, and e-mail accounts) to fulfill your requests, such as "Show me how to get home from here." You must be connected to the Internet over Wi-Fi for Siri to work.

Siri learns your speech patterns and phrases over time as long as you leave Siri on. If you turn Siri off, it forgets everything and resets itself.

To activate Siri, press the physical Home button until the Siri microphone appears, as shown in Figure 18-4 (left side). (If you change your mind, you can cancel Siri by pressing the Home button again.) You can start speaking right away — the microphone glows in color from the bottom indicating that Siri can hear you.

Siri waits for you to stop talking before it digests what you said, or you can stop the conversation by tapping the microphone. You can also restart the conversation or reply to Siri by tapping the microphone. When you stop, Siri displays what it heard and provides a response. You can scroll up to see the entire conversation. If Siri doesn't understand what you said (such as my first comical request, which it interpreted as "Yackety-yack"), it presents the Search the Web button, which you can tap to automatically launch Safari and search the web. You can also tap your request to edit it, as shown in Figure 18-4 (center). (After changing my request to "Play Yakety-Yak by the Coasters," it found the song and started playing it.)

If Siri understands your request (such as "Remind me to take out the trash at seven-thirty"), it displays the response with a Confirm or Cancel button to confirm the action with the app, as shown in Figure 18-4 (right side) with the Reminders app. You can tap Confirm or say "Yes" to confirm the action.

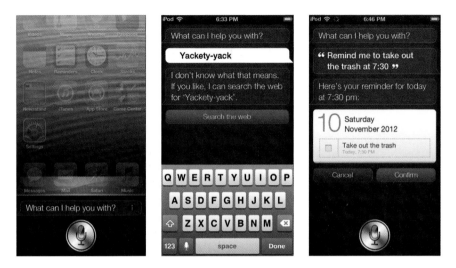

Figure 18-4: Talk to Siri (left) and edit your request (center); create a reminder (right).

There are many useful actions you can perform with Siri, such as making a FaceTime call to a friend in your Contacts app ("FaceTime Sam"), using Message to send a message telling a friend you're on your way ("Tell Dave I'll be right there"), setting up a meeting in Calendars ("Meet with Tim at noon"), tweet your location ("Tweet love this restaurant"), and post your Facebook status ("Write on my wall going to California"). Siri is well versed in sports, movies, and restaurants, and connects with Yelp and Open Table and other sources to provide more information.

Siri also has a few surprises up its sleeve — ask it "What's your favorite color?" and "What do you look like?" and see the responses. Don't forget to try "Open the pod bay doors, HAL."

Messaging with Your iPod touch

You can use the Messages app on your iPod touch to send and receive instant text messages with other iOS devices (such as iPhones, iPads, and other iPod touches) and Macs running Mountain Lion or newer operating systems. Messages uses the iMessage protocol. Unlike cellphone texting (SMS and MMS), iMessage is completely free and works over Wi-Fi. You can even send photos, videos, locations, and contacts with your messages. It's easy to conduct conversations with people because you can see when each person is typing a message (and there's no shouting, although you're welcome to use ALL CAPS).

To send a message to a contact who uses an iPod touch, iPad, iPhone, or Mac, you can select the e-mail address for that contact, as long as that person has designated that e-mail address as one that can receive messages. (You can also send a message to an iPhone's phone number, but this may incur charges for the iPhone user.)

When you first set up your iPod touch (as I describe in Chapter 2), the Messaging screen appears as part of the setup screens showing your e-mail addresses. You can select any or all of your e-mail addresses that others can use to send messages to you. You can also do this at any time by choosing Settings⇨Messages⇨Send & Receive, and selecting your e-mail accounts. You can also select which e-mail account to use as the From account for new messages.

When your iPod touch receives a message, it can automatically display an alert on your lock screen (unless you turn this option off — choose Settings⇨Messages to turn the View in Lock Screen option on or off). Slide the slider to go right into the Messages app, where you can reply to the message, if you want.

You can view and send messages by tapping the Messages app. The Messages screen appears with a list of conversations. A blue dot appears next to any conversation that has one or more unread messages.

Tap a conversation to see its messages, which are organized into conversations as shown in Figure 18-5 (right side). Outgoing messages appear in colored balloons, and incoming messages appear in white balloons. You can tap the message entry field at the bottom of the screen to bring up the onscreen keyboard and add a reply to the conversation. The reply is sent to all who received the conversation.

Scroll the conversation screen to the top (or tap the status bar to get there quickly) to see the rest of the messages in the conversation. If there are many messages, the Load Earlier Messages button appears; tap it to see earlier messages. To return to the Messages screen, tap Messages in the upper-left corner.

To send a new message, follow these steps:

1. **Tap the create message icon in the upper-right corner of the Messages screen (refer to Figure 18-5, left side).**

   The New Message screen appears with the onscreen keyboard and the To: field.

2. **Tap the plus (+) icon to add a contact to the To: field.**

   Your contacts appear.

Create message

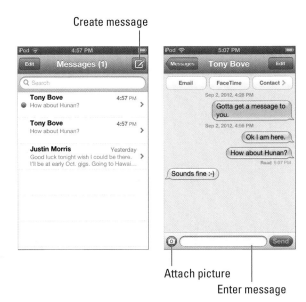

Attach picture

Enter message

Figure 18-5: The Message app's list of conversations (left) and a single conversation (right).

3. **Tap a contact, and then tap an e-mail address or iPhone phone number.**

   The contact is added to the To: field. If a red exclamation point appears next to the contact in the To: field, the contact has not designated the e-mail address or phone number for receiving messages.

   You can repeat Steps 2–3 to continue to add more contacts for a group conversation.

4. **Enter the message and tap Send.**

   Use the onscreen keyboard to enter the message (see Chapter 3 for details on using the keyboard).

To send a photo or video with your message or with a reply, tap the camera icon on the left side of the message entry field (refer to Figure 18-5, right side). You can then tap Take Photo or Video to use the iPod touch camera, or tap Choose Existing to choose an existing picture from your iPod touch photo albums or Camera Roll. (See Chapter 14 for details on taking pictures.)

To send your location from the Maps app in a message, tap the location icon in Maps to find your location, tap the pin for your location to show the Location screen, tap Share Location, and then tap Message. For more about Maps, see Chapter 17.

Phoning with your iPod touch

The iPhone gets all the glory for its communicating abilities with its phone and text-messaging services provided by the service carrier, but the iPod touch is no slouch in this department — in fact, the iPod touch can make you carrier-free. All you need to do is go online with a Wi-Fi connection that accesses the Internet (see Chapter 4). Not only can you use FaceTime to make video calls to other FaceTime users (as I show in the "Communicating with FaceTime" section), and use the Messages app to send and receive instant text messages (as I describe in the "Messaging with Your iPod touch" section), but you can also use other apps to make Internet phone calls or send instant messages.

Skype (shown in the following figures) is a service that lets you make phone calls over the Internet. Calls to other Skype users are free, but calls to landlines and mobile phones require some money on your part. The Skype app (free)

gives you phone service, video chat, and instant text messages to anyone else on Skype. For voice calls, all you need is a Wi-Fi connection.

Messages is fine for iPod touch, iPhone, iPad, and Mac users running Mountain Lion, but if you need instant messaging with others who don't use those iOS devices, try the AOL Instant Messenger (AIM) app, which is popular in the United States. You can send and receive instant messages on your iPod touch (and with Mac users with Messages or iChat), view your buddy list, and rearrange the entries in groups or separate them as favorites. And Yahoo! Messenger folks are just a chat away (with the free Yahoo! Messenger app). And, of course, you can send and receive messages using the Facebook and Twitter apps (see the "Socializing on Networks" section), as well as use apps for other social networks.

You can delete part of a conversation or an entire conversation from the Messages app without disturbing the other conversations. Tap Edit in the top-right corner of the conversation screen (refer to Figure 18-5, right side) to see the editing screen. Tap to select each part of the conversation that you want to delete, and then tap Delete at the bottom of the editing screen. To clear an entire conversation, tap Clear All in the upper-left corner of the editing screen.

 You can also forward an entire conversation to someone else. Tap Edit in the top-right corner of the conversation screen, select each part of the conversation that you want to forward, and then tap Forward at the bottom of the editing screen.

 Want to let the others in a conversation know that you read their messages? Choose Settings⇨Messages and turn on the Send Read Receipts option.

You can use Emoji characters in your messages by activating the Emoji keyboard, and then tapping the globe symbol on the keyboard to show the Emoji characters. To find out how to add an international keyboard (such as Emoji), see Chapter 20.

Socializing on Networks

Connecting socially by computer isn't new, but connecting on a digital network anytime and from anywhere makes social networking more instant and gratifying. You can use your iPod touch to stay in touch with your connections on the leading social networks, including Facebook and Twitter — viewing and typing messages, chatting, uploading and sharing photos, joining groups, and so on.

You've got a Facebook friend

Facebook is the fastest-growing free-access social networking site as of this writing, with hundreds of millions of active users worldwide. If you're one of them (as I am), you already know that you can add friends, send them messages, and update your personal profile with photos, videos, and links. Although you can do all this using a browser on your computer and using Safari on your iPod touch, the site itself is far too cumbersome for easy access that way.

Facebook is integrated with the iPod touch so that you can share photos directly from the Photos app, share your location directly from the Maps app, share contact information from the Contacts app, share web links from the Safari app, and even see your Facebook events and birthdays in the Calendar app.

To set up your Facebook account with your iPod touch, choose Settings⇨Facebook. The Facebook settings screen appears as shown in Figure 18-6 (left side). Enter your username and password, and tap Sign In. The screen changes to show more settings, as shown in Figure 18-6 (right side).

Figure 18-6: Set up your Facebook account (left) and change its settings (right).

You can allow or disallow the Calendar and Contacts apps to use your Facebook account by tapping the On/Off switch. If you allow Calendar to use your account, the Facebook Events and Birthdays calendars appear in the Calendar app (as I explain in the earlier section, "Using Calendar on an iPod touch"). If you allow Contacts to use your Facebook account, the All Facebook group appears in your groups of contacts, so that you can see all of your contacts that are also on Facebook.

You can also tap the Update All Contacts button at the bottom of the screen to update the e-mail addresses and photos all of your contacts that are also in Facebook.

To change settings for your Facebook account on the iPod touch, tap Settings (refer to Figure 18-6, right side). The Settings screen appears. In the Chat and Message Alerts section, you can turn the Vibrate and Play Sound options on or off for incoming chat and message alerts. (To set your push notification settings for Facebook, use the Facebook app and tap Account Settings.) You can also enable HD video recording from within the Facebook app by tapping the Off switch for the Record HD Video option to turn it on.

After setting up your Facebook account with your iPod touch, you can then share items such as photos and video clips (which I call "pictures") with your Facebook friends using the Photo app. As I show in Chapter 14, you can view a picture and then tap the options button to see the sharing sheet, and tap the Facebook icon on the sharing sheet. The Facebook sheet appears, as shown in Figure 18-7 (left side), with a thumbnail of the picture you're post-ing to Facebook, a notes-style text entry field and onscreen keyboard for entering a message to go with it, and the Add Location and Friends buttons. Here's how you use these optional features for posting to Facebook:

- ✔ **Thumbnail:** Tap it to assign the picture to one of your Facebook photo albums. You can select any album that you've already set up in Facebook.

- ✔ **Message field:** Enter a message to accompany the picture using the onscreen keyboard.

- ✔ **Add Location:** After tapping this, a request to access your current location appears. Tap OK, and your location information accompanies the picture.

- ✔ **Friends:** Tap this to choose the audience for your picture. You can then select Friends, Only Me, Friends Except Acquaintances, Public, or any groups associated with your Facebook account.

To post your picture (and optional message), tap Post in the upper-right corner (refer to Figure 18-7, left side).

Figure 18-7: Sharing a picture from Photos on Facebook (left); using the Facebook app (right).

You can also use the Facebook app to upload pictures and even record HD video. The app also displays your friends' status updates and photos, and lets you start a conversation in Facebook Chat.

Setting up Facebook in Settings automatically downloads the Facebook app to your iPod touch. Tap the Facebook icon on whichever Home screen it downloads to. If this is your first time using the app, a dialog appears asking whether you would like Facebook to push notifications, such as alerts, sounds, and numeric icon badges, whenever your Facebook account receives messages and notifications. (See Chapter 4 for details on setting app notifications.) Tap OK to allow notifications or tap Don't Allow to stop them from happening. (You may want to disallow them to save battery power.)

Figure 18-7 (right side), shows the Facebook main menu. Tap the News Feed tab to see your news feed. If you have messages in your inbox, a number appears on the Messages tab; tap it to see your messages. If you have notifications or invites, they appear in the Nearby or Events tabs. Tap them to see who's nearby or which events you've been invited to. Tap your Facebook name to show your profile or tap the Friends tab to see your friends. Tap a friend, and then tap Message, to send a message.

The Facebook app even lets you upload and share photos and videos. Tap the News Feed tab, and then tap Photo at the top. You can then tap Take Photo or Video to take a picture, or Choose From Library to choose one from your iPod touch photo library.

Dedicated follower of Twitter

Twitter is a free social messaging service for staying connected with people in real time. With Twitter, you can post and receive messages that are 140 characters or fewer — called *tweets.* All public tweets are available to read on the public timeline, or you can read just the ones posted by the Twitter members you follow. You can post a tweet that can be read by all of your followers and by anyone reading the public tweets.

Members use Twitter to organize impromptu gatherings, carry on a group conversation, or just send a quick update to let people know what's going on. Companies use Twitter to announce products and carry on conversations with their customers.

Twitter is integrated with your iPod touch apps so that you can tweet directly from apps that offer an options or sharing button with the Twitter option — such as the Safari browser (which I show in Chapter 15) for sharing web links, and the Photos app (which I describe in Chapter 14) for sharing photos and videos.

To set up one or more Twitter accounts with your iPod touch, choose Settings⇨Twitter. The Twitter settings screen appears, as shown in Figure 18-8 (left side). You can add multiple accounts — tap the Add Account button to add each Twitter account. The Add Account screen appears, and you can tap the User Name field to enter your Twitter account name, the Password field to enter your password, and the Sign In button to sign into Twitter. If you don't have a Twitter account, tap the Create New Account button to sign up for one. You can also tap the Update Contacts button on the Twitter settings screen (see Figure 18-8, left side) to add Twitter usernames and photos to your contacts who also use Twitter.

Figure 18-8: Setting up your Twitter accounts (left); sending a tweet with a photo (right).

After setting up your Twitter account with your iPod touch, you can then share with your Twitter followers such things as web links from Safari, and photos and video clips (which I call "pictures") from the Photo app. As I show in Chapter 14, you can view a picture and tap the options button to see the sharing sheet, and tap the Twitter icon on the sharing sheet. The Twitter sheet appears, as shown in Figure 18-8 (right side), with a thumbnail of the picture you're posting as a tweet, a notes-style text entry field and onscreen keyboard for entering a tweet, and the Add Location button. Enter the text of the tweet using the onscreen keyboard, and tap the Add Location button to include your current location. After tapping it, a request to access your current location appears. Tap OK.

To post your tweet, tap Send in the upper-right corner (refer to Figure 18-8, right side).

Setting up a Twitter account in Settings automatically downloads the Twitter app to your iPod touch, which you can use to easily flip through all your messages with the flick of a finger. Tap the Twitter app icon on the Home screen it downloads to, and the Twitter app logs you in to your account. If you set up multiple Twitter accounts with your iPod touch, you can tap the Sign In button to log in to one of your accounts. After logging in or signing in, you can see recent tweets, search the Twitter timeline, post new tweets, send direct messages and replies to others on Twitter, and add new friends (called *followers*).

And wherever you go, "tweetness follows." Twitter can use the iPod touch's built-in location services so that, with your permission, it can let your followers know where you are and let you know when your followers are posting from a nearby location. Tweet dreams!

Joining the Game Center

For socializing at a faster pace, nothing beats gaming with friends. You can discover new games and new friends from around the world in the Game Center. You can invite friends to join, or choose people you don't know, and use an alias if you want — it's the safest way to interact with strangers.

To join Game Center, tap its icon on the Home screen. If your nickname and photo don't appear, you need to tap Sign In and provide your Apple ID and password, or tap Sign On to set up an account (to set up an account, see Chapter 6). As a first-time gamer, you see the New in Game Center screen with a Friend Recommendations section with the Contacts option. On this screen you can also add or change your photo and enter your status. Turn on Contacts to upload your contacts to the Game Center to get friend recommendations, and then click Done to proceed.

If you have already set up your Facebook account, as I describe in the "You've got a Facebook friend" section, earlier in this chapter, Game Center asks if it can find new Game Center friends among your Facebook friends. Tap Allow to allow it or Later to postpone the decision (you can postpone it indefinitely).

To change your Game Center account settings, tap the account button (the one with your account name), and then tap View Account in the pop-up menu that appears. Game Center then displays your account screen, where you can turn on or off the Game Invites option to allow friends to invite you to play games. You can also turn on or off the Public Profile option (which makes your name visible to other players). The Email section of the screen lets you set an e-mail address to receive friend requests. Tap Done in the upper-right corner of the screen to finish changing your account settings.

Tap the Games icon along the bottom row of icons to see the Games screen with a list of games you already have. To find more games in the App Store that are developed for use in Game Center, tap Find Game Center Games at the bottom of the Games screen.

To play a game, tap the game to see the information screen, and then tap the Play button in the upper-right corner. For many games, you can tap the Leaderboards button to see how others score in the game, the Achievements button to see a list of game goals, and the Players button to find someone to play against. You can challenge people to play a game by tapping their scores. If you are challenged, tap the Challenges icon in the bottom row of icons to answer the call to battle.

To invite a friend to play a game, tap the Friends icon in the bottom row of icons. Tap an existing friend's name, or tap Add Friends and enter an e-mail address to send a friend request. If you have games in common with your friend, tap a game in your friend's list of games, and then tap the price of the game below its name at the top of the screen. If you don't have games in common, tap Send Friend Request to send a request. To reply to friend requests, tap the Requests icon.

Communicating with FaceTime

I saved the best for last: making and receiving video calls with Apple's truly innovative FaceTime technology. No matter how we communicate, it helps sometimes to have a little face time. Apple has engineered a solution that lets you make video calls over Wi-Fi to an iPad 2 or later, iPhone 4, another iPod touch (fourth-generation or later), or a Mac running Mountain Lion or a newer operating system. You can use either the front or back camera with FaceTime — the front camera has just the right field of view and focal length to focus on your face at arm's length, but you can switch to the back camera to show what's happening around you. And FaceTime can use the cameras in either portrait or landscape orientation.

FaceTime calls are not any more intrusive than phone calls — your iPod touch rings (you can sync ringtones to your iPod touch, as I show in Chapter 4), and an invitation pops up on your screen asking if you want to accept the call. Tap Accept, and the video call begins.

To use FaceTime on an iPod touch, you need a fourth-generation or newer iPod touch and to be connected to the Internet over Wi-Fi, as I describe in Chapter 4. The person you're calling also needs to be connected to the Internet over Wi-Fi or cellular and using a device that can run FaceTime.

You also need to sign into FaceTime using the FaceTime app and an Apple ID (see Chapter 6 about getting an account). Once you've signed in, you don't need to do it again for every call.

Setting up your calling address

To sign in, tap the FaceTime icon on the Home screen, tap the Email Address and Password fields to enter your Apple ID and password, and then tap Sign In. If you don't already have an Apple account, tap Create New Account to set one up. You can then enter your account information on the New Account screen (see Chapter 6 for details on setting up an account).

You can then select an e-mail address that you use on your iPod touch, which is the address that others will use to call you in FaceTime. If you use more than one e-mail address on your iPod touch, you can add the others to FaceTime so that people can use them to call you. Choose Settings➪FaceTime, and then tap Add Another Email. Now others can call you using any of the e-mail addresses you provided. While you are in the FaceTime settings screen, you can also set a Reply With Message option to reply automatically when you can't answer a call (such as "I'll call you later"). You can also set the e-mail address to use as a caller ID in the Caller ID section of the settings screen.

Making a video call

You can start a FaceTime video call by tapping the FaceTime icon on the Home screen. You can then tap the following icons along the bottom of the screen:

- **Favorites:** Tap one of your favorites. (To add a contact to your favorites list, open the contact as I describe in the earlier section, "Using Your Contacts," and then tap the Add to Favorites button on the contact information screen.)

- **Recents:** If you've previously had a FaceTime video call with someone, you can make another video call with that person by tapping the Recents icon, and then tapping an entry in the Recents list that appears.

- **Contacts:** Tap to see your contacts, which appear just like they do in the Contacts app (see the earlier section, "Using Your Contacts"). You can then choose a contact, scroll the contact information screen to the bottom, and tap the FaceTime button.

FaceTime places the call and sends an invitation to the contact. If your contact taps the Accept button in this invitation, as shown in Figure 18-9 (left side), you then see the screen shown in Figure 18-9 (right side), with your contact's face on the other end (or in this case, his fingers, as he hadn't truly woken up yet). If you are receiving a call (see Figure 18-9, left side), you can tap Decline to decline it, Accept to accept it, or the no-video icon to accept it without a picture (just voice).

On the Notifications screen in Settings you can also tap Allow Calls From to specify which FaceTime calls you will accept. See Chapter 4 for details.

While communicating with your contact in FaceTime (refer to Figure 18-9, right side), a picture-in-picture window shows the image from your iPod touch that the other person sees. You can drag the picture-in-picture window to any corner. You can use FaceTime in portrait or landscape orientation — when you rotate the iPod touch, the image your contact sees changes to match.

Mute End the call

Switch cameras

Figure 18-9: Accept a FaceTime call (left) and start talking (right).

To avoid unwanted orientation changes as you move the camera around, lock the iPod touch in portrait orientation as I describe in Chapter 3.

To switch from the front camera to the back camera, tap the switch camera button once; tap it again to switch back to the front camera. You can also tap the mute button to mute your iPod touch microphone so that your contact can't hear you, although your contact can still see you, and you can still see and hear your contact. To end the video call, tap the End button.

Don't be shy about using another app during a FaceTime call, if you want to. Just press the Home button and choose any app. You can still talk with your contact over FaceTime, but you can't see each other. To return to the video portion of the call from another app, tap the green bar that appears at the top of the app's screen.

You can turn FaceTime off if you don't want to receive any calls — choose Settings⊃FaceTime, and then tap On at the top of the FaceTime settings screen to turn FaceTime off.

19

Resetting, Updating, and Restoring

In This Chapter

▷ Resetting your iPod
▷ Updating iPod software with the newest version
▷ Restoring your iPod touch settings
▷ Restoring an iPod to its factory condition

This no-nonsense chapter may not be fun, but it's necessary. Humans aren't perfect, and neither are the machines they make. If your iPod stops working as it should, or an app causes your iPod touch to freeze up, you can turn to this chapter. You also find out how to reset your iPod touch network settings and the keyboard dictionary.

This chapter also covers updating the firmware and software on your iPod. (*Firmware* is software encoded in hardware.) All software devices need to be updated now and then — it's a good thing because new versions fix known bugs and add improvements.

Finally, I describe how to restore your iPod to its factory default condition. Restoring to factory condition is a drastic measure that erases all of the content, information, and settings on the iPod, but it usually solves a software glitch when nothing else does, and it's a step you should take before selling or giving your iPod to someone else after you upgrade to a new one. You can then restore your settings for an iPod touch, and sync your iPod with your content and information.

Hitting the Panic Button

Sometimes problems arise with electronics and software that can prevent an iPod touch from returning from an app, or keep an iPod nano or iPod classic from turning on properly with all its content and playlists. Don't panic — there's a panic button for that, in the form of a reset operation.

Before resetting the iPod, you may want to connect it to a power outlet by using the AC power adapter. You can reset your iPod without connecting it to power if it has enough juice in its battery. However, if you have access to power, it makes sense to use it because the reset operation uses power, and starting up your iPod from scratch again also uses power.

Stopping a frozen iPod touch app

If your iPod touch freezes while running an app, touch and hold the Home button below the screen for at least 6 seconds or until the app quits.

If the app doesn't quit in 6 seconds or the iPod touch remains frozen, touch and hold the sleep/wake button on the top for a few seconds until a red slider that says Slide to Power Off appears on the screen. Slide the slider with your finger to turn off the iPod touch. Then press the sleep/wake button. The iPod touch starts up again.

If your iPod nano, iPod shuffle, or iPod classic itself freezes, you need to reset its system, as I describe later in this section.

Resetting an iPod touch

You probably won't be too surprised to discover that, on the off chance your iPod touch gets confused or refuses to turn on, you can fix it by resetting it and restarting the system — just like computers and other iPods. Resetting does *not* restore the iPod touch to its original factory condition, nor does it erase anything — your content and settings remain intact.

To reset the iPod touch, touch and hold the sleep/wake button and the Home button at the same time for at least 15 seconds, ignoring the red Slide to Power Off slider, until the Apple logo appears.

After you reset the iPod touch, everything should be back to normal, including your music and data files.

Resetting your iPod touch settings

You can reset all or part of your iPod touch settings while leaving your content and personal information intact. To see your resetting options, choose Settings⇨General⇨Reset from the Home screen (Reset is at the very bottom of the General settings screen). The Reset screen appears with the following options:

- ✓ **Reset All Settings:** To return your iPod touch to its original condition with no preferences or settings while still keeping your content or your personal information (including contacts, calendars, and e-mail accounts) intact, tap Reset All Settings.

- ✓ **Erase All Content and Settings:** To erase *everything,* first connect the iPod touch to your computer or a power adapter, and then tap Erase All Content and Settings. This operation can take a while, and you can't use the iPod touch until it finishes.

- ✓ **Reset Network Settings:** You can reset your network settings so that your previously used networks are removed from the Wi-Fi list. This type of reset is useful if you can't find any other way to stop a Wi-Fi network from connecting automatically to your iPod touch — just tap Reset Network Settings, and you're automatically disconnected from any Wi-Fi network. (Wi-Fi is turned off and then back on.) For more details about choosing Wi-Fi networks, see Chapter 4.

- ✓ **Reset Keyboard Dictionary:** To reset the keyboard dictionary, tap Reset Keyboard Dictionary. This erases all words that have been added to the dictionary. (Words are added when you reject words suggested by the onscreen keyboard and type the word — see Chapter 3 for details.)

- ✓ **Reset Home Screen Layout:** If you rearranged the icons on your Home screen (as I describe in Chapter 3), you may want to set them back to their original positions. To reset your Home screen to the default arrangement, tap Reset Home Screen Layout.

- ✓ **Reset Location & Privacy:** You can reset your location and privacy settings by tapping Reset Location & Privacy. To find out how to set your location, see Chapter 4, and for details on privacy settings, see Chapter 20.

Resetting an iPod nano and iPod classic

To reset an iPod nano, press the sleep/wake button and the Home button for six seconds, until the Apple logo appears.

To reset the iPod classic, follow these steps:

1. **Toggle the hold switch.**

   Slide the hold switch to the right, exposing the orange layer, to lock the buttons, and then slide it back to unlock.

2. **Press the Menu and select buttons simultaneously and hold for at least 6 seconds or until the Apple logo appears; then release the buttons when you see the Apple logo.**

   The appearance of the Apple logo signals that your iPod is resetting itself, so you no longer have to hold down the buttons.

Release the Menu and select buttons as soon as you see the Apple logo. If you continue to press the buttons after the logo appears, the iPod displays the low battery icon, and you must connect it to a power source before using it again.

To reset iPod nano or iPod classic settings, choose Settings⇨Reset Settings from the iPod nano Home screen or iPod classic main menu, and then select Reset (or Cancel to cancel). This resets all the items on the Settings menu to their default settings.

Resetting an iPod shuffle

To reset the iPod shuffle, first disconnect it from your computer (if you haven't already done so) and then slide the three-position switch to the Off position. The green stripe under the switch should not be visible. Wait 5 seconds and then switch the slider back to the Shuffle Songs or Play in Order position.

After resetting, everything should be back to normal, including your music and data files.

Updating Your iPod

You should always keep your iPod updated with new versions of the software that controls the device — which is iOS for the iPod touch, or the iPod system software for an iPod classic, iPod nano, and iPod shuffle. New versions often include bug fixes as well as new features. The following sections outline what you need to know to update your iPod.

Checking the software version

The fastest way to find out if the version of iOS on your iPod touch is the most recent version, choose Settings⇨General⇨Software Update. If a new version of the software is available, you see the Download and Install button, as I describe in the next section. If your version of iOS is current, the screen tells you so, and you don't see those buttons.

To see which version of iOS is installed on your iPod touch, choose Settings➪General➪About. Next to the word Version is information that describes the software version installed.

To see which version of the iPod system software is installed on an iPod nano or iPod classic, choose Settings➪General➪About from the iPod nano Home screen or Settings➪About from the iPod classic main menu. Next to the word *Version* is information that describes the software version installed.

You can also determine the software version on your iPod touch, iPod nano, iPod classic, or iPod shuffle by using iTunes. Connect the iPod to your computer and select it in the iTunes source pane (in the Devices section). The Summary page appears to the right of the source pane, and the software version appears next to Software Version at the top of the page.

Updating with newer software

To update your iPod touch software from iCloud, choose Settings➪General➪Software Update. If a new version of the software is available, you see the Download and Install button — tap it to install the new version of the software. The installation doesn't affect the music or data stored on it.

You need to use iTunes to install or update the software on an iPod nano, iPod shuffle, or iPod classic, and you can also use iTunes to update iOS on your iPod touch. Connect the iPod to your computer, click the iPod button (as I describe in Chapter 7), and you'll see the Summary sync page appear. iTunes automatically checks for updates of iOS or the iPod software and lets you update your iPod without affecting the music or data stored on it. iTunes includes updates for all generations of iPods and can detect which iPod models you have.

Make sure that you use the newest version of iTunes. To check for the availability of an updated version for Windows, choose Help➪Check for iTunes Updates. If you use a Mac and you enabled the Software Update option in your System Preferences, Apple automatically informs you of updates to your Apple software for the Mac, including iTunes. All you need to do is select which updates to download and then click the Install button to download them.

If an update is available, a dialog appears to ask permission to download it. Go ahead and click OK to update the iPod; you'll be happy you did. After you update the software, iTunes continues syncing the iPod until it is finished.

You can also check for a new version of iOS or new iPod software at any time by clicking the Check for Update button on the Summary sync page.

Restoring Your iPod

You can restore your iPod to its original factory condition. This operation erases its storage and installs the current version of iOS for an iPod touch, or iPod software for an iPod classic, iPod nano, or iPod shuffle. The restore operation returns the iPod to its out-of-box factory settings. It's the last resort for fixing problems, and it's the only choice if you intend to change the computer you're using for syncing your iPod, especially if you're switching from a Mac to a PC as your sync computer. You should also restore the iPod if you are giving it to someone else to keep.

The restore operation wipes out the content and apps on the iPod. For an iPod classic, iPod nano, or iPod shuffle, you need to replace the content that was erased by the restore operation by syncing your iPod from your computer's iTunes library, as I describe in Chapter 7. For an iPod touch, you can restore your settings from previous settings (see the next section), but you still have to sync your content and apps with iTunes, although you can also sync the content with iCloud.

Restoring previous settings on an iPod touch

iTunes provides protection and backs up your iPod touch settings so that you can restore them. This backup comes in handy if you want to apply the settings to a new iPod touch or to an iPod touch that you had to restore to its factory conditions. You can copy all the settings you use to customize your iPod touch and its apps, including Wi-Fi network settings, the keyboard dictionary, and settings for contacts, calendars, and e-mail accounts.

If you generally sync with your computer using iTunes, choose the Back Up to This Computer option in the Backup section of the iPod touch Summary sync page. (This option will already be chosen if you haven't synced from iCloud.)

If you sync from iCloud, as I describe in Chapter 8, you can use iCloud to back up your settings, and then restore your settings from the iCloud backup. Choose the Back Up to iCloud option in the Backup section of the iPod touch Summary sync page.

To restore your settings on your iPod touch, go through the process of setting up your iPod touch as I describe in Chapter 2.

If you are setting up your iPod touch wirelessly, after signing into your iCloud account, the setup process includes the Set Up as a New iPod touch option, but you can instead choose the Restore from iCloud Backup option (as I show in Chapter 2). Choose the option to restore the settings, and then tap Next to finish setting up your iPod touch.

You can also restore your settings while setting up your iPod touch using iTunes. Connect your new or restored iPod touch to the same computer and copy of iTunes you used before so that iTunes remembers the backup settings. iTunes should open automatically. (If it doesn't, open iTunes manually.) Then follow the step-by-step instructions in Chapter 2 for connecting your iPod touch to iTunes and setting it up. As you continue through the setup screens, iTunes provides the option to restore the settings from a previously backed-up iPod touch or to set up the iPod touch as new, as I show in Chapter 2. Choose the option to restore the settings and then click Continue to finish setting up your iPod touch. iTunes uses the previous settings for syncing the iPod touch.

To delete the backed-up settings for your iPod touch from iTunes on your computer, open iTunes and choose iTunes➪Preferences (on a Mac) or Edit➪Preferences (on a Windows PC). Click the Devices tab, select the iPod touch in the Device Backups list, and then click Remove Backup. You don't need to connect your iPod touch to do this.

Restoring to factory conditions

Restoring an iPod erases its storage and sets all settings to their original default values. To restore an iPod, follow these steps for both the Mac and Windows versions of iTunes:

1. **Connect the iPod to your computer.**

   iTunes opens automatically.

2. **Click the iPod button (as I show in Chapter 7).**

   The Summary sync page appears.

3. **Click the Restore button.**

   An alert dialog appears to confirm that you want to restore the iPod.

4. **Click the Restore button again to confirm the restore operation.**

   A progress bar appears, indicating the progress of the restore operation. iTunes notifies you when the restore is finished.

5. **Sync your iPod with content from your iTunes library or manually manage your content, as I describe in Chapter 7.**

You can sync an iPod touch with your iTunes Match library in iCloud or with your iTunes library on your computer, which I also show in Chapter 7.

6. **Sync your iPod with personal information, as I describe in Chapter 8.**

7. **When you finish syncing, eject the iPod by clicking the eject button next to its name in the source pane.**

Now, with your iPod restored, refreshed, and re-synced, you're ready to rock!

Part VI
The Part of Tens

*Y*ou've reached the last part, the part you've come to expect in every *For Dummies* book that neatly encapsulates just about all the interesting aspects of this book's topic. Like the compilers of other important lists — David Letterman's Top Ten, the FBI's Ten Most Wanted, the Seven Steps to Heaven, the 12 Gates to the City, the 12 Steps to Recovery, The 13 Question Method, and the Billboard Hot 100 — I take seriously this ritual of putting together the *For Dummies* Part of Tens.

And so, I offer in Chapter 20 the top ten tips (actually eleven) not found elsewhere in the book, including keeping your battery juiced and your screen clean, rating your songs, deleting apps and videos from your iPod touch, changing privacy settings, and adding onscreen keyboards for different languages.

In Chapter 21, the last chapter of this book, I've compiled the top ten apps for the iPod touch that shook the iPod world and changed it forever (and one more app that shook my world). These consist of the apps not mentioned elsewhere in this book that you can obtain from the App Store — many of them for free.

20

Eleven Tangible Tips

*T*his book is filled with tips, but in this chapter, I've put 11 truly handy ones that didn't fit in elsewhere but that can help make your iPod touch experience a completely satisfying one.

Saving the Life of Your Battery

Follow these simple rules:

- Don't keep an iPod in a snug carrying case when charging — that snug case can cause overheating.
- Top it off with power whenever it's convenient to do so.
- Set your iPod touch to automatically go to sleep by choosing Settings⇨General⇨Auto-Lock from the Home screen.
- Turn off Bluetooth on your iPod touch or iPod nano when you're not using a Bluetooth device.
- Set the iPod classic backlight to turn off automatically by choosing Settings⇨General⇨Backlight and picking the amount of time to remain on (or choosing Always On).

Everything else you need to know is in Chapter 1.

Keeping Your Screen Clean

If the iPod display has excessive moisture on it from humidity or wet fingers, wipe it with a soft, dry cloth. If it's dirty, use a soft, slightly damp, lint-free cloth — an inexpensive eyeglass cleaning cloth sold in vision care stores or pharmacies is a good choice.

Do not use window cleaners, household cleaners, aerosol sprays, solvents, alcohol, ammonia, or abrasives to clean the iPod display — they can scratch or otherwise damage the display. Also, try not to get any moisture in any of the openings, as that could short out the device.

Getting Healthy with Nike+

Use your iPod touch or iPod nano as a workout companion with people on the Nike+ website (www.nikeplus.com), where you can see all your runs and share motivation with runners across the world. Because both devices have accelerometers, you can track your pace, time, and distance from one workout to the next, and you can pick songs and playlists to match your workouts.

See Chapter 4 for details on working out with your iPod nano. You can upload your iPod nano workout data to the Nike+ site by syncing with iTunes (as I describe in Chapter 7), clicking Send to send your data, and following the instructions for signing in to or setting up a Nike+ account. After signing in to your account, the Nike + iPod tab appears in the sync options when you connect your iPod nano — click the iPod button to see the sync options, as I describe in Chapter 7. Click the Nike+ iPod tab to set your Nike+ iPod options. The option Automatically Send Workout Data to nikeplus.com is turned on by default, but you can turn it off to stop automatically sending your workout data.

For the iPod touch, use the Nike+ Running app available in the App Store. The app collects data from the sensor as you work out. You can track your pace, time, and distance from one workout to the next, and you can pick songs and playlists to match. The app automatically syncs your workout data with the Nike+ website.

Rating Your Songs on Your iPod

Ratings are useful — the iTunes DJ and Genius features are influenced by ratings, and you can define smart playlists with ratings to select only rated songs so you can avoid the clunkers and spinal tappers. In fact, when you try to put a music library on your iPod that's larger than the device's capacity, iTunes decides which songs to synchronize based on — you guessed it, *ratings*.

iTunes lets you rate your songs, but so does your iPod touch, iPod classic, and iPod nano. You can rate any song while you listen to it. Ratings you assign on your iPod are automatically synchronized back to your iTunes library when you connect your iPod again. If you sync your iPod touch with your iTunes Match library in iCloud, as I describe in Chapter 11, the ratings are synchronized with your iTunes Match library.

To assign a rating to a song on your iPod touch or iPod nano, follow these steps:

1. **Start playing a song (see Chapter 12 for details).**

   The Now Playing screen appears.

2. **Tap the screen on an iPod nano to see the row of buttons and scrubber bar.**

   You have to do this on an iPod nano, but not on an iPod touch.

3. **Tap the list button, which appears in the upper-right corner of the iPod touch screen and the right side of the row of buttons on an iPod nano.**

   A list of the album or playlist contents appears, with a row of five dots across the top, which is called the *ratings bar.*

4. **Tap the title of any song in the track listing or leave the song that's playing selected.**

5. **Drag across the ratings bar at the top of the track listing to turn each dot into a star.**

   You can turn all five dots into five stars (for the best) or one (for the worst).

On an iPod classic, press the select button three times, cycling through the scrubber bar and Genius Start button to reach the ratings bar (a row of five dots); then scroll the click wheel to turn each dot into a star (up to five stars).

Deleting Apps from Your iPod touch

If you use iTunes to sync your iPod touch, you can turn off the synchronization of certain apps in your iTunes library before syncing your iPod touch (see Chapter 7) so that the apps disappear from your iPod touch. But you can also delete apps directly from your iPod touch — except, of course, the bundled apps from Apple.

Touch and hold any icon on the Home screen until all the icons begin to wiggle (as though you're about to rearrange them or add Home screens). To delete an app, tap the circled *X* that appears inside the app's icon while it wiggles. Your iPod touch displays a warning that deleting the app also deletes all its data; tap Delete to go ahead and delete the app and its data, or tap Cancel to cancel.

To stop the icons from wiggling the Watusi, press the physical Home button on the front of the iPod touch, which saves any changes you made to your Home screens.

Deleting Videos from Your iPod touch

Need more room on your iPod touch? Videos take up the most space, but the good news is that you can delete a video directly from your iPod touch. Tap the Videos app to see your videos and TV episodes (as I describe in Chapter 13). Flick left or right across the video or TV episode, and then tap the Delete button that appears.

Your video is deleted from your iPod touch only. When you sync your iPod touch with iTunes, the video is copied back to your iPod touch. To prevent the video from appearing on your iPod touch again, deselect it before syncing your iPod touch, or switch to manually managing music and videos, as I describe in Chapter 7. *Note:* If you delete a rented movie from an iPod touch, it's gone forever (or until you rent it again).

Checking the Traffic in Maps on Your iPod touch

The Maps app on the iPod touch not only shows you the route to take, but in some areas, it can also show you traffic patterns so you can avoid the jams. The traffic data is constantly updated and aggregated from a variety of Internet sources.

To use Maps, tap the Maps icon on the Home screen. The Maps app appears. You can obtain directions first, as I describe in Chapter 17, or just display any location on the map that has highways. To show traffic information, tap the options button (the curled page in the bottom-right corner) to see a menu underneath the map, and then tap Show Traffic. Traffic jams appear as red dashes along main roads and highways, so you can quickly see at a glance where they are. If you don't see any red dashes on the map, you may need to zoom out to view highways and major roads.

To stop showing the traffic, tap the option button, and then tap Hide Traffic.

Adding Keyboards on Your iPod touch

You can change the layout and language settings for the onscreen keyboard by choosing Settings⇨General⇨Keyboard, and then tapping the Keyboards option. The Keyboards screen appears with a language button for the currently selected keyboard language (which is English on my iPod touch). Tap the language button to see layout options for the keyboard, separated into the Software Keyboard Layout and Hardware Keyboard Layout sections.

The Software Keyboard Layout section offers options for the onscreen (Software) keyboard. These include the AZERTY key arrangement rather than the typical QWERTY arrangement for English. The Hardware Keyboard Layout section offers the virtual layout options for an Apple Wireless Keyboard.

Tap the Keyboards button in the upper-left corner to return to the Keyboards screen.

From the Keyboards screen (choose Settings⟹General⟹Keyboard and tap Keyboards if you need to start again), you can add keyboards for different languages and use them simultaneously. Tap Add New Keyboard on the Keyboards screen to add another keyboard. A list of languages appears, including Emoji, the keyboard for emotional icons used in messages. Scroll the list to find the language you want and then tap the language. After you tap a language, the Keyboards screen appears with buttons for the languages you've chosen. You can add as many keyboards as you need or tap a language to change its keyboard layout, as I just described.

You can then switch keyboards while using the onscreen keyboard by tapping the globe icon, which appears when more than one keyboard is added. For example, the French keyboard appears in Figure 20-1 (left side) and the globe icon is next to the .?123 key. The Emoji keyboard appears in Figure 20-1 (right side) with the globe icon on the left side of the row of icons.

Each time you tap the globe icon, the keyboard switches to the next language you've turned on, in the order that the languages appear in the keyboards list. When you switch keyboards, the language of the newly added keyboard appears briefly in the spacebar.

For example, if you turned on English, French, German, and Emoji (for a total of four keyboards), tapping the globe icon switches from English to French. Tapping it again switches to German, and tapping it again switches to Emoji. Tapping the globe icon one more time switches back to English.

Figure 20-1: Switch to French (left) and use the French spelling suggestions (center); switch to Emoji while typing a message (right).

To remove a language you added, choose Settings➪General➪Keyboard, tap Keyboards, and then tap Edit in the upper-right corner. You can then tap the delete button (the red button with a dash) next to the language you want to delete. Tap Done in the upper-right corner to finish.

Keeping Your iPod touch Private

Surfing can be dangerous — on the web, that is. You may want to protect yourself from fraudulent websites or keep some websites from tracking your web surfing habits. And you may not want your apps to be able to use your contacts, your calendar, or other personal information on your iPod touch.

Consider web browsing with Safari. You usually leave a cookie trail when you visit websites. Websites use cookies to personalize your experience with the site (such as remembering your username and password). You can decide not to accept cookies or to only accept them from sites you visit. Some website pages won't load correctly unless you accept cookies from the site.

You can change the Safari web browser's privacy and browser settings on your iPod touch by choosing Settings➪Safari from the Home screen to show the Safari settings screen. In the Privacy section of the Safari settings screen, you can tap Accept Cookies to see the choices for accepting cookies from sites you visit:

- ✓ **From Visited:** Accepts cookies only from sites I've visited before, which is what I do most of the time.
- ✓ **Always:** Allows cookies from all sites.
- ✓ **Never:** Refuses all cookies.

To clear cookies from Safari, tap the Clear Cookies and Data button in the section underneath the Privacy section. If you need to clear the history of pages you visited, tap Clear History beneath the Privacy section.

Scroll the Safari settings screen to see more options. In the Security section, Fraud Warning is usually turned on. It warns you of a potentially fraudulent site and doesn't load the page. You can turn it off if you are sure that the site you are visiting is not fraudulent, but be careful!

To block or allow pop-ups, turn Block Pop-Ups on or off. Blocking pop-ups stops only those pop-ups that appear when you close a web page or open one by typing its address. Sorry, the option doesn't block pop-ups that can appear when you tap a link.

To block apps from using personal information in your iPod touch, such as contacts, calendars, and your location, tap Settings⊏>Privacy to see the Privacy screen. You can then choose the following options:

- **Location Services:** By tapping on/off switches, you can turn location services on or off, and turn on or off each app's capability to use this service, as I describe in Chapter 4.

- **Contacts:** Turn on or off each app's capability to use your contacts. For example, I use the Skype app for calling people, and I keep Skype's access to my contacts turned on. For details on using the Contacts app, see Chapter 18.

- **Calendars and Reminders:** Turn on or off each app's capability to use your calendar or reminder entries. For details on using the Calendar app, see Chapter 18.

- **Photos:** Turn on or off each app's capability to use the information stored with your photos, such as location, or the photos themselves. For details on using the Photos app, see Chapter 14.

- **Bluetooth Sharing:** Turn on or off each app's capability to share data via Bluetooth.

  To find out more about using Bluetooth, see "Tips on Using iPods and iPhones" in the free tips section of the author's website (www.tonybove.com/tips).

- **Twitter:** Turn on or off the capability for all apps to use your Twitter account to post tweets. For details on using Twitter, see Chapter 18.

- **Facebook:** Turn on or off the capability for all apps to use your Facebook account to post status updates, photos and videos. For details on using Facebook, see Chapter 18.

To quickly stop all intrusions from messages, FaceTime calls, and notifications, choose Settings and tap the on/off switch for the Do Not Disturb option. A crescent moon icon appears in the iPod touch status bar when this option is on.

Saying No to a Pesky Wi-Fi Service

Your iPod touch remembers your Wi-Fi connections and automatically uses one when detecting it within your range. If you've used multiple Wi-Fi networks in the same location, your iPod touch picks the last one you used. (For details on choosing a Wi-Fi network, see Chapter 4.)

But if your iPod touch keeps picking up a Wi-Fi network that you can't properly join, such as a private network that requires a password you don't know or a commercial network that charges for access, you can tell your iPod touch to *forget* this particular network, rather than turning off Wi-Fi itself. This is very useful if a paid service has somehow gotten hold of your iPod touch and won't let you move on to other web pages without typing a password.

Choose Settings⇨Wi-Fi from the Home screen and tap the circled right-arrow (>) button next to the selected network's name. The network's information screen appears. Tap the Forget This Network button at the top of the screen so that your iPod touch doesn't join the network automatically. Then tap the Wi-Fi Networks button at the top-left corner to return to the Wi-Fi Networks screen. You can always select this network manually, and you can still continue to use other Wi-Fi networks.

Capturing an iPod touch Screen Image

You too can capture images of the iPod touch screen and display them in a book or website, just as I have. No matter what application you're running, touch and hold the Home button and press the sleep/wake button at the same time, and release both buttons at the same time. The iPod touch screen flashes (and if your volume is turned up, you can hear a shutter click sound). This indicates that the screen was saved in Camera Roll — choose Camera Roll in the Photos app to see the image. You can capture as many screen images as you like, and sync them to Photo Stream in iCloud or directly to a photo application on your Mac (such as iPhoto) or Windows PC, as I describe in Chapter 14.

21

Ten Apps That Shook the iPod World

*1*t's not fair. Only ten apps? Hundreds of thousands of apps from almost as many software companies are competing for attention in the App Store. I could write an entire book about just the ones that have shaken *my* world — right down to the very routines I live by. (Maybe they'll let me write that book in the future.) Instead, the publisher dragged me kicking and screaming to the back of the book and told me we'd run out of room and that we had to keep it to ten.

How did I pick these ten? I included apps I think are important as an introduction to the iPod touch experience, along with the apps that I use every day. I also threw in the app I created as number 11 — while I don't think it shook the iPod world, I think it's pretty cool, and it certainly shook my world.

I left out of this list the ones I've already described in other chapters and on the online Cheat Sheets (www.dummies.com/cheatsheet/ipodanditunes and www.dummies.com/cheatsheet/ipodtouch) — Facebook, Twitter, and Skype (Chapter 18); Google Earth (Chapter 17); ABC Player, Netflix, Pandora, Spotify, Truveo, and other apps that stream music or video (Chapter 13); GarageBand for making music (Chapter 12); a variety of games that use the accelerometer (Chapter 3); and the apps for fun and travel. I also left out, of course, Apple's apps that are supplied with the iPod touch. And yet, all of these apps, and especially the ones from Apple, are responsible for shaking up the iPod world.

Remote

The Remote app from Apple (free) turns your iPod touch into a remote control for iTunes and Apple TV (better than the physical remote controller that comes with Apple TV). That may seem like no big deal, but it was the first app to demonstrate how the iPod touch can control other Apple entertainment devices, which shows the direction Apple is heading — into the living room entertainment center. The Remote app works with your Wi-Fi network, so you can control playback from anywhere in and around your home.

Enigmo

Voted the best game at the 2008 Worldwide Developers Conference and winner of various awards, Enigmo (not free) is a puzzle game in which you direct animated flowing streams of water, oil, and lava by using your iPod touch to move and rotate the various puzzle pieces in order to divert the flow of the falling droplets so that they can reach their target. I know quite a few early adopters of the iPod touch that were first hooked by this game. Enigmo 2 expands on this theme by offering puzzles in 3D. The game was originally developed in 2003 by Pangea Software for Macs, PCs, and PlayStation Minis.

Tap Tap Revenge

With a name obviously inspired by Japan's megapopular Dance Dance Revolution, Tap Tap Revenge, one of the first games on the iPod touch (now known as Tap Tap Revenge Classic), took its cues from the addictive Guitar Hero, putting your rhythmic skills to the test. The app from Tapulous lets you tap through the beats of the music or shake left and right as the arrows fall. Version 4 offers lots of new music tracks to download as well as global leaderboards with up-to-the-minute scores.

Angry Birds

This game has managed to stay at the very top of the charts far longer than other games, and its characters have appeared in TV shows and commercials, and even at theme parks. Angry Birds (not free) offers many hours of game-play in which you take revenge on green pigs who steal the birds' eggs and lay waste to their fortified castles. Rovio, its developer, has released half a dozen episodes over the last few years to augment the game. In Angry Birds Seasons, the feathery monsters celebrate different festive seasons around the world. Follow the creatures as they chase a giant claw into a wormhole and defy gravity in Angry Birds in Space. Rovio recently partnered with the band Green Day to create new levels of Angry Birds featuring all three members of the band. Angry Birds wins my prize for most influential game.

Ocarina

Ocarina (not free) is the most famous of the strange mobile apps that defy characterization. It turns your iPod touch into an ocarina — one of the oldest instruments of our civilization that makes a flute-like sound. Without any musical training, you can touch the holes of the ocarina to make music or blow into an external microphone, and the app also lets you share the music you make with others over the Internet. Variations on this type of app include Leaf Trombone and one of my faves, Harmonica. Smule, the developer, has also released Ocarina 2, Magic Piano, Magic Guitar, AutoRap, Sing!, Songify, and Beatstream.

Dropbox

Dropbox has saved my, er, *reputation* a few times by giving me access on my iPod touch to documents and files on my computer at home — I could easily find a document and e-mail it. Dropbox makes your iPod touch an extension of your computer — you can view photos, videos, documents, and presentations on your computer, as well as share and send files by e-mail. You can also use your Dropbox account (free) to sync files across multiple devices, share large files, and maintain an online backup of your most important files.

Google Mobile

Searching with Google has always been part of Safari (see Chapter 15). Google Mobile (free) lets you search by voice and provides instant access to Google Search, Gmail, Google News, Docs, Calendar, Talk, and other Google apps. You get relevant search suggestions as you type or speak, and you can use location search to find businesses, services, weather, and movie info, and then see these suggestions on Google Maps.

Shazam and SoundHound

Why am I listing two? Because if you're like me, and you hear a song in a store or restaurant, and you absolutely *need to know immediately* its title and artist, you might try both of these free apps. Shazam was the first to recognize songs using the internal iPod touch microphone. SoundHound also recognizes tunes it can hear, and you can also hum or sing into the microphone — and if you're good at karaoke, it may just find that song. SoundHound also provides lyrics and artist info, and both apps connect you to iTunes to buy the music. Both also provide premium versions for unlimited tagging, previews, and sharing music.

Stanza and iBooks

Okay, I have to list two again. The Stanza app (free) changed my reading habits — I not only read more classics now (which are mostly free), but I also read everywhere I go. You can download a vast selection of free classics and buy contemporary works, sort by title or author, and create custom collections to build reading lists and keep track of all your books. Although other readers have appeared (notably the Amazon Kindle Reader and Nook), Stanza was my favorite . . .

. . . until iBooks came along from Apple. (I'm now dividing my reading time between both apps.) iBooks offers the best reading experience — you flip through pages with a swipe or tap, and you can bookmark pages, add notes, find words and phrases, change the font size, and so on. It also offers access to Apple's online iBookstore. With the bookmark-syncing feature, I can keep my bookmarks, notes, and the current page in sync wirelessly with the iBooks app on my iPad and iPhone.

iMovie

People seem to pay more attention to video than to any other medium. As the wise sage (and wisecracking baseball player) Yogi Berra once said, "You can observe a lot just by watching." Now you have an app that you can use to make your own videos and show them to the world. The iMovie app (not free) from Apple is an incredible feat of software engineering. You can record videos on your iPod touch and then edit them along with videos you've already recorded, mixing in still images from your iPod touch photo library. You can trim the lengths of your clips, splice them into two clips, rearrange them in sequence, stylize them using one of several themes (such as Travel or Playful), add a soundtrack from your music library on your iPod touch, and export the edited video clip to the Camera Roll. You can then sync your iPod touch to a Mac and use the edited video clip in an iMovie project on your Mac.

Tony's Tips for iPhone Users

Tony's Tips for iPhone Users Manual (not free), developed and published by yours truly, is an app that provides helpful tips for using an iPhone or iPod touch with iTunes. I add new tips and revise the information in Tony's Tips regularly as Apple updates the software — the app lets you search quickly for topics, bookmark pages, and save pages for offline reading.

Index

• *B* •